RICHARD SAKWA is Professor of Russian and European Politics at the University of Kent, an associate fellow of the Russia and Eurasia programme at Chatham House, and a fellow of the Academy of Social Sciences. His main research interests are Russian domestic and international politics, European international relations and comparative democratisation. Recent books include *The Crisis of Russian Democracy: The Dual State, Factionalism and the Medvedev Succession* (2011), *Putin and the Oligarch: The Khodorkovsky–Yukos Affair* (I.B.Tauris, 2014) and *Putin Redux: Power and Contradiction in Contemporary Russia* (2014).

FRONTLINE UKRAINE

CRISIS IN
THE BORDERLANDS

RICHARD SAKWA

I.B.TAURIS
LONDON · NEW YORK

Paperback edition published in 2016 by
I.B.Tauris & Co. Ltd
London · New York
www.ibtauris.com

Hardback edition first published in 2015 by
I.B.Tauris & Co. Ltd

Cover image: Anti-government protesters in Independence Square, Kiev,
February 20, 2014 (Photo by Jeff J Mitchell/Getty Images).

ISBN: 978 1 78453 527 8
eISBN: 978 0 85773 804 2

A full CIP record for this book is available from the British Library
A full CIP record is available from the Library of Congress

Library of Congress Catalog Card Number: available

Text designed and typeset by Tetragon, London
Printed and bound in Great Britain by T.J. International, Padstow, Cornwall

CONTENTS

NOTE ON TRANSLITERATION AND TRANSLATION

The transliteration system employed in this book is a modified version of British Standard, and is used in all cases except those where convention decrees otherwise. Thus the Cyrillic letter 'ю' becomes 'yu', 'я' becomes 'ya', and at the beginning of names 'e' becomes 'ye' (i.e. Yevgeny rather than Evgeny). For the sake of reader-friendliness the '—ий' or '—ый' at the end of words is rendered simply as '—y' (i.e. Dmitry rather than Dmitrii); similarly, in forenames 'кс' has been rendered 'x' (i.e. Alexei rather than Aleksei). Diacritics representing the Russian and Ukrainian hard and soft signs have been omitted in proper nouns. Note also that the Ukrainian 'g' ('г') is pronounced as an 'h'; thus Lugansk is pronounced as Luhansk, and Tyagnybok is spoken as Tyahnybok.

In general, for ease of reading, proper names have been anglicised and the conventional forms applied: thus Oleksandr is mostly given as Alexander, Serhiy as Sergei and Andriy as Andrei, unless the context is clearly Ukrainian. In addition, Kyiv will be rendered Kiev, and other place names will conform to the majority language spoken in the region: thus we will have Lviv, the only one of Ukraine's ten largest cities with a Ukrainian-speaking majority; but Dnepropetrovsk, Kharkov and Odessa, where Russian is the majority language. No political or cultural preference is thereby implied.

Transliteration in bibliographical references will largely follow the more precise Library of Congress system (albeit with 'ya' for 'я' and 'yu' for 'ю'), and so the reader may at times notice variations between the spelling in the text and that found in the references.

All translations, unless otherwise indicated, are by the author.

PREFACE

In 2014, history returned to Europe with a vengeance. The crisis over Ukraine brought back not only the spectre but the reality of war, on the one hundredth anniversary of a conflict that had been spoken of as the war to end all war. The great powers lined up, amid a barrage of propaganda and informational warfare, while many of the smaller powers made their contribution to the festival of irresponsibility. This was also the seventy-fifth anniversary of the beginning of World War II, which wreaked so much harm on Central and Eastern Europe. The fall of the Berlin Wall 25 years earlier and the subsequent end of the Cold War had been attended by expectations of a 'Europe whole and free'. These hopes were crushed in 2014, and Europe is now set for a new era of division and confrontation. The Ukrainian crisis was the immediate cause, but this only reflected deeper contradictions in the pattern of post-Communist development since 1989. In other words, the European and Ukrainian crises came together to devastating effect.

The 'Ukrainian crisis' refers to profound tensions in the Ukrainian nation and state-building processes since Ukraine achieved independence in late 1991, which now threaten the unity of the state itself. These are no longer described in classical ideological terms, but, in the Roman manner, through the use of colours. The Orange tendency thinks in terms of a Ukraine that can finally fulfil its destiny as a nation state, officially monolingual, culturally autonomous from other Slavic nations and aligned with 'Europe' and the Atlantic security community. I describe this as a type of 'monism', because of its emphasis on the singularity of the Ukrainian experience. By contrast, Blue has come to symbolise a rather more plural understanding of the challenges facing Ukraine, recognising that the country's various regions have different historical and cultural experiences, and that the modern Ukrainian state needs to acknowledge this diversity in a more capacious constitutional settlement. For the Blues, Ukraine is more of a 'state nation', an assemblage of different traditions, but above all one where Russian is recognised as a second state language and economic, social and even security links with Russia are maintained. Of course, the Blue I am talking about is an abstraction, not the blue of Viktor Yanukovych's Party of Regions. The Blues, no less than the Orangists, have been committed to the idea of a free and united Ukraine, but favour a more comprehensive vision of what it means to be Ukrainian. We also have to include the Gold tendency, the powerful oligarchs who have dominated Ukraine since the 1990s, accompanied by widespread corruption and the decay of public institutions. Since independence, there has been no visionary leader to meld these colours to forge a Ukrainian version of the rainbow nation.

The 'Ukraine crisis' refers to the way that internal tensions have become internationalised to provoke the worst crisis in Europe since the end of the Cold War. Some have even compared its gravity with the Cuban missile crisis of October 1962. The world at various points stood close to a new conflagration, provoked by desperately overheated rhetoric on all sides. As I shall describe later, the asymmetrical end of the Cold War effectively shut Russia out from the European alliance system. The failure to establish a genuinely inclusive and equal European security system imbued European international politics with powerful stress points, which in 2014 produced the international earthquake that we call the Ukraine crisis. There had been plenty of warning signs, with President Boris Yeltsin, the Russian Federation's first leader, in December 1994 already talking in terms of a 'cold peace', and when he came to power in 2000 President Vladimir Putin devoted himself to overcoming the asymmetries. The major non-state institution at the heart of the 'architecture' of post-Communist Europe, the European Union (EU), only exacerbated the tensions rather than engaging in transformative conflict resolution. The EU represented the core of what in this book I call 'Wider Europe', a Brussels-centric vision of a European core that extended into the heartlands of what had once been an alternative great-power system centred on Moscow. The increasing merger of Wider Europe with the Atlantic security system only made things worse.

Russia and some European leaders proposed not so much an alternative but a complementary vision to the monism of Wider Europe, which I and others call 'Greater Europe': a way of bringing together all corners of the continent to create what Mikhail Gorbachev in the final period of the Soviet Union had called the Common European Home. This is a multipolar and pluralistic concept of Europe, allied with but not the same as the Atlantic community. In Greater Europe there would be no need to choose between Brussels, Washington or Moscow. In the absence of the tensions generated by the post-Cold War 'unsettlement', the peace promised at the end of the Cold War would finally arrive. Instead, the double 'Ukrainian' and 'Ukraine' crises combined with catastrophic consequences.

This book is both personal and political. The Cold War division of Europe is the reason I was born and grew up in Britain and not in Poland, but, even before that, war and preparations for war had scarred the family. In the interwar years my father, an agronomist by profession but like so many of his generation also a reservist in the Polish army, marched up and down between Grodno and Lwów (as it was then called). He told of the 25 kilograms he had to carry in his backpack, with all sorts of equipment and survival tools. The area at the time was part of the Second Polish Republic, and for generations had been settled by Poles. These were the *kresy*, the borderlands of Europe grinding up against the ever-rising power of the Russian Empire. With the partition of Poland in the eighteenth century, Grodno and what is now the western part of Belarus was ceded to Russia, while Lemberg (the German name for Lwów) and the surrounding province of Galicia became part of the Austro-Hungarian Empire. On gaining independence in 1918 and with Russia and the nascent Ukrainian state in the throes of revolution and civil war, the various armies repeatedly marched back and forth across the region. In the end the Polish state occupied an enormous territory to the east of the Curzon Line.

These were the lands occupied by Joseph Stalin, following the division of the area according to the Molotov–Ribbentrop Pact of 23 August 1939. Poland was invaded on 1 September and against the overwhelming might of Adolf Hitler's armies the Polish forces fell back, only for the Soviet Union to invade on 17 September. My father's unit soon came up against the Soviet forces, and when greeted initially by the Poles as coming to support them against the Germans, they were asked to disarm. My father escaped to Hungary, but many of his reservist comrades were captured, and eventually murdered in Katyn and other killing sites. My father subsequently joined the Polish Second Corps under General Anders, and with the British Eighth Army fought at El Alamein, Benghazi, Tobruk and then all the way up Italy, spending six months at Monte Cassino. At the end of the war Poland was liberated, but it was not free. Unable to return to the homeland, the family was granted refuge in Britain. In the meantime, the Soviet borders were extended to the west, and Lwów became Lvov. These were territories that had never been part of the Russian Empire, and when Ukraine gained independence in 1991 became the source of the distinctive Orange vision of Ukrainian statehood. Today Lvov has become Lviv, while its representation of what it means to be Ukrainian is contested by other regions and communities, notably the Blues, each of which has endured an equally arduous path to become part of the modern Ukrainian state.

As for the political, being a product of an ideologically and geographically divided Europe, I shared the anticipation at the end of the Cold War in 1989–91 that a new and united Europe could finally be built. For a generation the EU helped transcend the logic of conflict in the western part of the continent by binding the traditional antagonists, France and Germany, into a new political community, one that expanded from the founding six that signed the Treaty of Rome in March 1957 to the 28 member states of today. The Council of Europe (CoE), established in 1949, broadened its activities into the post-Communist region, and now encompasses 47 nations and 820 million citizens, as its website proudly proclaims. The European Convention of Human Rights (ECHR) and its additional protocols established a powerful normative framework for the continent, policed by the European Court of Human Rights (ECtHR), based in Strasbourg. Russia in the 1990s actively engaged with the EU, signing a Partnership and Cooperation Agreement (PCA) in 1994, although it only took effect on 30 October 1997 following the first Chechen war, and the next year Russia joined the CoE.

However, another dynamic was at work, namely the enlargement of the North Atlantic Treaty Organization (NATO). Also established in 1949 to bring together the victorious Western allies, now ranged against the Soviet Union in what had become the Cold War, NATO was not disbanded when the Soviet Union disintegrated and the Cold War came to an end. This was the source of the unbalanced end to the Cold War, with the Eastern part dissolving its alliance system, while NATO in the 1990s began a march to the east. This raised increasing alarm in Russia, and, while notionally granting additional security to its new members, it meant that security in the continent had become divisible. Worse, there was an increasing perception that EU enlargement was almost the automatic precursor to NATO expansion. There was a compelling geopolitical logic embedded in EU enlargement. For example, although many member states had reservations about the readiness of Bulgaria and Romania to join, there was a fear that they could drift off and become Western versions of Ukraine. The project of European economic integration, and its associated peace project, effectively merged with the Euro-Atlantic security partnership, a fateful elision that undermined the rationale of both and which in the end provoked the Ukraine crisis that is the subject of this book.

The failure to create a genuinely inclusive and symmetrical post-Communist political and security order generated what some took to calling a 'new Cold War', or, more precisely in my view, a 'cold peace', which stimulated new resentments and the potential for new conflicts. It became increasingly clear that the demons of war in Europe had not been slain. Instead, the Ukraine crisis demonstrates just how fragile international order has become, and how much Europe has to do to achieve the vision that was so loudly proclaimed, when the Berlin Wall came down in November 1989, of a continent united from Lisbon to Vladivostok. The Ukraine crisis forces us to rethink European international relations. If Europe is not once again to be divided, there need to be new ideas about what an inclusive and equitable political and security order encompassing the whole continent would look like. In other words, the idea of Greater Europe needs to be endowed with substance and institutional form. Unfortunately, it appears that the opposite will happen: old ideas will be revived, the practices of the Cold War will, zombie-like, come back to life, and once again there will be a fatal dividing line across Europe that will mar the lives of the generation to come. This is far from inevitable, but to avoid it will require a shift in the mode of political intercourse from exprobration to diplomacy, and from denunciation to dialogue.

Thus the personal and the political combine, and this is as much an exploration of failed opportunities as it is an account of how we created yet another crisis in European international politics on the anniversaries of the start of two world wars and a moment of hope in 1989. My father's generation suffered war, destruction and displacement, and yet the European civil war that dominated the twentieth century still inflames the political imagination of the twenty-first.

It is my pleasure to acknowledge the support of the James Madison Trust within the framework of the project 'New Architectures of Europe'. I much appreciate being an honorary senior research fellow at the Centre for Russian, European and Eurasian Studies (CREES) at the University of Birmingham, which provides access to Russian-language electronic materials but above all to a community of scholars still committed to the best traditions of 'bourgeois objectivity'. As always, my friends, colleagues and staff at the University of Kent make it a stimulating and congenial place to work, while the partnership with the Higher School of Economics in Moscow adds enormously to our common intellectual endeavour. The list of those who have helped in the preparation of this work is endless, but I would like in particular to thank Nicolai Petro, who generously hosted my visit to Odessa, and my colleagues at the Kyiv-Mohyla University, in particular Andriy Meleshevich and Volodymyr Kushnirenko, who helped make my visit to Kiev so challenging and interesting.

I am most grateful to Iradj Bagherzade and Jo Godfrey at I.B.Tauris for the support and encouragement they have given me in the preparation of this book. The production team at Tauris have once again been outstanding, and I would like to thank in particular Alex Billington, Alex Middleton and Sara Magness. David Johnson's highly informative electronic newsletter 'Russia List' has been of immeasurable help in keeping up with facts and opinions as the Ukrainian and Ukraine crises have unfolded, and I am most grateful for his courageous commitment to balance and circumjacence. Everyone involved in the study of this crisis has been criticised by one side or the other and occasionally both, and I have no doubt this will continue. The temper of the times is angry and assertive (what I call 'axiological'), but only a 'dialogical' approach can guarantee the scholarly commitment to hearing the arguments of all positions while holding strong views of our own. This book will undoubtedly rile many, yet only the expression of doubt and the posing of difficult questions will allow Europe to find a path to peace with itself and others.

RICHARD SAKWA
CANTERBURY, NOVEMBER 2014

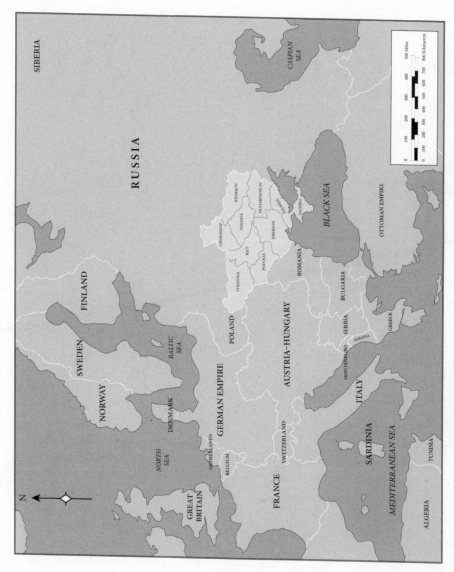

MAP 1: Europe and Ukraine in 1914

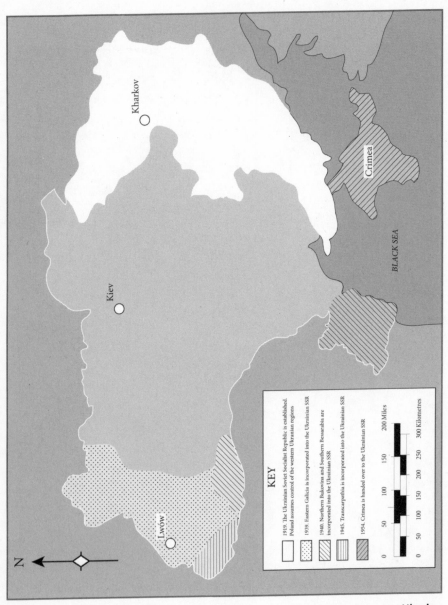

KEY

1919. The Ukrainian Soviet Socialist Republic is established.
Poland assumes control of the western Ukrainian regions

1939. Eastern Galicia is incorporated into the Ukrainian SSR

1940. Northern Bukovina and Southern Bessarabia are
incorporated into the Ukrainian SSR

1945. Transcarpathia is incorporated into the Ukrainian SSR

1954. Crimea is handed over to the Ukrainian SSR

Kharkov

Kiev

Lwów

Crimea

BLACK SEA

N

0   50   100   150   200 Miles

0   50   100   150   200   250   300 Kilometres

MAP 2: Interwar Ukraine

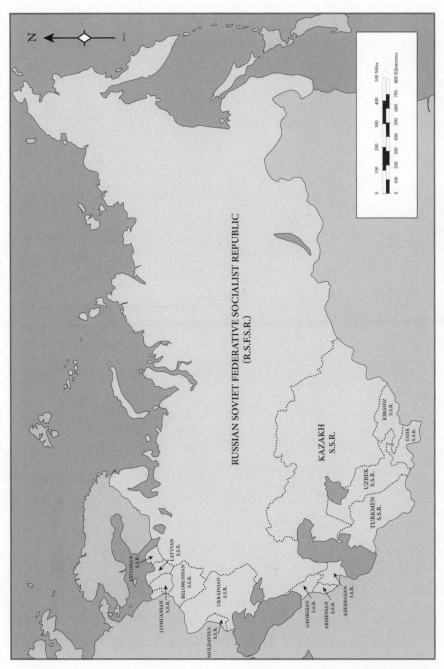

MAP 3: The USSR in 1991

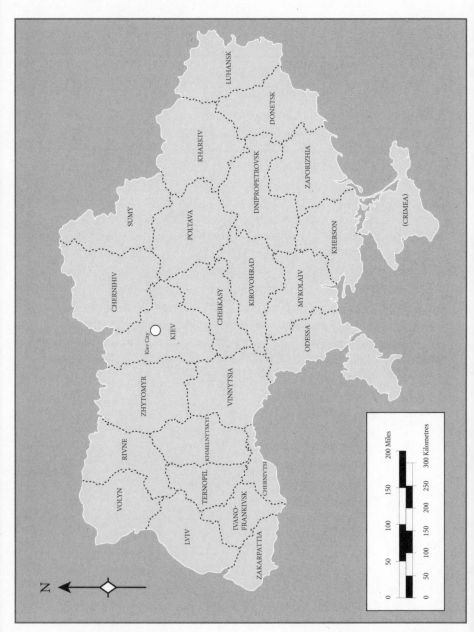

MAP 4: The Regions of Ukraine

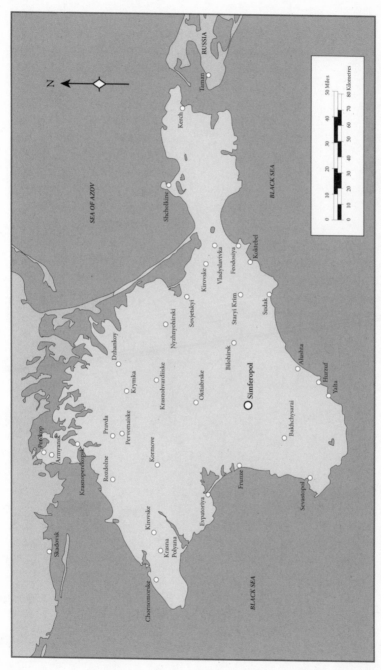

MAP 5: Crimea

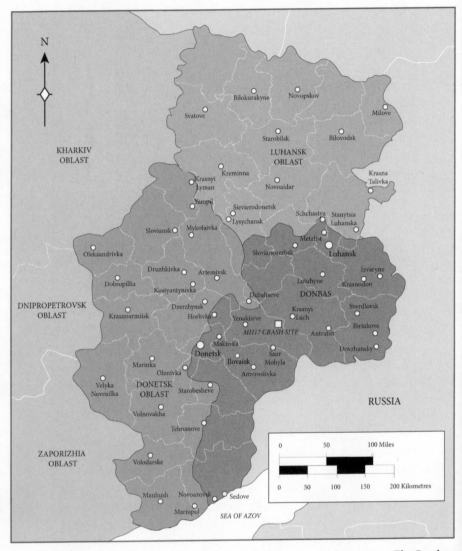

N

KHARKIV
OBLAST

Bilokurakyne
Novopskov
Svatove
Milove

Starobilsk
Bilovodsk

LUHANSK
OBLAST

Kreminna
Krasnyi
Lyman
Novoaidar
Krasna
Talivka
Yampil
Sievierodonetsk
Schchastya
Stanytsia
Lysychansk
Luhanska
Slovianoserbsk
Metalist
Luhansk

Sloviansk
Mykolaivka

Oleksandrivka
Izvaryne

Druzhkivka
Artemivsk
Lutuhyne
Krasnodon

Dobropillia
DONBAS

Kostyantynivka
Debaltseve
Sverdlovsk

DNIPROPETROVSK
OBLAST
Krasnoarmiisk
Dzerzhynsk
Krasnyi
Luch
Biriukove

Horlivka
Yenakiieve
Antratsit

Makiivka
MH17 CRASH SITE
Dovzhansky

Donetsk
Saur
Marinka
Ilovaisk
Mohyla
Olenivka
Amvrosiivka
RUSSIA
Velyka
Novosilka
DONETSK
OBLAST
Starobesheve

Volnovakha

Telmanove

ZAPORIZHIA
OBLAST
Volodarske

Manhush
Novoazovsk
Sedove
Mariupol
SEA OF AZOV

0   50   100 Miles

0   50   100   150   200 Kilometres

MAP 6: The Donbas

CHAPTER 1

COUNTDOWN TO CONFRONTATION

On the one hundredth anniversary of World War I and the seventy-fifth anniversary of the start of World War II, and 25 years after the fall of the Berlin Wall in 1989, Europe once again finds itself the cockpit of a great-power confrontation. How could Europe have allowed itself to end up in this position, after so many promises of 'never again'? This is the worst imbroglio in Europe since the 1930s, with pompous dummies parroting glib phrases and the media in full war cry. Those calling for restraint, consideration and dialogue have not only been ignored but also abused, and calls for sanity have not only been marginalised but also delegitimated. It is as if the world has learned nothing from Europe's terrible twentieth century.

SHADOWS OF WAR

The slew of books published to commemorate the start of the Great War reveals the uncanny similarities with the situation today. The war cost at least 40 million lives and broke the back of the continent, yet in certain respects was entirely unnecessary and could have been avoided with wiser leadership. If key decision makers had not become prisoners of the mental constructs that they themselves had allowed to be created, and if the warning signs in the structure of international politics had been acted on, then the catastrophe could have been averted. The assassination of Archduke Franz Ferdinand and his wife in Sarajevo on 28 June 1914 could well have remained a localised incident if Europe had not already been poised for conflict. Margaret MacMillan demonstrates in *The War That Ended Peace* that there were plenty of contingent factors that precipitated conflict in summer 1914, but the structural factors had been created over the previous two decades.[1]

A febrile atmosphere of exaggerated moral indignation and 'axiological' truths predominated. By this term I refer to the assertion of what are purported to be unchallengeable (axiomatic) realities, not susceptible to debate or repudiation, a central feature also of the present crisis. Geoffrey Wawro's *A Mad Catastrophe* exposes the reckless unfolding of the logic of conflict, while Sean McMeekin's *July 1914: Countdown to War* is unsparing in its condemnation of all leaders and countries. Christopher Clark's *The Sleepwalkers: How Europe Went to War in 1914*, an updated version of Barbara Tuchman's classic *Guns of August*, shows how none of the actors really wanted an all-out conflict but stumbled into hostilities that destroyed them all in one way or another.[2] More specifically, Thomas Otte's *July Crisis: The World's Descent into War, Summer 1914* shows how the century-old system of great-power politics collapsed in a matter of weeks. He asks 'how and why the civilized world, seemingly so secure in its material and intellectual achievements, could have descended into a global conflict'.[3] Social-Darwinist ideas rendered war a noble and cleansing ideal, but in the end it is the squalidity of the actual war and its catastrophic consequences that are remembered.

This is a salutary warning to those who argue that the military-alliance system forged in the wake of World War II will endure into the twenty-first century, in conditions that have changed unrecognisably from those of the bipolar confrontation of the Cold War years from the late 1940s to 1989. The contemporary crisis, of which the Ukrainian events are only one of the most intense manifestations, is very much worse because of the peril of nuclear catastrophe hanging over humanity. Deterrence has averted a global war so far, but that is no guarantee that the recklessness that affected the ruling classes of Europe a century ago will not once again lead the sleepwalkers to war. The actual fighting in 1914 was only an epiphenomenon of a broader cultural and psychological readiness to engage in conflict. Germany had long been demonised in the British press, above all for its perceived challenge to British naval supremacy, while France was still smarting over the loss of Alsace-Lorraine in the Franco-Prussian war of 1870. The list could go on – just as it could today.

The groundwork of the Ukrainian conflict has been latent for at least two decades. It was laid by the asymmetrical end of the Cold War, in which one side declared victory while the other was certainly not ready to 'embrace defeat'.[4] Unlike Germany and Japan in 1945, who acknowledged that they had been at fault and used the moment of destruction as the starting point of their transformation into Western-style liberal democracies, Russia did not in the least consider itself a defeated power.[5] This did not prevent the alleged victors after the Cold War believing that the Soviet collapse vindicated not only the institutions that had been created to wage the struggle but above all the ideology in whose name it had been fought. This gave rise to the triumphalism of the 'end of history', which effectively replaced one ideology with another, namely the belief in the inexorable advance of liberal democracy and the 'European choice'. Marxist historicism was replaced by liberal historicism, the belief that the telos – or purpose – of history was knowable. This rendered all those who resisted (in the Russian case, not so much the substance of the ideas but the manner of their imposition) as not only mistaken but in some way fundamentally evil, thus closing down space for pragmatic debate, diplomacy or even common sense. This helps explain how Europe in 2014 has once again become the crucible of international conflict, harking back to an era that has so often been declared to be over. Today, Ukraine acts as the Balkans did in 1914, with numerous intersecting domestic conflicts that are amplified and internationalised as external actors exacerbate the country's internal divisions.

One of the central themes of this book is the idea that the Ukraine crisis has escalated because of the multiplicity of power centres, contested narratives and divergent understandings of the nature of the post-Cold War order. As outlined earlier, two fundamental processes have intersected to devastating effect: the 'Ukrainian' crisis has emerged out of the contradictions of the country's nation- and state-building since independence in 1991, while the 'Ukraine' crisis is the sharpest manifestation of the instability of the post-Cold War international system.[6] Here we will briefly outline both, beginning with the Ukraine crisis, with the arguments developed in later chapters.

THE UKRAINE CRISIS AND PROBLEMS OF INTERNATIONAL ORDER

The Ukraine crisis reflects the continuation in new forms of what used to be called the East–West conflict, the focus of the next chapter. After the end of the Cold War in 1989–91, as a result of Mikhail Gorbachev's reform of the Soviet Union, which was based on the ideas of the 'new political thinking', no inclusive and equitable peace system was established. The Napoleonic Wars ended with the Congress of Vienna in 1815, when the victors came together to map the shape of a new Europe and established a peace system that effectively lasted until 1914, interrupted by the Crimean War of 1853–6 and the Franco-Prussian War of 1870–1. World War I ended with the Paris Peace Conference, which resulted in the Treaty of Versailles in 1919, which imposed punitive conditions on what was taken to be a defeated Germany. Russia was not invited to attend at all, having defected from the Allies following the Bolshevik seizure of power in October 1917 and then having been wracked by civil war between 1918 and 1920. Germany's refusal to accept the status of a defeated power fuelled a powerful revisionist strain that helped propel Hitler to power in 1933. In other words, the way one war ends determines the shape of the next.

There was no peace conference after the end of the Cold War, and instead an uneven peace was imposed on Europe. The Soviet Union disintegrated in December 1991, and Russia emerged as the 'continuer state', assuming the burdens, treaty obligations and nuclear responsibilities of the Union of Soviet Socialist Republics (USSR). As far as Russia was concerned, the end of the Cold War had been a shared victory: everyone stood to gain from overcoming the end of the division of Europe, symbolised by the fall of the Berlin Wall in November 1989. The institutions of the Cold War in the East were dismantled, above all the Warsaw Treaty Organisation (the Warsaw Pact), but on the other side the institutions of the Cold War were extended. Above all, NATO, established in 1949, sought to find a new role, which it did by going 'out of area' (notably in Afghanistan) and enlarging to encompass a swath of former Soviet bloc countries. Poland, Hungary and the Czech Republic joined in March 1999, and then in a 'big bang' enlargement in March 2004 the Baltic republics (Estonia, Latvia and Lithuania), Bulgaria, Romania, Slovakia and Slovenia joined, followed by Albania and Croatia in April 2009.

Despite repeated warnings by Russia that bringing NATO to its borders would be perceived as a strategic threat of the first order, the momentum of NATO enlargement continued. At the Bucharest NATO summit in April 2008 Georgia and Ukraine were promised eventual membership: 'NATO welcomes Ukraine's and Georgia's Euro-Atlantic aspirations for membership in NATO. We agreed today that these countries will become members of NATO.' However, Membership Action Plans (MAPs) were deferred because of German and French concerns that encircling Russia would be unnecessarily provocative, especially since Gorbachev had apparently been promised that NATO would not advance to the east. From Russia's perspective, there was no security vacuum that needed to be filled; from the West's perspective, who was to deny the sovereign choice of the Central and Eastern European states if they wished to enter the world's most successful multilateral security body?

In the end, NATO's existence became justified by the need to manage the security threats provoked by its enlargement. The former Warsaw Pact and Baltic states joined NATO to enhance their security, but the very act of doing so created a security dilemma for Russia that undermined the security of all. A security dilemma, according to Robert Jervis, is when a state takes measures to enhance its own security, but those measures will inevitably be seen as offensive rather than defensive by other states, who then undertake measures to increase their own security, and so on – in this case provoking the Ukraine crisis.[7] This fateful geopolitical paradox – that NATO exists to manage the risks created by its existence – provoked a number of conflicts. The

Russo-Georgian war of August 2008 acted as the forewarning tremor of the major earthquake that has engulfed Europe in 2013–14. As Mikhail Margelov, the head of the Foreign Affairs Committee of the Russian Federation Council, put it, noting the West's surprise at 'Russia's firm stance on Ukraine, given that everything has been pointing in that direction for the last decade':

> Since the beginning of the Ukrainian crisis, the West has failed to forsake the principle according to which only Western interests are legitimate. Nor has it learned the lesson of the events of August 2008, when Russia intervened in the war unleashed by the regime of Mikheil Saakashvili, in order to enforce peace in the region. The Georgian crisis should have made clear to everyone that Russia is not only ready to make its voice heard, but is also prepared to use force when its national interests are at stake.[8]

The unbalanced end of the Cold War generated a cycle of conflict that is far from over. An extended period of 'cold peace' settled over Russo-Western relations, although punctuated by attempts by both sides to escape the logic of renewed confrontation. This is what I call a mimetic cold war, which reproduces the practices of the Cold War without openly accepting the underlying competitive rationale.[9] Structurally, a competitive dynamic was introduced into European international relations, despite the best intentions of both sides. At worst, the revanchists in the post-Communist countries of Eastern Europe, encouraged by neoconservatives in Washington and their vision of global transformation on a global scale, fed concerns about Russia's alleged inherent predisposition towards despotism and imperialism. The Trotskyite roots of US neocon thinking are well known, and for them the world revolution was not cancelled but only transformed: the fight now was not for revolutionary socialism but for capitalist democracy – to make the world safe for the US. This became a self-fulfilling prophecy: by treating Russia as the enemy, in the end it was in danger of becoming one. NATO thus found a new role, which was remarkably similar to the one it had been set up to perform in the first place – to 'contain' Russia.

Much of the discussion of the 'Ukraine' crisis externalises responsibility – in other words, it looks for a scapegoat. This book argues that the crisis has been generated by structural contradictions in the international system, but for the scapegoaters Russia is, quite simply, held responsible. The corollary is that the West needs to find an adequate response, which means only intensifying the contradictions that provoked the crisis. Thus Andrew Wilson argues that Russia's alleged 'covert ambition since 2004 to expand its influence within the Soviet periphery, and over countries that have since joined the EU and NATO, such as the Baltic states', accompanied by 'American inattention', is the root cause of the crisis.[10] This sort of analysis, predominant among the Orangists within Ukraine, is wrong-headed in conceptualisation and dangerous in its consequences. It deflects attention from the tensions within the Ukrainian state-building project by externalising responsibility for the country's failures, and, by demonising Russia, forecloses opportunities for constructive engagement and the solution of common problems, most notably those facing Ukraine itself, but also at the European and global levels.

The contrast with post-war Germany is stark, a country that was also 'contained', but within the framework of a set of institutions, above all the EU and NATO. Russia has effectively been left out in the cold since the end of the Cold War. There were serious attempts to mitigate the outsider effect, but in the end they were not enough to overcome the security dilemma. In the 1990s there was not much that Russia could do about the asymmetrical end of the Cold War, since it was economically weak and engaged in an intensive period of internal transformation as it became something approximating a market economy. Putin's accession to the presidency in 2000 coincided with the beginning of an extended period of high prices for raw materials, above all for oil and gas, as China's boom translated into an insatiable demand for materials to fuel its factories, allowing the West to deindustrialise and to take advantage of an extraordinary period of cheap consumer goods. The Western working classes, and with them the trade unions and other forms of mutuality, were marginalised, allowing corporate capitalism and the financial services to enjoy an extended boom on the back of cheap labour. Although marked by several periods of turbulence, the system thrived – until the great recession.

Russia shared in the good years, enjoying annual growth of 7 per cent up to 2008. The state greatly increased its extractive capacities, with tax revenues rising on the back of the defeat of the oligarchic model of capitalism, notably through the 'Yukos affair' from 2003 that saw the Yukos oil company expropriated and transferred into the hands of state-owned Rosneft, while its head, Mikhail Khodorkovsky, spent a decade in jail.[11] Putin himself stepped down in 2008 after the two terms allowed him by the constitution, and for four years the country was governed by the relatively liberal Dmitry Medvedev. The latter promised to revive the country's democratic institutions, which had been increasingly suffocated by the system of 'managed democracy'. Medvedev achieved only modest success, but he established an agenda for the reform of the Putinite system that remains active to this day. In the end it was perceived foreign-policy threats, notably the Western intervention in Libya in 2011, which ensured Putin's return to the presidency in 2012. In the UN Security Council vote on 17 March 2011 to establish a no-fly zone, Russia abstained, allowing the Western powers to overthrow Muammar Gaddafi by the end of the year. This was another instance of the 'regime change' that alarmed Russia so much, and which already had provoked a 'tightening of the screws' internally in the mid-2000s, in response to the various 'colour' revolutions.[12]

The Putinite defeat of the oligarchs, accompanied by the humbling of the 'barons' in the regions and enormous energy rents, shifted Russia onto a very different path of development from Ukraine. Ukraine endured societal upheaval and political crisis every few years, while Russian stability provided space for economic growth and societal development, but at the price of the heavy-handed tutelage of Putin's administrative regime. By the time Putin returned to the presidency in May 2012 Russia was much stronger, and ready to assert itself in world politics. What Ickes and Gaddy represent as the 'missing quadrant' was being filled in: a strong but 'bad' Russia, not the weak and good Russia of the 1990s, the weak and bad Russia presented by its critics, or the good and strong Russia extolled by its friends.[13] Oil and other natural-resource rents filled Russian coffers and allowed the Putin administration to co-opt most societal interests. In the wake of the problems exposed by the Georgian war, the armed forces became the object of a grand programme of reform and re-equipping, and in April 2014 Dmitry Rogozin, the head of the military–industrial complex, announced that Russia would invest $560 billion in the coming years in modernising its army and navy, and $85 billion in modernising its defence plants. As will be detailed below, Russia under Putin presented itself as not so much anti-Western as a complement to the West, a type of 'neo-revisionism' that sought not to change the fundamentals of international order but to ensure that Russia and other 'rising' powers were treated as equals in that system.

WHAT IS UKRAINE?

The path to Ukrainian statehood has been exceptionally long and arduous.[14] In the modern era the country has enjoyed only a brief period of statehood following the collapse of the Russian Empire in 1917. At a time of revolution and civil war, a precarious independent state was established, but it was overthrown in 1919. With the victory of the Bolsheviks under Vladimir Lenin, the country was reconstituted as a federation. Ukraine was one of the founding nations of the USSR in December 1922, and following World War II was granted a seat in the UN (together with Belorussia), even though it was no more than a 'union republic' of the USSR. Throughout the vicissitudes of war, division and domination, the idea of Ukrainian nationhood was never extinguished, but it was balanced by commitment to the larger Soviet project, which brought with it industrialisation, urbanisation and the creation of a relatively modern and educated society.

Two models of Ukrainian statehood, the monist and the pluralist, have long been in contention. They correspond to the long struggle in Ukrainian history between those who assert that the country is an autochthonous cultural and political unity in its own right, and those who believe that common ancestry in Kievan Rus, a loose federation of East Slavic tribes from the ninth to the thirteenth century ruled by the Rurik dynasty, means that they are part of the same cultural, and by implication, political community. The conversion to Orthodoxy in AD 988 by the Kievan Prince Vladimir the Great, moreover, endowed the modern Russian, Ukrainian and Belarusian nations with a shared religion. However, the early Slav state was already fragmenting when the Mongol invasion of 1240 destroyed Kiev and separated the various peoples. Putin's view that Russia and Ukraine are just two aspects of a single civilisation is widespread in Russia, whereas Ukrainian nationalists argue that their country long ago set out on its own developmental path (more on this later in this chapter).

This tension has played out in manifold struggles and conflicts over the centuries. Notably, from the late eighteenth century Ukraine was often described as 'Malorossiya' (Little Russia), derived from Byzantine maps that referred to the territory as Lesser Rus or Rus Minor. Malorussianism views Ukraine as an emanation of the Greater Russian identity, and thus from the nineteenth century sought to standardise the country's language to what had become the Russian Slavic norm. This was the view of Nikolai Gogol, who, although an ethnic Ukrainian, wrote in Russian. This is countered by the long tradition of Ukrainism, which argues that the Ukrainian version of the East Slavic language represents the emergence of a wholly distinct ethnic identity. The name 'Ukraine', like the term Malorossiya, derives from cartographical toponyms and is translated literally as 'borderland'. Taras Shevchenko, who wrote mostly in Ukrainian, is the best exemplar of this tradition.[15]

In our era, Alexander Solzhenitsyn is a good example of someone who embodied the tension between monist and pluralist conceptions of Ukraine. In his powerful 1990 analysis, *Rebuilding Russia*, he argued: 'We do not have the energy to run an Empire. Let us shrug it off'; but when it came to Ukraine he advocated the creation of a 'Russian union' with Ukraine at its heart.[16] For Ukrainists, the main challenge of independence is precisely to repudiate such thinking, to rid the country of the 'imperial' legacy and to carve out a wholly separate Ukrainian nation, whereas the Malorussian tradition represents an entirely different model of statehood, one that encompasses multiple civilisational experiences, languages and cultures, while respecting the Ukrainian inflection of all of these. The post-Communist struggle for democracy, good governance, economic transformation and civic dignity became entwined in this deep-rooted cultural conflict.

Winston Churchill once quipped that the Balkans produces more history than it can absorb, and in certain respects this is equally applicable to Ukraine. There is a surfeit of unresolved historical and national issues that remain scabrous and contested, and thus Ukraine has not yet reached the point where it can be considered to have passed Ernest Renan's test, according to which a nation is made up as much by what is forgotten as that which is remembered. History is raw and alive. For example, the 2014 crisis has brought the notion of 'Novorossiya' (New Russia) back into popular discourse.[17] Between 1764 and 1917, Novorossiya was a distinct administrative unit of the Russian Empire along the entire Black Sea coast from Transnistria in the west to Mariupol in the east, and to this day remains predominantly Russian-speaking. Equally, there are other historic entities, such as the old Sloboda Ukraine centred on Kharkov, and Zaporozhia focused on Dnepropetrovsk. Overarching this is the constant tension between Eastern and Western influences. As Andrew Wilson puts it: 'Ukraine's entire history could be written in terms of its oscillation between the two sides, with the Russians decisively surpassing the Poles in importance only in the nineteenth and twentieth centuries.'[18] Thus the present contest between 'Europe' and Russia is one that goes back centuries, and is a constituent element of Ukraine's historical DNA (see Map 1).

The modern stage of this conflict begins in 1991 with the break-up of the Soviet Union. Contrary to expectations, when the Soviet Union disintegrated it was Russia that led the way. Its Declaration of State Sovereignty on 12 June 1990 was followed on 16 June by that of Ukraine, which stressed the alliance-neutral status of the country. In the all-union referendum on transforming the Soviet Union into a confederation of sovereign republics of 17 March 1991, 70.5 per cent of Ukrainians voted in favour of retaining a renewed union, although in a second question inserted by the Ukrainian authorities, asking whether 'Ukraine should be part of a Union of Sovereign States on the basis of the Declaration of State Sovereignty of Ukraine', 80.2 per cent also said yes. As in all revolutionary situations, time was compressed and events moved at a dizzying pace. The attempted coup of 18–21 August 1991 by a group of conservatives, hoping to undo the drift of reforms towards a more pluralist democracy and decentralised state, acted as the catalyst for the disintegration of the state they were hoping to save. The putsch swiftly unravelled, and in its wake Ukraine declared independence on 24 August. In the last months of 1991 Gorbachev frantically sought to save the union, but the overwhelming Ukrainian poll on 1 December, in which 90.3 per cent voted for Ukrainian independence, inflicted the death blow on the USSR. The traditionalists were discredited, and on the same day the Communist-turned-nationalist Leonid Kravchuk was elected Ukraine's first president with 63 per cent of the vote. On 7–8 December the leaders of Russia, Belorussia and Ukraine met in the

Belavezha Pushcha in the country now known as Belarus and, as founding members of the original USSR, agreed to dissolve the union and establish the Commonwealth of Independent States (CIS). The Soviet Union was dead, and 15 independent states now began their distinctive paths to modernity and nation statehood (see Map 3).

Like many modern nation states, Ukraine is an agglomeration of territories, peoples and languages. The newly independent republic encompassed various territories and peoples that had at various points been part of neighbouring states, and comprised a society that had endured massive changes and traumas. When the Russian Empire collapsed in 1917 the population of Ukraine included 32.9 million Ukrainians (67.7 per cent), 5.4 million Russians (11.1 per cent) and 4.3 million Jews (8.8 per cent). The Soviet census of 1989 registered the changes on the eve of the Soviet collapse. Out of a total population of 51.7 million, 37.4 million (72 per cent) were Ukrainians and 11.4 million (22 per cent) were Russians, while the number of Jews had fallen tenfold to 486,628.[19] The figures for the 2001 census found that there were 37,541,700 Ukrainians, constituting 77.8 per cent of the population, and 8.3 million Russians (17.3 per cent) (see Table 1.1).

Ethnic Russians were distributed unevenly, being concentrated in the eastern and southern regions, comprising 39 per cent of Lugansk, 38.2 of Donetsk, 25.6 of Kharkov, 24.7 per cent of Zaporozhe and 20.7 of Odessa, while in the cities the proportion of Russians is even higher. There are even greater inter-regional disparities when it comes to language use. The 2001 census found that 67.5 per cent stated that their native language was Ukrainian, 29.6 per cent (including 14.8 per cent of ethnic Ukrainians) said it was Russian, and 2.9 per cent named other languages. Russian-speakers were concentrated in the south-east, with 90.6 per cent of people in Sevastopol claiming Russian as their native language, 77 per cent in Crimea, 74.9 per cent in the Donetsk region and 68.8 per cent in the Lugansk region, as well as making up about half the population in several other regions, while Kiev is a preponderantly Russian-speaking city. Surveys reveal that these figures underestimate the proportion of Russian-speakers, with between one-third and a half using Russian at home and in social and professional communication. Once again there are regional differences, with western Ukraine mostly using Ukrainian with some Surzhyk (a mix of Russian and Ukrainian in common use across central Ukraine) and Russian; people in the centre and some southern regions (Mykolaiv and Kherson) mostly speak Ukrainian, but with a large proportion using Surzhyk, with Russian predominating in the large cities, including Kiev; the Donbas (short for Donets Basin, comprising the Donetsk and Lugansk regions) and Crimea are overwhelmingly Russian-speaking; while the other eastern and southern regions of Ukraine are predominantly Russian-speaking, with the common use of Surzhyk and bilingualism.[20]

TABLE 1.1 Ukrainian population census 2001

	POPULATION (THOUSANDS)	AS % OF THE TOTAL		2001 AS % OF 1989
		2001	1989	
Ukrainians	37541.7	77.8	72.7	100.3
Russians	8334.1	17.3	22.1	73.4
Belarusians	275.8	0.6	0.9	62.7
Moldavians	258.6	0.5	0.6	79.7
Crimean Tatars	248.2	0.5	0.0	530
Bulgarians	204.6	0.4	0.5	87.5
Hungarians	156.6	0.3	0.4	96.0
Romanians	151.0	0.3	0.3	112.0
Poles	144.1	0.3	0.4	65.8
Jews	103.6	0.2	0.9	21.3
Armenians	99.9	0.2	0.1	180
Greeks	91.5	0.2	0.2	92.9
Tatars	73.3	0.2	0.2	84.4
Gypsies	47.6	0.1	0.1	99.3
Azerbaijanis	45.2	0.1	0.0	122.2
Georgians	34.2	0.1	0.0	145.3
Germans	33.3	0.1	0.1	88.0
Gagauzians	31.9	0.1	0.1	99.9
Other	177.1	0.4	0.4	83.9
TOTAL	48052.3			

Source: All-Ukrainian Population Census [website].
Available at http://2001.ukrcensus.gov.ua/eng/results/general/nationality/.

Contemporary Ukraine is the product of many changes (see Map 2). In the south-east the Donbas is the most industrialised. The city of Donetsk was founded in 1879 by the Welsh industrialist John Hughes, and is famous for its mines, oligarchs and football team (Shakhtar Donetsk). Already the 1897 tsarist census revealed that the majority in the Donbas identified themselves as 'Malorussians' (that is, Ukrainians), and were not simply Russians who adopted the Ukrainian ethnonym in the Soviet period.[21] In other words, despite the extensive links with Russia and ethnic intermingling, the region had an identifiable sense of belonging to the Ukrainian community. This is balanced by the retention of intense historic links with Russia across the border, reinforced by common experiences and patterns of economic interaction. The industrialisation of the region in the Soviet period drew in workers from across the USSR, and their detractors in western Ukraine insist that they retain a 'sovok' mentality, a dependence on the state and an orientation towards Russia. Nevertheless, opinion polls confirmed that before the war the population of the south-east identified as Ukrainians, but of a special sort. A 2005 Razumkov Centre survey, for example, found that 67 per cent of citizens in Ukraine's east answered positively to the question 'Do you consider yourself a patriot of the Ukraine?' and other studies had similar findings. Separatism barely registered, and the majority considered the Ukrainian state their home, but there were deep-seated grievances – notably over the status of the Russian language in state and educational institutions – accompanied by hostility to NATO membership and geopolitical reorientation to the West. It was the failure to give constitutional form to this distinctiveness and the perception that the February 2014 revolution brought hostile forces to power that provoked the rebellion.

In the west of Ukraine, at least three major regions can be identified. The area known as Galicia (currently the regions of Lviv, Ternopil and Ivano-Frankivsk) formed part of the Austro-Hungarian Empire until 1918, and thereafter was ruled by Poland in the interwar years. Western Ukraine only finally joined the Soviet Union in 1944, when taken from the Germans, but for 400 years it had been ruled by Poland and then Austro-Hungary. Lwów was seized by the Soviet Union in 1939 under the terms of the Molotov–Ribbentrop Pact of 23 August, but two years later was occupied by the Germans (returning to Lemberg), until it was taken by the Red Army in 1944 and integrated into the Ukrainian Soviet Socialist Republic (SSR) – as Lvov – becoming Lviv at independence in 1991. The region considered the Russians as invaders and occupiers, deep sentiments that flourish to this day. This is presented as a 'civilisational' choice that transcends day-to-day politicking. Transcarpathia was part of the kingdom of Hungary for a thousand years, until 1919, when it was assigned to the newly created Czechoslovakia as punishment for Hungary's role in the Great War. The region was annexed by the Soviet Union in 1945 and assigned to the Ukrainian SSR. In 1919 Lenin also assigned extensive territories to the east and south to what would become Ukrainian jurisdiction. However, it was Stalin who was the greatest Ukrainian state-builder, adding extensive territories to both the east and the west. In cultural terms, however, in the mid-1930s he reversed the cultural renaissance of the period of 'Ukrainisatsiya' of the 1920s, when the policy of korenizatsiya (indigenisation) encouraged teaching and the publication of books in native languages. (For contemporary Ukrainian regions, see Map 4.)

The Crimean peninsula is the heartland of Russian nationhood. It was here in Khersones that Prince Vladimir adopted Orthodoxy as the official religion of the people of Rus. Following the Mongol invasion, the Crimean Khanate ruled the peninsula from 1441, whose territories at one point encompassed a large part of the northern Black Sea littoral. From 1736 Russia started its push to take over the region, prompted in particular by the desire to put an end to the raids on the Slavic parts to the north. Catherine the Great's push against the Ottoman Empire saw Crimea occupied by Russian forces in 1783, and on 2 February 1784 it formally entered the Russian Empire as Taurida Oblast. In turn, the Tatar population now faced successive waves of deportation, including in response to the threat from Napoleon in 1812, when they were sent to Siberia, and then in 1855, towards the end of the Crimean War, when they were branded as enemy agents and tens of thousands were sent to Turkey. From the 1860s the imperial authorities launched a new wave of deportations, accompanied by attempts to Russify the northern Black Sea region. The worst deportation was Stalin's, on 18–20 May 1944. The whole population, some 230,000, including 40,000 who had served with distinction in the Red Army, were sent to Siberia and Central Asia, with at least 100,000 expiring en route of hunger and thirst. They had been accused of collaboration with the Nazi occupiers, but given the purges of the 1930s, which had wiped out much of the Crimean Tatar elite, surprisingly few (some 2,000) joined 'defence teams' rather than be sent to work in Germany. Tatars now make up 13 per cent of the Crimean population, whereas before the Russian occupation of 1783 they comprised 80 per cent.[22] In 1954 the region was transferred from Russian to Ukrainian jurisdiction, a decision that was contested from the first, above all because Russians made up the majority of the population. The 2001 census revealed that 1.45 million (57 per cent) out of a total population of 2 million claimed to be Russians, 576,000 Ukrainians and 245,000 Tatars, while some 77 per cent were registered as native Russian-speakers. It was the return of Crimea to Russia in March 2014 that transformed the Ukrainian crisis into a major European confrontation (see Chapter 5).

The pattern of religious affiliation is equally complex. Some 68 per cent of Ukrainians identify themselves as Orthodox Christians, 7.6 as Greek Catholics (Uniates), 1.9 as Protestants and evangelicals, 0.9 as Muslims, and 13 per cent do not identify with any of the above faiths.[23] The Uniates, who observe Orthodox rites but render allegiance to the Pope in Rome, are concentrated in the seven regions of western Ukraine, overwhelmingly in the Lviv, Ivano-Frankivsk and Ternopil regions (Galicia). Orthodoxy itself split in 1989, when the Ukrainian Autocephalous Orthodox Church (UAOC) once again took on a legal identity, and then in 1992 split away under the leadership of Metropolitan Filaret (who in June 1990 lost the battle to become Moscow Patriarch) to create the Ukrainian Orthodox Church – Kiev Patriarchate (UOC-KP), with Filaret becoming its Patriarch in October 1995. The split provoked some undignified tussles over parishes, with about half remaining loyal to Moscow, especially in the Russophone regions, now registered as the Ukrainian Orthodox Church – Moscow Patriarchate (UOC-MP). In 2013–14 Filaret has been an enthusiastic supporter of the pro-European protesters, a stance that has put him at odds with the Moscow-oriented Church. There have been numerous incidents of pressure against Moscow-affiliated congregations following the revolution of February 2014. Although the Moscow Patriarch, Kirill, is often accused of being too close to the Putin regime, when it comes to Ukraine he has sought to steer a path towards reconciliation and dialogue.

Thus the fundamental question facing the newly independent Ukrainian state in 1991 was to find an adequate political form in which to institutionalise and represent this diversity. Countries like Belgium and Canada have used federalism to provide a constitutional framework for diversity. Others, like Spain and the United Kingdom, remain unitary but have a great degree of quasi-federal devolution of powers. In the end, after a divisive debate, Article 2.2 of the 1996 constitution declared that Ukraine is a unitary state and that its territory is indivisible and inviolable. Ukraine is far from being the only country facing the problem of managing diversity, but the internal developmental impasse and the incipient new East–West division of Europe that runs across its historically diverse territories has made the task immeasurably more problematic.

TWO MODELS OF UKRAINIAN STATEHOOD

I mentioned earlier that there are two contrasting visions of statehood, and ultimately the Ukrainian crisis of 2013–14 is a battle between the two. The first is *monist national-ism*, driven by the idea that after several centuries of stunted statehood the Ukrainian nation has had to seize the opportunity to join the front ranks of nation states. The Pereyaslavl treaty uniting Ukraine with Russia, signed by Hetman Bogdan Khmelnitsky in 1654, was to be undone, along with the succeeding centuries of Russianisation, which only in the late nineteenth century turned into a conscious programme of Russification. Ukrainisation entailed above all giving priority to the titular language as the single most important token of nationhood. This form of Ukrainian national-ism affirms the link between ethnicity and the state, although couched in the civic language of modern governance. The tension between nationalising ambitions and recognition that in fact Ukraine is a fragile ensemble of peoples and territories pro-voked exaggerated fears about the country's cohesion. For this reason the Ukrainian nationalising elite insisted on creating a unitary state, fearing for the territorial integrity of the country. Thus the monist model is one of integrated nationalism, in which the state is a nationalising one, drawing on the tradition of Ukrainism to fill the existing borders with a content sharply distinguished from Russia. It would be officially monolingual, unitary and culturally specific.

The monist vision of Ukrainian statehood draws in part on the ideas of Dmytro Dontsov, a Ukrainian nationalist writer whose radical ideas shaped the thinking of the Organisation of Ukrainian Nationalists (OUN), established in Vienna in 1929. Like so many of his generation, Dontsov was traumatised by the collapse of the government of Hetman Pavlo Skoropadsky, in which he served, in 1919. Ukraine's failed attempt to establish its independent statehood in the period of revolution and civil war radicalised later thinking and influences policy to this day. In the interwar years Ukrainian-populated areas were divided between Poland, Romania, Czechoslovakia and Bolshevik Russia. The Soviet part was granted the institutions of federal statehood, but like the other Soviet republics, this was overlain by the unitary power of what would become the Communist Party of the Soviet Union (CPSU). Dontsov wrote withering critiques of the failure of Ukraine to sustain its independence between 1917 and 1921, including severely personal attacks on the leading Ukrainian figures of that time. He repudiated the socialism of his youth and instead embraced a radical Ukrainian nationalism that excluded the possibility of consensus and cooperation with Russia. He proposed a new 'nationalism of the deed' and a united 'national will' in which violence played an essential part in overthrowing the old order. He excoriated the Russianism, Polonism or Austrianism of parts of Ukrainian society, and instead advocated the creation of a 'new man', who with 'hot faith and stone heart' would destroy Ukraine's enemies. A national culture in his view was sacred and should be defended by all means necessary.

Dontsov did not become a member of the OUN but his writings provided much of the inspiration for the movement, and he remains a revered figure today in the pantheon of integral Ukrainian nationalism.[24] Liberalism, democracy and the lack of political will were held responsible for the failure to establish an independent Ukrainian state and encouraged a turn to fascism.[25] Fascist ideas about national rebirth took deep root, and despite the inherent fractiousness and contradictions of the ideology, Ukrainian ultra-nationalism conforms to Roger Griffin's definition of generic fascism: 'bent on mobilising all "healthy" social and political energies to resist the onslaught of "decadence" so as to achieve the goal of national rebirth, a project that involves the regeneration (palingenesis) of both the political culture and the social and ethical cultures underpinning it'.[26] While elitism, strong leadership, militaristic values and mass mobilisation are core elements, racism and anti-Semitism are not necessarily part of what Ernst Nolte calls the 'fascist minimum'.

In the early 1930s the OUN, headed by Andriy Melnik, led the resistance to Polish rule. In June 1933 Stepan Bandera became head of the OUN's national executive in Galicia, territory that became part of Poland after the Great War. Bandera led a vicious campaign against Polish officials and policies. Released from a Polish jail in September 1939, he moved to Krakow, the capital of the German General Government of occupied Poland. Here the OUN split into a more conservative faction headed by Melnik (OUN-M) and a more radical wing headed by Bandera (OUN-B). By the terms of the Molotov–Ribbentrop Pact of August 1939 Galicia for the first time became part of the Soviet Union. The peace lasted barely two years, and the German invasion of 22 June 1941 was at first welcomed by the Ukrainian nationalist movement, anticipating that Germany would re-establish some form of Ukrainian statehood.

Bandera espoused a virulent form of integral nationalism, an exclusive and ethnically centred definition of the Ukrainian nation, accompanied by the murderous denigration of those who allegedly undermined this vision, notably Poles, Jews and Russians, the last of whom in his view were the worst. Bandera's supporters argue that in fact he advocated an inclusive policy of nation-building, including Jews and others as long as they supported his goals. This is true to the degree that the participation of the OUN in the slaughter of Jews in the early period of German occupation was motivated less by virulent anti-Semitism than by the situational alliance with the Nazis.[27] By late 1941 some of their violence was directed against the Germans. The OUN's goal was the creation of an independent Ukrainian national state to unite ethnic Ukrainians, and they were willing to accept support from any source in pursuance of this goal. Zaitsev defines integral nationalism as

> a form of authoritarian nationalism that regards the nation as an organic whole and demands the unreserved subordination of the individual to the interests of his or her nation, which are placed above the interests of any other group, other nations, and humanity as a whole.[28]

The other side of the coin is the denial of the common historical path of Russia and Ukraine accompanied, in Dontsov's words, by 'unity with Europe, under all circumstances and at any price – that is the categorical imperative of our foreign policy'.[29] All of this has deep resonance today, although of course intellectual filiation is never direct but a tangled skein of complex interactions.

On 30 June 1941, in Lviv, Bandera announced the formation of the Ukrainian state, appointing his associate Yaroslav Stetsko as prime minister. The OUN fought with the Germans, committing atrocities against the Jews, Poles and Russians. Nazi Germany proved a fickle ally, and on 5 July Bandera and his colleagues were arrested and they spent the rest of the war in German concentration camps. Bandera was taken to a special wing of the Sachsenhausen concentration camp for political prisoners (Zellenbau), from where he was released in September 1944 when the Germans thought that he could once again prove useful against the advancing Soviet forces. Even without him the Banderites (Banderovtsy) organised the Ukrainian Waffen SS Nachtigall and Roland divisions that together with the Galicia division by some estimates were responsible for the deaths of some half a million people, typically attended by extreme brutality. The military wing of OUN-B, the Ukrainian Insurgent Army (Ukrayinska Povstanska Armiya, UPA), was organised in Volyn in 1943 to fight for an independent Ukraine after the war. In the first instance this entailed a radicalisation of the long-standing Polish–Ukrainian civil war. Beginning on 'bloody Sunday', 11 July 1943, the UPA slaughtered some 70,000 Poles, mainly women and children and some unarmed men, in Volyn, and by 1945 it had killed at least 130,000 in Eastern Galicia. Whole families had their eyes gouged out if suspected of being informers, before being hacked to death. After Ukraine was liberated by Soviet forces in summer 1944, the Ukrainian nationalist resistance movement (OUN-B and UPA) continued a partisan war against the Polish and Soviet authorities, apparently with British intelligence service (MI6) support, which lasted into 1949. Bandera himself was assassinated by the KGB in Munich in October 1959.[30]

When the Soviet Communist overlay disappeared in 1991, what had become a rather large Ukrainian proto-state gained independence. The Soviet institutions of governance were replaced by liberal-democratic forms, and the Soviet economy began the long transition to a market system. However, the traumas associated with the struggle for independent Ukrainian statehood remained etched in the national consciousness. In October 2007 the city of Lviv erected a statue in Bandera's honour, and dozens of other cities in western Ukraine followed suit. As the leading scholar of right-wing extremism Andreas Umland puts it: 'The OUN is a – if not the – major historical source of inspiration for all Ukrainophone nationalist parties, especially the more radical ones.'[31] At the height of the protests on Independence Square (Maidan Nezalezhnosti, henceforth Maidan), the centre of Ukrainian civic life in the heart of Kiev, on 1 January 2014 a 15,000-strong torchlit procession celebrated his one hundred and fifth birthday, a march supported not only by the nationalist Svoboda (Freedom) party but also by Yulia Tymoshenko's Batkivshchyna (Fatherland) party. All of this was alien and incomprehensible to the large Russophone populations in the south-east, for whom the Soviet period was one of development and progress. It was also the time when the modern Ukrainian state was given its territorial shape by the Soviet Union, encompassing contested territories to the west and east, as well as Crimea in the south.

The red and black UPA flag was once again displayed as the symbol of radical Ukrainian nationalism. Monist nationalism draws on a naturalistic, historicist and restitutive narrative of Ukrainian statehood, suggesting that Ukraine has finally come together naturally after the deviations and mistakes of history. As in some other post-Communist states, notably the Baltic republics, the model of state-building is restorative: the attempt to re-establish some lost ideal of what the new state and nation should look like. In the case of Estonia and Latvia, for example, the idea was to return to the pre-war republics, and thus only those who lived there at the time and their descendants gained the automatic right to citizenship. The tens of thousands of Russians who had arrived since to build the new industries and to serve in the armed forces, who now hoped to live out their pensionable years in peace in their homeland, had to win the right to citizenship through language and history tests. Ukrainian state-building also operated with an attenuated restorative model at its heart. Although all those living in Ukraine in 1991 automatically gained the right to citizenship, including many stationed there in the armed forces, the nationalising state was nevertheless biased towards the view that ultimately the society would have to be 'Ukrainised', above all through the monolingual imposition of Ukrainian. This view was incorporated, after intense debate, in the 1996 constitution.[32] Article 10 was studious in its denigration of the status of Russian: 'The state language in Ukraine is the Ukrainian language. […] in Ukraine the free development, use and protection of Russian, other languages of national minorities of Ukraine is guaranteed'. The comma after 'Russian' was particularly symbolic of the new priorities, as was lumping Russians together with other 'national minorities'.

The new state sought to create its attendant symbolism and myths, but there was no single national narrative. Indeed, much of the discussion over the last two decades has been about the weakness of Ukrainian ethno-nationalism and Ukrainisation, registered by Russophones more as an annoyance than a major impediment. Ukraine developed as a pluralistic community, in which Ukrainian in culture and the arts may actually have diminished. The deep cultural struggle continued, however, with contrasting mythologies, memory politics and calendars of secular saints used as the currency of political exchange. As with so many of the former Communist Eastern European states, nation-building was accompanied by a pronounced cult of victimhood, the seedbed for new conflicts. In particular, the Holodomor (meaning 'hunger extermination') was crucial for the nation's self-identification. More than 2 million died in the famine of 1932–3 in the wake of Stalin's vicious collectivisation campaign, which saw peasants uprooted from their land and the so-called kulaks (rich peasants) exiled to Siberia. Even as food production collapsed, exacerbated by a severe drought, the Soviet regime continued to export grain to buy machine tools and other equipment to push forward the campaign of accelerated industrialisation. The famine affected the heartlands of Ukraine nationhood, and the Stalinist elite may well have sought to destroy the spirit of the nation; but the famine was not restricted to Ukraine alone, with millions more dying in the Kuban and the lower Volga.

A further symbol of the Ukrainisers was Bandera, the leader of the OUN from the 1930s. The defeat of Nazi Germany in 1945 did not bring peace to Galicia, and the Soviet forces fought a vicious war against the insurgent army of the Banderovtsy. After his death this strain of militant Ukrainian nationalism lived on in the emigration abroad, combined with a pronounced anti-Russian ideology. Stetsko took over the leadership of the Ukrainian government in exile following Bandera's death in 1959, and led the organisation until his own death in 1986. Many leading Ukrainian nationalists were associated with the organisation, including Viktor Yushchenko, president from 2005 to 2010. The émigré movement inspired the creation of the Captive Nations Committee, which in 1959 persuaded the US Congress officially to acknowledge a Captive Nations Week. This recognised Nazi creations such as Idel-Ural and Cossackia as being captive, with Russia portrayed as the captor. Irrespective of their ideology, in this tradition Russia is viewed as inherently evil, and thus the fall of Communism did not make the slightest difference: Russian imperialism was considered oppressive before Communism and after.[33] This feeds the irreconcilable anti-Russianism of part of the monist nationalist tradition, which has considerable resonance in Washington, impeding constructive and pragmatic relations between the two countries.

Yushchenko's second wife Kateryna, an American citizen, briefly headed the Captive Nations Committee, writing a famously anti-Russian letter to the *Washington Times* (no longer available online). Her career included working for the State Department and the White House during Ronald Reagan's presidency, and after Ukrainian independence she was a co-founder and vice president of the US–Ukraine Foundation. Yushchenko was the first Ukrainian president to support the rehabilitation of the OUN and Bandera, its controversial leader. In one of his most divisive acts, on 22 January 2010 Yushchenko awarded Bandera the title of 'Hero of Ukraine', a move that was widely condemned, including by the European Parliament and the Simon Wiesenthal Center. Exactly a year later the new president, Viktor Yanukovych, officially annulled the award. A giant portrait of Bandera was positioned to the left of the stage (from the viewer's perspective) during the Maidan protests, understandably alienating the Russophone population. The struggle for democracy and the 'European choice' was overlain by a radical nationalist mobilisation.

Equally, Yushchenko made recognition of the genocidal nature of the Holodomor one of the central planks of his presidency. In 2006 the Verkhovna Rada (parliament) adopted a resolution referring to the Holodomor as an 'act of genocide against the Ukrainian people'. The move was bitterly divisive, with the prime minister, Yanukovych, and over 200 MPs from the east abstaining or not taking part in the vote. The next year Yushchenko sought to make Holodomor and Holocaust denial a criminal offence, although parliament did not vote on the bill. On assuming the presidency in 2010, Yanukovych told the Parliamentary Assembly of the Council of Europe (PACE) that the Holodomor was not genocide: 'Recognising the Holodomor as an act of genocide, we think, will be incorrect, unjust. It was a tragedy, a common tragedy of the states that made up the Soviet Union.' The implication was that the partisans who considered the Holodomor to be genocide were not only condemning the Stalinist regime, but also couching it in anti-Russian terms. Instead of a common disaster for all Soviet peoples, monists made it a uniquely Ukrainian tragedy. The question divided the western from the eastern part of the country and is yet another example of the 'genocide wars', which include the struggle over the recognition of the Armenian massacres in 1916 and 1988 as 'genocides'.[34] This was another divisive issue in the debate over the formulation of Ukrainian national identity.

The model of integrated nationalism shares some of the concerns of the classic ideas of integral nationalism – the latter denoting the creation along fascist lines of a united people with a single language, culture and mythology – but it is important to stress the differences. Integrated nationalism is fundamentally oriented towards a civic model of state development and is tolerant of diversity and rights. There is little evidence that the civic rights of Russian-language-speakers were systemically abused, even at the height of the mobilisations in 2004 and 2014. As Kuzio argues, civic development and nationalism are not necessarily opposed and can complement each other.[35] This is the fundamental argument long advanced by Michael Ignatieff, who distinguishes civic from ethnic nationalism. For him, nationalism can be a constructive force as it brings a people together to create the institutions of a modern representative state, but in extreme forms it can lead to a collective escape from reality in which the rhetoric of noble causes and tragic sacrifices in the name of some primordial entity inflicts agony on others and subverts civic idealism.[36] The collapse of Tito's socialist state in Yugoslavia in 1989–91 unleashed the demons of war and extreme nationalism, and the post-Communist phenomenon of 'new nationalism' is now evident in Ukraine.

However, civic inclusion was partial and integrated nationalism could not find a formula to include the country's diversity on a constitutional basis. Ukrainian was the sole state language, and thus all official documents, notices and signs were in that language alone. Not everyone could understand the state documents that they had to read and sign, and even at election time all the instructions are in Ukrainian alone. Such inconveniences and demonstrative assertion of Ukrainism provoked a constant sense of resentment. Russian for the most part was not proscribed, but was rendered the language of private life. Ukrainian nationalists like to sneer that Russian is the 'kitchen language', not worthy of use in civic and professional life. In practice, even during the protests on the Maidan in 2004 and again in 2013–14, the predominant language was Russian. In addition, plenty of Russian-speakers endorse the nationalising model of state development, as do a certain quotient of ethnic Russians, but at the level of state development the problem remains. Identities are so mixed that the majority of the population comfortably live with multiple identities, yet this represents social adaptation and not the resolution of the political question at the constitutional level.

The core of the problem is an ideological one. At the heart of the monist model, as noted, is a restitutive understanding of re-established statehood. In other words, the aim is not to reflect existing realities, above all the different histories of the territories making up contemporary Ukraine, but to restore some idealised vision of that statehood. As we have seen the model is also applied in Estonia and Latvia, where the post-Communist national elites gave automatic citizenship only to those with roots in the pre-war independent republics, while all the rest (overwhelmingly the Russians who had moved there in the post-war years) had to demonstrate their eligibility for citizenship, typically through a language test. Like all ideologies, the restitutive model seeks to impose an external pattern on reality.

Not surprisingly, the model of restitutive nationalism could assume highly intolerant forms. At the extreme, it took on aspects of the integral nationalism espoused by the classic fascist movements of the twentieth century. This was the case with the militantly nationalist Svoboda party. Established as the Social–National Party of Ukraine (SNPU), an obvious reference to Hitler's National Socialist Party, in Lviv in 1991 by Oleg Tyagnybok, Andriy Parubiy and others, the group was distinguished by 'its openly revolutionary ultranationalism, its demands for the violent takeover of power in the country, and its willingness to blame Russia for all of Ukraine's ills'. It was also the first party 'to recruit Nazi skinheads and football hooligans'.[37] In 2004 the party changed its name to Svoboda, replaced its neo-Nazi *Wolfsangel* (Wolf's Hook) official symbol by a stylised trident (the emblem of Ukraine) consisting of three fingers, and Tyagnybok became sole leader (while Parubiy went on to join Yushchenko's Our Ukraine). Until 2013 they were happily distributing Ukrainian versions of Nazi tracts. In a debate in 2012 about the Ukrainian-born American actress Mila Kunis a Svoboda spokesman, Igor Myroshnichenko, argued that she was not Ukrainian but a 'Jewess'.[38] Anti-Semitism was deeply embedded in the party, but the intensity of its Russophobia was far greater. Svoboda is allied with France's Front National and the Italian neo-fascist group Fiamma Tricolore.

The great recession from 2008 hit Ukraine with particular intensity, exacerbating social and political divisions, redounding to the advantage of right-wing populism. The more mainstream Batkivshchyna party also strongly reflects the monist Ukrainian nationalist aspiration of creating a culturally uniform Ukrainian-speaking nation, by contrast with the pluralist concept of Ukraine as culturally and linguistically diverse. A welter of radical nationalist parties made electoral advances, notably Svoboda. Viacheslav Likhachev rightly predicted 'the final escape of right-wing extremism from the marginal niche that it occupied for the first twenty years of the political history of independent Ukraine'.[39] In the 28 October 2012 parliamentary election Svoboda won 10.44 per cent in the proportional part of the vote, taking 25 list candidates to the Rada and another ten from single-mandate districts. Parliament became a rostrum 'for the fight against Yids, Russkies, and other filth'.[40] A resolution of the European Parliament at that time condemned the party as xenophobic, anti-Semitic and racist.

The nationalising agenda could take both a civic and a more harshly accentuated, exclusivist nationalist form. This explains the paradox that even the Ukrainian nationalist parties, unlike their right-wing, populist counterparts in Western Europe, supported accession to the EU. For them, it was not so much the institutional and normative structures of the EU that were attractive, but the Wider European representation of political space. The enlargement of Wider Europe to the post-Soviet area and Ukraine meant pushing back Russian influence and limiting its geopolitical pretensions. In other words, for Svoboda and others of that ilk the EU came to be associated not with the normative values of human rights and good governance, and, above all, with the overcoming of the logic of conflict, but with the projection of Western European geopolitics, reinforced by the power of the Euro-Atlantic security community. The nationalists favour the EU not for its principles but because it embodies a set of interests that increasingly run counter to those of Russia. In other words, the exclusive and proprietary nature of 'Wider Europe' amplified the exclusivity of the integrated-nationalism project.

The Russophobia of monist Ukrainian nationalism does not acknowledge that Russia was both victim and perpetrator. Russia still has to come to terms with its Stalinist past (just as Britain does with many remaining dark spots of colonialism), but one-sided condemnation by its former 'fraternal nations' in the USSR does not help, especially since each of these countries played their part in Bolshevik crimes. Three Soviet general secretaries came from mixed Russian–Ukrainian stock: Nikita Khrushchev – who was born on the Russian side close to what is now the Russo-Ukrainian border, grew up in the Donbas and spent most of his early career in Ukraine – is often perceived as a Ukrainian, especially since his wife, Nina

Kukharchuk, was fully Ukrainian; Leonid Brezhnev, who became the party boss in Dnepropetrovsk, was born there and used it as his political base even when in Moscow; and Konstantin Chernenko, who came from a Russified Ukrainian family born in Siberia. Mikhail Gorbachev is half Ukrainian, as was his wife, Raisa Titarenko. The post-colonial model can shed some light on the tangled history of the two peoples, but the issue of competing identities runs far deeper. Even if one accepts that the Ukrainian nation has its own thousand-year history, distinct but complementary to the history of the Russian nation, the political question of the foundation of relations between the two countries still has to be resolved. The post-colonial model by definition emphasises the self-assertion of the former subaltern element, but this is only the other side of the coin to those who stress the 'fraternal' nature of the relationship between the two countries. One stresses separation, the other unity, whereas in fact 'normal' relations in the end will only be established through a combination of the two.

This brings us to the second paradigm of Ukrainian state development, which I call the *pluralist* to denote its appeal to broad principles of national inclusiveness. At root, this model proposes that the post-Communist Ukrainian state is home to many disparate peoples, reflecting its long history of fragmented statehood and the way that its contemporary borders include territories with very different histories, but that they all share an orientation to a civic Ukrainian identity. The borders of Ukraine, as we have seen, have changed considerably over the years. In particular, the boundaries of the interwar Ukrainian SSR were very different to those of today.

A path not taken is that represented by Vyacheslav Chornovil. He was one of the leaders of the 'dissident' movement in Soviet Ukraine, and then the most articulate of the leaders of the national-independence movement known as 'Rukh' in the final period of the Soviet Union. Rukh led the movement towards Ukrainian independence, but as with similar movements in Russia, it was quickly marginalised by more powerful players once independence was achieved. Chornovil fought passionately for the rebirth of Ukrainian nationhood, but he was sensitive to the pluralistic nature of the society. His vision of reborn Ukrainian statehood was inclusive and multidimensional, but it was overshadowed by the 'nationalisers' and partisans of a narrower monism. Chornovil spent the 1990s on the margins, but was set for a comeback when he was killed in a suspicious traffic accident in 1999. Chornovil's ideas appealed to all segments of Ukrainian society while challenging the powerful 'third force' – the oligarchs. Chornovil remains a hero for those who believe that Ukraine can develop as a confident pluralistic society on good terms with all of its neighbours.

Thus Valentin Yakushik argues that Ukraine is 'bicivilisational', with Ukrainians and Russians as equals in the state, together with a rich variety of other peoples, notably Ruthenians, Gagauzians, Hungarians, Jews, Romanians and Crimean Tatars.[41] Nicolai Petro refers to the Russian-speaking population as 'the Other Ukraine', and stresses that the current tension goes back generations. It is fundamentally a dispute about who gets to define what it means to be Ukrainian. From this perspective Ukraine is not one culture but many; not simply a 'cleft' society, as Samuel Huntington put it in his infamous lecture 'The Clash of Civilizations?', but a richly diverse society.[42] Equally, although the various Orthodox congregations are split, the tension was exacerbated by the myth-making of the nationalisers. For the pluralists multiple religious and linguistic orientations do not represent a danger to the state, as the nationalists would have it, but the opposite: the diversity contributes to a rich and multifaceted culture. This did not necessarily entail turning Ukraine into a federal state, but it did mean that it would have to evolve into some sort of 'consociational' entity in which the voice of its multiple identities was given some sort of legally defended constitutional status.

The pluralist model argues that all the peoples making up contemporary Ukraine have an equal stake in the development of the country, and thus opposes the nationalising strain, although without repudiating some of its concerns. For example, few would deny the need for special programmes to reassert the centrality of the Ukrainian language, including ensuring that it is taught to all children and can hold its own in further and higher education, the professions and government. This would not necessarily exclude linguistic competency tests for civil servants to ensure that Ukrainian is not overwhelmed by Russian – but it does repudiate the idea that the new state should officially be monolingual. One of the great riches of Ukraine is precisely its diversity, and, as far as the pluralists are concerned, there is no reason why this should not be constitutionally entrenched. The very 'borderness' of the country adds to its complexity, not as a problem to be managed but as an endowment to be celebrated. Thus the pluralists condemn the nationalists for failing to find a political form in which this diversity could be embedded in an inclusive constitutional order.

The tension between these two representations of Ukrainian state formation has a clearly delineated spatial dimension. The monist view is obviously stronger in the western part of the country, while the pluralist approach is stronger in the east and the south. There is also a cross-cutting temporal dimension, that is, different representations of the past and future. As well as calling for a pluralistic form of statehood, the south-east also appeals to neo-Soviet sentiments, recalling the good times of the Soviet period when jobs were plentiful, welfare (however minimal) was guaranteed and the borders between Russia and Ukraine were wide open, with numerous inter-marriages and a genuine 'Soviet' people beginning to emerge. The change of regime in February 2014 thus played out against the background of already intense divisions. As a recent unequivocal study puts it: 'the culture, language, and political thinking of western Ukraine have been imposed upon the rest of Ukraine'. The goal ostensibly is the unification of the country,

> but in fact the objective has been to put down and humiliate Ukraine's Russian-speaking population. The radical nationalists of western Ukraine, for whom the rejection of Russia and its culture is an article of faith, intend to force the rest of the country to fit their narrow vision.[43]

This may be putting it rather strongly, but the division is real.

CHAPTER 2

TWO EUROPES

The struggle for the lands between Russia and Western Europe has endured for as long as the modern European state system has existed.[1] For centuries Russia and Poland contested a territory with shifting boundaries and evolving identities. In our era Ukraine suffered inordinately from the clash between the two great totalitarian despotisms of our time, Nazi Germany and Stalin's Soviet Union. The larger region became what Timothy Snyder calls the 'bloodlands' (what are today the modern states of Poland, Belarus, Ukraine, Russia and the Baltic states) in which some 14 million non-combatants were killed between 1933 and 1945, with Germany responsible for twice as many deaths as the USSR. Even before then, what Snyder calls 'the Soviet famines' in the early 1930s saw at least 3.3 million die of hunger in Ukraine and the Kuban as Stalin allowed whole peoples to perish.[2] This catastrophe of almost unimaginable proportions affected Ukraine most deeply, and is today represented by nationalists as the Holodomor, the deliberate genocide of the Ukrainian people. As late as 1989 Melvin Croan identified the region as the seismic fault line across the continent.[3] It remains so to this day. The Ukraine crisis has signalled the return of the Baltic–Black Sea conflict system, described as 'the Intermarium' by Vadim Tsymbursky. It is here that two visions of Europe come into contention: on the one side there is 'Wider Europe', with the EU at its heart but increasingly coterminous with the Euro-Atlantic security and political community; and on the other side there is the idea of 'Greater Europe', a vision of a continental Europe, stretching from Lisbon to Vladivostok, that has multiple centres, including Brussels, Moscow and Ankara, but with a common purpose in overcoming the divisions that have traditionally plagued the continent. Two actual and potential orders in Europe interact and clash in Europe today, generating contestation in the borderlands.

THE TWO EUROPES

Wider Europe is associated with the year 1989, when the Berlin Wall was torn down and geopolitical fluidity returned to European affairs. The Soviet 'empire' collapsed and the former Communist countries in Central and Eastern Europe once again gained autonomy and sovereignty. For most, joining Wider Europe was the natural choice. This is the model of Europe that is focused on Brussels, with concentric rings emanating from the Western European heartlands of European integration. European integration in the 1950s was inspired by two fundamental principles: of transcending the logic of conflict, above all between France and Germany, and of ensuring equitable well-being for the continent's citizens. Since the signing of the Treaty of Rome by the six founding members of the European Economic Community on 25 March 1957, the association has grown to encompass 28 members, with the latest entrants coming from the former Communist part of the continent.

As the Communist systems collapsed from autumn 1989 onwards, there was a fundamental consensus in countries such as Poland and the Czech Republic in favour of liberal democracy, market reform and, above all, the 'return to Europe'. There were domestic debates, setbacks and contradictions, but overall political, social and geopolitical goals lined up. The accession wave of May 2004 included not only the Central and Eastern European states of Poland, Hungary, the Czech Republic, Slovakia and Slovenia, but also the Baltic republics of Estonia, Latvia and Lithuania (together with the Republic of Cyprus and Malta). In 2007 Bulgaria and Romania joined, and in July 2013 Croatia. This was an exemplary manifestation of the 'Wider Europe' model of development, and it undoubtedly delivered substantial benefits to the countries concerned. No less important, there was no external resistance at this point to EU enlargement. On its own it posed no security threat to Russia, and it was only later, when allied with NATO enlargement and the aggressive promotion of Western democracy, that expansion encountered resistance.

The idea of a 'Greater Europe' asserts a different model of European internal politics. Instead of concentric rings emanating from Brussels, weakening at the edges but nevertheless focused on a single centre, it posits a multipolar vision, with more than one centre and without a single ideological flavour. This is a pluralistic representation of European space, and draws on a long European tradition: the vision of pan-European unification. Plans for the integration of the continent have a long pedigree. Richard Coudenhove-Kalergi's notion of 'pan-Europa' before the war, Gaullist ideas of a broader common European space from the Atlantic to the Pacific, Mikhail Gorbachev's dream of a 'Common European Home' transcending the bloc politics of the Cold War era, Nicolas Sarkozy's idea of establishing 'an economic and security common area' with the EU to create a new bloc 'of 800 million people who share the same prosperity and security',[4] and the Valdai Club's idea of a 'Union of Europe', are all moments giving voice to this aspiration.

The symbolic date of the second model is 1991, the year in which the Communist system in the Soviet Union dissolved and the country disintegrated. The 'project of 1991' is broader than this, however, since it also denotes aspirations for democracy, constitutionalism and international integration in Russia and the other CIS countries. However, unlike the 1989 countries, those on the 1991 trajectory found that very little lined up: certainly, for Russia 'democracy' came to be associated not only with the chaos of the 1990s, the rise of the 'robber baron' oligarchs and an economic decline that surpassed anything endured by any country in the great depression of the 1930s, but above all with the loss of great-power status and international influence. The various aspirations were orthogonal to each other, provoking confusion over national identity and the country's destiny. In Russia this ultimately provoked a remedial programme of state activism, the attempt led by Putin to rectify what were perceived to be the internal excesses of the 1990s and Russia's external loss of status. At its extreme, the remedial programme in March 2014 took the form of the 'restitution' of Crimea to Russian jurisdiction, responding to what had long been the deepest sore in Russia's representation of its territoriality and nationhood.

The price to pay for the relatively peaceful and bloodless collapse of the Soviet Union was the entrenched position of the Soviet-era elites, officialdom and corporations. The vast security apparatus remained lodged in the post-Communist Russian body politic like a fish bone in the throat. The *siloviki*, those with a security service background or affiliation, had already under Boris Yeltsin in the 1990s emerged as a powerful counterweight to the oligarchs, and under Putin pushed for more repressive domestic policies and a more assertive foreign policy. Above all, the fundamental difference between 1989 and 1991 lies in contrasting geopolitical perspectives. Russia considers itself a 'great power' and an alternative, although not necessarily adversarial, civilisational and geopolitical pole in world politics. Thus Russia could not simply become part of the 'Wider Europe' focused on the EU, let alone slip easily into the Euro-Atlantic security community. It did attempt to join both, but its size, awkwardness, autonomy and aspirations to great-power status prevented any easy integration. Instead, the Greater European idea represented a way of negotiating what in the best of circumstances would have been a complex and difficult relationship.

The anti-Communist revolutions of 1989 drew their inspiration and reference points from developments in the West, notably the EU and ultimately NATO. Russia had no such clear direction, with membership of NATO excluded almost by definition by its own conflicted identity and Western fears of diluting the Euro-Atlantic alliance. Even relations with the EU soured as the Wider and Greater European agendas clashed. Russia was on a different track to the Eastern European states. If the goals were clear for the 1989 countries, in the 1991 countries the Soviet legacy is far deeper and the desired model of social and political organisation far more contested. After over two decades of 'transition' and reform, at least 11 out of the 15 countries emerging out of the USSR are authoritarian to one degree or another, including Russia. Even Estonia and Latvia, now members of NATO and the EU, can be charged with serious violations of civic rights as well as tolerating right-wing movements that verge on the fascistic. The tortured history of multiple occupations during World War II, each brutal but in a different way, has prompted virulent 'memory wars' today, as each side seeks to impose its own version of the dominant national narrative. These memory wars are one of the central issues that divide Ukraine, reflecting the different historical experiences of various parts of the country.

As Russia's estrangement from Wider Europe intensified, it placed ever-greater emphasis on the Greater European idea. As Yeltsin put it, 'Europe without Russia is not Europe at all. Only with Russia can it be a Greater Europe, with no possible equal anywhere on the globe.'[5] In other words, Russia was a vast and relatively underdeveloped country rich in natural endowments, while Western Europe had advanced technologies but needed energy and other resources. The two complemented each other, but no political form could be found to encompass the two halves of the continent. While the Russian leadership expended considerable effort to devise a new 'architecture' for a united Europe, the other countries saw no need for new ideas since, as far as they were concerned, 'Wider Europe' was a perfectly viable model, complemented not by Russia but by the US.

Among the Greater European plans mooted by Russia was the idea of a new European Security Treaty, announced by Medvedev in a speech in Berlin on 5 June 2008, which called for the creation of a genuinely inclusive security system to ensure that new dividing lines were not drawn across the continent. The initiative was greeted with polite contempt by the Western powers, although the 'Corfu process' was established to assess the proposal. In keeping with his original strong European leanings, in a speech in Berlin on 26 November 2010 Putin called for the geopolitical unification of all of 'Greater Europe' from Lisbon to Vladivostok, to create a genuine 'strategic partnership'.[6] Eurasian integration was the big project of Putin's third term, but he insisted that the planned Eurasian Economic Union (EEU) was not an alternative but a complement to European integration.[7] Rather surprisingly, given the crisis in Ukraine and the souring of relations with the EU, Putin returned to the idea of creating a free-trade zone from the Atlantic to the Pacific at the Russo-EU summit in Brussels on 28 January 2014.[8] Despite the Ukraine crisis, the Greater European cooperative path of development is not dead.

Russia's Greater European initiatives were typically seen in the West as being little more than a cover for the establishment of a 'Greater Russia' by stealth. The Atlantic community is intensely vigilant against attempts to 'drive a wedge' between its two wings, North America and Western Europe, and it has been so since various Soviet plans for European security were advanced by Khrushchev in the 1950s. This Cold War view prevails to this day, with the constant fear that any idea emanating outside the NATO system is potentially divisive and dangerous. This also includes a deep ambivalence about the EU taking greater control of its Common Foreign and Security Policy (CFSP). This has resulted in the effective 'militarisation' of the EU; in the sense that enlargement has become part of the broader process of the expansion of the Euro-Atlantic community, in which security, good governance and economic reform go hand in hand. In other words, EU enlargement paves the way to NATO membership. For historical reasons a number of EU countries are not members of NATO – Austria, Ireland, Finland and Sweden – but even this neutrality is being questioned. Since 1989 all new members of the EU have also become members of NATO. The Treaty of Lisbon (the 'Reform Treaty') of 13 December 2007, which came into effect in 2009, made this explicit. Accession countries are now required to align their defence and security policies with those of NATO. Despite the aspirations for a united continent at Communism's fall, new dividing lines have been established in Europe.

RUSSIAN NEO-REVISIONISM

The Ukraine crisis cannot be understood unless the evolution of Russian thinking is analysed. From a country that up to the early 2000s sought to align itself with the EU and NATO, after the Iraq war of 2003 Russia became increasingly alienated and developed into what I call a 'neo-revisionist' power, setting the stage for the confrontation over Ukraine. On coming to power in 2000, Putin sought engagement and accommodation with the West through the policy of 'new realism', and was perhaps the most pro-European leader Russia has ever had. Russia sought autonomy in its foreign policy, but this would not be based on anything approaching neo-Soviet notions of Russia as the core of an alternative geopolitical or ideological bloc.[9] After 2007 Russian foreign policy entered a new phase, that of neo-revisionism. Its behaviour became more assertive, in part derived from economic recovery bolstered by windfall energy rents, political stabilisation and a growing alienation not so much from the structures of hegemonic power but from its practices. From a status quo state Russia became a distinctive type of neo-revisionist power, claiming to be a 'norm-enforcer' and not just a norm-taker.[10] The essence of neo-revisionism is not the attempt to create new rules or dangle a vision of an alternative international order, but the attempt to ensure the universal application of existing norms.

Russia's neo-revisionism was provoked by a number of issues. First, the gradual deterioration of the relationship with the EU. The EU's conditionality always irked Russia, which considered itself by right a European country and was thus resentful of an organisation that claimed the prerogative to decide what was and what was not European, as well as condemning Russia's democratic inadequacies.[11] According to Sergei Yastrzhembsky, the deterioration in Russo-EU relations was provoked by the accession of the former Communist countries, who allegedly 'brought the spirit of primitive Russophobia' to the EU.[12] Different visions of integration collided. As Sergei Karaganov, the founding president of the Council for Foreign and Defence Policy (SVOP), put it, as Europe and Russia drew closer they realised just how different they were: 'Russia was moving towards the Europe of de Gaulle, Churchill and Adenauer, and when it got closer, it saw the Europe of the Brussels bureaucracy and new political correctness.'[13] Continued conflicts in the post-Soviet space, the inability to establish genuine partnership relations with the EU and disappointment following Russia's positive démarche in its attempt to reboot relations with the US after 9/11 all combined to sour Putin's new realist project.

The second key issue was the gradual breakdown of an inclusive pan-European security system in which Russia could act as an autonomous yet cooperative partner. For example, William Hill, who served two spells as head of the Organisation for Security and Cooperation in Europe (OSCE) Mission to Moldova in 1999–2006, reveals how Russia was systemically excluded from being able to contribute to the resolution of the Transnistria issue, undermining the long-standing canard that Russia prevents 'frozen' conflicts from being resolved in order to maintain leverage against the countries concerned. This may well be the practical consequence, but as most experts on each of the conflicts note, Russia's attempts to find constructive solutions are consistently blocked. As the reviewer of Hill's book puts it:

> Another important finding of the book is the author's acknowledgement that Western capitals displayed insufficient sensitivity toward Russia and denied her an independent diplomatic and political role in the region that had once been hers exclusively. [...] The problem of Russia being denied agency is also outlined when the author stresses that Russia–NATO problems were not caused by the very fact

of its enlargement, but by the fact that Moscow was prevented from meaningfully participating in or influencing decisions of the most important political and security questions in Europe.[14]

The point is a crucial one and has broader relevance. Thus, for example, the deepening of trade and other links between the EU and Ukraine is a natural and potentially beneficial process for all concerned, including Russia, but became problematic when Moscow was denied effective agency in managing the process, since it would clearly have a direct and massive impact on Russia.

Putin's frustrations were vented in his speech at the Munich Conference on Security Policy on 10 February 2007. He stressed the 'universal, indivisible character of security' and warned against the dangers of establishing a 'unipolar world [...] in which there is one master, one sovereign', while noting 'those who teach us [about democracy] do not want to learn themselves'. Putin listed a range of strategic problems, including the marginalisation of the UN, failure to ratify the adapted Conventional Forces in Europe (CFE) Treaty, the remilitarisation of Europe through missile defence development, NATO enlargement – which represented 'a serious provocation that reduces the level of mutual trust' – the weakening of the non-proliferation regime and the attempt 'to transform the OSCE into a vulgar instrument designed to promote the foreign policy interests of one or a group of countries'.[15] The 57-member OSCE remains one of the most important European bodies defending human rights and, in particular, monitoring elections, through its Office for Democratic Institutions and Human Rights (ODIHR), although its focus on the former Soviet states has drawn criticism from Russia. Under the 'chairmanship in office' of the Swiss president Didier Burkhalter, the OSCE has been one of the few independent bodies offering a crucial mediating role during the Ukraine crisis. On 21 March 2014 it created a Monitoring Mission to Ukraine, with the first observers arriving on 25 March.

Third, Russia and a number of other 'rising powers', notably China, have challenged American claims to 'exceptionalism' and global leadership. We shall return to this issue at various points, but here should stress that for the most part these countries are happy to work with the US on issues of common concern, but when American leadership turns into hegemonism the problems start. Russia is certainly not planning to create a counter-bloc to the Western alliance system, but it does reject the assumption that the Atlantic security order is universally benign and of global application. Even the former secretary of defence Robert Gates condemned 'the arrogance, after the collapse [of the USSR], of American government officials, academicians, businessmen, and politicians in telling Russians how to conduct their domestic and international affairs [...] [which] led to deep and long-term resentment and bitterness'.[16] In her study of Russo-American relations since the end of the Cold War, Angela Stent comes to a similar conclusion, noting that 'since 1992, a central Russian objective has been to regain its status as a great power and be treated as an equal by the US – a goal that was constantly frustrated'. She urges American policy makers to recognise that the Russian worldview differs from that of the US, and thus should 'exercise restraint in publicly commenting on developments in Russia'. She notes that the 'Bush administration focused considerable attention on Russia's neighbours, viewing its policies through a Russian prism – the more distanced from Russia the country was, the better. It wanted NATO membership for Ukraine more than Ukraine itself wanted it'. She lists a number of issues of mutual concern, including counter-terrorism and counter-proliferation, where the two countries could work together.[17]

A very different approach was adopted by Hillary Clinton as Secretary of State in President Barack Obama's first administration from 2009 to 2013. In her mem-oirs *Hard Choices* she stresses US global leadership and the country's commitment to democracy and human rights, which is hardly surprising, but more disturbing is the harsh inability to understand the logic of Russian behaviour. As long ago as 2008, during her failed presidential bid, Clinton asserted that Putin, as a former KGB agent, 'doesn't have a soul', to which Putin riposted that anyone seeking to be US president 'at a minimum […] should have a head'. She interpreted actions in support of independent Russian political subjectivity as an aggressive challenge to American leadership, rather than the normal expression of great-power autonomy in what Russia considers a multipolar world of independent nation states. She takes a consistently hawkish view of the world, urging Obama to take stronger action in Afghanistan, Libya and Syria, but when it comes to Russia her views are particularly harsh and unenlightened. She considers Putin a throwback to a nineteenth-century world of zero-sum realpolitik, intent on rebuilding the Russian Empire through Eurasian integration. Through this prism, she interprets Russian actions in Georgia in 2008 and in Crimea in 2014 as part of an aggressive strategy, rather than as defensive reactions to perceived challenges.

Clinton's view of the 'reset', the attempt by Obama in his first term to place rela-tions with Russia on a new footing, was minimalist. She engaged the more liberal Medvedev to pursue matters of common concern, such as managing nuclear arsenals and non-proliferation, but the policy lacked a vision of the strategic relationship between the two countries. The attempt to drive a wedge between Medvedev and Putin was doomed to fail, and the whole policy had run out of steam by the time Putin returned to power in 2012. Her Cold War stance is reflected in her parting injunction to Obama that 'the only language Putin would understand' is 'strength and resolve'. She doubts that internal protest will overthrow Putin, and instead argues that only the geopolitical challenges posed by the rise of China and the threat from radical Islam will force the Russian president to understand that Russia's best interests lie with the West and in 'charting a peaceful and profitable future as part of Europe rather than as its antagonist'.[18] Putin certainly understood this and in his early years had tried to find practical ways to become 'part of Europe', but it was the failure to find an appropriate formula that set Russia on its path of neo-revisionism, which was provoked precisely by the policies that she advocates.

This brings us to the fourth catalyst for Russian neo-revisionism. This is the ideology of 'democratism', which is distinct from the practices of democracy itself, instead assuming that if democracy is the best possible form of government and the one that is liable to make allies of the states concerned, then all practicable measures should be employed to achieve the desired end. The perception that the West was using democracy promotion as a cover to advance its strategic objectives, including regime change, aroused a host of defensive reactions in Russia. The main instrument for this came to be seen as 'colour' revolutions, popular mobilisations against attempts to 'steal' elections, whose classic exemplar was the events in Ukraine in autumn 2004 (on which more below). This form of regime change was not limited to the post-Soviet area. At the Moscow International Security Conference on 23 May 2014 Russian and Belarusian officials described how over the past decade the US and some NATO allies had allegedly overthrown governments in Ukraine, Georgia, Kyrgyzstan, Afghanistan, Iraq, Syria, Egypt, Libya and Yemen.[19] The ideology of democratism is backed up by an extensive network of civil-society associations sponsored by the US and European countries. For Russia and other countries the gripe is not so much with democracy as a *practice*, but its advancement as a *project* on other countries is perceived to be aggressive, expansionist and ultimately subversive of state sovereignty. Certainly, the critique of 'democratism' can be used as a cover for 'the society of despots', but it is also an appeal for a pluralist international order that recognises alternative types of development and different models of modernity.

These four factors turned Russia into a neo-revisionist power. Russia makes no claim to revise the existing international order, but demands that the leading powers abide by the mutually established rules of the international system, as well as claiming a no less leading place in that system. Russia is far from being a consistently revisionist power, and endorses American hegemony as long as what it perceives to be its vital interests and prestige are recognised. Russo-American cooperation over Syria and Iran is precisely the sort of relationship to which Russian neo-revisionism aspires. In September 2013 Putin and Sergei Lavrov, the Russian foreign minister, together with his American counterpart John Kerry, had brokered an international agreement on the destruction of Syria's chemical weapons of mass destruction. Russia's various initiatives in the field of security and norm-modification are intended not to repudiate the existing order but to make it more inclusive and universal.[20]

EURASIAN INTEGRATION

One of the core elements of Russian neo-revisionism is the attempt to give substance to Eurasian integration, limited at first to a small number of post-Soviet states but with an expansive dynamic that ultimately encompassed broader Asian integration. Aspirations for Greater European integration had run into the sand, and to compensate Russia advanced increasingly ambitious plans for Eurasian integration, which only exacerbated the division of Europe. Eurasian integration is not intended to undermine aspirations for Greater European unity, but does reflect the stymied nature of inter-European affairs and the dead end in Russo-EU relations. Russia and its partners began to develop Eurasia as a distinct pole in world affairs by providing the institutional framework for an alternative integrative project. For some nationalists this fulfilled ambitions to create a 'Greater Russia', although traditionally Eurasianist and Russian nationalist tendencies are antithetically opposed. One is based on the Russian nation, while the other envisages Eurasia as the basis for an alternative civilisational entity, anti-Western and anti-liberal.[21] What is important for our purposes is that geopolitical contestation returned to the heart of the continent. Wider Europe presented itself as the dominant force on the continent; Greater European ideas lacked substance; and Eurasian integration plans began to take institutional form. It is in the crosshairs of these competing projects that the Ukraine crisis has unfolded.

The CIS, as the successor to the Soviet Union, sought to maintain some of the earlier links between states, including visa-free travel and labour mobility, but it was unable ultimately to provide a vision of reconstituted economic, let alone political, community. The Tashkent Collective Security Treaty (CST) agreements of 1992 were transformed into the Collective Security Treaty Organisation (CSTO) on 7 October 2002, uniting Armenia, Belarus, Russia, Kyrgyzstan, Kazakhstan and Tajikistan, while Uzbekistan periodically joined and left. Through the CSTO Russia has supplied its partners with armaments at preferential domestic prices. The CSTO sought to give institutional form to the creation of a regional security complex, as described by Buzan and Waever.[22] The existence of such a complex was intended to provide a platform for the pursuit of Russia's broader goals, notably opposition to NATO enlargement, as well as to reinforce Russia's claims to be an autonomous great power. Attempts to mediate the tension between integration processes in eastern and western parts of the continent by establishing links between the respective security organisations were vetoed by the US. It was reported that the NATO Secretary General Anders Fogh Rasmussen sought to explore the possibility of cooperation between the CSTO and NATO, but when the US mission in Brussels got wind of this, the American ambassador to NATO Ivo Daalder was instructed to block any moves in this direction, because 'it would be counterproductive for NATO to engage with the CSTO, an organisation initiated by Moscow to counter potential NATO and US influence in the former Soviet space'.[23] Rasmussen began his term in office in 2009 with a bold attempt to engage with Russia, but by the time of the Ukraine crisis had turned into one of Russia's most virulent critics. This trajectory was shaped by the structural impasse derived from the asymmetrical end of the Cold War.

After a slow start the practical implementation of integration covering a large part of the Eurasian land mass moved with remarkable speed. On 25 January 2008 Russia, Belarus and Kazakhstan signed a tripartite customs union consisting of nine trade agreements covering tariffs, anti-dumping statistics and taxation issues. In summer 2009 agreements were signed to create the Eurasian Customs Union (ECU), formally launched on 1 January 2010, with most barriers removed by July. In the next stage, a 'Single Economic Space' came into effect on 1 January 2012, and by 1 January 2015 the two were to combine to create the Eurasian Economic Union (EEU). After a period of intense bargaining against the background of the Ukraine crisis, the EEU treaty signed on 29 May 2014 dropped plans for political cooperation, common citizenship, foreign policy, inter-parliamentary cooperation, passports and visas, and common border protection, as well as the idea of creating a common customs authority. There was no provision for a common currency or common social policy and pension system. The EEU agreement systematised the provisions already contained in the ECU and the CES, including free movement of goods, capital and labour, and harmonisation of regulation in 19 areas. The main innovation was the establishment of a common market for services, starting with less important sectors and gradually expanding to cover sectors like telecommunications, transportation and financial services. By the mid-2020s the EEU planned to establish a common financial–banking regulatory and monitoring authority located in Kazakhstan. The most ambitious proposals were postponed, notably the liberalisation of markets in a number of sensitive goods, including pharmaceuticals, and the creation of a common oil, gas and electricity market.[24]

Important steps were thus taken towards what in due course is anticipated to become a fully fledged Eurasian Union (EaU), with its own *acquis* covering technical, labour, mobility and other norms that would, like the EU, improve economic governance throughout the region. The three founding states cover about three-quarters of the post-Soviet region and have a combined population of 170 million and a total GDP of around $2.3 trillion (compared to the EU's GDP of $16.6 trillion), and contain 20 per cent of the world's gas and 15 per cent of oil reserves. It was initially anticipated that Uzbekistan, Kyrgyzstan and Tajikistan would join as equal members, although only the last two were serious candidates. There is also a plethora of other integrative projects. The Shanghai Cooperation Organisation (SCO) maintains a secretariat in Shanghai and is increasingly becoming a pole of attraction for countries far beyond its original Moscow–Beijing axis. From being no more than a catchy acronym, the BRICS countries (Brazil, Russia, India, China and South Africa) have begun to institutionalise their relationship. Although it lacks a permanent secretariat, it does have the makings of a serious international organisation. There are also ambitious schemes for pan-Asian integration encompassing Russia, China, South Korea and many countries in between – variations of the Silk Road idea. The intensity and scope of these plans for spatial integration vary greatly, yet all are groping to find a formula that brings together various combinations of states in post-European integrative endeavours. The degree to which sovereignty will be ceded to the institutions of integration remains fundamentally contested. Together they suggest an alternative architecture to that of Wider Europe and offer some substance to the idea of Eurasia and Asia aligning along a different axis to that of the West. The surge in macro-continental regionalism reflects the attempt to find mediating institutions in a world lacking the stable bipolarity of the Cold War and aspirations to overcome the asymmetries in the international system that arose in its place.

THE IN-BETWEEN LANDS AND THE EASTERN PARTNERSHIP

Between the 1989 and 1991 projects there are what can be called the '1990' countries, the 'in-between' lands, namely Belarus, Moldova and Ukraine, and the three South Caucasian states of Armenia, Azerbaijan and Georgia. These are countries which in one way or another sought to escape the geopolitical and governance limitations of 1991 while engaging with the EU and other partners to improve economic performance. These are not just in-between lands, but actively contested 'overlapping neighbourhoods'. Ukraine is the sharpest example of this in-between status. Located in the geographical heart of Europe and once known as the breadbasket of the continent, the country is torn internally and caught between two emerging blocs externally.[25] This was the inevitable consequence of the failure of Greater European ideas and the expansionist dynamic of Wider European countered by the development of Eurasian integration. Russia encouraged Ukraine to join the various pan-Eurasian regional economic integration projects, but from the very beginning Ukraine was wary of these invitations, fearing being turned away from its European aspirations.

Indeed, for some the Ukrainian nation state can only develop by shedding its dependency on Russia. Taras Kuzio, for example, calls these lands the 'post-Soviet colonial space', in which national self-affirmation inevitably comes into conflict with Russian attempts to retain a central role in the region.[26] This assumes that the historical relationship with Russia was a colonial one, a natural corollary of the 'Ukrainising' position. This a priori excludes a 'civilised' relationship with Moscow, condemning the region to contestation. For the monist Ukrainisers, the fundamental challenge was to 'desovietise' as quickly as possible, including dismantling the Soviet social-security system, economic links and bureaucratic traditions. The decolonisation model sustains monist Ukrainising forms of national development. The 'Malorussian' perspective insists, on the contrary, that the retention of traditional economic and personal links is one of the conditions of building sovereign nation states in the region.[27] This spills over into the cultural sphere, where Russia's double identity as both victim and perpetrator generates a more complex understanding that all the countries in the region both suffered and inflicted wounds on others.

After successive waves of enlargement, the problem remained of what to do with the countries on the EU's periphery. The enlargements of 2004 and 2007 placed an enormous strain on EU institutions, in part reformed by the Treaty of Lisbon. What is colloquially known as 'enlargement fatigue' set in, exacerbated by the great recession from 2008. Turkey's aspirations for membership had already effectively been put on hold, despite the beginning of accession negotiations in October 2005. The European Neighbourhood Policy (ENP) was launched in 2004 as an 'alternative to traditional geopolitics'.[28] Initially called the 'Wider Europe' strategy, the ENP sought to move beyond traditional foreign policy to allow a more strategic and intensified relationship with the EU's neighbours. As the former president of the European Commission Romano Prodi put it on 6 December 2002, they would 'share everything with the Union but institutions'. Designed to prevent new dividing lines between the EU and its neighbours, the idea was to create a 'ring of friends' engaged in an integration process that would not necessarily result in accession. The EU offered financial incentives in exchange for governance and economic reforms. Russia was initially invited to become part of the ENP, but that particular vision of being part of a Western-centred Wider Europe was anathema to those who considered Russia a great power and a centre of integration in its own right. Instead, in 2004 Moscow and Brussels pursued the 'common spaces' strategy, although this soon ran into the sand (despite some significant technical achievements), with mutual recrimination over human rights, energy politics and business practices.

Russia's fears were exacerbated by the development of the Eastern Partnership (EaP) from May 2008, targeting the six former Soviet states on the EU's borders. In the same year France and the EU's southern member states launched the Union of the Mediterranean (UoM), otherwise known as the Barcelona process, to forge closer links with the North African and Middle Eastern states, although the whole project was derailed by the onset of the Arab Spring in late 2011. At first glance, the EaP was just another variant of the Barcelona process, but whereas partnership to the south was not challenged by an alternative hegemonic power, Russia and its CIS partners had long-standing cultural, economic and political links with the EaP countries. The EaP, like the UoM, was not considered as a step towards EU membership for its participating states, but sought to create a comfort zone along the EU's borders by tying these countries in to a Western orientation.

The EaP was the brainchild of the Polish foreign minister Radosław (Radek) Sikorski, but he then drafted in his Swedish counterpart Carl Bildt to give the idea greater heft in intra-EU negotiations. Instead of finding ways to transcend the deepening lines of division in the continent, the two set about giving these divisions institutional form. The initial idea was to reinforce the Eastern dimension of ENP with the ultimate aim of bringing countries like Ukraine and Moldova into the EU. However, the strategy later changed: 'Indeed, without the Russian intervention in Georgia in 2008, in the opinion of one Commission official, the Eastern Partnership might have amounted to rather less in the way of substance.'[29] The previous pattern of bilateral relations was retained but deepened, with Association Agreements (AAs) to be signed with individual Eastern European countries, which were then to be reinforced by the deepening of bilateral economic relations through the establishment of a 'Deep and Comprehensive Free Trade Area' (DCFTA). The EaP has been criticised on a number of grounds, notably the lack of an articulated perspective for ultimate EU membership, as well as the relatively limited financing undergirding its aspirations, but it represented a return of bloc politics to Europe.

The Poles had long sought to make their diplomatic mark by claiming a special expertise in relations with their eastern neighbours, and in particular Ukraine, yet other member states took some convincing to believe that Poland had been adequately socialised not only in the procedures but also in the normative foundations of the EU. As Copsey and Pomorska put it:

> what surprised some officials in Brussels was that the Poles repeated persistently that the initiative was not anti-Russian and that it had nothing to do with the membership perspective for the countries involved. However, some of Poland's partners in the Union thought that the Polish government was protesting too much – after years of

presenting itself as a steely, sceptical cold warrior vis-à-vis Russia and emphasising the geopolitical imperative of preventing Russian expansion, the Polish government lacked credibility in arguing that there was nothing anti-Russian in the EaP.[30]

The Russian intervention in Georgia in August 2008 changed the tone of the discussion and bolstered the Polish argument that Russia's western neighbours needed stronger links with the EU, 'partly for their own security and partly for the security of the EU'.[31] Most Western accounts of the Georgian conflict have been tendentious, too often swallowing uncritically the line put out by the Georgian president from 2004 to 2013, Mikheil Saakashvili. Russia's response to the Georgian attack on the South Ossetian capital, Tskhinvali, included the temporary occupation of part of Georgia proper followed soon after by the recognition of the independence of South Ossetia and Abkhazia. This may have been disproportionate and ill-judged, yet in broad terms was a response to the threat of NATO enlargement. Misrepresentations of this conflict led directly to the Ukraine crisis. Sikorski and Bildt worked assiduously to ensure that the wrong lessons were drawn from the Russo-Georgian war. Sikorski, in the words of one perceptive commentator, 'really is another East European fruitcake. [...] Apparently, he is still back in 1939, imagining that somehow Putin and Merkel are Stalin and Hitler, about to conspire to divide Poland once again.'[32] The goal was to engineer Ukraine's separation from Moscow to steer it into the Western camp. From 2010 negotiations began on an Association Agreement with the country, specifying reform priorities, while the DCFTA would eliminate tariffs and trade quotas between the EU and its partner. The Association Agreement was initialled on 30 March and the DCFTA on 19 July 2012, but the plan to sign it at the third summit of the EaP in Vilnius on 28–29 November 2013 provoked the gravest European crisis in a generation.

On the face of it the EaP was analogous to the UoM, a deeper set of interactions between a regional subgroup of the ENP, but the context is very different. Whereas the UoM sought to forge links between hitherto disparate countries and where there was no putative alternative hegemon, the EaP had a profound geopolitical logic from the first. In Eastern Europe the dynamic of spatial contestation was already well established, as the 2008 war amply demonstrated. Although the EaP was presented as just another attempt to give a sub-regional dimension to a broader policy encompassing the EU's neighbours, it was in practice a way of forcing the countries between to choose. Its partisans insisted on the sovereign right of these states to join the alliance system of their liking. The concept of 'choice' thus became deeply ideological and was used as a weapon against those who suggested that countries have histories and location, and that choices have to take into account the effect that they will have on others. This is not a postulate of cynical realpolitik or pragmatism, but plain common sense, a commodity that has been signally absent in the Ukraine crisis.

As Russia developed its own integrative project, 'the EaP has therefore gradually become the most contentious issue between the EU and Russia'.[33] Russia had not traditionally been opposed to (non-Baltic) former Soviet states developing links with the EU, but the EaP represented a qualitatively different level of interaction that effectively precluded closer integration in Eurasian projects, and indeed had a profound security dynamic that effectively rendered the EU as much of a threat in Russian perceptions as NATO. It would certainly set back what Christopher Marsh and Nikolas Gvosdev call 'Putin's Eurasian dream', the ambition to create a Russian-dominated sphere in Eurasia that would be able to hold its own in the global geopolitical struggle with the US and China.[34]

The EU was launched on the path of geopolitical competition, something for which it was neither institutionally nor intellectually ready. Not only was the Association Agreement incompatible with Ukraine's existing free-trade agreements with Russia, but there was also the Lisbon requirement for Ukraine to align its defence and security policy with the EU. This was an extraordinary inversion: instead of overcoming the logic of conflict, the EU became an instrument for its reproduction in new forms. This is not the EU that a whole generation of idealists, scarred by the memory of European civil wars, sought to build. It also deeply alienated Russia, shattering the post-Cold War European security system. Not surprisingly, as soon as the Ukraine crisis escalated, the burden of geopolitical leadership shifted to the US, which was far more organisationally and temperamentally suited for this sort of conflict. Although the EU did devise elements of its own CFSP, and through the creation of the European External Action Service (EEAS) as a result of the Lisbon Treaty had a clear hierarchy about who was responsible for its foreign policy, as a collective actor it was overshadowed by its Atlantic partner. Lady Catherine Ashton, the first high representative of the EU for foreign affairs and security policy at the head of the EEAS, had some notable achievements to her credit, in particular helping regulate Serbian–Kosovar relations, and was indefatigable in representing Europe diplomatically, but it has been clear as the Ukraine crisis has developed that she is unable to articulate an independent policy that could temper the militant rhetoric emanating from Moscow, Washington and Kiev. The EU has been marginalised – in a conflict that its actions have provoked and that is taking place in its 'neighbourhood'.

Russia's various proposals for the trilateral regulation of neighbourhood matters were consistently rebuffed. At the time of the Prague summit in May 2009 launching the EaP, Putin suggested creating a tripartite structure to modernise the Ukrainian gas pipeline system, but this was brusquely dismissed, as were all Russia's later tripartite and Greater European initiatives.[35] As a result, relations with José Manuel Barroso, the head of the European Commission, seriously deteriorated and he was not trusted in Moscow. His belated attempts to place detailed discussion of association issues on the agenda of the six-monthly EU–Russia summits were considered as the substitute for real discussion of problematic questions. Tensions were exacerbated by the selective application of conditionality, notably in the case of Belarus, when before the 2010 election it looked as if relations with Russia were souring. Indeed, the EU was prepared to sign the Association Agreement with Ukraine even though its own condition that Yulia Tymoshenko be released from jail had not been met.

Each of the borderland former Soviet republics adapted to the problem of being trapped in two opposing gravitational fields in its own way. Belarus, led by President Alexander Lukashenko since 1994, was formally the closest to Russia, and engaged in an endless process of creating a 'union state'. Based on the rhetoric of 'Slavic unity' and the shared Soviet past, the process dragged on for years. Russia continues to fund the Belarus economic model, but relations are far from easy. There have been various gas conflicts, milk wars and mutual media attacks. Ultimately, however divided Belarusian identity may be, fewer than 30 per cent wish to reunify with Russia.[36] Following the Ukraine crisis and the annexation of Crimea, concern about Russian 'imperial' ambitions have increased. At least half the population opposes Belarus merging in one way or another with Russia, a figure that is comparable to those favouring membership in the EU. Belarus looks both ways, as would be expected from a borderland country.[37] Authoritarian leadership is perpetuated by the geopolitical stand-off in the centre of Europe.

Much the same applies to Armenia, whose position is made all the more precarious by its long-standing conflict with Azerbaijan over the Nagorno-Karabakh territory. On 3 September 2013 the president of Armenia, Serzh Sargsyan, initialled an agreement with the EEU, and thus turned his back on signing up to an Association Agreement with the EU. Moscow had placed a lot of pressure on Armenia to turn away from the EU, but given its strategic vulnerability when faced by Azerbaijan's attempts to regain Nagorno-Karabakh and the intense economic relations with Russia, the move was logical. The tragedy for Armenia, as it was for Ukraine, was to have been placed in a position where it was forced to choose.

INTEGRATION DILEMMAS

The EaP expressed in accentuated form the basic principle of Wider Europe: that cooperation between the EU and its eastern neighbours, including on security issues, would provide mutual benefit for all concerned. In return for bringing their legislation into line with EU standards and making the appropriate regulatory and governance reforms, the countries would gain access to European markets and a range of other benefits, while the EU would gain better governed and more prosperous neighbours, and thus enhance the security of all. There is little not to like about such a scenario, except for three problems. First, the transitional period would impose profound strains on the reforming country, and, in the absence of massive support from the EU, would threaten stability. The actual economic assistance that was offered to Ukraine in the run-up to the Vilnius summit was miserly. Second, the prospect of accession to the EU had been tangible and realistic for the Central European countries, but now the EU was suffering from a palpable enlargement fatigue. Having grown to 28 members with the accession of Croatia and endured the after-effects of the most profound economic crisis in its history, there was no appetite for further territorial growth. Turkey's accession process looked like dragging on for yet more decades. The absorption of a country the size and complexity of Ukraine is simply not on the agenda for this generation. Hence the incentives to undertake structural reforms are much weaker than in countries such as Poland, where EU membership was relatively uncontested.

Third, and most important, the advance of the EU into Eastern Europe came up against an already existing network of economic and other partnerships, and thus entered contentious territory. EU policy could find no way to take into account the interests of other actors, and instead its approach was characterised by 'a rather naive, Eurocentric attitude'.[38] The argument that 'the EU should not accept Russian rules for the relationship but set and enforce its own rules' was a recipe for confrontation, albeit one tempered by the view that 'the EU should use and apply existing instruments in a less ideological, but more pragmatic way'.[39] The sentiment is echoed by Sergei Glazyev, Putin's chief advisor on Eurasian integration, who argues that 'the European bureaucracy, a new political force with interests and leverage of its own, is behind the emerging EU trend to politicise ongoing integration'. He goes on to argue that 'a constructive way out of the growing contradictions between the alternative integration processes in Eurasia would be to depoliticize them into mutually beneficial economic cooperation'.[40] Instead, tensions between Russia and the Atlantic alliance increasingly took on a geopolitical aspect.

An 'integration dilemma' emerged, by analogy with Jervis's classic concept of a security dilemma, whereby 'one state's gain in security inadvertently threatens others'. As Charap and Troitskiy note, the purely defensive actions by one state can be seen as aggressive by another. They argue that an integration dilemma emerges 'when one state perceives as a threat to its own security or prosperity its neighbours' integration into military alliances or economic groupings that are closed to it'.[41] Exclusivity is the key, since the dynamic of insider and outsider imbues the process of what is usually considered a positive process into a zero-sum game for the excluded country. Although the leaders of the EEU insist that there is no fundamental incompatibility between their integration project and the Western European one, the EU insists that countries have to choose. It is this assertion, redolent of the Cold War spirit, which typifies the way that the EU has degenerated from an institution designed to transcend the logic of conflict to one that perpetuates it in new forms. The 'in-between' countries now face a stark choice: the EU or EEU? The 'common neighbourhood' has become a zone of contestation.

A DIVIDED EUROPE

The tension between the wider and greater representations of Europe is compounded by the struggle between continental and Atlanticist approaches to European security. In strategic terms, these now solidified into two putative new blocs, with a contested territory between them. The rift between 'Wider' and 'Greater' representations of Europe's future was compounded by the growing gulf between the idea of Europe as a continent in control of its own destiny, and that of Europe as, ultimately, simply part of a larger Euro-Atlantic community. As the Cold War drew to a close in 1989 the 'hour of Europe' was declared to have struck. The idea was that Europe could emerge from the superpower 'overlay' that had covered the continent for several decades. The aspiration was for Europe to take control of its own affairs, and thus the long shadow of World War II, accompanied by the 'occupation' of the two halves of the continent by the superpowers, would give way to a Europe 'whole and free'. This aspiration can be called 'continentalism', the idea that with the end of the Cold War Europe could take control once again of its own future. Instead, no form was found in which to institutionalise aspirations for Greater European integration. The post-Cold War anticipation of the unification of the continent on an inclusive and equal basis foundered on the fragmented nature of the new security order.

Instead, the dominant trend has been the Atlanticism embedded in NATO. At the time of German unification commitments were given by Western leaders that the eastern part of the united Germany would not become militarised. At a meeting in Moscow on 9 February 1990 Secretary of State James Baker promised Gorbachev that if Germany joined NATO and Russia pulled out its 24 divisions, 'there would be no extension of NATO's jurisdiction one inch to the east', but this referred only to the former GDR. The question of NATO enlargement to the other Soviet bloc countries simply did not enter anyone's head and was not discussed.[42] On that day the German foreign minister Hans-Dietrich Genscher told the Soviet foreign minister Eduard Shevardnadze that 'one thing is certain: NATO will not expand to the east'.[43] Although it was East Germany that was in question, the commitment reflected an understanding that NATO enlargement was a neuralgic issue for the Soviet Union. However, under President Bill Clinton NATO began its path of enlargement, gradually threatening to encircle Russia to the east and south. There was no deal prohibiting NATO's advance since it had appeared utter insanity even to conceive of such a thing in 1990. Given Russian weakness in the 1990s, Yeltsin could do little else but acquiesce. On coming to power in 2000, Putin toyed with the idea of Russia joining not only the EU but also NATO. On a visit to Britain in 2000 he was asked by David Frost about the possibility of Russia joining NATO, to which Putin responded: 'Why not?' The answer was not so much a serious bid for membership as a signal (as Putin put it in the same interview) that 'Russia is part of European culture and I can't imagine my country cut off from Europe or from what we often refer to as the "civilized world" [...] seeing NATO as an enemy is destructive for Russia.'[44]

However, there was no road that could lead to Russian membership. The existing members feared that it would not only impair NATO's military effectiveness but also threaten its viability. As an insider Russia would be able to shape decisions, forcing the US to share its leadership with Russia, something it certainly had no intention of doing. In NATO, as the Chinese put it, there could be 'only one tiger on the mountain'. Equally, NATO membership is conditional on meeting certain standards of democracy, the lack of border conflicts, and in general a certain level of state consolidation, which in the Russian case, with two Chechen wars and domestic turbulence, was lacking. Nevertheless, a path to membership could no doubt have been found if there had been the will to do so. NATO would then have become an instrument for peace in Europe and lived up to its proclaimed goals, as articulated in Article 1 of its founding charter. In the post-Cold War era, in any case, it had become a looser organisation complemented by various 'coalitions of the willing'. Instead, as its first Secretary General, Lord Ismay, put it in 1949, NATO remained a mechanism 'to keep the Russians out'. NATO remained the cornerstone of an Atlantic security system that preserved dividing lines rather than transcending them.

The implications of NATO enlargement were substantively debated. In an interview with Thomas Friedman in 1998, the doyen of international diplomacy and the architect of the original policy of 'containment' of the Soviet Union in the post-war years, George Kennan, was unsparing in his condemnation. Kennan spoke with dismay about the Senate's ratification of NATO expansion plans:

I think the Russians will react quite adversely and it will affect their policies. I think it is a tragic mistake. There was no reason for this whatsoever. No one was threatening anyone else [...] This expansion would make the Founding Fathers of this country turn over in their graves. We have signed on to protect a whole series of countries, even though we have neither the resources nor the intention to do so in any serious way.

Not for the first time the 'superficial and ill-informed' nature of Congressional discussion was condemned. Equally, he added words that remain a portent for today:

I was particularly bothered by the references to Russia as a country dying to attack Western Europe. Don't people understand? Our differences in the cold war were with the Soviet Communist regime. And now we are turning our backs on the very people who mounted the greatest bloodless revolution in history to remove that Soviet regime.[45]

Kennan was not alone, and in July 1997 an open letter from senior American statesmen to the White House echoed his warning that enlargement would be a 'policy error of historic proportions'. They argued that it would be bad for NATO, since it would 'inevitably degrade its ability to carry out its primary mission', it would be bad for Russia since it would strengthen the non-democratic opposition, it would be bad for Europe since it would 'draw a new line of division between the "ins" and "outs" and foster instability', and it would be bad for the US since it would 'call into question the US commitment to the alliance'.[46]

The liberal universalism of the Bill Clinton presidency dominated the discourse and swept aside realist objections. The idea was that by bringing the former Communist states into the 'civilising institutions and prosperity of the West', they would be transformed, just as Germany had been after the war, and that eventually the same would apply to Russia. The problem was that Russia was not a defeated power and considered itself a great power in its own right, very unlike post-war Germany, and if brought into NATO it would seek to exercise leadership, something that the other states would not readily contemplate. The talk at the time that NATO enlargement put an end to the division of Europe appeared oblivious to the fact that Europe's largest country remained a growling and increasingly dissatisfied presence outside. One can imagine how Poland would have felt if Russia had been invited to join while it was left out in the cold. Kennan could have added that by creating new dividing lines in Europe, the security of all was thereby diminished. When Russia did finally respond in the manner anticipated by Kennan and other critics, it was taken as justification for the need for NATO consolidation. This is the essence of the Ukraine crisis.

The Western powers did seek to sweeten the pill. Russia was included in NATO's Partnership for Peace programme in 1994, and the NATO–Russia Founding Act on Mutual Relations of May 1997 'defined the goals and mechanisms of consultation', including the creation of the NATO–Russia Permanent Joint Council. NATO committed itself not to station troops permanently in the newly acceded countries. In 2002 the NATO–Russia Council (NRC) was established as a forum to advance cooperation, in which Russia was meant not to be one against the others but part of an expanded security community. However, at moments of crisis the NRC turned out to be useless as a forum of conflict resolution, isolating rather than engaging with Russia.

The perceived promise of NATO membership granted to Georgia and Ukraine at the Bucharest NATO summit on 2–4 April 2008 raised the stakes on all sides. Ukraine's non-bloc status is enshrined in its constitution, yet this seemed to matter little to advocates of enlargement. The summit radicalised the Russian position, with Putin strengthening the military, diplomatic and aid links with Abkhazia and South Ossetia. Equally, Bucharest endowed the Georgians with what turned out to be ill-founded optimism that they had, even if informally, come under Western protection. Saakashvili apparently sabotaged all attempts to de-escalate the growing conflict not only between Tbilisi and its two breakaway regions but also between Tbilisi and Moscow. The Russian action, very simply, can be called 'the war to stop NATO enlargement'.[47] It was an issue of existential security importance for the country, and in that light Russian actions can be considered defensive. However, instead of drawing the appropriate lessons, the ferocious propaganda put out by the Saakashvili regime about 'Russian aggression' shaped Western perceptions. The British Foreign Secretary, David Miliband, visited Kiev and pledged Britain's support, dooming the country to become the next epicentre of the artificially constructed struggle for mastery in Europe.

The tension between a continental vision of European security and what appeared to be the inexorable enlargement of NATO prepared the stage for the Ukrainian confrontation of 2014 that was, as Stephen Cohen repeatedly warned, two steps from another Cuban missile crisis and three steps from World War III. Greater Europe and continental approaches to the management of European affairs were dismissed as the 'Gaullist heresy', and discussion was thereby rendered illegitimate. Atlanticism became the new ideology to contain Russia. This was vividly manifested in the open letter of 15 July 2009 to Obama, in which leading intellectual and former politicians from across Central and Eastern Europe warned him not to take the region's 'transatlantic orientation' for granted. The letter noted that 'twenty years after the end of the Cold War, however, we see that Central and Eastern European countries are no longer at the heart of American foreign policy', and went on to warn that if this neglect continued the region could cease to be a 'pro-Atlantic voice within the EU' under pressure from a 'revisionist' Russia that was 'pursuing a 19th-century agenda with 21st-century tactics'. The letter was blunt in its condemnation, claiming that Russia 'uses overt and covert means of economic warfare, ranging from energy blockades and politically motivated investments to bribery and media manipulation in order to advance its interests and to challenge the transatlantic orientation of Central and Eastern Europe'.[48] The shocking feature of the letter was its view that the EU was no more than a component of the Atlantic security system, rather than a peace project on the European continent. In this respect, events proved them right, and the EU was unable to transcend its roots as one of the instruments of the Cold War.

Although the authors of the letter were condemned by many in the West at the time as 'confrontational neocons', the events in Ukraine appear to have justified their plea to Obama to maintain American engagement with the region.[49] Indeed, from this perspective it is the weakness of Atlanticism rather than its consolidation that encouraged Russia in its aggressive actions. However, as I have argued above, the precise opposite is the case. The persistent delegitimation of Russia's security concerns, the anti-Russianism of the new NATO members, the failure to overcome the asymmetries in the Cold War settlement, the consolidation of a monological Wider European agenda of EU enlargement and its effective merger with the Atlantic security system, and the dismissal of Russian and other ideas for Greater European unity, have all conspired to create the conditions for the confrontation of 2014. The failure of Europe to outline a strategy to prevent the imposition of new dividing lines, as reflected in the axiological tone of the open letter, predictably led to the crisis; which in turn only aggravated the conditions that provoked the conflict.

The Atlantic security partnership began in ideological terms to merge with the EU's Wider Europe. While Russia had initially taken a relatively benign stance on EU enlargement, the increasing coincidence of Atlanticist and Wider European identities became a matter of concern. In effect, EU enlargement became the harbinger of the NATO enlargement. The failure to sustain a 'Gaullist' narrative of European security, separate from although allied with the US, meant that the two very different institutions effectively became one. Karaganov notes that 'the Ukraine crisis has exposed the failure of post-cold war policies'. He was shocked by the intense anti-Russian sentiments in the Western media in the two years before the February 2014 Sochi Olympics:

This refreshed memories of the double standards and lies that have been characteristic of the West's behaviour for the past 20 years. We were reminded of the eastward expansion of NATO, over the pleas and protests of a weakened Russian state. Had Ukraine been absorbed into the alliance, Russia's strategic position would have become intolerable. When calls for reason proved powerless to stop NATO's expansion, Russia halted it instead with an iron fist. In 2008 Russia responded to an attack by Georgian troops that killed Russian peacekeepers and scores of Ossetian civilians. Ukraine has since designated itself a nonaligned state, although NATO officials continued to try to lure it. It is against this background that Russia's actions […] must be seen. The iron fist is once again being shown to revanchists seeking consolation for the geopolitical and moral loses of the last decade.[50]

The boycott of the opening ceremony by major Western leaders was a turning point in the attitude of many Russians to the West, and has shaped subsequent events in Ukraine. Equally, just as in the Russo-Georgian war, EU enlargement was seen as the harbinger of NATO's extension to the region, and with it the renewed policy of containing Russia.

CHAPTER 3

UKRAINE CONTESTED

The previous chapter analysed the tensions in the post-Cold War international system, in which Western enlargement came up against an intractable Russia, with security and civilisational concerns of its own. No inclusive and mutually beneficial European order was established. This chapter examines how these tensions interacted with Ukraine, a country with its own contradictory patterns of historical and national development. As we saw in Chapter 1, Ukraine has a complex balance of ethnic and linguistic intermingling, and finds itself a genuine borderland between two increasingly antagonistic blocs. The Ukrainian crisis is essentially a struggle between different visions of what it means to be Ukrainian and who is to decide, and, following on from that, what is Ukraine's proper place in the world. As early as the 1990s Anatol Lieven asked whether it was wise to try to force Ukraine to choose between integration into Western institutions, notably NATO, and its traditional orientations to the East.[1] The imposition of such a choice in the end turned 'fraternal rivalry' into deadly contestation that threatened to tear the country apart and endanger world peace.

LEADERS AND POWER

The two contrasting models of statehood and visions of nationhood – the monist and the pluralist – have been contested since Ukraine became an independent state. While I have stressed the divisions, on many issues the two tendencies are agreed, above all on the imperative of developing Ukraine as a sovereign nation state. Despite the many linguistic, cultural and historic differences, all regions, with the exception of Crimea, were committed to the idea of Ukraine. The sentiment expressed repeatedly by the Belarusian president Alexander Lukashenko that Belarusians and Russians are 'one nation' is one that is not repeated in the Ukrainian context;[2] as the second Ukrainian president, Leonid Kuchma, famously wrote: 'Ukraine is not Russia.'[3] David Marples dubbed Belarus a 'denationalised nation', with the implication that Russia and Belarus were one nation divided into two states.[4] By contrast, Ukraine was one state divided into many nations, among whom the Russian component (according to the Ukrainisers) was just one; whereas the Malorussian tendency stresses the centrality of Russian influence. The continuing challenge is to find an adequate constitutional form to institutionalise this diversity while creating a governable polity. Constitution-making and politics are always irretrievably interwoven, but in Ukraine this took extreme forms as leadership change and constitutional shaping became entwined.

With independence in 1991, the difficult times began. The former leader of the Ukrainian Communist Party (CPU), Leonid Kravchuk, had, like Gorbachev, shifted to become president of the republic, and he remained in office until 1994. The election in that year prefigured the tensions that were to characterise all presidential contests until 2014. The south and east supported the more 'pro-Russian' candidate from Dnepropetrovsk, Leonid Kuchma, while the centre and west inclined to the more assertive nationalist rhetoric coming from Kravchuk as he sought to renew his mandate. Kuchma was elected for a second term in 1999, but thereafter his presidency degenerated into scandal and controversy. Kuchma was alleged to have requested the silencing of the investigative journalist Georgiy Gongadze in September 2000, whose decapitated body was found shortly afterwards. Audiotapes emerged of Kuchma, Vladimir Lytvyn and other top officials discussing the need to stop his investigations into high-level corruption. The murder provoked the first wave of popular mobilisation in Ukraine, with mass rallies against Kuchma and attempts to organise a national referendum to impeach him.

With no natural successor and limited to two terms by the constitution, in September 2004 Kuchma reluctantly endorsed Viktor Yanukovych as the regime candidate. Yanukovych was already a controversial figure. He had acquired a criminal record in his youth, when at the age of 17 in 1967 he was sentenced to three years in jail for robbery and assault, and then in 1970 he was convicted for a second time and given a two-year sentence for assault. Notwithstanding, in 1997 he was appointed governor of the Donetsk region, apparently at the behest of the local oligarch, Rinat Akhmetov. His governing style was a mix of co-optation and coercion, although not totally devoid of a rational pragmatism tempered by corruption and cronyism. He left the governorship to become prime minister on 21 November 2002, serving until 31 December 2004.

He came up against Viktor Yushchenko, the candidate of the radical nationalists. He was in alliance with Yulia Tymoshenko, the head of the liberal nationalist Bloc

Yulia Tymoshenko (BYuT), and promised her the post of prime minister if he won. The top two candidates in the first round held on 31 October 2004, Yushchenko and Yanukovych, proceeded to the run-off on 21 November. Following the contested vote on that day, with Yanukovych prematurely declared the winner and absurdly congratulated as such by Putin, Tymoshenko called on the population to come to the Maidan and to spread the Orange symbol, the colour of Yushchenko's campaign. On 22 November, led by the youth group 'Pora' ('Enough'), massive protests gathered across the country, with at least half a million people assembling in the centre of Kiev. Many of them stayed in a tent city for several weeks, despite the bitter cold, although they were generously supported with warm food and supplies. On 3 December the Supreme Court invalidated the run-off result and announced a rerun on 26 December. Yushchenko was elected president with 52 per cent of the vote against Yanukovych's 44.2 per cent. Thus protest against electoral irregularities provoked what came to be known as the Orange Revolution.[5] This was a decisive instance of 'people power', but it also involved powerful elite conflicts. The structures of 'oligarch democracy' were not challenged, and hence the question posed by David Lane as to whether it was a 'people's revolution' or a 'revolutionary coup' remains pertinent to this day.[6]

Reflecting the political indeterminacy and tensions in the state-building project, the constitution itself became the plaything of political intrigue and immediate advantage. Amendments were introduced on 8 December 2004 that significantly increased the powers of parliament. From 1 January 2006 the president lost the power to nominate the prime minister, who was now chosen by the parliamentary majority, or to dismiss cabinet ministers, but retained the right to appoint the minister of defence and the foreign minister. However, the president gained the right to dissolve parliament if no coalition could be mustered to appoint the prime minister; the president could then call new parliamentary elections.

Despite the mass mobilisation and the enthusiasm attending Yushchenko's victory, his administration stumbled from crisis to crisis amid bitter personal conflicts, confused policy making and corruption. His first prime minister was Tymoshenko, known as the 'gas princess' for the way that she made a fortune out of energy-trading in the 1990s. Entering office on 24 January 2005, Tymoshenko brought only one of her bloc colleagues into the government, Alexander Turchynov, a Baptist minister, who was appointed head of the Security Service of Ukraine (SBU). A report published by WikiLeaks reveals that the US Assistant Secretary of State for European and Eurasian affairs, Daniel Fried, hurried to Ukraine,

> to deliver a message of USG [US government] commitment to Ukraine's sovereignty, its future as a free nation, and its right to make its own choices about its place in the

world. The Poles and the Balts had successes in asserting such rights in the face of Russian pressure and opposition, and Ukraine would as well, as long as its leaders were strong enough to continue reform.

Fried 'emphasized US support for Ukraine's NATO and Euro-Atlantic aspirations'.[7] In other words, democratic protest against electoral fraud was inextricably bound up with geopolitical contestation, a fateful combination that would have devastating consequences in 2014.

Tymoshenko's administration lasted a bare eight months, and was marked by controversy and conflicts with the president. It ended with the resignation of several senior officials, including Petro Poroshenko, the head of the National Security and Defence Council (NSDC). Her government was dismissed by Yushchenko on 8 September 2005. Live on air, he claimed that Tymoshenko was serving the interests of certain businesses, and that her plan to reprivatise the Nikopol Ferroalloy Plant, previously owned by Kuchma's son-in-law Viktor Pinchuk, Ukraine's second-richest oligarch, 'was the last drop' that prompted him to dismiss the government. He accused her of betraying the ideals of the Orange Revolution. The personal antagonism between Yushchenko and Tymoshenko continued. In the 2006 parliamentary elections the BYuT group did remarkably well, outpolling Yushchenko's Our Ukraine, winning 129 seats to the latter's 81. Yushchenko's poll ratings began the disastrous slide that saw him gain a miserable 5 per cent in the 2010 presidential election. Tymoshenko once again sought to become prime minister, but this was conditional on her long-time opponent Poroshenko becoming speaker of parliament. After long manoeuvring this was blocked by Alexander Moroz, the leader of the Socialist Party of Ukraine, who wanted the position himself. He achieved this on 6 July 2006. Immediately afterwards, a coalition of the Party of Regions (PoR), the Socialist Party of Ukraine and the CPU allowed Yanukovych to become prime minister once again from 4 August 2006 to 16 December 2007. This was a remarkable turnaround for the man against whom the popular uprising had been directed in 2004. Yanukovych was rehabilitated as a political figure, despite his chequered past and nefarious role in the electoral fraud of autumn 2004.

In the preterm parliamentary election of 30 September 2007 Tymoshenko's party (BYuT) once again did well, in part by gaining seats in the industrial east, the heartland of Yanukovych's PoR. This allowed the Yushchenko–Tymoshenko alliance to be put together once again. A new government was formed by the end of the year and Tymoshenko became premier for a more extended second period, from 18 December 2007 to 4 March 2010. A cable sent by the American ambassador, William B. Taylor, was typically ambivalent: 'She continues to say many of the right things on economic matters, yet some of her populist campaign promises convey a different message.'[8] The gas relationship with Moscow was at the centre of her activities, finally pushing her long-term rival Dmytro Firtash and his RosUkrEnergo (RUE), established by Putin and Kuchma as the main gas trade between the two countries at a meeting in Yalta in July 2004, out of the gas intermediary business, but only after an extended gas shut-off in January 2009.[9] The messages reveal how excruciatingly hard it was to establish a direct gas-trading relationship between Turkmenistan and Ukraine.[10] In his study of Ukraine's energy dependence, James Sherr argues that no Ukrainian government tried to break the pattern of dependency, opacity, rent-seeking and preferential pricing, since this would have broken the close ties between big business and power.[11] The issue was at the centre of government concerns, taking the form of one group of oligarchs seeking to displace another, accompanied by accusations of corruption and subservience to the Kremlin.

Other cables demonstrate how febrile the energy relationship between Moscow and Kiev was, with almost permanent negotiations and threats of shutdowns. For example, in February 2008 the ambassador noted: 'Gazprom has indicated it had grown tired of Ukraine's inability to sign and implement the February 2008 gas agreement announced by Putin and Yushchenko and threatened to reduce gas supplies to Ukraine by 25 percent beginning on March 3.'[12] Yushchenko and Putin met on 12–13 February without Tymoshenko and hammered out a deal, followed soon after by Tymoshenko's angry visit to Moscow. As a cable notes: 'GOR [government of Russia] officials expressed dismay at the complicated dynamics between Yushchenko and Tymoshenko, which required "delicate balancing" on its part.' The report goes on to make the crucial point, which endures to this day: 'Moscow analysts view bilateral relations as hostage to Ukrainian domestic political games.'[13]

The problems were compounded by Ukraine's NATO aspirations, which provoked harsh statements from Moscow. A Russian foreign-ministry statement on 13 January 2008 'warned that further expansion of NATO could produce a serious political–military upheaval that would affect the interests of Russia'. Potential integration with NATO, an issue that was to be discussed at the Bucharest summit in April, 'would force Russia to undertake "appropriate measures"'. In his 14 February annual press conference, Putin, in the words of the cable, 'lashed out against Ukraine's MAP [Membership Action Plan] request, saying that the majority of Ukrainian citizens were against their country's NATO membership but Ukrainian leaders did not ask their opinion[.] "What kind of democracy is this? he asked."'[14] Bucharest backed off the immediate issuance of a MAP, but Ukraine's NATO aspirations were recognised. The Americans had been clearly warned just how concerned Moscow was about potential NATO enlargement to its borders, yet it took the combined efforts of the French and

Germans to dissuade President George W. Bush from starting the process of Ukrainian and Georgian accession then and there. The Russo-Georgian war of August 2008 was in effect the first of the 'wars to stop NATO enlargement'; the Ukraine crisis of 2014 is the second. It is not clear whether humanity would survive a third.

An unstoppable force was hitting an immovable object. As a cable later that year put it:

> President Yushchenko has a reputation as a visionary. Even his critics concede that his commitment to seeing Ukraine join NATO is sincere and unwavering. He has been the driving force behind Ukraine's request for a MAP and tireless in making the case both at home and abroad. In Yushchenko's view, NATO membership is the only thing that can guarantee Ukrainian sovereignty and territorial integrity for the long run. He has stated that recent events in Georgia reinforce the need for collective security arrangements for Ukraine. Yushchenko has a close relationship with Georgian President Saakashvili, and is the godfather to Saakashvili's son.[15]

As the Russo-Georgian war progressed, on 12 August Yushchenko visited Tbilisi and issued two decrees more closely regulating Russia's Black Sea Fleet (BSF) operating out of Sevastopol, and reaffirmed that the basing rights agreed in 1997 would be terminated in 2017. The issue could hardly have been more painful for Moscow, but the torture was enhanced by making the announcement in Georgia. Yushchenko was indeed a 'visionary' in his inability to put himself in the shoes of the other. The cables demonstrate that, for the US, Russian concerns were not so much ignored as simply not considered worthy of consideration. This blindness was prevalent among the monists in Kiev, compounded by the campaign, spearheaded by Yushchenko, to obtain international recognition of the Holodomor as genocide. On the other side, those who were more inclined to take Russian concerns into account were associated with corruption and bad governance practices. What was lacking was a substantive political expression of Ukrainian pluralism, sensitive to the potentially devastating consequences of NATO enlargement on relations with its eastern neighbour, but committed to a more equitable pattern of economic development. In the event, although NATO enlargement was not on the immediate agenda, the effective merger of EU security integration with the Atlantic security community meant that Ukraine's association with the EU, which by most reckonings could only be considered benign, took on dangerous security connotations, as well as challenging Moscow's own plans for economic integration in Eurasia.

In the 17 January 2010 presidential election Tymoshenko came second with 25 per cent of the vote, while Yanukovych took first place with 35 per cent. In the run-off on 14 February, Yanukovych won 48.95 per cent against Tymoshenko's 45.47 per cent. Once again the division in political geography came to the fore, with 16 western regions and Kiev voting for Tymoshenko, while nine south-eastern regions and Sevastopol voted for Yanukovych. Tymoshenko appealed against the outcome, arguing that at least a million votes were stolen, and she resigned as prime minister, with Yanukovych assuming the presidency on 25 February. The Orangists describe Yanukovych's election as a '*coup d'état*', although international observers considered the election relatively free and fair. In the event, the consequences were indeed coup-like. It remains a matter of surprise that a man with Yanukovych's record could have been returned to the presidency. As Kuchma commented to the new American ambassador, John F. Tefft, in a document dated 2 February 2010, the choice between Tymoshenko and Yanukovych was between the 'bad and very bad'; Kuchma praised the candidate eliminated in the first round, Arseniy Yatsenyuk.[16] Yatsenyuk is a Greek Catholic (Uniate) and is typically considered a technocrat, but proved to be one of the harshest exponents of monist nationalism. With Yanukovych coming to power it was clear that relations with the US would not be warm. President Obama focused on the 'reset' with Medvedev (but not with Putin, who at the time was prime minister), and let the EU make the running on Ukrainian policy. The US came racing back to take the lead once the protests against Yanukovych gathered pace in late 2013.

Yanukovych proceeded to establish a party-based patronage system accompanied by misrule on a grand scale. The PoR consolidated its position across the east and south by proclaiming its opposition to the politicisation of linguistic and cultural differences by the previous Orange administration. The party's identity increasingly focused on defence of the Russophone population, intensifying the already powerful cleavage between monism and pluralism. The party sought to raise the legal status of the Russian language, establish closer ties with Russia, maintain neutrality and devolve power to the regions. On 1 October 2010 Yanukovych suborned the Constitutional Court and forced a reversion to the original presidential system stipulated by the 1996 constitution, thus nullifying the 2004 'Orange' amendments that gave more power to parliament. With his new powers, Yanukovych gained the right to appoint and dismiss a wide range of executive officials. The chair of the PoR, Mykola (Nikolai) Azarov, was appointed prime minister, while throughout the country regional governors were replaced by PoR appointees. This was standard practice in Ukraine following a change of president, but Yanukovych took the purge of old officials to new extremes.

Tymoshenko subsequently faced a barrage of criminal charges, including that she had allegedly tried to bribe Supreme Court judges and had misappropriated funds received by Ukraine within the framework of the Kyoto Protocol. A third case was opened against her in April 2011 concerning the alleged abuse of power during the 2009 Russo-Ukrainian gas dispute. Her trial in the 'gas' case began on 24 June 2011, and on 11 October she was convicted of embezzlement and abuse of power and sentenced to seven years in prison, as well as being ordered to pay the state $188 million in compensation. The case was considered to be politically motivated.[17] Her former interior minister, Yury Lutsenko, was also jailed. Tymoshenko remained leader of the Batkivshchyna (Fatherland) party, which in the 2012 election came second, winning 101 of parliament's 450 seats. The 2012 election was controversial, being marked, in the words of a Bertelsmann Stiftung report, by 'the lack of a level playing field, by the abuse of state resources, by the lack of a transparent campaign and party financing, and by the lack of balanced media coverage'. State-controlled media devoted nearly half of its coverage to Yanukovych's PoR.[18] Yanukovych's slide into authoritarianism had begun.

It was clear that Yanukovych would face an uphill struggle to win the 2015 presidential election. His support plummeted from 46 to 26 per cent by the end of his first year in power, and never recovered. His support had faded even on his home turf in the Donbas, and polls suggested that he would be beaten by Vitaly Klitschko, the head of the Ukrainian Democratic Alliance for Reform (UDAR) party. From jail Tymoshenko urged the Ukrainian government to sign the EU Association Agreement and the DCFTA, which had long been negotiated and was due to be signed in Vilnius on 29 November 2013. One of the EU's conditions was Tymoshenko's release, but as the signing approached it was clear that the EU, in its eagerness to extend its influence in Ukraine, was willing to sign in any case. This placed Yanukovych in a quandary, being urged by Russia to maintain its traditional links with the CIS free-trade area, if not to sign up to the Eurasian Customs Union (ECU) that was being transformed into the Eurasian Economic Union (EEU). Russia in the end offered $15 billion in immediate support, and preferential gas tariffs, much more generous than what the EU offered.

On 21 November 2013 Yanukovych announced that he would postpone signing, and the crowds once again gathered on the Maidan. The decision was far from predetermined. Yanukovych maintained the long Ukrainian tradition of tacking between East and West, the venerable 'multi-vector' policy enunciated by Kuchma. In an attempt to break out of the impasse, Yanukovych tried to bring in China as a counterweight to Russia and the EU, offering generous economic concessions to attract Chinese corporations into the energy and manufacturing sector. Equally, in January and November 2013 Ukraine signed production-sharing agreements (PSAs) with Shell and Chevron to exploit unconventional gas with the use of fracking technologies in the Yuzivska and Oleshka shale-gas fields. The shale-gas revolution could free Ukraine from natural-gas imports. When it came to the EU, even his chief of staff, Sergei Levochkin, headed a group of advisors urging him to sign and fight the presidential contest as a reformer.[19] This was quite feasible, since relations with Russia during his presidency had never been easy. He had consistently refused to sign up to the ECU, while gas prices remained high. In the months before the Vilnius summit, fearing a flood of tariff-free EU goods and undermining domestic producers, Russia imposed various restrictions on Ukrainian exports. I will return to this below.

CONSTITUTIONAL INDETERMINACIES

The constitution adopted on 28 June 1996, after intense debate, encapsulated a particular vision of Ukrainian statehood. Three issues were particularly contentious. The first concerned the territorial character of the state – whether it should be unitary or federal. Fears about the fragility of the bonds holding the country together led to the creation of a unitary state. Article 132 asserts that 'the territorial structure of Ukraine is based on the principles of unity and indivisibility of the state territory'. This was accompanied by the appointment of regional governors, who are subordinated to the president and can be dismissed by him. The administrative and territorial structure of Ukraine consisted of 24 oblasts (regions), the two cities of Kiev and Sevastopol, and the Autonomous Republic of Crimea. Following the early attempts at separatism and struggles to return Crimea to Russian jurisdiction, the constitution devoted a whole chapter to the republic. Article 134 stressed that it is 'an inseparable constituent part of Ukraine and decides on the issues ascribed to its competence within the limits of authority determined by the Constitution of Ukraine'. A range of devolved powers were listed, including management of agriculture and forestry, land reclamation, tourism, culture, transport and health services. In Crimea the prime minister fulfilled the role of governor.

The second concerned the national language. Once again, the agenda of the Ukrainian 'nationalising' elites prevailed, and Ukrainian was instated as the sole national language, relegating Russian simply to the language of personal communication. As we have seen, Article 10 was unequivocal in its statement that 'the state language of Ukraine is the Ukrainian language', but went on to note that 'the free development, use and protection of Russian, and other languages of national minorities of Ukraine, is guaranteed'. The description of Russian as the language of a 'national minority', in a country where 80 per cent described themselves as Russian-speakers, was galling to say the least. Defenders of this approach argue that Ukrainian had long been suppressed and marginalised, and now needed extra support to re-establish itself as the language of the nation. There is substance to this view, since in the nineteenth century the tsarist authorities had relegated Ukrainian to little more than a folkloric residue. Its use had revived at the time of Ukraine's first attempts at independent statehood during the Russian Revolution and civil war. The Soviet policy of *korenizatsiya* (indigenisation) lasted until the mid-1930s, encouraging the revival of native languages and cultures, but Stalin from the late 1930s moved against national elites.

By the end of the Soviet period there were few schools teaching the Ukrainian language, and higher education, the professions and politics were conducted almost entirely in Russian. While the 2001 census found that only 17 per cent considered themselves ethnically Russian, various surveys found that up to 80 per cent of the population used Russian as the primary language of communication. The category of so-called Russian-speakers was much larger than the identifiable group of ethnic Russians. Petro cites a 2012 study that 'found that over 60 percent of newspapers, 83 percent of journals, 87 percent of books and 72 percent of television programs in Ukraine are in Russian', a cultural predominance that was reinforced by the internet.[20] There was thus a gulf between practice and policy. Yushchenko's presidency signalled the radicalisation of the integrated nationalism model, and the implicitly repressive policy towards the Russian language became more overt. Official documents are only in Ukrainian, including birth and death certificates and other binding legal documents. There are plenty of cases in which Russian-speakers sign documents, including legal contracts, not knowing the precise meaning of the texts. There was now a campaign of place-name changes, and there were many cases of Russians forced to Ukrainise their name when changing passports. As Deema Kaneff puts it: 'Ukrainisation is a form of repression experienced on a daily basis.'[21]

All the major presidential candidates promised to make Russian a second state language during their campaigns, but failed to deliver – against the ferocious opposition of the Ukrainian nationalisers – once in office. Yanukovych came closest to fulfilling his promise, and in July 2012 forced through a law that allowed any local language spoken by at least a 10 per cent minority to be declared official within that region. The Kolesnichenko–Kivalov language law, as it is officially called, was bitterly resisted by the monists, although it did not displace or downgrade Ukrainian as the official language. The law applied not only to Russian but to a total of 18 languages, notably Hungarian, Romanian and Moldovan. As a result of the law, 13 of Ukraine's 27 regions adopted Russian as a second official language. However, the granting of regional status to 'minority' languages did not address the problem of the civil service, military and politics, where the use of Ukrainian is mandatory, or the bias in higher education that effectively precludes doctoral dissertations being written in Russian. Ukrainian pluralists endlessly cite the experience of other multilingual societies, notably Finland and Canada, where official bilingualism has enhanced the unity of the state. The monists will have none of it. In a misjudged moment of triumphalism after their victory in the Maidan, one of the first revolutionary acts of parliament on 23 February 2014 was to vote for its abolition, restoring Ukrainian as the sole state language at all levels, although the measure was not signed into law. The incident demonstrates just how important the language issue is and how ferociously Ukrainisers¯ fight to defend linguistic pre-eminence.

The third contentious issue is whether Ukraine should be a presidential or parliamentary republic, or something between the two. In the end a semi-presidential system was introduced, with a popularly elected president with significant powers elected for a five-year term, but accompanied by a prime minister appointed by the president but confirmed by parliament, the 450-member Verkhovna Rada elected for a four-year term. The country's unitary character was reinforced by the creation of a unicameral parliament – there is no second or upper chamber to represent the regions or to act as a check on the Rada.[22]

This made the role of the 18-member Constitutional Court even more important, but in the event it has been repeatedly abused and ignored. The court was not consulted over the constitutional reform prompted by the Orange Revolution in late 2004, which as we have seen weakened the presidency and gave greater powers to parliament, and the changes offered inadequate checks and balances. With Yanukovych's assumption of the presidency in 2010, the constitution once again became the plaything of the leadership. On 1 October 2010 the Constitutional Court overturned the 2004 amendments, declaring them unconstitutional. The decision was extremely controversial, and came amid claims that four members of the court had been forced to resign in the run-up to the vote as a result of executive pressure. No less controversial was the restoration of the 2004 amendments on 22 February 2014, the day of Yanukovych's fall, adopted by a simplified procedure in a single session by an overwhelming majority of MPs (351 of the nominal 450), without preliminary debate or discussion in committee. Of course, Yanukovych was in no position to ratify the restoration, and thus the reversion represented yet another revolutionary act of the mobilised people. All of this undermined the consolidation of Ukrainian statehood, threatening in the end the very existence of the polity.

OLIGARCH DEMOCRACY

While the two models of Ukrainian state development, the monist and the pluralist, quarrelled, the bureaucratic–oligarchic plutocracy ran off with the cream. A plutocracy is defined as a small group at the top, owning a large part of a nation's wealth, exercising an effect on politics that is totally out of proportion to their number.[23] One hundred people control some 80–85 per cent of Ukraine's wealth. The detailed study by Sławomir Matuszak describes how 'the Ukrainian oligarchic system developed into its ultimate shape during Leonid Kuchma's presidency (1994–2004)', and how, although it evolved, the system 'appears to be very durable'.[24] He describes in detail the various clans and the shifts in power, notably the eclipsing of other clans by Yanukovych's 'family' as their power and wealth swiftly increased following his election in 2010. Andrei Kluev, who headed the NSDC, was the head of one of the numerous 'clans' that surrounded Yanukovych, along with others with leadership positions in the PoR who competed with each other for access to the president and control over resources. Other major clans were led by Rinat Akhmetov and Dmytro Firtash.

Despite repeated radical political turbulence, the basic model of how the system works is remarkably immune to change. The major oligarchic groupings became 'regional business clans', of which four were the most enduring and important: Donetsk, Dnepropetrovsk, Lviv and Kiev.[25] Oligarchy entails an asymmetrical relationship between business and politics, typically based on some rent-extraction mechanism. The territorial aspect inserted certain regions into the 'vertical of power', permitting a degree of bargaining within the system that recognised the special weight of the specific clan. The leaders of these clans were economic oligarch and regional baron rolled into one. In the early 1990s many of them favoured decentralisation and even outright federalisation as a way of protecting their regional fiefdoms from central interference, but as they gained broader markets and exercised national influence they repudiated their earlier separatism.[26]

Yulia Tymoshenko made her fortune in the gas-trade business in the 1990s, becoming one of the richest oligarchs in the country. Born on 27 November 1960 in Dnepropetrovsk, she is one of Ukraine's most colourful business and political leaders. With her trademark braided hair, she is both charismatic and divisive. Her United Energy Systems of Ukraine (UESU) was a forerunner of RUE in acting as a privately owned intermediary that imported Russian natural gas to Ukraine from 1995 to 1 January 1997, the period when she gained the moniker of 'gas princess'. In 1999 she formed her own party, Batkivshchyna (Fatherland), and soon after became the deputy prime minister for the fuel and energy sector, locking horns with the oligarch groups that controlled the economy. In 2001 she was dismissed and prosecuted for gas-smuggling and tax evasion, being placed under arrest for 42 days. Later, an FBI investigator, Bryan Earl, provided vivid insight into how the system worked:

> When he [Pavlo Lazarenko] was the chairman of Dnepropetrovsk Oblast, he visited all the successful businessmen and said: 'give me 50% of your profits [...] if you

give me the money, I'll guarantee that you'll stay in business and that your business will be successful.' Later Lazarenko moved higher up the political ladder, becoming deputy prime minister and then prime minister. [...] When he emerged on to the national stage, he began to extensively manipulate the structure of natural gas imports. Whereupon, virtually overnight, Yulia Tymoshenko and her company became Ukraine's largest gas importer.[27]

In the end, in February 1999 Lazarenko fled to the US, where he was later sentenced to eight years' imprisonment for extortion and money-laundering. Tymoshenko appears in these proceedings as a 'co-conspirator', but was never sentenced, an anomaly that remains unexplained.

UESU was replaced by Itera, headed by Igor Makarov, a company that worked closely with Gazprom to supply Russian and Central Asian gas to Ukraine. When Tymoshenko became deputy prime minister responsible for fuel and energy on 30 December 1999, a position she held until 19 January 2001, she supported Itera, but was dismayed when EuralTransGaz (ETG), whose co-owner was Firtash, began to act as an intermediary to supply Central Asian gas to Ukraine from 2003. He offered Naftogaz more favourable terms and soon Itera was squeezed out of the market, arousing Tymoshenko's hostility. RosUkrEnergo was established in early 2004 as a joint venture in which Gazprom held a 50 per cent share, and Firtash and his partner Ivan Fursin 45 per cent and 5 per cent respectively. The idea was to replace ETG, which had become the object of controversy and Tymoshenko's attacks. The new business started operating from 1 January 2005, and was in direct competition with Tymoshenko. From this arose the various gas conflicts, including the two shut-offs in January 2006 and January 2009. Tymoshenko was at the centre of interminable conflicts with Yushchenko, Poroshenko and other oligarchs. Although she was the presumed heir of the Orange Revolution, her election platform in 2010 did not make 'a liberal economic platform a part of her current campaign for Ukraine's presidency. Instead, her platform promises a strong role of the state, both in the social sector and in economic development'.[28] Her campaign presciently warned that 'Yanukovych is a criminal and front man for rapacious economic interests, whose election would be a humiliation for Ukraine'.[29]

Meanwhile Firtash had diversified his holdings. Firtash controls Group DF, an international conglomerate of companies ultimately owned by Group DF Ltd, a British Virgin Islands holding company established in June 2007. Group DF companies include Ostchem Holdings AG, an Austrian company working in mining and processing minerals, including titanium; Global Energy Mining and Minerals Ltd, a Hungarian company; and Bothli Trade AG, a Swiss company, in which Global

Energy Mining and Minerals Ltd was the majority shareholder. As co-owner of RUE, once Ukraine's sole importer of Russian natural gas, Firtash was the obvious target for reprisals following the February revolution. Overall, Group DF employs 100,000 people in Ukraine. He owned eight television stations, and in 2013 paid $2.5 billion for the InterMedia Group, which operates the country's leading television channel.

By far the richest Ukrainian oligarch is Rinat Akhmetov. The son of a coal-miner, he amassed his fortune in the 1990s and was ranked by Forbes as the world's ninety-second richest person, with a net worth of $12.4 billion. His System Capital Management (SCM) has vast holdings in coal and steel, assets that he acquired in the cut-throat and semi-criminal era of privatisation in the 1990s. The two corporations Metinvest and DTEK Krymenergo are overseen by SCM. Metinvest was Ukraine's largest metallurgical and mining holding. According to fellow oligarch Sergei Taruta, it was Akhmetov who personally convinced Kuchma to appoint Yanukovych governor of Donetsk in 1997.[30] The rise of Firtash's RUE from 2006 led to increased influence in the PoR, which Akhmetov vigorously resisted. His business thrived in the Yanukovych years and now makes up about a quarter of Ukraine's GDP. In the troubles that engulfed the country after the fall of Yanukovych he tried to maintain neutrality, but this soon became untenable.

The regional oligarch model became prevalent under Kuchma, but polarised after 2005 between those favouring 'Orange' politics and those who gravitated towards the 'Blue' of the PoR. The 'Gold' faction was unable to sustain an autonomous position. At the same time, business conglomerates extended out of their original bases to encompass neighbouring regions, a development particularly noticeable in the eastern half of the country, and with their added weight were able more effectively to lobby their interests at the national level.[31] The formal labels of pro-Western or pro-Russian, or even the formal political labels, have little substantive traction. These symbols are important, but no less important are the battles between regional clans. The tension between Yanukovych and Tymoshenko was real, but the fact that she had inherited the Dnepropetrovsk mantle from her former rival Kuchma, while Yanukovych represented Donetsk and the Donbas heartlands, was no less important.

The structure of the economy remained overwhelmingly oligarchic. The comparison with Russia is instructive. On coming to power in 2000 Putin reduced the influence of the most egregiously political of the oligarchs, notably Boris Berezovsky and Vladimir Gusinsky, and by 2001 both were in exile. The policy of 'equidistance' of oligarchs from the state thereafter held for a couple of years, but in October 2003 Mikhail Khodorkovsky was arrested and soon after his giant Yukos oil company passed into the hands of the state. The political power of the oligarchs was broken, and thereafter business leaders aligned themselves with the concerns of the Putinite state. Russia became a far less pluralistic polity, with the media also brought into the statist fold now that independent oligarchs had disappeared; but what Russia lost in democratic competitiveness and accountability, it gained in managerial coherence.

The existence of powerful oligarchs imbued Ukrainian politics with a pluralism that is missing in Russia. One such figure is Poroshenko, who built a business empire out of the debris of the post-Soviet economy. He was born in Bolgrad in the Russian-speaking region of Odessa, but when he was nine his family moved to the Moldovan town of Bendera (hence his critics call him a 'Bendera-ite'). They later moved to Vinnytsya, where he started his business and political career and which remains his political stronghold. Starting in consulting and importing cacao beans, he assembled a powerful financial and industrial group of more than 50 companies. Chief among them is the Roshen confectionery corporation, established in 1996, which is large even by world standards. Roshen produces some 320 different products, including chocolate bars that are popular across the CIS. The name is drawn from the middle letters of Poroshenko's name, and in turn this has given him the moniker of 'the chocolate king'. About 40 per cent of his business is related to Russia, with one of his largest factories located in Lipetsk. A mysterious holding company called UkPromInvest manages many of his other interests, including bus-manufacturing, car distribution, shipyards, banking and electrical cables. Forbes estimated his wealth at $1.6 billion in March 2013. Like most of Ukraine's oligarchs, he owns an impressive mansion, in his case on the banks of the River Dnieper (which illegally cut off access to the shoreline along his property), 'complete with a white portico and columns that recall, not at all subtly, the White House, surrounded by a yellow brick wall'.[32]

He was an experienced MP, first entering parliament in 1998 after he became a founding member of the Party of Regional Revival, which later became the Party of Regions (PoR). Political pragmatism allowed him to cross the various political divides and factional conflicts. Kuchma in 2003 offered him the post of first deputy prime minister, but by then Poroshenko had entered the opposition camp. From 2001 he headed Viktor Yushchenko's pro-Western Our Ukraine electoral bloc. In that capacity he was at the centre of the Orange Revolution in 2004 that brought Yushchenko and Tymoshenko to power. He took on the post of secretary of the NSDC to balance Tymoshenko, although he had clearly expected to become prime minister himself. This marked a decisive turning point and the beginning of an enduring feud with Tymoshenko, even though he served in her administration later. The arrangement soon ended in tears and mutual recriminations, with Tymoshenko's government collapsing in September 2005 after only eight months. A number of senior positions then followed for Poroshenko: head of the board of the National Bank of Ukraine (NBU) from 2007 to 2012; minister of foreign affairs 2009–10 in Tymoshenko's second administration, which lasted rather longer than the first, from December 2007 to March 2010; and then minister of economic development and trade in Azarov's government for nearly a year, up to December 2012.

Poroshenko thus had a long record in government, but as the protests against Yanukovych unrolled he was unaffiliated with any of the country's political parties and instead threw his not inconsiderable weight in support of the 'pro-European' opposition. His speeches have consistently been of a pro-European orientation, and he has repeatedly denounced corruption while prospering in a corrupt state. He is mentioned over a hundred times in the WikiLeaks cables, often in less than compli-mentary terms. Most refer to the period 2006–9, when he was an MP and council chair of the NBU. The enmity between him and Tymoshenko is repeatedly noted, while in a cable of 16 February 2006 the American ambassador, John Herbst, described Poroshenko as a 'disgraced oligarch'. Other cables reveal that when he was foreign minister he opposed rapprochement between Kiev and Moscow. For example, in December 2009 at a meeting of the NATO–Ukraine commission he urged his Western colleagues to resist Russian attempts to retain influence in the region and called on them not to oppose his country's NATO-membership aspirations. According to the American ambassador, John Tefft, it was Poroshenko who convinced Yanukovych to make his first presidential visit to Brussels rather than to Moscow. The cable notes that Poroshenko 'urged the US not to read too much into language in Yanukovych's speeches favourable to Medvedev's proposal for new security architecture', and, instead, that 'NATO membership remains an aspiration, albeit a distant one'.[33] Thus it is hardly surprising that as the protests gathered pace on the Maidan from November 2013, Poroshenko unequivocally sided with the demonstrators, using his Channel 5 to advance their views. His chameleon-like ability to blend in with the existing system allowed him to thrive in a turbulent environment, accompanied by an attitude that was not so much anti-Russian as 'post-Russian', considering Ukraine's future as unequivocally lying in the West.

A number of other oligarchs have shaped Ukrainian development. Igor Kolomoisky is the latest manifestation of the 'Dnepropetrovsk clan', although in a radically new form. The former Soviet leader Leonid Brezhnev had worked in the region and drew on its cadres when he was the Soviet leader between 1964 and 1982. Kuchma had been director of the giant Yuzhmash plant in the region before becoming president of Ukraine between 1994 and 2004. Kolomoisky's giant financial–industrial group 'Privat' grew out of his 'PrivatBank', established in 1992, and now encompasses some 100 enterprises in Ukraine and the CIS. His conglomerate covers some of the core parts of the economy, including metallurgy, machine-building, oil extraction and chemicals. He has extensive media holdings, including the largest Ukrainian media group, '1+1

Media' and the news agency Unian, as well as various internet sites that served to mobilise Ukrainian public opinion to serve his causes, including the demonisation of Yanukovych and Putin. Kolomoisky is famous for his alleged 'corporate raiding', managing to wrest control of enterprises from the Tatarstan authorities and even, as Putin noted in his press conference of 4 March, from Russian oligarchs: 'This is a unique crook. He even managed to cheat our oligarch Roman Abramovich two or three years ago. Scammed him, as our intellectuals like to say.'[34] Kolomoisky is active in Jewish politics, funding various projects from Jerusalem to his native Dnepropetrovsk to restore Jewish monuments and buildings, and serves as the president of the Jewish community in Ukraine. In 2010 he became president of the European Council of Jewish Communities (ECJC), following generous donations, but his appointment was condemned by other ECJC members as an Eastern European-style 'hostile takeover', and he was forced to resign, after which he set up his own European Jewish Union. The Ukrainian crisis endangered his metals holding in Lugansk, but he was compensated by the exclusive contract he gained to supply the military with fuel, and the possibility that this could be extended to supply the agro-industrial complex. Kolomoisky has undoubtedly been one of the victors of the 2014 revolution.

The fastest route to personal enrichment is political office. Once ensconced in the presidency, Yanukovych exploited the predatory character of Ukrainian politics to the full, and the Yanukovych 'family' soon became the country's leading clan. His eldest son, Alexander, owned Mako Holding, which soon became the fastest-growing company in Ukraine, with interests in a number of energy-, gas- and coal-producing companies, the Marinservice construction company, the Artyomovsk and Artvin winery as well as the Ukrainian Development Bank. Other clans came under threat as the distribution of rent focused on a narrowing group of individuals. This, as much as the civic movement for dignity, in the end predisposed a number of oligarchs to defect and join the anti-Yanukovych movement. Alexander's associate, the secretive Sergei Kurchenko, who quickly became a multi-billionaire, in 2013 bought the United Media Holding (UMH), after one of its journals, *Forbes Ukraine*, exposed his activities in an article called 'The gas king of all Ukraine'.[35] UMH was the last of Ukraine's media holdings not owned by an oligarch, and was the country's second-largest in the field, enjoying a quarter of the print audience and 45 per cent of online readership, and included such prestigious titles as *Korrespondent*, the country's most popular weekly. Its planned takeover by the family, which had hitherto lacked any serious media companies, would have helped shape public opinion in the run-up to the 2015 presidential election.[36] As noted, the largest television channel, Inter, was sold by Valery Khoroshkovsky, a former director of the security services, to Sergei Levochkin, the head of Yanukovych's presidential administration, and Firtash.

The growing gulf between an irresponsible elite and the mass of the people was the crucial precipitating factor for the protest movement from November 2013. The 'European choice' acted as the proxy for blocked domestic change. State officials and the business class acted with impunity. The case of the MP from Tymoshenko's BYuT faction, Viktor Lozinsky, who was sentenced to 15 years in jail on 20 April 2011 for premeditated murder after he shot a villager dead in 2009 when out hunting with the local head of police, was a rare case when immunity was lifted. In a country with the fourth-lowest per capita income in Europe, the case illustrated 'the crisis of legitimacy that Ukraine's democracy finds itself facing, with officials and parliamentarians perceived as an elite caste rather than a political class'. Deputy status granted millionaire business leaders immunity and networks to advance and protect their interests, with parliament's committees offering unique opportunities for rent-seeking. In his nine years in parliament the businessman and MP from the PoR Mykola Lisin has not made a single political speech, or even interview, but 'this is par for the course: MPs in Ukraine are not actually required to have an interest in public politics'. The closed-list system means that most MPs do not have to campaign for their seats, or even to turn up to vote. The bloc-voting system allows colleagues to vote on behalf of the group, with the well-tuned system of 'piano-playing' allowing the electronic voting cards to be used in the name of others. The day after he died in a car crash on 17 April 2011, Lisin was registered to vote in the chamber.[37]

RUSSO-UKRAINIAN RELATIONS

As the Soviet Union disintegrated, one of the fundamental principles that quickly became established was that the existing Soviet borders between republics were inviolable, however arbitrary and unfair they may have been. Russia declared its state sovereignty on 12 June 1990, and thereafter under Boris Yeltsin effectively sponsored the sovereignty declarations of the other union republics. Already on 11 March 1990 Lithuania had declared independence, leading what became a cascade of independence declarations. Following Ukraine's declaration of independence on 24 August 1991, Yeltsin's press secretary, Pavel Voshchanov, warned that independence could prompt revisions to borders: 'if any republic breaks off Union relations with Russia, then Russia has the right to raise the question of territorial claims'.[38] The storm that attended his comment intensified when he clarified that he meant only regions that had formerly been part of Russia, among which he listed the Donbas. Gorbachev added his view that there 'cannot be any territorial claims within the Union, but their emergence cannot be ruled out when republics leave the Union'.[39]

The status of Crimea had already long been a matter of concern to Russian nationalists. As we shall see in more detail in Chapter 5, the transfer of the peninsula from Russian to Ukrainian jurisdiction in 1954 by Nikita Khrushchev had always been contested by 'restorationists' in Russia, and this was an issue on which the fragmented patriotic movement united. Above all, the Sevastopol naval base in 1954 had been recognised as separate and remained an 'object of all-union significance', to use the parlance of the day. Throughout autumn 1991 Yeltsin was urged to push for the return of Crimea, and the issue was latent at the Belavezha meeting that dissolved the USSR. As far as Yeltsin was concerned, the CIS would effectively mean the continuation of the Soviet community, above all in security and defence matters, and hence it would make little difference to which republic the peninsula belonged. In the event, plans for a common military swiftly dissolved, and the republics set on their path of differentiation and divergence. Russia was formally recognised as the 'continuer' (not successor) state to the USSR by the UN in December 1991. This technically meant that everything that belonged to the Soviet Union came under Russian jurisdiction. Thus Sevastopol, as an 'object of all-union significance', automatically reverted to Russian jurisdiction. Russian nationalists have never forgiven Yeltsin for not having pressed this claim at the time.

A further contentious issue was the status of nuclear weapons deployed on the territories of Belarus, Kazakhstan and Ukraine. The first two quickly agreed to join the Non-proliferation Treaty as non-nuclear states, and the rockets and other installations were moved to Russia, mostly for destruction supervised by international observers. However, in Ukraine nationalists quickly realised that a nuclear arsenal would immeasurably enhance Ukraine's international status, and act as a deterrent against Russia. The tone of the debate demonstrated the intense strain of Russophobic nationalism that attended the birth of the new state. Russia, after all, had taken the lead in the destruction of the Soviet Union and could in effect be called the midwife of the new republics. There are also technical issues involved, since Ukraine only hosted the launch pads but had no access to the launch codes, effectively rendering the arsenal useless. However, since many of the rockets were built in Ukraine, notably at the enormous Yuzhmash plant in Dnepropetrovsk, technicians may have been able to devise a way to circumvent the Moscow codes. In the end Ukraine, together with Belarus and Kazakhstan, joined the Non-proliferation Treaty through the Lisbon Protocol in 1992, and its nuclear warheads were taken to Russia for disposal. Leonid Kravchuk agreed to relinquish the weapons in exchange for international guarantees of Ukraine's security and borders. This took the form of the Budapest Memorandum of 5 December 1994, signed by the leaders of Russia, the US, the UK and Ukraine. It did not have the status of an internationally binding treaty, yet signalled that the signatory states would give up any territorial pretensions and defend Ukraine's independence. Accompanying the memorandum was a joint statement confirming the importance of commitments undertaken within the framework of the OSCE on countering the growth of aggressive nationalism and chauvinism, a point that Russia, following the February revolution, was quick to seize on as ostensibly invalidating the memorandum.

The Budapest agreement did not resolve the issue of the status of what had now become Russia's fleet based in Sevastopol. There had been attempts by Kravchuk to 'nationalise' the whole Soviet BSF based there, but Admiral Vladimir Kasatonov resisted and instead raised the Russian flag, turning him into a Russian nationalist hero. Thus the anomalous situation arose of Russia owning a large collection of vessels but having nowhere to take it. Although a vast land-based territory, Russia has historically lacked access to warm-water ports. Over the years the facilities at Russia's major commercial port on the Black Sea at Novorossiisk were developed to take some naval vessels, but it simply does not have the capability to house a major naval fleet. During storms even commercial vessels have to ride out the turbulence in open water. Unlike the US, which still occupies Guantánamo Bay, wrested from Cuba in 1903 and kept despite demands since 1959 for it to be restored to Cuban sovereignty, and the UK, which ensured that the Akrotiri and Dhekelia bases remained sovereign British territory (although restricted to exclusively military purposes) after Cyprus became independent, Russia had failed to achieve a similar result.

Instead, the status of the fleet in Sevastopol remained contentious until Russia's annexation of the territory in March 2014. Article 17 of the Ukrainian constitution prohibits foreign bases on its territory. The issue bedevilled negotiations for the Treaty on Friendship, Cooperation and Partnership. Already mooted in late 1991, negotiations began in 1993, but it was only finally signed, after years of mutual recriminations and insults, by Kuchma and Yeltsin on 31 May 1997. The treaty codified the principles of Russo-Ukrainian relations, based on mutual respect of sovereign equality, territorial integrity, the inviolability of borders and the non-use of force. However, the ratification process in Russia provoked enormous controversy and divisions. Political society was deeply split, with the realist–statists, liberals and most neo-imperialists in favour of ratifying the treaty, whereas the ethnic nationalists and part of the neo-imperialist group – including Vladimir Zhirinovsky's Liberal Democratic Party of Russia (LDPR), the mayor of Moscow Yury Luzhkov, Sergei Baburin (the head of the Russian All-People's Union) and Alexander Lebed – were bitterly opposed. The key issue for them was that the treaty would confirm that Crimea belonged to Ukraine. The advocates argued that good relations with Ukraine should take precedence: this was the line pushed by the leading realist–statist, Yevgeny Primakov (prime minister from September 1998 to May 1999), and he convinced the State Duma to ratify the treaty in 1999.[40]

Ukrainian statehood is built in opposition to what constructivists would call the 'significant other': in this case, Russia. In the end this was to lead to war in 2014, but it is an essential element of the monist tradition. Russia is distrusted to the degree that it is difficult to establish sustained diplomatic relations based on trust. Instead, too often it appears that Russia is held responsible for all Ukraine's problems. This externalisation means that inadequate attention is devoted to finding negotiated domestic solutions to domestic problems. Tymoshenko, for example, was an apostle of the 'containment' of Russia, although this did not prevent her signing the controversial gas deal with Russia in 2009. In 2007 Tymoshenko argued that 'the West must seek to create counterweights to Russia's expansionism and not place all its chips on Russian domestic reform'.[41] The view of Russia as an expansionist power was unsubstantiated, but the argument reflected the stereotypes at the heart of the monist version of Ukrainian development. When Yushchenko and Tymoshenko were trading mutual imprecations, their worst insult was 'acting in the interests of Russia'. In other words, domestic contradictions were rendered homologous with the broader divisions in Europe, and fed on each other.

Russo-Ukrainian relations in the post-Communist period were never easy, but were driven into a pathological state by global tensions. As a WikiLeaks cable from the American ambassador to the State Department noted in April 2009:

> Ukraine's relationship with Russia has remained tense and complicated. Since the August 2008 Georgia–Russia conflict, Ukrainian perceptions of the potential security threat presented by Russia have come into greater focus, particularly against the backdrop of continuing opposition by some NATO members to MAP status for Ukraine. Changing US policy toward Moscow has led to speculation that the US has softened its support of Ukraine as the price of improving US–Russia relations.[42]

In other words, any rapprochement between Washington and Moscow was perceived as a threat in Kiev and other Eastern European capitals. Equally, the logic of NATO enlargement appeared inexorable, with no appreciation of the effect that this would have on other parties. Worse, the cable noted that

> for the most part Ukrainian officials remain committed to pursuing Euro-Atlantic integration. How long they will continue to do so in the face of the continuing lack of Ukrainian public support (at only about 25%) for NATO membership is not clear.

Joining NATO clearly seemed to be the 'democratic' thing to do, even if the demos itself was not in favour.

At the time of the attempt to improve relations at the beginning of Obama's first term when Medvedev was president, a cable noted that 'many of our interlocutors have questioned whether "the reset button" signals a departure from our policy of strong support for Ukraine's Western orientation, including its Euro-Atlantic integration'. It seemed that the worse relations were between Russia and the West, the better for Ukraine. The events in Georgia in 2008 had already 'raised specific worries about Russia's intentions toward Crimea, and whether Russia intends to pursue a "South Ossetia strategy" in this autonomous Ukrainian region'. Another contentious issue was also raised, namely 'the lack of progress in regular negotiations regarding the Black Sea Fleet', accompanied by concern that Russia was issuing passports to citizens in Crimea. Yushchenko had been one of the fiercest critics of Russian actions in Georgia, although the cable noted that 'officials occasionally lament that Saakashvili's actions in August have caused discord in Ukraine–Russia relations'. The issue of new security guarantees for Ukraine was raised, with Tymoshenko at the March 2009 Munich Security Conference calling for greater Ukrainian participation in the European Security and Defence Policy.[43] The cables expose a shocking lack of appreciation of Russia's legitimate security concerns or of its historic and economic links with Ukraine. Instead, the logic of Euro-Atlantic security expansion became a hermetic project: nothing could affect the rationality in which it was embedded. It was this logic that visited discord and conflict upon Ukraine, and has brought Europe to war in 2014.

The demarcation of the 2,295-kilometre-long border was another contentious issue, and to this day the border remains porous. On 21 April 2010 Medvedev and Yanukovych signed an extension to the lease on the Sevastopol naval base for another 25 years, granting Russia use until 2042, with the option for a five-year extension. In return, the 'Kharkov Accords' provided Ukraine with a discount of $100 per 1,000 cubic metres (tcm) of natural gas. The contract price in the January 2009 deal, bringing to an end the second of Russia's gas shut-offs to Ukraine, was $486.50 per tcm, and the discount saved the Ukrainian exchequer billions, although as we shall see became the subject of various claims and counter-claims in 2014. The discount did nothing to help Ukraine resolve the severe problems in its energy sector, which undermined the financial viability of the state oil and gas trading and production company Naftogaz Ukrainy, which pumps over 97 per cent of the oil and gas in the country. Domestic gas prices for the general population and municipal heating companies were well below the import price, bridged by enormous state subsidies to Naftogaz. Even then, a large proportion of domestic consumers were unable to meet their bills. At the same time, attempts by Ukraine to exploit its own potential oil and gas reserves were held back by complicated legal procedures, bureaucracy and corruption.

TOWARDS THE EUROCRISIS

In his meeting with the American ambassador on 8 December 2008, Firtash was reported as having warned that

> Yushchenko made a possibly fatal political error during the Orange Revolution in that he and Tymoshenko propagated the concept of two Ukraines – an orange, more democratic Ukraine, and a blue Ukraine represented by the Party of Regions (PoR) and more focused towards the status quo. He added that this divisiveness through-out Ukraine is exactly what Russia hoped to cultivate in order to control Ukraine.[44]

There was also a third Ukraine, that of the oligarchs (which I have designated as Gold), and it was in this arena that Yanukovych thrived. He turned out to be neither a nationalist nor a pluralist, even though he did deliver the language law of July 2012. Yanukovych was a competent representative of the bureaucratic–oligarchic centrist trend in Ukrainian politics, accompanied by a crude kleptocratic opportunism concerned with his personal enrichment and that of his family. He had some achievements to his credit, including the successful staging (in partnership with Poland) of the 2012 European football championship, the beginning of energy diversification, and the restoration of modest economic growth. However, he not only failed to deal with the fundamental governance problems facing the country, but exacerbated them. This was reflected in the deepening alienation of voters. A poll in April 2011 showed support for the PoR crashing in the space of a year from 38 per cent to 14 per cent, but the main opposition force, Tymoshenko's BYuT, did not benefit, with its own support falling to 10.6 per cent. At that time 64 per cent believed that the situation in the country was heading in the wrong direction, with only 10.6 per cent supporting the president while 49 per cent disapproved. All this demonstrated 'a deep-seated disillusionment among the Ukrainian people'.[45] Ukraine was one of the few democracies in the post-Soviet area, yet it was overlain by an oligarchic system that fostered corruption and undermined the legitimacy of the elite.

Ukraine appeared to be stuck in a developmental stalemate. It is one of only two post-Soviet countries (the other is Kyrgyzstan) whose GDP has not yet recovered to its 1991 level. The comparative statistics are quite shocking. In 1992 its per capita gross national income was higher than that in Latvia or Romania, and comparable to Poland's, but by 2013 Poland's had increased threefold whereas Ukraine's economy was still smaller than it had been in 1991. In 2012 Ukraine's GDP was $176 billion in nominal terms, or $335 billion if adjusted to global prices (or 'purchasing power parity' terms). Today, its closest neighbours in the rankings are Iraq and El Salvador. Ukraine's population has fallen by 10 million to 44 million, one in three is below the poverty line, and unemployment in the first quarter of 2014 stood at 9.3 per cent, and it would be even higher if millions had not left to work in Russia and the EU. Inflation in 2014 was at least 20 per cent, and the country's foreign debt by mid-year reached $151 billion. In 2012 Ukraine exported only $63.3 billion of goods, while neighbouring Slovakia, with a population of only 5.4 million, exported $88.3 billion. Even unreformed Belarus recorded exports of $36.6 billion, with a quarter of the population.[46]

The record looks even worse when compared with the country's undoubted economic potential. It is the world's sixth-largest exporter of military and transport aircraft, and has a sophisticated rocket industry. Its shipbuilding is one of the world's most advanced, including natural-gas tankers. The Zorya–Mashproekt plant in Mykolaiv is the main supplier of naval turbine engines to Russia's state-owned United Shipbuilding Corporation. Ukraine comes fourth in terms of IT professionals, and has a very well-educated workforce, with 90 per cent of the population connected to the internet. It has a strong motor-, truck- and public-bus-manufacturing base. Above all, the country has 30 per cent of the world's black earth soil (*chernozëm*), producing grains, sugar and vegetable oils. It also has significant energy resources, including conventional gas fields and potentially enormous shale-gas reserves. But Ukrainian leaders did little to tackle the underlying factors that inhibited sustained economic growth. In particular, successive governments made little attempt to wean the country off its wasteful energy addiction. Ukraine is at the extreme end of the scale when it comes to total primary energy consumption per dollar of GDP. The UK takes 3.8 thousand British thermal units (btu) per year, Germany 4.7 and the US 7.5; the world average is ten. Poland takes 10.6, China 26.3 and Russia 32.4, while Ukraine takes an astonishing 56.3, 15 times more than Britain. Household gas subsidies came to 7.5 per cent of GDP in 2012, or $13 billion. Natural gas constituted 36.9 per cent of primary energy supply in 2011, coal 32.7, nuclear 18.7, oil 9.7 and renewable a measly 2 per cent.[47] More than two decades of misrule had allowed services to decay, with average monthly wages falling to some $200, four times lower than in neighbouring Poland and nine times lower than in Moscow.

The endless oligarch wars and self-enrichment of the elite were thus accompanied by declining living standards, exacerbated by the onset of 'stealth authoritarianism'. The quality of Ukraine's law enforcement degraded, the state apparatus disintegrated, corruption and misappropriation destroyed the armed forces, while the country's politics became more toxic than ever. The criminal charges brought against Tymoshenko and the former interior minister, Yury Lutsenko, of exceeding their powers while in office, broke the unwritten rule of Ukrainian politics: that you do not prosecute your predecessors. Their imprisonment was only the tip of the iceberg of repression against opposition figures. Crude methods of physical coercion were applied, of the sort that Yanukovych had long practised in Donetsk but which were new to Ukraine as a whole, and exceeded anything seen in Putin's Russia. Freedom House in January 2011 shifted Ukraine from the 'free' to the 'partly free' category, and a whole raft of human-rights organisations voiced their concerns.

The deep disillusionment was reflected in the 28 October 2012 parliamentary election. This was the least free and fair election in Ukraine's history, and was accompanied by rampant fraud. The classic political parties appeared to be exhausted. For example, in earlier years Viktor Medvedchuk's Social Democratic Party of Ukraine (SDPU) gave expression to a moderate centrism, but this had gradually become the voice of a particular type of oligarch capitalism allied with Russia. Putin was godfather to Medvedchuk's daughter. The disillusionment boosted the right-wing parties. As noted, Svoboda won 10.4 per cent of the proportional part of the vote, giving it 25 seats, having adapted its rhetoric to reflect a more urban, pro-democratic, pro-NATO electorate. The distinctive geopolitics of Ukraine meant that the typical stance of such parties in Western Europe – anti-EU and anti-NATO – was inverted. This is quite understandable when examined through the prism of my model, where monist nationalists favour the Wider European agenda in contrast to ties with Russia. This effect was amplified by the deep governance problems facing the country and the slide into authoritarianism.

The Association Agreement was the cornerstone of the EU's effort to integrate Ukraine into Wider Europe. For three years the negotiations had been conducted in a deeply technocratic way, and the text was not even available in Ukrainian until the last moment. In keeping with the EU's traditions, this was integration by stealth. At the heart of the agreement was the sweeping liberalisation of EU–Ukraine trade, with the Ukrainian economy reducing and in due course removing tariff and non-tariff barriers to become more open for goods and services from the EU. Unlike the equivalent agreements with the Central and Eastern European states, there was no promise of eventual membership. Ukraine would not gain 'candidate status', and thus the AA/DCFTA was very much a second-tier agreement, offering many of the sticks but few of the carrots. For its partisans, this was compensated by what the agreement offered in symbolic terms: a 'civilisational' alternative to Russia as part of the country's 'European choice'. Looking over the EU's shoulder, the president of the National

Endowment for Democracy in Washington, Carl Gershman, declared in September 2013 that Ukraine represented 'the biggest prize', but beyond that was an opportunity to put Putin 'on the losing end not just in the near abroad but within Russia itself'.[48]

The agreement was about far more than just free-trade but required Ukraine to adopt a large part of the EU *acquis communautaire*, the 100,000-odd pages of law and regulations, which were economically exclusionary towards Russia. In addition, the agreement's foreign policy and security protocols meant that Ukraine would have to align its foreign and security policy towards the West. The Ukrainian border at its closest is a mere 480 kilometres from Moscow, and thus the whole issue assumed an existential character. Ukraine matters to Russia as an issue of survival, quite apart from a thousand years of shared history and civilisation, whereas for Brussels or Washington it is just another country in the onward march of 'the West'. The Russian military has traditionally used space to give it strategic depth, and this advantage would now be lost. As for the 'European choice', signing up would in the long term probably help improve governance, economic performance and reduce corruption, but of itself it would not mean that Ukraine had left its dark past to become more 'civilised'. As Mark Adomanis notes, 'in reality the Association Agreement [is] [...] a highly technocratic bit of economic liberalization. There is no "European" way to end gas subsidies, and no "civilized" way to cut pensions.'[49]

There is no agreement over the extent to which the DCFTA was compatible with Ukraine continuing its links with the CIS. Russia remained Ukraine's largest trade partner, accounting in 2013 for 24 per cent of its exports and 30 per cent of its imports. Natural gas made up a large part of the imports, while metals (including pipes), machinery and agricultural goods made up a large part of exports. Russia bought Ukraine's industrial goods that could find no market in the West. The Ukrainian and Russian economies are highly complementary, having been part of a single unit for so many centuries and shared patterns of Soviet industrialisation. Ukrainian manufactured exports include railway equipment and a whole range of military-related items, notably helicopter engines, produced at the Motor Sich plant in Zaporozhia. Almost all the helicopters produced in Russia use these engines, as does most of the Afghan fleet. The above-mentioned plant in Mykolaiv is the sole producer of power units for Russian naval ships; Russia had heavily co-invested in modernising Antonov transport aircraft, based in Kiev; and, far from least, Russia's SS-18 (Voevoda, designated by NATO as 'Satan') intercontinental ballistic missiles (ICBMs) were produced and maintained by the Yuzhmash plant in Dnepropetrovsk, although the category was near retirement and was being replaced by new classes of missiles. The Donbas alone made up a quarter of all Ukraine's manufactured exports, but the region had been badly affected by global price trends even before the collapse of the Yanukovych regime. In the first quarter of 2014 Russia's share in Ukraine's total trade turnover reached 21.7 per cent, while China's share was 6.8 per cent and Germany's 4.9 per cent. According to the NBU, Ukraine's imports from Russia came to $4 billion, while exports were $2.7 billion.[50] Overall, industrial output fell by 12.1 per cent in July 2014 year on year, with Donetsk suffering a 28.5 per cent fall in output.

Political and economic matters were deeply entwined. However, it was a third element that provoked no less concern in Moscow: the surprising degree of security concerns. The Wider European agenda, as argued above, united not just the EU's traditional political and economic interests, but collapsed into the Euro-Atlantic security partnership. This was a dangerous elision, and now produced bitter fruit. A number of clauses in the Association Agreement inevitably raised concerns in the Kremlin. Article 4 talks of the 'Aims of political dialogue', with section 1 stressing that

> political dialogue in all areas of mutual interest shall be further developed and strengthened between the Parties. This will promote gradual convergence on foreign and security matters with the aim of Ukraine's ever-deeper involvement in the European security area.

Article 7 called for EU–Ukrainian convergence in foreign affairs, security and defence, while Article 10 on 'Conflict prevention, crisis management and military–technological cooperation' notes in section 3 that 'the parties shall explore the potential of military and technological cooperation. Ukraine and the European Defence Agency (EDA) will establish close contacts to discuss military capability improvement, including technological issues.' Thus the EU asserted exclusivity in security matters, which would have become operative as soon as Ukraine signed up at the Vilnius summit. Although couched in classic European language of peace and development, the agreement in effect announced a formal state of contestation with Russia over the lands between. The EU 'slid involuntarily into competition with Russia'.[51] By the same token, yet another step was taken in the EU's move away from being a peace project to perpetuating conflict in new forms, and thus undermining the credibility of the European project in its entirety.

Since the establishment of the EaP, Putin had repeatedly advanced various formats for trilateral discussion between Moscow, the EU and the respective partnership countries. Various plans had been proposed to modernise Ukraine's gas transit network and to manage the trade issues that would arise from signing the DCFTA. Such ideas were repeatedly rebuffed, with for example Barroso being quoted by news agencies as late as 29 November 2013 as saying: 'Russia's inclusion in the talks on setting up an Association Agreement between the EU and Ukraine is wholly unacceptable.' It is in this context that Moscow expended an extraordinary amount of effort to dissuade Kiev from signing the agreement, including various sanctions and trade bans. The ultimate goal was to encourage Ukraine to join what was planned to become the EEU, but this did not necessarily exclude closer association with the EU. Ways no doubt could have been found to ensure compatibility between the two free-trade zones, and indeed, if there had been the will, Ukraine could have acted as the bridge between the two.

There were also 'sentimental' factors at work, with 3 million Ukrainians living in Russia, tied together by a plenitude of cultural and human ties. Emigrant remittances totalled some $10 billion a year, some 4 per cent of Ukrainian GDP. In 2012, Andrei Kostin, the head of VTB Bank, had already sought to convince Ukrainian politicians that the EU deal was an 'arranged marriage', whereas association with Russia offered the country 'real love'. Putin repeatedly warned of Russia's worry that once the Ukrainian market was opened to EU goods, the Russian market would be flooded by lower-quality Ukrainian items seeking new markets to the east. From July 2013 various crude sanctions were imposed, including a ban on imports of Poroshenko's Roshen confectionery, on the grounds that they failed to meet food-safety standards. In September a ban was imposed on the import of railway wagons. Medvedchuk and what had now become his Ukrainian Choice party sponsored a publicity campaign to convince Ukrainian society that association with the EEU was in Ukraine's best interests. The hardest line of all was pursued by Sergei Glazyev, Putin's advisor on Eurasian integration, who in 2013 repeatedly warned Ukraine that signing the agreement could provoke social unrest and the possible secession of pro-Russian regions.[52]

Equally, on the other side, Štefan Füle, the commissioner for enlargement and European neighbourhood policy, stressed that Ukraine really did face a choice, and that the two free-trade areas were incompatible. In September 2013 he noted that the approaching Vilnius summit was 'wrongly' perceived 'in some quarters' as a threat, and 'as a result, we have seen enormous pressure being brought to bear upon some of our neighbours'. He insisted that the aim was to work with the eastern partners to 'build a zone of prosperity and stability in our continent'. However, he conceded that

it is true that the Customs Union membership is not compatible with the DCFTAs which we have negotiated with Ukraine, the Republic of Moldova, Georgia, and Armenia. This is not because of ideological differences; this is not about a clash of economic blocs, or a zero-sum game. This is due to legal impossibilities: for instance, you cannot at the same time lower your customs tariffs as per the DCFTA and increase them as a result of the Customs Union membership.

He went on to warn:

The development of the Eurasian Economic Union project must respect our partners' sovereign decisions. Any threats from Russia linked to the possible signing of agreements with the European Union are unacceptable. [...] The European Union will support and stand by those who are subject to undue pressures.[53]

In other words, the EU would forge ahead irrespective of Russian concerns, while appealing to universal principles of choice and sovereignty.[54] Few in the abstract would challenge these principles, but for the first time in the EU's history they were running up against the *finalité* of the EU, fizzling out in the ragged conceptual and territorial frontier between the Atlantic and Eurasian worlds. The EU had never before encountered opposition from an external power to its enlargement plans, and simply lacked the experience and language to maintain dialogue with a power that challenged the advance of the Brussels-centric Wider Europe.

Despite all the governance and economic problems, it was clear that the EU was intent on getting Yanukovych to sign up in Vilnius. The EU set the deadline of May 2013 for Tymoshenko to be released, and when she remained in jail the Polish and German governments sought to broker a deal whereby she could go to the West for medical treatment. Since May 2012 she had been in Kharkov Central Clinical Hospital No. 5 to treat her spinal disc herniation. Complicating the situation was the accelerating pace of Eurasian integration. On 31 May 2013 Yanukovych signed a memorandum on deepening cooperation with what was taking shape as the EEU. Putin later commented on how he saw the situation:

Ukraine was supposed to sign an Association Agreement with the EU. Using absolutely modern diplomatic tools, we proved that the document is at least inconsistent with Russian interests since the Russian and Ukrainian economies are closely intertwined. We have 245 Ukrainian enterprises working for us in the defence industry alone.

The 'diplomatic tools' were on the rough side, yet sought to register Russian concerns. Instead, as Putin put it:

They told us to mind our own business. Excuse me, I don't want to hurt anyone's feelings, but it's been a while since I heard anything that snobbish. They just slammed the door in our face telling us to mind our own business.[55]

Instead, Ukraine was posed with a stark choice, one that it had tried to avoid for two decades. The failure to reform the energy sector, sluggish economic performance and poor governance compounded its geopolitical ambiguity. The Association Agreement promised a shock to the system that was intended to address the internal problems, but it was embedded in a larger geopolitical project that placed Ukraine in an impossible position. Yanukovych was not particularly 'pro-Russian', but he understood that the Association Agreement would force the country to undertake radical changes that could threaten his own position. It became clear that the EU's conditionality in the Tymoshenko case was itself conditional, and that Yanukovych would be allowed to sign even while she languished in jail. Although demonised later, Yanukovych was clearly acceptable as a partner if the EU was so keen to sign him up for the Association Agreement. Yanukovych was running out of road.

On 21 November 2013 he announced that he would not sign the document as it was presently constituted, and needed more time to study the effect it would have on Ukraine. A number of factors weighed in the decision to postpone accession. It was certainly not simply because he was a pro-Russian 'puppet', although he had come under brutal pressure not to sign the Association Agreement. Putin, who had very little respect for Yanukovych personally, showed him the work of Glazyev and others demonstrating just how damaging it would be to Ukraine's economy. Like most other Ukrainian leaders, Yanukovych had long been playing Moscow off against Brussels, in an attempt to get the best of both worlds. He now realised that the EU in fact had placed very little on the table that would be of immediate benefit, while the reforms would destabilise an already precarious situation. Moscow, on the other hand, offered a $15 billion loan and a hefty discount on the gas price. On 17 December the deal was signed, and an addendum was signed to the gas agreement of 19 January 2009 that reduced the price of natural gas for Ukraine by one third, from $410 to $268.5 per tcm. The deal with Russia, however, did not mean that in Yanukovych's mind the door was closed to the EU, and he certainly planned to return to Brussels. He also played the Chinese card, a country that he visited in December, hoping that it would offer an escape route from the impasse in relations with Ukraine's neighbours. In the event, things blew up in his face.

The crisis was the culmination of sharpening domestic contradictions and deteriorating international relations. Ukraine had long exploited the contradictions between Russia and the West, but in the end this proved a dangerous game. Ukraine mattered to Russia more than any other country, and now there was the danger of a permanent estrangement. As Dmitry Efremenko notes, 'the Eastern Partnership policy, which had been conceived by its proponents as a dislodging of Russia's influence in the Western part of the post-Soviet landscape, inevitably drew the EU into a competitive geopolitical conflict'.[56] Relations between the US and Russia also worsened. Putin considered the Orange Revolution a geopolitical challenge, as well as a model of political change that he feared could spill over into Russia. By then it was clear that the US had moved to become Russia's main opponent. The September 2013 G20 summit in St Petersburg was marked by a bitter chill in relations between the two countries, exacerbated by attempts in Washington to lead a boycott of the Sochi Olympics, scheduled for February 2014. Equally, it was clear that the EU had blundered badly in its Ukraine policy. It had been unable to temper the partisan agendas of its 'new Europe' members allied with the more virulent Atlanticist countries elsewhere. The EaP in principle served an important purpose, but its implementation proceeded within the worst paradigm of competitive geopolitics.

All the conditions were in place for the 'perfect storm' that hit Europe in late 2013. There was a deepening 'Ukrainian' crisis, with a president who had already destroyed civil society when he had been governor in Donetsk, and who was now generalising these corrupt practices to the country as a whole. The bureaucratic-oligarchic system of rule was also being destabilised by the greed of his 'family'. This provoked a radicalisation of public opinion, as reflected in the 2012 parliamentary-election results. At the same time, the 'Ukraine' crisis was also gathering pace as the Atlantic and Eurasian integration poles radicalised their positions. The catalyst was the Association Agreement with the EU, but this was only the culmination of a broader failure to negotiate a mutually acceptable structure to post-Cold War European international politics. The country's central position meant that when the two crises intersected there would be a rapid escalation of both. Tony Wood summarises the situation nicely:

> For the US and Europe, the aim has all along been relatively straightforward: to wrest the country from Russia's sphere of influence and continue the joint eastward expansion of NATO and the EU. [...] For Russia, the basic goal has until recently been a symmetrical pushback: to keep Ukraine out of Western security and economic structures, leaving it as at the very least a neutral state, if not an active member of a 'Eurasian Union' dominated by Russia.[57]

The two trains were hurtling towards each other.

CHAPTER 4

THE FEBRUARY REVOLUTION

Following Yanukovych's announcement on 21 November 2013 that he would not after all sign the Association Agreement, Mustafa Nayyem, a journalist for the online news site *Ukrainska Pravda*, called on Facebook for people to gather on the Maidan to protest. Starting with a relatively small gathering, the numbers soon swelled. The Maidan became a symbol not only of protest but of the direct expression of popular sovereignty. The language of the 1989 movements that brought an end to the Communist systems in Eastern Europe was heard once again, including a romantic but also extremely effective belief in the power of the people and civil society. Disappointed by what was perceived to have been the betrayal of the ideals of the Orange Revolution after 2004, the 'people' this time would not disperse until they had achieved a fundamental reordering of the Ukrainian political system.

THE PEOPLE ARMED

Ukrainian society has repeatedly demonstrated a capacity for mass mobilisation and engagement in political protest. The 'granite' student strike movement in 1990 forced the republic's Communist leadership to pursue sovereignty and then independence, while protests against Leonid Kuchma had engulfed the country in 2001. In the autumn of 2004 the Maidan was occupied for several weeks, forcing an unprecedented third round to the presidential elections. Now once again the Maidan became the epicentre of a movement that would sweep away the president and provoke a major European crisis. This was a time when a wave of popular protest broke on the rocks of authoritarian stabilisation. The Arab Spring of 2011–13 saw long-time dictators swept from office in Egypt, Tunisia, Yemen and Libya, but not in Syria, where the country was engulfed in civil war. In Russia, Putin's return for a third presidential term provoked a protest movement. The distortion of the result of the parliamentary ballot of 4 December 2011 brought thousands on to Bolotnaya Square, the site of a confrontation later with the police on the day before his inauguration on 6 May 2012.[1] The Kiev Maidan, like Tahrir Square in Cairo and Bolotnaya Square in Moscow, became the site of putative civic renewal and the restoration of popular accountability.

Demonstrations across the country on 24 November gathered some 300,000 people, but thereafter the protests appeared to be on the wane. However, the ill-judged attempt by the police to disperse the crowd on the Maidan on the night of 29–30 November, under the pretext of putting up a Christmas tree, prompted renewed mobilisation. Over half a million came out on Sunday 1 December. The swirling crowd occupied the centre of the city, and pulled down the statue of Lenin off the main street, Khreshchatik. The police action was the key blunder, and later the Ukrainian authorities admitted that they had overreacted. The four main opposition parties – Tymoshenko's Batkivshchyna (Fatherland), Vitaly Klitschko's UDAR, Arseniy Yatsenyuk's Front for Change and Oleg Tyagnybok's Svoboda – had already formed an alliance, with Yatsenyuk as leader, in anticipation of the 2015 presidential election, and they now worked together in opposition to Yanukovych. On 11 December the square was once again attacked, provoking violent conflicts but still no deaths. On 24 December the opposition journalist Tetyana Chornovil was savagely beaten up on her way home from a village near Kiev where her parents lived. At this stage the protesters were mainly middle-aged and middle class, drawing on social media and the internet for information, looking to the EU to escape from economic and political stagnation. Although students were well represented, two-thirds of protesters were over 30 years of age. The median protester was male, between 34 and 45, and with a full-time job. The ethnic make-up broadly reflected the country's national composition, with 92 per cent of the demonstrators ethnic Ukrainians, while a large group of Russians also joined, motivated by the same concerns as their Ukrainian counterparts – corruption and misgovernance.[2]

The atmosphere on the square has now become legendary. The sweet smoke from wood-burners was tempered by the acrid fumes from burning tyres, while purposeful platoons marched intent on their business of saving Ukraine. What appeared to be a funeral pyre became a monument to freedom. Stepan Bandera looked down from his giant portrait and would no doubt have approved of the frequent bursts of singing the national anthem and cries of 'Glory to Ukraine. Glory to the Heroes!' Impassioned speakers took to the stage to excoriate the authorities, to rally the troops and to organise what soon turned into an insurrection. The surrounding buildings were occupied and provided shelter and warmth, and the encampment reached far up the main boulevard, the Khreshchatik, and on occasions flowed into government buildings in the surrounding streets. This was more than just another Orange Revolution, since the Blues had a direct stake in a better governed and less corrupt Ukraine, and even some of the Gold oligarchs threw in their lots and supported the insurgency with money, food and tents. For those who participated, this was a transformative experience, while observers could not but be concerned about what sort of Ukraine would emerge as a result.

The major escalation took place after 16 January 2014, when the Verkhovna Rada adopted a bundle of 12 'anti-protest laws' (technically called the Bondarenko–Oliynik bill but soon dubbed the 'dictatorship laws'), which aroused popular fury and accelerated the drift towards violence. The laws imposed draconian penalties against demonstrations, with the 'organisers of mass unrest' facing 10 to 15 years in jail. The measures were not discussed in committee, and were adopted in a tumultuous parliamentary session by a show of hands. They were signed into law immediately by the speaker, in contravention of the rules. At the same time, the moderates in Yanukovych's team were dismissed, notably Sergei Levochkin, the head of the presidential staff, who favoured dialogue with the opposition. The first demonstrator was killed on 22 January, transforming the protest movement into a revolution. From 23 January insurgents took over regional state administration buildings, effectively ending governmental control. In Lviv armed protesters occupied several government buildings, including City Hall, which was festooned with Nazi banners, and also seized a military arsenal. They dispatched up to several hundred armed forces daily to the Maidan, who participated in the escalating violence. In three regions, Volyn, Lviv and Ternopil, a new government structure called the Narodna Rada (People's Council) came to power.

The defence of the square increasingly took on a quasi-military form. In other words, a civic protest movement turned into an armed struggle in the space of just a few weeks. The head of the *samooborona* (self-defence committee) was known as 'commandant', the post taken up by the veteran nationalist Andriy Parubiy, one of the founders of Svoboda, and the lightly armed units making designated *sotnyas* (squadrons, literally 'hundreds'). The radicalisation of the square marginalised the traditional party leaders. Klitschko came in for particular criticism from the radicals, with Tymoshenko in jail and Tyagnybok in his element in fomenting revolution. The trade union building adjacent to the square was taken over by militant groups and provided field kitchens, a press centre, meeting space and first-aid facilities. Entrance to the square was strictly controlled to stop 'provocateurs' entering, in particular the so-called '*titushki*', young men in civilian clothes hired by the regime to support the security forces and intimidate the opposition through kidnappings and beatings. The Orange Revolution endured for 17 days, whereas the Maidan revolution lasted 100.

Svoboda was now joined on the nationalist flank by Right Sector (Pravy Sektor), a coalition of small groups which took the lead in organising the defence of the Maidan. It is reputed that Kolomoisky was one of the main funders of the Maidan movement, and in particular Right Sector, a party that began as a loose grouping of radical right-wing movements that led the confrontations with the riot police on the Maidan, 'organically combining militaristic organisation, nationalist ideology and Christian doctrine'.[3] Born in the territorial configuration of the defence of the right-hand segment of the square, Right Sector came together on 26 November 2013 and proved the most resolute militant fighting force. It combined such groups as the Stepan Bandera All-Ukrainian Organisation Trident (the trident being the symbol of Ukraine), the Ukrainian National Assembly (UNA), White Hammer and the avowedly fascist Social–National Assembly. It set up headquarters in the trade union building overlooking the square, until it was burned out on the night of 18–19 February. At the peak of the protests it numbered at most a few thousand, devoted to Yanukovych's overthrow, and after successfully achieving that it transformed itself into a political party. Its leader, Dmytro Yarosh (also the head of Trident), fought the 25 May presidential election. Typical of the distorting effect of Eastern European post-Communist politics, the group supported Ukraine's association with the EU, not because of any respect for the values traditionally associated with that organisation but because it symbolised separation from Moscow.[4] Yarosh had been a member of UNA, but like the movement had developed a more eclectic post-Communist ideology. Right Sector inherited the Bandera philosophy that Russia was the main enemy in all circumstances and at all times, a credo that destroyed the possibility of diplomacy and rational political debate, and which seeped heavily into the new regime after February.

The authorities used force three times, and in each case it provoked a powerful counter-mobilisation and an escalation of violence. Three protesters were killed in the third week of January, one of whom showed signs of torture. Protest supporters were being kidnapped, tortured and murdered. The rhetoric on both sides revealed cleavages that presaged the civil war to come. Even the prime minister, Mykola Azarov, described the demonstrators as 'extremists and terrorists', although when resigning on 28 January he stated that he did so to allow a peaceful resolution of the civil unrest. The pro-government Lugansk MP Arsen Klintshaev said that it was 'totally right' that the first demonstrators had been killed, since they had turned against the country's leadership and urged 'a much harder line against the protesters'. On the other side, Svoboda activists argued that that 'the EU is the only possibility for us to defend ourselves against Russian pressure'. As a perceptive report noted, 'without the nationalists' tight organisation, the revolt on Maidan Square would long since have collapsed. But Svoboda also embodies the greatest danger to the protest movement.'[5] The battle on the square became a civilisational struggle, with the hardliners on both sides squeezing out the middle ground where monists and the pluralists could meet on a common platform of anti-corruption and democratic renewal.[6]

A range of popular initiatives welled up from below, bypassing the traditional parties and giving shape to citizen activism. A Maidan Council was established early on to coordinate actions and to advise leaders. A number of self-defence organisations were created following the beating of Chornovil, the first step in the institutionalisation of the Maidan. One such group, the AutoMaidan, became responsible for transporting protesters safely to and from the Maidan, while a night guard group sought to prevent injured protesters being removed from hospitals by the security forces. EuromaidanSOS was established after the beating of the students on 30 November to provide legal and other support for those who had suffered at the hands of the Berkut (Golden Eagle), the special police force, and to help find missing people. It was based on the Centre for Civil Liberties, thus reinforcing the point that much of the activism in 2013–14 has its roots in movements spawned by the Orange Revolution a decade earlier. It provided a list of lawyers willing to provide their services, monitored the fate of those who went missing, and created mobile groups in Sevastopol and south-east Ukraine after the Crimean events. The opir.org website warned activists of how to avoid Berkut emplacements. In short, the new social media that had helped launch the protest movement was then used to organise activities and to support the participants.

However, these aspirations were later overshadowed and the revolution became a mockery of its original ideals. The focus broadened out from European issues to become an insurrection against the corruption, nepotism and general malfeasance of the Yanukovych regime. The 'revolt' element became more salient, above all against abuse of the constitutional system and the exercise of power over law. This was now less of a movement 'for' some ideal but a revolution 'against' the regime. The Maidan protest became radicalised, in large part because of the incompetence and irresolution of the regime's response. Just enough coercion and violence was used to strengthen the spirit and numbers of the protest movement, but not enough to achieve the goal of clearing the Maidan and the city centre of protesters. The 42 self-defence units of the Maidan managed and defended the square, three of which were all-female. Traditional gender roles, however, were asserted as the militarised agenda of national liberation began to overshadow the civic aspirations of the early protests. The Ukrainian 'revolution' was now dominated by neo-Leninist bodies of armed men strutting across the square, foreclosing pluralist options and undermining the representative institutions of the state. The radical nationalism that came to predominate was later generalised to the rest of the country.[7]

This played into the hands of the more radical elements in the protest movement, notably the activists grouped around Right Sector. Unlike the Svoboda party, this was less an ideological, right-wing movement than an eclectic front of militants. Hence it is always easy to point out that it contained some Jews, to counter claims that Right Sector was anti-Semitic; that it contained ethnic Russians, to refute claims that it was Russophobic; that it brought together people from the Donbas, to deny that it was exclusively Galician, and so on. Despite its ideological and social heterogeneity, the predominant spirit undeniably was an extreme form of monist Ukrainian nationalism. The age profile of Right Sector was higher than the average on the Maidan, including some Afgantsy (those who had fought in the Afghan war in the 1980s) and veterans of the Chechen wars, and the predominant language was Russian.[8] Right Sector's relative prominence reflected the contradiction in the Maidan between liberal-democratic aspirations for civic dignity and democratic governance, and anti-liberal monistic representations of the nation. The rising tide of Ukrainian nationalism subordinated the struggle for individual rights to the collective aspirations of the nation. The various battles for the Maidan generated militancy as a distinct form of political behaviour, and thus gathered under its umbrella all sorts of activists, many of whose views were antithetical to each other.

The Maidan became a pilgrimage site for advocates of Western democratism. As Victoria Nuland, assistant Secretary of State for European and Eurasian affairs, revealed in her remarks to the US–Ukraine Foundation conference at the National Press Club on 13 December 2013, she had travelled to Ukraine three times since the protests had begun. Visiting the Maidan on 5 December, she famously handed out 'cookies' to the demonstrators, although Catherine Ashton, who was in attendance, demonstrated European independence by not following suit. Nuland describes how

in the wee hours of December 10th, we witnessed the appalling show of force by government forces who turned riot police, bulldozers and tear gas on the Maidan demonstrators as they sang hymns and prayed for peace. Ukrainians of all ages and backgrounds flooded to the Maidan to protect it. Secretary Kerry wasted no time in expressing the United States' disgust at this decision of the Ukrainian government and by morning the riot police had been forced to retreat.

She revealed that the US had 'invested' over $5 billion in democracy-promotion in Ukraine since 1991. Her remarks took it as a given that 'Ukraine's European future' was the only possible option, and thus she commended 'the EU for leaving the door open on the Association Agreement and for continuing to work with the Ukrainian government on a way forward'.[9] It did not appear to have crossed her mind that the occupation of a city centre square in any other major city would long ago have been broken up, or that Ukraine was genuinely torn between East and West.

By early February, Yanukovych's position was becoming untenable. A leaked telephone call between Nuland and the ambassador, Geoffrey Pyatt, revealed the close involvement of the US in choosing his successor. The transcript was placed on YouTube on 6 February, and was part of a larger conversation. Its veracity was not challenged by the American authorities, although they blamed Russia for the interception and leak. Although the mantra of the Atlantic powers was that Ukrainian sovereignty should be respected, the tape revealed that the US had clear ideas on who should assume power. The leadership potential of Vitaly Klitschko, the head of UDAR, was assessed, but he was considered to be rather pro-German (EU), with Nuland summing up: 'I don't think Klitsch should go into government. I don't think it's necessary. I don't think it's a good idea.' Pyatt agreed and feared that it would be hard 'to keep the moderate democrats together', but Svoboda head Tyagnybok was identified as a problem, to which Nuland responded: 'I think Yats is the guy who has got the economic experience, the governing experience', clearly expressing the wish to see Arseniy Yatsenyuk become the country's prime minister.

The two then discussed how this could be achieved. They considered how to manage the Ukrainian opposition and how to get the UN involved, and noted that high-level reinforcement was waiting in the wings in the form of US vice president Joe Biden, who could move the process along at the appropriate time. Nuland stressed the importance of the UN: 'I think, to help glue this thing and to have the UN help glue it and, you know, fuck the EU.' This is certainly a sentiment shared by many Eurosceptics, but in this case it refers to the hesitancy of the EU to go along with American militancy on the Ukraine crisis, as well as its own divisions that inhibited the formulation of a coherent policy. The tape also reveals concern about Russia: 'You can be pretty sure if it [the deal] does start to gain altitude, that the Russians will be working behind the scenes to try to torpedo it.'[10] There are many disturbing elements about the intercept, quite apart from its provenance, one assumes, as part of the Russian secret intelligence service's attempts to discredit its opponents. It reveals the high degree of US meddling in Ukrainian affairs, and the way that the concerns of its ostensible allies and partners are dismissed with a profanity.

The country edged towards civil war. On 18 February 28 people were killed, including ten policemen from the Berkut riot police. The bloody clashes culminated in mass violence on 20 February. This was the day of sniper shootings, targeting both protesters and police, with at least 39 protesters and 17 police officers killed. The angle of some of the shots suggests that they came from buildings occupied by the insurgents. Shots killing both protesters and police were fired from the Philharmonic Hall, a building under the full control of the insurgents. Parubiy was in charge of the building, and in general he ensured strict control on who could enter or leave the square. Surprisingly, Right Sector activists escaped mostly unharmed, even though they were actively involved in the fighting. The Maidan doctor Olga Bogomolets is reported to have suggested that the same type of bullets that killed the protesters also killed the police. Overall, between 30 November and 20 February at least 15 police officers and 77 activists (later commemorated as the 'heavenly hundred') were killed, and around 900 people were injured.

With violence spreading, on the night of 20–21 February the foreign ministers of Germany (Frank-Walter Steinmeier), Poland (Radosław Sikorski) and France (Laurent Fabius, who soon left for a visit to China), together with the head of the continental European department of the French foreign ministry, Eric Fournier, flew to Kiev and brokered a deal with Yanukovych. At 4 p.m. on 21 February in the building of the presidential administration the agreement was signed by Yanukovych, Yatsenyuk, Klitschko and Tyagnybok, and witnessed by the three EU ministers and Vladimir Lukin, Russia's former ambassador to the US and then human-rights ombudsman, who was now Putin's special representative. There were six key provisions:

i. within 48 hours Yanukovych was to sign a bill to return the country to the 2004 constitution, which would allow the Rada to form a 'government of national unity' within ten days;

ii. the unity government was to draft a new constitution by the end of spring 2014 that would further limit presidential powers;

iii. early presidential elections were to be held as soon as the new constitution was adopted, no later than December 2014, with a new electoral law and electoral commission;

iv. an investigation was to be conducted into the recent bout of violence, to be overseen by the authorities, the opposition and the Council of Europe;

v. the authorities would not introduce a state of emergency and all sides would renounce the use of force accompanied by the withdrawal of government forces from the Maidan and the disarming of the Kiev street militias;

vi. the various foreign ministers and representatives called for an immediate ceasefire.[11]

These were significant concessions and offered a peaceful and constitutional way out of the crisis. The security services melted away and Yanukovych was left defenceless.

That evening the deal was fulsomely rejected by the Maidan, whose leaders demanded Yanukovych's immediate resignation, the release of jailed protesters, signing of the Association Agreement and reversion to the 2004 constitution.[12] When the three opposition leaders went to the demonstrators to sell the deal, the Maidan squadron (*sotnia*) leader Vladimir Parasyuk responded furiously:

> We don't want to see Yanukovych in power. We don't want deals with them. On Saturday [22 February] at 10am he must step down. And unless this morning you come up with a statement demanding that he steps down, then we will take arms and go, I swear.[13]

Party leaders of maturity would have argued that the deal offered a peaceful way out of the crisis, but instead Klitschko even apologised for having shaken hands with Yanukovych. The next day insurgents took advantage of the removal of government forces to assert their control of the city and to occupy parliament. On that day statues of Lenin across the country were destroyed (part of the process known as the 'Leninopad'). Undoubtedly, Yanukovych's position was already shaky, and thus he was not a strong foundation on which to base a deal, yet with the Western powers and Russia as guarantors and less populism from the opposition, it could have worked. The revolution by then had a dynamic of its own, and, just as in February 1917 in Russia, a regime that looked so powerful crumbled in a matter of hours.

The details remain unclear, but on the night of 21–22 February Yanukovych left Kiev to attend a conference of PoR in Kharkov. He had already been packing and sending his goods towards Russia.[14] Putin warned Yanukovych against leaving Kiev, but it was already clear that his life was in danger. As Yanukovych left the city there were at least four assassination attempts. Yanukovych stayed briefly in Kharkov before making his way to Crimea, and then escaped to Rostov with Russian help. As with Saddam Hussein in Iraq and Colonel Gaddafi in his ill-fated flight from Tripoli, the extreme personalisation of the system meant that when the tyrant fled, the regime effectively collapsed. Hussein ended up being hanged by the victorious allies, and Gaddafi met a gruesome fate at the hands of the insurgents, but Yanukovych has been given shelter, although reputedly has little influence on Russian policy. Later it was claimed that Yanukovych and his entourage took some $32 billion in cash to Russia.[15] The physical task of transporting such a sum would require at the minimum some 20 large trucks, which were not available at the time. Some of this money was allegedly used to finance the resistance in the Donbas, while the government sought to recover some of his assets lodged in Western banks. More immediately, Yanukovych's 350-acre estate at Mezhyhirya was opened up. Acquired from a former nature reserve in 2007, he built a grotesque mansion in a style now dubbed 'Donetsk rococo', a private zoo and garages for an extensive fleet of cars and a large boat. The scale of his opulence was a source of wonder, as was his spectacular bad taste.

THE RIDDLE OF THE MAIDAN

The first stage of the Maidan protest was a movement for the EU and the Association Agreement, and was quickly dubbed the 'Euromaidan', with the focus on expressions of commitment to Ukraine's European destiny. By definition this was a concern that was limited both geographically, mainly to the west and centre, and socially – those in the 'creative' classes who would benefit from closer ties with Western Europe. This represented an attempt to shift Ukraine's trajectory out of the '1990' rut, with its endless ambiguities and indeterminacies, and to set the country firmly on the path to the agenda of '1989' and Wider Europe. It would mean that Ukraine would escape joining the club of 'dictators for life', since Yanukovych would certainly have tried to manipulate the presidential elections due in March 2015. It was rumoured that he had already accumulated a campaign war chest (known colloquially as the *obshchak*) of at least $3 billion before he was overthrown. The Euromaidan sought to reorient Ukraine away from the indeterminacy of the '1990' impasse, and certainly to avert Ukraine's joining the '1991' group of countries. The idea of '1989' came to represent a whole interconnected package: economic modernisation, improvement of governance and alignment with the Euro-Atlantic security community.

The economic integration of Ukraine into the EU is a natural process, just as it is for Russia, but the EaP had politicised the issue while pretending it to be no more than a trade deal. It was later discovered that between 2004 and 2013 the EU had spent €496 million in Ukraine on 'subsidising front groups'. As Patrick Armstrong puts it: 'Brussels and Washington lit the fuse, the fire is burning. Easy to start; hard to finish.'[16] Despite this, the impulse that generated the Euromaidan for civic dignity, accountable government and a 'European future' was genuine and continued to inspire protesters to the end. The struggle for good governance and constitutionalism was something in which the whole country had a stake, and it was on this basis that significant numbers from the south-east joined the Maidan protesters. The movement of popular mobilisation represented a moment of national unity and the uniting of the two traditions of nation-building on the basis of civic renewal for all.

For all of its undoubted spirit of popular participation and civic engagement, the Maidan movement reflected a particular strain of Ukrainian nationalism. Stephen Shenfield notes the attempt on 6 February by a group of 41 *engagé* scholars led by Andreas Umland to refute allegations that the Maidan was 'being infiltrated, driven or taken over by radically ethnocentrist groups'. They denied that 'ultra-nationalist actors and ideas are at the core or helm of the Ukrainian protests', since these claims only fed the Kremlin propaganda mill. The refutation in Shenfield's view was weak, since no one would dispute that the Maidan movement was politically diverse and dynamic, but this does not explain 'how a Banderite slogan became the main motto of the Maidan'. In other words, the radical nationalism of Galicia was becoming gen-eralised to become the new normal of Ukrainian state development. A conservative, Russophobic nationalist ideology came to predominate. As Shenfield notes, 'what is perhaps most shocking is not the presence of ultra-rightists or even their numbers but the fact that (with few exceptions) they are broadly accepted as a legitimate part of the Maidan'. In addition the political ethos of the Maidan became axiological, with the 'forces of absolute good' ranged against the 'forces of absolute evil', with legitimate disagreements, for example over the scope of relations with the EU, 'glossed over for the sake of unity', accompanied by a proclivity towards conspiracy theories. Russian-speakers were characterised as '*sovoks*', people still influenced by Soviet attitudes. The endless repetition of the idea of the 'European choice' was reminiscent of Gorbachev's set phrase of 'the socialist choice of the Soviet people'; in both cases, 'the word "choice" is actually used to deny choice'.[17]

The spirit of the Maidan was not limited to Kiev, and prompted a wave of civil-society development across the country. Everywhere civic associations were estab-lished to hold officials and administrators accountable, to investigate corruption and malfeasance, and to advance positive projects for social amelioration. The lustration (from the Roman lustrum purification rituals) campaign gathered pace, focusing not on the Communist past of officials but on their honesty, probity and competence in office. Integrated nationalism was united as never before, and the patriotic fervour brought it new adepts from the Russian-speaking community. In the philosophy of the monist nationalists, Russia was always the implicit 'other' against which the nation was forged; but now what had been feared became real, in part because of the philosophy itself. As the pluralists had long warned, treating Russia as an enemy would in the end become a self-fulfilling prophecy. The dynamic of conflict embedded in integrated nationalism was now amplified by the exclusivist ambitions of the Wider European project. Those favouring a more pluralist expression of Ukrainian nationhood and mediating conflict through Greater European institutions were marginalised. Ukraine was hit by a perfect storm of competing ambitions.

The long-promised independent inquiry into the sniper shootings of 20 February, in which 50 people were killed, has still not been reported, allowing conspiracy theories to flourish. The initial assumption was that the shooting came from Yanukovych's forces, but in a leaked phone call of 26 February between the Estonian foreign minister

Urmas Paet (who had visited the Maidan on 25 February) and Catherine Ashton, which emerged on 5 March, he told her that 'there is now stronger and stronger understanding that behind the snipers, it was not Yanukovych, but it was somebody from the new coalition'. The substance of the charge is astonishing, but no less surprising is Ashton's calm response, as if she was not surprised by the revelation that Maidan leaders may have been responsible for the killing: 'I think we do want to investigate. I mean, I didn't pick that up. Gosh.' He goes on to note that a certain Olga (who turned out to be the Maidan activist, the doctor Olga Bogomolets) had stated that

> all the evidence shows that people who were killed by snipers from both sides, among policemen and people from the streets, that they were the same snipers killing people from both sides. It's really disturbing that now the new coalition, that they don't want to investigate what exactly happened.

In other words, the Maidan leaders were not interested in discovering the source of the sniper fire, since it helped rally the opposition. He sums up: 'So there is a stronger and stronger understanding that behind snipers it was not Yanukovych, it was somebody from the new coalition.'[18] Paet is not stating this as his view, but reporting what he heard on his visit to Kiev, while Bogomolets later distanced herself from the inferences drawn from her reported statements.

A German public television (ARD) investigation into who killed the 'heavenly hundred' on 20 February came to similar conclusions on both counts. It reported on 10 April that shots appear to have come also from the Ukraine Hotel, to which only the insurgents had access, thus shooting demonstrators from behind.[19] Aired on the main German channel, the report noted that six weeks after the events, no attempt had been made to get to the bottom of things, and instead the interim Ukrainian prosecutor general, Oleg Makhnitsky (a member of Svoboda), simply asserted that Yanukovych was to blame, while the interior minister Arsen Avakov claimed that Russian Federal Security Service (FSB) agents were directly involved in the killing. A recent scholarly analysis by Ivan Katchanovski comes to the opposite conclusion:

> Analysis of a large amount of evidence in this study suggests that certain elements of the Maidan opposition, including its extremist far right wing, were involved in this massacre in order to seize power and that the government investigation was falsified for this reason.[20]

If confirmed, this would make the credulous partisanship of the Western powers all the more irresponsible.

The repudiation of the 21 February deal marked the moment when protest turned into revolution. Across the country statues of Lenin were demolished, and Svoboda even advocated the removal of a monument honouring General Mikhail Kutuzov, the architect of victory over Napoleon. Over 100 statues of Lenin were toppled, mostly in the south-east, since already in June 2009 Yushchenko had called for the erasure of Communist symbols, provoking a wave of monument destruction in western Ukraine, so there were few left now. The campaign continued throughout the year. On 28 September 2014 vigilantes destroyed the statue of Lenin in the centre of Kharkov – which the mayor, Gennady Kernes, promised to restore. All of this provoked a Blue counter-mobilisation from February 2014. Anti-Maidan sentiments across the Russophone areas of the country were inflamed, and in the Donbas so-called 'pro-Russian' militants began to seize government buildings, copying the tactic of the Maidan militants. Yanukovych continued to argue that his dismissal represented a 'coup', although his opponents argue that his flight represented an abdication. A 'coup' is rather too narrow a definition of the seismic changes, although 'revolution' is probably too broad, since the structure of power was not challenged and neither was the social basis of the bureaucratic–oligarchic order. Nevertheless, it is appropriate to talk of the 'February revolution', since the events represented a critical juncture. The overthrow of a legally elected president by a mobilised people represents a turning point of the first magnitude. The usurpation would have grave consequences in regions where there had been enduring dissatisfaction with the nationalising strain of Ukrainian state-building. The 'anti-Maidan' movement across the south and the east in defence of the pluralist reading of Ukrainian politics adopted as its symbol the St George ribbon, the black and orange pattern introduced in 2005 to commemorate the Great Patriotic War, that is, the struggle against Nazi Germany, but which in Ukraine became a sign of resistance to the February revolution. Anti-Maidan sentiment was strongest in Crimea, leading to its incorporation into Russia, which will be discussed in the next chapter, as well as in the putative 'Novorossiya' in the Donbas, which will also be discussed later.

THE SQUARE AND THE CASTLE

The Maidan now constituted itself as a 'people's parliament', acting not just as a check on the new authorities but also to advance policies of its own, notably the lustration of officials considered too close to the old regime, or corrupt, or both. The 'square' of people's power sought to control the 'castle' of government. The square as we have seen was far from homogeneous, and the various contradictions would ultimately be fatal for the revolution. The key contradiction was between the idealism of the middle-class 'revolutionaries', fighting for dignity and responsible government, and the militants, who tended to come from the margins of society and drew on the ultra-nationalist traditions of interwar Galicia. Both groups aspired to overcome the obvious political and economic stagnation of the country, yet their alliance was trapped in a palpable dilemma: if unity was maintained, then the whole revolution would be tainted by the 'fascistic' features of the right-wing militants; but if it fell apart, then the revolution would be usurped by the restoration of bureaucratic–oligarchic power or diluted by concessions to the pluralists (by now considered tantamount to capitulation to the Kremlin). With the country's territorial integrity under threat, the militant part of the square prevailed over the more pacific 'bourgeois' element – although the territorial threats were in part a response to the militancy of the square in the first place. The alliance was maintained, but the square ultimately brought to the castle little more than a reconfigured form of bureaucratic–oligarchic power, although now espousing the rhetoric of civil society and its ultra-nationalist inflections.

What had begun as a movement in support of 'European values' now became a struggle to assert a monist representation of Ukrainian nationhood. The amorphous liberal rhetoric gave way to a much harsher agenda of integrated nationhood, and the euphoria prompted a rash of ill-considered policies. In the flush of victory, the triumphant opposition forces undertook a number of fateful steps. First, the impeachment of Yanukovych on 22 February was accompanied by armed insurgents strutting around the debating chamber. The formal procedure required the establishment of a dedicated investigatory committee by the procuracy, its conclusions to be reviewed by parliament and then a vote in favour of impeachment if so decided, followed by a decision of the Constitutional Court and the Supreme Court, and, finally – most importantly – a vote by no fewer than three quarters of the constitutional total of the Verkhovna Rada (338 MPs). Instead, MPs were simply instructed to 'sack' Yanukovych. Even then, the vote did not reach the required majority: 328 of 447 MPs (73 per cent), many from the PoR, voted to remove Yanukovych from the presidency on the grounds that he was unable to fulfil his responsibilities, even though an hour earlier on television Yanukovych insisted that he would not resign and at that point had not left the country. Article 111 of the constitution lists four circumstances in which an incumbent president may leave office – resignation, a serious health condition, impeachment, and death – none of which applied in this case.

Second, a 'coup-sponsored' government was created (as its critics put it) by parliament. Parliamentary speaker Alexander Turchynov was selected as acting president, and he in turn appointed Yatsenyuk acting prime minister. This brought to the fore the man already 'pre-selected' by Nuland, rather than the putative German (European) candidate for the post, Klitschko, giving the new administration the appearance of being little more than an American project. These were far from being a new generation of politicians. Turchynov was a close Tymoshenko ally, having served as SBU head when she was prime minister from February to September 2005. As an old comrade of Tymoshenko's he had been deeply involved in the various 'gas wars' between Firtash's RUE and Tymoshenko's Itera as the gas-trading intermediary between Russia and Ukraine, a battle that had been fought on and off for five years from 2004 and which caused immeasurable damage, including gas cut-offs in January 2006 and January 2009, ending with the deeply flawed settlement of 19 January 2009. Ministers now had to seek approval from the Maidan before being ratified. The square claimed to constitute the 'sovereign' people as a 'people's parliament', overshadowing the discredited Rada. Some 70 MPs from Yanukovych's PoR fled to the east, while 30 crossed the floor to join the victorious coalition. The party as a whole was divided between the Akhmetov and Firtash factions, although both these oligarchs had facilitated 'regime change' by shifting their support away from Yanukovych at the decisive moment. Two days later the Rada dismissed five Constitutional Court judges, a clear infringement of the idea of separation of powers, for allegedly violating their oaths in acquiescing to Yanukovych's demand in 2010 to restore the 1996 constitution.

The so-called 'unity government' turned out to be anything but a unifying force. There was gross imbalance in ministerial appointments, designed to consolidate the victory of the Maidan but thereby alienating the proponents of a more pluralistic interpretation of Ukrainian development. Only two ministers from the entire south and east, covering half the country, joined the 21-person cabinet. Between five and eight (depending on changing affiliations) core ministerial positions were taken by Right Sector and Svoboda, including the top national-security, defence and legal (prosecutor general) posts. The minister of justice and deputy prime minister came from the Russophobic Svoboda party, while its founder, Parubiy, became secretary of the NSDC, and Yarosh, no less, was nominated as his deputy, although he turned it down in anticipation of a higher post. Parubiy as we have seen had a long history of ultra-nationalist activism, having been one of the founders in 1991, along with Tyagnybok, of the Social–National Party of Ukraine, which evolved into the Svoboda party. Parubiy's appointment to head the NSDC was by any measure astonishing, placing him in charge of the country's security policy. Five positions alone were taken by members of the radical Svoboda party, although at the time the party held only 8 per cent of seats in parliament, and another seven were from Batkivshchyna. No posts were given to PoR, even though at the time it held 27 per cent of the seats in the Rada. In addition, five governorships were taken by Svoboda, covering a fifth of the country. It is not unprecedented to have extreme right-wing parties in government, notably the

Northern League in Italy, as well as various groups in Poland and Slovakia, but their radical populism everywhere challenges the foundations of liberal constitutionalism. Svoboda remained an alienating and divisive force.

Third, the ethos of the new government, although liberal on economic issues and keen to adopt IMF stringency on the road to Europe, was conservative and 'romantic' nationalist in social matters. On 27 February the Svoboda MP Alexander Sych was appointed deputy prime minister, a man who had sponsored a bill in April 2013 to ban abortion and who was infamous for his comments that, if women did not wish to risk rape, they should not drink alcohol in questionable company. These traditionalist, conservative views were intended to revitalise the Ukrainian nation, but later took on a more sharply militaristic tone as part of the struggle against the insurgency in the Donbas. The cult of violence as a necessary crucible to forge a cleansed nation took on fascistic symbolism. The representation of Ukraine as a young woman garlanded with a crown of braids, victimised by an oppressor, became universal across the Maidan, and was drawn from the playbook of romantic-nationalist associations of the nineteenth century and integral-nationalist movements of the twentieth. This in turn reinforced a highly traditionalist representation of the role of women in society, and opposed the 'demo-liberalism' of the West with its espousal of gay marriage and non-traditional diversity. As long as the focus was on suppressing 'pro-Russian separatism' and the fight against 'terrorism' in the Donbas these contradictions were suppressed, but came to haunt the new regime, although tempered by the pragmatism of the bureaucratic–oligarchic establishment.

Fourth, in policy terms, the government began with perhaps the worst of all possible moves, given the fragile unity of the country. The law of July 2012 granting regions the right to instate a second official language where there was at least a 10 per cent minority had been forced through against the bitter resistance of the nationalists. On 23 February parliament voted by an overwhelming majority to rescind the law. This was not just an attack on Russia but an assault against all of the country's minority nations, and above all against the Russian-speakers in Crimea and the Donbas. In the ensuing uproar, Turchynov (after an unconscionable delay, during which time power was transferred in Crimea) on 28 February refused to sign and thus effectively vetoed the act, but the damage was done. This was attended by virulent anti-Russian rhetoric in the chamber, and a slew of proposals consolidating the victory of the radicals.

Fifth, the armed militants were given a quasi-official status, patrolling the streets and allegedly providing security in conditions of regime collapse. This did not prevent, for example, them breaking into the headquarters of the CPU and trashing their files and meeting rooms. Two waves of military 'reform' under Yanukovych left the regular army even more unreliable, ill-equipped and poorly trained. To compensate, in mid-April the interim interior minister, Arsen Avakov, announced the creation of a new National Guard. The Maidan turned into a military recruiting centre, absorbing many of the militants. Although the volunteers were meant to operate under the aegis of the interior ministry, several oligarchs funded their own militias, who were sent to fight the insurgents in the Donbas, imbuing the conflict with elements of a civil war. On 1 May conscription was reintroduced. The Ukrainian revolution moved through all the standard stages of a revolution in an accelerated, almost farcical and certainly tragic manner: from genuine popular enthusiasm for a democratic cause, to radicalisation and the emergence of a revolutionary elite, followed by the seizure of power and punitive operations against 'enemies of the revolution', resulting in counter-mobilisation and civil war. The final phase is accompanied by denunciations of 'fifth columnists' and the fostering of the peculiarly intense hatreds when brother fights against sister, until the revolution implodes in a frenzy of recriminations and an authoritarian stabilisation takes place imposed by a new dictator, either the 'man on horseback' or some foreign-backed usurper.

The interim government sought to bring the Maidan self-defence groups, notably Right Sector, under control. One of the leaders of Right Sector, Alexander Muzychko (better known as Sashko Bily), was infamous for his anti-Semitic, as well as anti-Polish and anti-Russian, rhetoric. On 24 March he was killed in a shoot-out with police in Rovno in western Ukraine. He had earlier been seen on video threatening a local council meeting with a pistol and striking an official. His supporters swore to avenge his death, which they believed was a political assassination ordered by Avakov. Avakov now insisted that all the unofficial armed groups were acting illegally and should turn in their weapons. Instead, on 27 March hundreds of Right Sector militants marched on parliament demanding Avakov's resignation and an explanation for Muzychko's death. Parliament voted for the 'immediate disarming of illegally armed groups' while acting president Turchynov warned that they were trying to 'destabilise' Ukraine, and others warned that they were 'discrediting' the revolution.[21] Muzychko's killing had the desired effect, and thereafter nationalists eschewed anti-Semitic language and instead focused their rhetorical violence on Russia.

Power moved from the square to the castle, and then leaked back to squares across the country. In Odessa in March and April a series of demonstrations and counter-demonstrations were held, accompanied by the creation of an anti-Maidan tent encampment in Kulikovo Pole (Kulikov Field) with some 300 activists. On 2 May a pro-Maidan demonstration was organised in the city centre, including nationalist 'ultra' fans from the Chernomorets Odessa and Metalist Kharkov football teams, who had played earlier. Permission was granted to hold what would obviously be a controversial event. Some 1,500 demonstrators marched through the city centre chanting 'Glory to Ukraine' and 'Death to enemies', as well as the now obligatory 'Knife the Moskals' ('Moskals' being a derogatory term for Russians), long the slogan of nationalist students in Lviv and elsewhere. The procession was assaulted by people allegedly from the anti-Maidan group. The attackers, as well as some policemen, were marked with red tags – and it was precisely these who began the shooting. They were let through the police chain, and when the shooting started there are pictures of such red-tagged provocateurs standing with police officers. On the other side, the Maidan militants were led by Right Sector, some 500 of whom had arrived earlier in the city, along with the Maidan leader, Parubiy.

Several hundred ultras now assaulted the encampment in Kulikov Field, burning the tents and driving the anti-Maidan protesters into the adjacent five-storey, Soviet-style trade union building. Right Sector militants threw Molotov cocktails and set fire to the building, and beat back protesters with clubs and knives as they tried to escape the flames. There are suggestions that the protesters were beaten, raped and killed before the fire took hold, with a strange pattern to the flames, concentrated on the first and third floors. Those trapped inside heard the Ukrainian nationalists compare them to the black-and-red-striped potato beetle called Colorado, the colour of the St George ribbons: 'Burn, Colorado, burn.' They clubbed to death those who survived when they jumped out of windows, accompanied by chants of 'Glory to Ukraine!' and 'Death to enemies!' The official figures state that 48 died (seven women and 41 men) and 247 were injured, whereas local reports suggest that several hundred were consumed by the fire or died by violence. Two days later the police headquarters was stormed to release the 67 pro-Russian activists who had been detained in the fighting. The website of the Right Sector leader Dmytro Yarosh hailed the massacre as 'another bright day in our national history', while a Svoboda MP exclaimed, 'Bravo, Odessa [...] Let the devils burn in hell.'[22] The vigilante violence that began on the Maidan now affected the rest of the country. This was a terrible crime by people masquerading as 'democrats' on the road to Europe.

Yatsenyuk revealed the brutal insensitivity for which he would become famous when he argued that 'what happened in Odessa was part of a plan by the Russian Federation to destroy Ukraine and its statehood [...] Russia sent people here to create chaos.'[23] Even worse, the event evoked remarkably little response in the West and was swept under the carpet in Ukraine. Despite the creation of at least four commissions to investigate the event, the details remain murky, accompanied by a media blockade by the Kiev authorities. The parliamentary report presented on 9 September 2014 missed out important episodes, including the involvement of Parubiy and the 500 Maidan militants bussed into Odessa on the eve of the massacre. On 6 May Turchynov appointed one of Kolomoisky's closest associates, Igor Palitsa, governor of the Odessa region, and the violence continued. The nationalists set up 'block-posts' and patrolled the city: 'Though the city is predominantly Russian-speaking, a fierce grass-roots anti-Russian movement now has de facto control of the streets, owing to careful organisation over the past two months.'[24] It is this which the separatists in Crimea and the Donbas argue that they averted. Odessa is famous for its tolerant and relaxed lifestyle, but these events traumatised the city. It took on the character of an occupied territory as Maidan 'democrats' established offices to monitor the local population. There were no more anti-Maidan protests.

The option of evolutionary, although extraordinary, change was lost, and instead the events were construed by opponents as a 'coup' by the Maidan against the legitimately constituted authorities. The black and red colours of the Bandera movement confronted the black and orange St George ribbon as monists and pluralists marched and counter-marched in squares across the country. For the Kremlin, 21 February was the turning point, with the EU unwilling or unable to honour its own agreements and condoning the illegal seizure of power. The 'Ukrainian' crisis at this point became internationalised and turned into the 'Ukraine' crisis, with the Kremlin enraged by the coming to power of Russophobic nationalists. The seizure of power by monist nationalists allied with unsavoury right-wing elements alienated pluralists and raised fears that the exclusive form of nationalism, whose features had already been well articulated under Yushchenko, would now be given free rein. In Crimea, Odessa and above all the Donbas the scene was set for confrontation, loss of territory and civil war.

CHAPTER 5

THE CRIMEAN GAMBIT

The events of February 2014 came as a shock to Moscow. The repudiation of the EU-brokered deal and Yanukovych's unceremonious removal meant that business could not continue as usual. For at least a couple of months Putin had been distracted by the Sochi Winter Olympics, and Russian hawks argue that Moscow's low-key approach emboldened the protesters and their foreign backers, in the end provoking regime change. It was only then that Moscow reacted, and implemented what from its perspective was a counter-coup, the remarkably smooth and peaceful takeover of Crimea. Putin's choices were effectively limited to two: do nothing, which itself involved a whole series of risks, or act decisively. In chess a gambit is when a player accepts the loss of a piece to win positional advantage. Putin was willing to damage his international reputation and risk isolating Russia and alienating Ukraine to gain what for him was a crucial 'piece', Crimea, and with it the Sevastopol naval base. In chess the gambit may be declined, but for that you need to be a skilled and imaginative player.

RETURN TO RUSSIA

We noted in Chapter 1 that in 1954 Crimea was transferred from Russian to Ukrainian jurisdiction, a decision that remains mired in controversy.[1] The region had been devastated in World War II, and well into the 1950s it remained sparsely populated and barely functioning. The transfer took place at the time when the major watercourses were being built from Ukraine proper, and it seemed sensible to have a single republican administration for both. Without irrigation Crimea would be an arid desert, and the cities of Simferopol (the capital), Sevastopol, Kerch, Sudak, Evpatoriya, Feodosiya and others would not be viable (see Map 5). The republic is dependent on the water it gets from the River Dnieper via the 400-kilometre-long Northern Crimean Canal, which since 1961 has been channelling water from the Kakhovka reservoir to the peninsula. The republic has developed an extensive rice, fruit and vegetable industry, as well as extensive wine plantations. The transfer was voted for by the USSR Supreme Soviet without debate or consulting the people involved, allegedly prompted by a semi-inebriated Khrushchev, the general secretary who just a year earlier had taken over from Stalin. He was up to his elbows in blood, and had spent much of his career in Ukraine, and the transfer was seen as a form of expiation.

At the time of the Soviet Union's disintegration Crimea was very much on the minds of the Yeltsin leadership. There had been a vociferous movement since 1956 to allow the Tatars to return to their historic homeland, accepted by the Soviet Council of Ministers in July 1990. As purely administrative internal boundaries became the borders of independent states, one of the fundamental principles was the inviolability of existing borders, however arbitrary. Crimea was always understood, particularly by Russian nationalists, as a special case. Russia became the 'continuer state' of the USSR, assuming its responsibilities, treaty obligations and privileges. Even at the time of the transfer in 1954 Sevastopol had been recognised as an 'object of all-union significance', and thus technically should have reverted to Russia as the continuer state when Ukraine became independent. Yeltsin did not pursue the issue, assuming that the CIS would allow visa-free and other links between the former Soviet republics to continue uninterrupted. In the event, Ukraine had gained the most in terms of transfer of territory from the Russian Soviet Federated Socialist Republic (RSFSR), but turned out to be the least willing to work within the framework of the CIS, a contradiction that would be exposed in 2014.

The first years of independence were marked by extreme tensions in the region. As Ukraine gained independence, this was challenged immediately by 'secession within secession' as Crimea sought greater autonomy, if not independence. In a referendum of January 1991, 93 per cent voted in favour of creating a separate 'Crimean Republic'. In December 1991 Crimea voted along with the rest of Ukraine for independence, although by a far smaller margin than the rest of the country – 54 per cent as opposed to 91 per cent nationally. On 26 February 1992 the Crimean Supreme Soviet renamed the peninsula the Republic of Crimea and on 5 May declared self-government, to be ratified in a referendum, which in the end was not held although the republic later strengthened its constitutional autonomy and created an executive presidency, a post taken by Yury Meshkov. On 17 March 1995 the Ukrainian parliament scrapped the constitution and abolished the post of president, and in 1996 incorporated the peninsula as an 'Autonomous Republic', granting extensive devolved powers. Tensions thereafter eased but the 'culture wars' continued, especially when a NATO military exercise was planned for the region in 2006. A major demonstration on 24 August 2009 was provoked by fears over the status of the naval base. This was, until 2014, the most powerful institutional expression of the 'other Ukraine', which at this time 'saw itself as part of a broader but diffuse imagined community'.[2]

The Ukrainian state had not recognised Tatar proprietary objects, let alone granted Tatar the status of a state language alongside Ukrainian. Crimea was allowed to have its own constitution and enjoyed considerable autonomy within Ukraine. The city of Sevastopol repeatedly proclaimed itself a Russian city, a cause that the Moscow mayor, Yury Luzhkov, made peculiarly his own. He was one of the most active proponents of the idea that Crimeans had never technically lost their status as citizens of the USSR and the RSFSR, and were thus entitled to Russian citizenship, encouraging the issuance of Russian passports to Crimean citizens. He was loudest in defence of Russophone culture in the republic, helping Moscow State University open a branch there. For all of its undoubted potential, Crimea was a huge burden on the Ukrainian exchequer. By 2013 at least two-thirds of its budget was made of transfers from Kiev, and there is a widespread view that the peninsula has stagnated since independence, much like the rest of the country.[3]

Crimea was important to Russia for a number of reasons, but above all for its strategic significance. Sevastopol was the home of the Black Sea Fleet (BSF), and the fear was that after the February revolution Russia would be evicted, even though a 'status of forces agreement' had been signed with Ukraine. Sevastopol is more than just a naval base but an extensive network of airfields, radar stations and ship repair yards. From the Russian perspective, the expansion of Wider Europe opened the door to Ukraine's accession to NATO, something promised at the Bucharest summit in 2008 and never repudiated. Although after Bucharest NATO membership had been placed on the back burner and was not an immediate issue, the security implications of the Association Agreement with the EU were not lost on Moscow. The Orange movement not only condemned the extension of the lease to 2042, but also questioned the basing rights to 2017, which potentially allowed external forces to be invited in on a bilateral basis. Losing the use of Sevastopol would be a devastating blow to Russia. It had spent years trying to find an alternative warm-water port, including extending the naval facilities at Novorossiisk and establishing basing rights in Ochamchira in Abkhazia, but neither even begins to match Sevastopol. Worse, Russia faced the prospect of Sevastopol being taken over by units of the US Sixth Fleet, currently based in Naples. NATO may well no longer have been Russia's enemy, but the prospect of its ships, missile defence units and various other bases along Russia's borders represented a strategic defeat and existential threat of the first order.

As the tensions in Kiev reached breaking point, in early February Vladislav Surkov, the former deputy head of the presidential administration and now an advisor to Putin on the Caucasus, was dispatched to Crimea, although his mission was shrouded in secrecy. Commentator Valery Solovei wrote on 3 March that Putin personally took the decision to take over Crimea in consultation with only five or six top security officials, which the *New York Times* on 7 March suggested included Sergei Ivanov (head of the presidential administration), Alexander Bortnikov (head of the FSB) and Nikolai Patrushev, the secretary of the Russian Security Council. The plan soon rolled into action. In the days following Yanukovych's flight, pro-Russian forces in Crimea began signing up volunteers for self-defence militias, amid reports that armed Ukrainian nationalists would descend on the region. On 26 February the region's parliament met to discuss staging a referendum on loosening ties with Kiev, accompanied by mass demonstrations for and against the new regime. The lack of a quorum meant that no vote could be held. Early next morning pro-Russian insurgents seized the building and deposed the prime minister appointed by Yanukovych, Anatoly Mogilev. He was a member of the ruling PoR, which held 80 out of the 100 seats, and supported autonomy within Ukraine. That evening 53 MPs voted to replace Mogilev with Sergei Aksenev, and 61 voted to hold a referendum on 'sovereignty'. The circumstances attending this decision, like the earlier ones, breached all sorts of parliamentary rules, and the session was held in secret. Aksenev was reputed to have links with the criminal underworld, acquiring the moniker 'Goblin'. His party, Russian Unity, won only 4 per cent of the vote to the Crimean parliament in the 2010 election, giving it three seats. Russian Unity was the political wing of one of the most ardent pro-Russian groups, the Russian Society of Crimea, headed by Sergei Tsekov, who now became deputy speaker. Various polls between 2011 and 2014 have found that support for joining Russia ranges between 23 and 41 per cent, which is rather a lot or little, depending on one's perspective.

On 28 February unidentified soldiers took control of Simferopol airport. The stated concern was the threat to Russians in Crimea, although this was more preemptive than responsive, since there were no reported cases of ethnic persecution. Right Sector did threaten to send a 'train of friendship' to Crimea, the character of which is not hard to imagine. Armed personnel in uniforms without insignia, later identified as members of the Russian armed forces, seized control of strategic objectives in a remarkably well-organised operation. Russia denied having sent in forces, and since Russia was allowed to have 25,000 personnel in the region in accordance with the Sevastopol basing agreement, technically Russia was not violating the letter of the law, although the armed forces were deployed in ways that contravened the basing agreement, operating beyond the leased area. There had been some 12,500 service people stationed in the peninsula, so there was scope to draft in more. Wearing green uniforms without insignia, the men claimed to be local volunteers and were soon dubbed 'little green men'. In fact, they were highly trained Russian special forces using advanced technologies to achieve the bloodless takeover of the peninsula.[4]

Debate rages over the causality of the events. In a press conference on 4 March Putin declared that Russia had no intention of annexing Crimea, although he insisted that the residents had the right to determine the region's status in a referendum. The issue initially was over enlarging the sphere of Crimea's autonomy, but when the Kiev authorities launched criminal investigations into Crimea's new leaders a new dynamism was introduced. Timely concessions over the Russian language, federalisation and other core long-term demands may have been enough to avert the region's secession, and indeed the subsequent conflict in the Donbas. However, with militant gestures coming from the new authorities in Kiev, Aksenev organised another vote in which parliament appealed to Russia to annex the republic. Already on 4 March Putin stressed the peaceful nature of the takeover: 'There was not a single armed conflict, not a single gunshot.' When asked about cases of people 'wearing uniforms that strongly resembled the Russian Army uniform', he asserted that 'those were local self-defence units'. He also raised some broader issues about forced regime change:

> I sometimes get the feeling that somewhere across that huge puddle, in America, people sit in a lab and conduct experiments, as if with rats, without actually understanding the consequences of what they are doing. Why did they need this? Who can explain this? There is no explanation at all for it.[5]

The referendum was brought forward to 16 March, and after much debate over the wording, the ballot in the end consisted of two simple questions (printed in the Russian, Ukrainian and Tatar languages): 'Are you in favour of the reunification of Crimea with Russia as part of the Russian Federation?' and 'Are you in favour of restoring the 1992 constitution and the status of Crimea as part of Ukraine?' According to the referendum commission, 83 per cent of Crimea's eligible voters cast their ballot (1,274,096), of whom 96.7 per cent backed reunification with Russia (1,233,002). Thus, 82 per cent of the total Crimean population apparently voted in favour. There were no independent Western observers, and thus the vote inevitably attracted widespread criticism. A report of the Russian Presidential Council for Civil Society and Human Rights later estimated that turnout was in fact only between 30 and 50 per cent, of whom 50–60 per cent voted for unification with Russia, with a higher turnout of 50–80 per cent in Sevastopol, the overwhelming majority of whom voted in favour. Thus in the peninsula as a whole, only between 15 and 30 per cent of the total population voted to join Russia.[6] Kiev and the Tatar Mejlis, the presidium of the traditional Crimean Tatar parliament, the Qurultay, urged voters to boycott the referendum, and if turnout fell below 50 per cent the vote would automatically have been invalidated, and the majority of Tatars apparently abstained. Nevertheless, it is reasonable to assume that even in perfect conditions a majority in Crimea would have voted for union with Russia, and in Sevastopol the vote would have been overwhelming.[7]

On 18 March Crimea formally became part of the Russian Federation. Before the treaty signing ceremony, Putin delivered an impassioned speech in the Kremlin. As he entered, the select audience, including members of the Federal Assembly, government ministers and representatives from Crimea, broke into a spontaneous and enthusiastic standing ovation, reminiscent of the congresses of the Soviet years. Putin condemned the post-Yanukovych authorities in Kiev as the 'ideological heirs of Bandera, Hitler's accomplice during World War II'. He justified Crimea's attempt to escape, noting that

> those who opposed the coup were immediately threatened with repression. Naturally, the first in line here was Crimea, the Russian-speaking Crimea. In view of this, the residents of Crimea and Sevastopol turned to Russia for help in defending their rights and lives, in preventing the events that were unfolding and are still under way in Kiev, Donetsk, Kharkov and other Ukrainian cities. Naturally, we could not leave this plea unheeded; we could not abandon Crimea and its residents in distress. This would have been a betrayal on our part.

He outlined Russia's response:

> First, we had to help create conditions so that the residents of Crimea for the first time in history were able peacefully to express their free will regarding their own future. However, what do we hear from our colleagues in Western Europe and North America? They say that we are violating norms of international law. First, it's a good thing that they at least remember that there exists such a thing as international law – better late than never.

He insisted that Russia had not exceeded the personnel limit of Russian armed forces in Crimea. He then proceeded to lambast the West, reprising the grievances that he had first outlined in his Munich speech in 2007, now adding some more: the high-handed and insulting treatment of Russia as a defeated power, the bombing of Belgrade in 1999, Iraq, Afghanistan, Kosovo, Libya, Syria, missile defence, NATO enlargement to Russia's borders, and the attempt to impose an either/or logic on EU enlargement, forcing countries to choose between Brussels and Moscow. Without beating about the bush, he noted: 'We have been lied to many times.'[8]

Most importantly, a new theme entered his discourse, namely the defence of 'Russian-speaking Crimea', and he talked about the 'compatriots' (*sootechestvenniki*) concentrated in neighbouring countries, in part confused with 'ethnic Russians' (*etnicheskie russkie*), 'Russian-speakers' (*russkoyazychnye*) and 'Russian citizens' (*rossiiskie grazhdane*). Putin veered towards the ethnicisation of Russian foreign policy, with his speech reflecting the confused identity questions that have haunted Russia since independence. Considerable resources had been devoted to the 'soft power' strategy of supporting the 'Russian world' (*Russkii mir*), including the establishment of a foundation of that name, to advance Russian-language teaching and the like, but the addition of an 'ethnic' dimension represented a departure for Putin. Although the law on 'compatriots' of 2010 had pledged support for all individuals with cultural, historic and even spiritual ties with Russia, the new emphasis represented a shift from a realist and pragmatic foreign policy to a more romantic-nationalist inflexion. In keeping with his profound 'Malorussian' understanding of Ukrainian statehood, Putin went on to argue:

> Our concerns are understandable because we are not simply close neighbours but, as I have said many times already, we are one people. Kiev is the mother of Russian cities. Ancient Rus is our common source and we cannot live without each other.
>
> Let me say one other thing too. Millions of Russians and Russian-speaking people live in Ukraine and will continue to do so. Russia will always defend their interests using political, diplomatic and legal means. But it should be above all in Ukraine's own interest to ensure that these people's rights and interests are fully protected. This is the guarantee of Ukraine's state stability and territorial integrity.[9]

There was an implicit threat here, but also a reasonable assumption of mutual responsibility.

Russia's disillusionment with the West, not only with the US but also with the EU, was total. The Crimean takeover marked a watershed in Russian foreign policy. The country perceived that it had been in retreat ever since 1991, and had allowed endless 'red lines' to be crossed, above all NATO enlargement and Western interventions in the Balkans and the Middle East, and although it had fired a warning shot when pushed in Georgia in 2008, only now was it ready to push back. What for Moscow was a defensive reaction, above all to prevent a replay in Crimea of what it considered a putsch in Kiev, confirmed in the West already deep-seated prejudices about Russia's potential to challenge the Western-dominated international order. The resistance narrative against Western hegemony and irresponsibility had been gaining ground since at least Putin's Munich speech in 2007, and it was now translated into action, while the West had gradually relegated Russia from 'partner' to enemy. Both processes had been latent in the cold peace since 1991. On both sides the media war reached frenetic levels. The new head of what had been RIA Novosti but was becoming Russia Today, Dmitry Kiselev, used his weekly *Vesti Nedeli* broadcast to excoriate the West, warning on 16 March that only Russia had the capacity to turn the US into 'radioactive dust'.

The Russian parliament (State Duma) enthusiastically endorsed reunification on 20 March, with only one vote cast against (by the Just Russia MP Ilya Ponomarev), a move endorsed by the Federation Council the next day. The federal constitutional law of 21 March stipulated that the peninsula would join Russia as two separate regions – the Republic of Crimea became Russia's twenty-second republic, while Sevastopol joined Moscow and St Petersburg as a 'city of federal significance' (Article 65 of the Russian Federation constitution).[10] With the port now part of Russia, on 2 April Putin abrogated the Kharkov Accords of April 2010, which had extended Russia's lease of the naval facilities in Crimea by 25 years, accompanied by a hefty discount on the gas price. Contrary to his designation as 'pro-Russian', Yanukovych had extracted a very high price. The basing agreement cost Russia some $45 billion and rendered Putin 'apoplectic': 'I would be willing to eat Yanukovych and his prime minister for that sort of money. No military base in the world costs that much.'[11] When Yanukovych fled to Russia, Putin did not initially deign to meet him. Polls revealed that the overwhelming majority of Russians endorsed Crimea's incorporation into Russia and considered it 'legal, irreversible, and desirable'.[12]

It is likely that after the Russo-Georgian war of 2008 military plans were laid down for various contingencies in Ukraine, and as the Maidan protests unfurled, no doubt the General Staff in Moscow was brushing them up. In 2013, special forces had already been created to defend ethnic Russians in the 'near abroad', but that was the enhancement of capacity rather than intent. When it came to the takeover, Russia's actions were not so much premeditated as an opportunistic reaction to developments on the ground. With the Sochi Olympics over on 23 February, Putin turned his attention to Ukraine. The Kharkov Accords, giving Russia leasing rights up to 2042, were threatened, and even the treaty allowing Russia to use the base to 2017 came under threat. This argument is often countered by the existence of the 'Return of Crimea' medal awarded by the Russian Ministry of Defence to those who had assisted the process, with the dates 20 February to 18 March on the reverse. This is taken to prove that the operation started before the change of government in Kiev, especially since the notice was soon after taken down from the ministry's website. In practice, all the medal shows is that the forces were on alert, which is hardly surprising, but the decision only came later.

The Russian media undoubtedly exaggerated the threat to Crimea's Russophone population, but they were, in the light of later events in Odessa, not entirely unfounded. The early actions of the interim government in Kiev hardly inspired confidence that the monists in power would temper their policies with an adequate dose of civic pluralism, accompanied by clear signals that they were committed to a geopolitical reorientation that could have deprived Russia of basing rights. Russian actions were prompted by 'realist' geo-strategic motives, but these were supplemented by 'ethno-national' concerns based on the idea of the 'Russian world', a sphere of Russophone interests. This reflected a long-term trend towards couching Russian concerns about the imbalances in global power and the asymmetrical end of the Cold War in cultur-ally conservative terms.[13] This shift also represented a concession to the swelling tide of nationalist sentiment in Russia, in part sponsored by the regime itself. A perceived foreign-policy success certainly consolidated domestic support for the regime, but this was not the driver of Russian actions.

Critics argue that the referendum violated the Ukrainian constitution and inter-national law, but the reunification was defended by Russia on a number of grounds, leaving aside the argument that the Ukrainian constitution had been rendered null and void by the 'putsch' of 22 February. First, there is the procedural point, arguing that the transfer of the peninsula following the decision of the Presidium of the CPSU Central Committee of 25 January 1954 had not even followed the correct Soviet for-malities. The decision was ratified by the Presidium of the RSFSR Supreme Soviet on 5 February, and then by the Presidium of the USSR Supreme Soviet on 19 February. The adoption of the law on the transfer by the USSR Supreme Soviet on 26 April 1954 simply rubber-stamped decisions taken earlier. At no point were the full assemblies involved in taking the decision to transfer territory, as should have been the case according to the RSFSR constitution of the time.[14] In addition, the port of Sevastopol had since 29 October 1948 been an 'object of all-union significance', so even when the peninsula changed jurisdictions, Sevastopol remained under the direct control of Moscow. When the Soviet Union broke up, Russia as the 'continuer state' automati-cally retained sovereignty over the city. As noted, this was pointed out to Yeltsin when Ukraine declared independence on 24 August 1991, and provoked enormous debate among the Russian leadership. Appeals were made to the Russo-Ukrainian treaty of 19 November 1990 about the inviolability of borders, but Russian critics insisted that its terms only applied to administrative divisions within a single Soviet state, not to independent countries. In the end, Yeltsin insisted that with the formation of the CIS on 8 December 1991, accompanied by plans for a single CIS military command, the formal status of Sevastopol did not matter. As I mentioned earlier, this is one of Yeltsin's 'betrayals', for which Russian nationalists will not forgive him.

Second, there was the preventative argument, couched in terms of averting attacks against the Russian-speaking population of the peninsula. There had been some threatening political actions, notably the attempt to abolish the 2012 language law, but no direct threats by that time. Later events, notably the Odessa massacre and the disproportionate violence with which the war was pursued in the Donbas, suggest that fears were not entirely misplaced, yet the separatism of Crimea no doubt intensified the violence of the response elsewhere. The anticipatory 'responsibility to protect' argument in this case is not enough to justify the abrogation of international law unless it is considered in the context of long-term dissatisfaction in Crimea of attempts to impose the cultural hegemony of the monist vision of Ukrainian state-hood. Crimea had its own constitution, but this was a much-diluted rendition of the 1992 version and did not meet the aspirations of a solid portion of the Crimean population. If the opportunity presented by the February revolution had been used to begin a genuine debate about the constitutional foundations of a more pluralist state system, then the later divisions could have been averted. Instead, it appeared that the revolution represented the intensification of the monism that had already provoked intense dissatisfaction among the Russophone and minority populations.

The third argument would stress the right of peoples to self-determination, a cardinal principle of modern international law (*jus cogens*). However, no procedure is articulated whereby this declared right can be actualised, and the presumption is against secession unless a clear and transparent popular mandate has been achieved, usually through a referendum or as a remedial response to persecution, as in Kosovo and East Timor (Timor-Leste). The two referendums in Quebec in 1980 and 1995 and the one in Scotland in September 2014 are a model of how this should be done, irrespective of the outcomes. The referendum in Crimea certainly did not meet these standards. Not only were armed troops on the ground, but the vote was arranged in a hurry, there were no independent international observers and the counting was held in far from transparent circumstances. In addition, the vote breached the stipulations of the Ukrainian constitution and was opposed by the incumbent government. The partisans of Crimean secession argue that it is precisely the last point that vitiates the other doubtful features of the referendum. The forcible seizure of power by radical nationalists represented the breakdown of the constitutional order in Kiev; and if the constitution had been repudiated in the centre, then on what basis could it be defended in the regions? For the defenders of Crimea's choice, this would be the worst form of selective justice. It is clear that the majority of the Crimean population favoured unification with Russia, and the opportunity presented by constitutional breakdown was seized. However, the lack of a clear and transparent ballot undermines the legitimacy, quite apart from the issue of the legality, of the process.

The fourth argument draws on the Kosovo precedent, whereby secession can be justified by facts on the ground and the realities of international power politics. Russia had earlier condemned Kosovo's unilateral declaration of independence from Serbia on 17 February 2008, without staging a referendum. Putin had threatened that there would be consequences, and on 26 August of that year Russia recognised the independence of Abkhazia and South Ossetia. In part this was because by then many Western countries, with the US in the lead, had recognised Kosovo's independence, despite repeated UN resolutions upholding the territorial integrity of Yugoslavia (notably Resolution 1244 of 10 June 1999). In addition, the infamous advisory opinion of the International Court of Justice (ICJ) of 22 July 2010 argued that Kosovo's declaration of independence 'did not violate general international law', a finding immediately endorsed by the US and its allies (although they stressed that Kosovo was a unique situation) and quoted by Putin in his speech of 18 March. The Kremlin repeatedly referred to the ICJ judgment on Kosovo, suggesting that Russia was doing no more than following the Kosovo precedent. It may have been politic for the UN General Assembly once again to ask the ICJ for an advisory opinion on the Crimean case, to allow the matter to be tested in court.

CONSEQUENCES

Crimea relies on Ukraine proper for some 85 per cent of its water. By late April 2014 Ukraine had built a dam in the Kherson region, about 40 kilometres from the border with Crimea, blocking supplies through the Northern Crimean Canal. The shortage of fresh water destroyed the 2014 rice crop and sharply reduced the soybean and maize harvest. The Ukrainian water agency claimed that consumers had not paid their debts for the previous year, and stated that it could reopen the canal if Crimea paid the $143 million debt.[15] The 124 water-operating companies in Crimea found themselves without legal contracts with Ukraine's State Water Resources Agency, running up large debts while the system of payments was blocked. As for electricity, about 82 per cent of the region's supplies come from thermal power plants in Zaporozhe and Kherson. Some of the major plants were owned by oligarchs, notably Rinat Akhmetov's DTEK Krymenergo, a major supplier to the republic. As with water, the legal uncertainty allowed large debts to build up to suppliers, notably DTEK Krymenergo. Crimean power stations at full stretch can supply no more than 25 per cent of the peninsula's electricity needs. At the minimum, two or three major new power plants will need to be built as well as connecting the republic with high-capacity power links to the Russian mainland via the Kerch Strait. All this will cost a minimum of $3.5 billion. Aksenev estimated that it would take at least five years to achieve the full adaptation of the Republic of Crimea to Russian legislation. In addition, a bridge is planned to provide a fixed link with the Russian mainland across the Kerch Strait, an agreement about which has already been signed, in December 2013.

The annexation of Crimea jeopardised the work of Dmytro Firtash's two major plants in the region, Krymsky Titan (Crimean Titanium) and Krymsky Sodovy Zavod (KSZ, Crimean Sodium Works). Krymsky Titan is the largest producer of titanium dioxide in Eastern Europe, and accounts for 2 per cent of the world market for titanium dioxide pigment, able to produce some 120,000 tonnes a year. It is used in the production of varnish and paint products, plastic, resin, rubber, paper and other goods. About 20 per cent of the plant's output went to the Russian market, annoying Russian competitors. The same applies to KSZ, which sells some 40 per cent of its output to Russia. The new Crimean authorities, at Russia's behest, could cut off access to the peninsula's natural resources – Krimsky Sodovy takes its water from the Sivash saltwater lake. Up to September 2014 the plants were working at full capacity, but there were some major challenges, above all affecting supplies, access to markets, and the legal, tax and regulatory framework. The plants had previously been closely integrated into the Ukrainian economy, but are now located on declared Russian territory. They are less reliant on gas than the mainland plants, but still make up about 15 per cent of the production costs in the two plants.

The key problem in the first instance is exporting the finished product, which previously used Crimean ports, but the 'grey' status of the territory renders this problematic. Using mainland Ukrainian ports would add significantly to costs. The issue of tax payments is also complicated. The two plants contribute an astonishing 60 per cent to Crimea's GDP. They previously paid taxes to the Ukrainian authorities, but if they reregister as Russian enterprises they will automatically come in for European and American sanctions. At the same time, they will become vulnerable to being taken over by a major Russian player. Under Russian law an enterprise's accounts can be frozen and bankruptcy proceedings initiated if a certain amount of unpaid tax accumulates. This is one reason why Firtash preferred to maintain Ukrainian registration in the interim, and thus pay taxes to the Ukrainian government. The Crimean authorities appeared to have no plans to nationalise the plants, but instead sought to have them reregistered. In the words of one analysis: 'This indicates Moscow's support for Firtash.' His mainland companies also struggled to maintain supplies of gas, the feedstock for his chemical plants, notably Rovnoazot in Cherkassy, the Severodonetsk Azot plant and the Stirol concern in Gorlovka.[16] The financial stability of the group was underwritten by one of Firtash's partners, the Russian billionaire, owner of Gazprombank and president of the Russian Judo Federation, Vasily Anisimov.

On 21 April 2014 a presidential decree formally rehabilitated the Crimean Tatar people, a demand that had first been advanced when Crimean Tatars demonstrated on Red Square in 1986. Now Tatar, alongside Russian and Ukrainian, was accorded the status of a state language, and there was a raft of initiatives to resolve the long-running problem of landownership. This did not entirely bring the Tatars over to the side of the new authorities. Resistance was led by Mustafa Dzhemilev, a Soviet-era dissident and latterly head of the Mejlis, which he had revived in 1991. He warned that the annexation of Crimea was 'damaging to the basic interests of Russia and the Russian people', and 'a path to catastrophe, isolation and loss of respect' for the country.[17] He urged Russians to leave Crimea, while being tolerant of extremism among Crimean Tatars. It was reported that he was banned from entering Crimea for five years. He was accused of betraying the genuine concerns of the Crimean Tatar people and of ramping up tensions to serve the authorities in Kiev. When the authorities in May banned a national rally to commemorate the seventieth anniversary of the deportation in Simferopol, the new head of the Mejlis, Refat Chubarov, agreed on a number of local events, which passed without incident. Other Tatar organisations welcomed the reunification with Russia. One such group, Milli Firka, argued that Kiev had done little to rehabilitate the Crimean Tatars in the 23 years of independence: 'In less than two months Russia has done far more for the Crimean Tatars than Ukraine ever did. Only after Crimea became part of Russia did Kiev even remember that we exist,' said Vasvi Abduraimov, Milli Firka's chair.[18] Nevertheless, tensions with the Tatar community continued, leading to the impoundment of the Mejlis building in September.

As far as Russia is concerned, Crimea is now firmly part of the Russian polity. On 14 September 2014 Crimea, along with over two dozen other Russian regions, held elections to the regional parliament and district assemblies. In the Crimean parliamentary election, the United Russia party list headed by Aksenev received 70.4 per cent of the vote, while the strength of nationalist sentiment was reflected in the 8.9 per cent received by the LDPR. For the first time the Communists, who had been in every Crimean parliament since 1991, failed to clear the 5 per cent threshold. Turnout was 53.6 per cent, which was above the national average but lower than the stratospheric figure recorded for the March referendum. On 17 September Putin nominated three candidates apiece to the gubernatorial posts, including the acting head of Crimea, Aksenev, and the acting head of Sevastopol, Sergei Menyailo, both of whom were duly selected.

Overall, the notion of a Russian 'land grab' is misleading if understood as a long-term plan to seize Crimea and annex it to Russia. Even after the fall of Yanukovych,

Russian policy was hesitant, initially contemplating the creation of another 'frozen' conflict through the secession of Crimea or just the takeover of Sevastopol. The idea of separating the naval base and its hinterland was quickly understood to be unworkable for technical reasons, hence the shift from secession to annexation. While resolving one problem, although controversially, this did not resolve the larger problem of Ukraine's geopolitical status. Thus Russia was sucked into the Donbas conflict and relations with Kiev and the West were further poisoned. As Mankoff puts it: 'Far from dissuading Ukrainians from seeking a future in Europe, Moscow's moves will only foster a greater sense of nationalism in all parts of the country and turn Ukrainian elites against Russia, probably for a generation.'[19] It also alarmed Russia's partners in the EEU, who now insisted that the Eurasian Union (EaU) would be no more than a free-trade area and rebuffed plans for deeper political integration.

CRIMEA AND INTERNATIONAL POLITICS

The reunification of Crimea and actions in the Donbas provoked a wave of sanctions (see Chapter 8). More immediately, since Russia wielded veto power in the UN Security Council, on 27 March the US sponsored a vote in the UN General Assembly to support 'the territorial integrity of Ukraine' and condemning the annexation. One hundred voted in favour, while 11 voted against, including Cuba, North Korea, Venezuela and other 'leftist' Latin American states like Bolivia and Nicaragua. The 58 who abstained included some major states, notably China and the other BRICS countries, with Brazil joined by the other Latin American states of Argentina, Uruguay and Ecuador. In other words, Latin America was becoming increasingly non-aligned, if not sympathetic, to Russian perspectives. In one of their most significant démarches, the BRICS countries issued a statement condemning the international community for isolating Russia. The sixth BRICS summit in Brazil, held on 15–17 July 2014, agreed to establish a New Development Bank based in Shanghai and a currency reserve pool. While these plans had long been aired, the Ukraine crisis gave them greater urgency. As one Russian scholar put it: 'The summit showed that the unipolar world system, that the Americans and Europeans cling to, is already not effective any longer.'[20] The BRICS countries refused to criticise Russia for its actions in Ukraine, but neither were they willing to agree the measures, urged by Putin, to prevent 'sanctions attacks' by the US to 'harass' countries opposing its policies.[21] China adopted a position of benevolent neutrality over the Russian takeover, which given its own problems with separatist challenges in Tibet and Xinjiang effectively meant a tacit endorsement of border adjustments, of the sort it desired in the South

China Sea. For China, the Western-supported overthrow of a democratically elected leader raised real fears about what these powers could do against what it had now taken to calling 'autocrats'.

Other states were placed in a considerable dilemma by the annexation of Crimea, as they had been over Kosovo's declaration of independence. Most immediately affected was Turkey, home to at least half a million people with Crimean Tatar roots, although most had long ago assimilated. Turkish foreign policy had long lost the lustre associated with the 'no problem' strategy of its academic foreign minister Ahmet Davutoğlu, and instead it was confronted with setbacks on all fronts, notably in neighbouring Syria. Turkish policy now was about 'limiting the damage of decisions taken elsewhere rather than exercising some sort of leverage on either the West or Moscow'. As for Crimea: 'There is also a grudge in Ankara against the EU for inserting Ukraine into a zero-sum game with the Vilnius Summit and unduly provoking Russia.'[22]

A view prominent in Western commentary, greatly magnified following the Crimean events, suggests that Putin was bent on rebuilding the Russian or Soviet empire. Thus his support for the insurgency in the Donbas was considered just the first step to recreate 'Novorossiya'. General Philip Breedlove, the Supreme Allied Commander in Europe (SACEUR), at this time talked of Russia sweeping through the Donbas and the rest of Novorossiya to link up with the Moldovan breakaway region of Transnistria. Transnistria is home to some 300,000 people, overwhelmingly Russian, who separated from Moldova when the republic gained independence in 1991. In mid-1992 over 1,000 people were killed in a brief war when Transnistria, backed by Russia, resisted absorption into Moldova, fearing it planned to reunite with Romania, and since then some 1,500 Russian troops have been permanently stationed there, ostensibly to guard the vast Soviet-era weapons dumps. Transnistria staged two referendums on self-determination, in 1991 and 2006, and both passed with overwhelming support. The second moved beyond assessing the level of support for state independence and now asked explicitly: 'Do you support the course towards independence for the Transnistrian Moldovan Republic and its subsequent free unification with the Russian Federation?' On a 78 per cent turnout, 97 per cent voted in favour. If Russia really was the land-grabbing expansionist state that its critics suggest, then this would have been more than enough to move towards the accession of the entity.

This is a classic 'frozen' conflict, in which Russian attempts to broker a deal are blocked by the West, and vice versa. Soon after Crimea was reunited with Russia, the Transnistrian Supreme Soviet sent an official request to Moscow to join the Russian Federation. Neo-Soviet nationalists may well have been enthused by fantasies of neo-imperial enlargement, but this is something that the Russian leadership since

Yeltsin has avoided (Crimea is considered an exception). Only if there were a full-scale Ukrainian state collapse would a territorial rearrangement be on the cards. The idea that Putin's comment in his state-of-the-nation speech of 25 April 2005 that the break-up of the Soviet Union represented 'the greatest geopolitical catastrophe' of the twentieth century and a 'tragedy for the Russian people' has too often been taken out of context, and taken to mean the exact opposite of what Putin went on to say – that there could be no question of restoring the Soviet Union.[23]

This misinterpretation fed into a narrative – peddled furiously in Saakashvili's Tbilisi, Maidanite Kiev, a raft of Russophobic former Soviet bloc states, *The Economist* and the US State Department – that Russia is hell-bent on destroying world order because of some innate destructive impulse. In this account Russian motivations and concerns are automatically excluded, and instead some primitive cultural urge renders Russia a spoiler and destroyer. For supporters of this view, the only response is sanctions, more sanctions and isolation. As an editorial in the *Kyiv Post* put it:

> More than two months after Russia destroyed the post-Cold War order by invading and annexing Crimea, European heavyweights France, Germany and even Great Britain continue to dither in the face of Vladimir Putin's aggression. Their weakness has shown that business lobbies in the three nations are willing to turn a blind eye to Moscow's war crimes as long as their companies are making money. Now we understand better why two world wars started in Europe and the dangers of appeasement. The EU still hasn't grasped the reality that Russia is not a partner but rather a threat to world peace, with the Kremlin richly deserving isolation and the harshest economic sanctions for its assault on Ukraine. This means that the West should punish Russia's energy, finance, military and hi-tech sectors – all of which the three nations play key parts in feeding.[24]

Nothing less than utter humiliation and destruction would do, and the idea that there could be principled rather than venal reasons prompting the caution of Germany and France is denied. The pragmatists understood the complexity of motivations that had provoked the crisis, and were aware that sanctions should be a weapon of last resort. Instead, the new Cold War ideologues had a field day, rubbishing the pragmatists and denying their bona fides. *The Economist* condemned 'Ostpolitik' as 'naive' and warned that it 'risks undermining Germany's transatlantic and European alliances'.[25] These alliances have brought Europe once again to the edge of war, so quite the opposite conclusion may have been warranted.

This was countered by an important group who sought to understand the dynamics that provoked this act of outright revisionism, by a state that had hitherto been a conservative status quo power – although, as I argued earlier, increasingly laced with elements of neo-revisionism. The zero-sum logic of the Cold War, and indeed of classic great-power politics, was firmly reinserted into European international affairs, in the most brutal manner possible. Putin had come to power stressing the primacy of economic development in Russian foreign policy, yet he had now reverted to a situation where geopolitics shaped decision making. Anders Fogh Rasmussen argued that Russia had become a revisionist power, 'willing to use force to extend its influence and control over independent sovereign states in blatant disregard of international law',[26] but his argument is misleading since it fails to take into account the factors that had taken Russia to this point. The extremism of Ukrainian monist elites fed into international discourse, rendering diplomacy meaningless and only fuelling conflict. This was the real revisionism that played on Western sentiments to sublimate the contradictions in Ukrainian state-building (as they had earlier with the contradictions within Georgia) to provoke a crisis of world peace. Post-Communist revanchist pathologies were magnified, turning Russia from what had been at most a relatively defensive, conservative neo-revisionist power in this instance into a genuinely revisionist state. Arguments in favour of engagement, dialogue and a little understanding are met with a barrage of imprecations and false historical analogies (Munich, appeasement, and the like).

The seizure of Crimea reflected the failure to create a 'Greater Europe' as well as the limits of the EU's aspirations to establish an arc of allies to its east. The tensions generated by the asymmetrical end of the Cold War were now exposed. Russia under Putin had been the opposite of a land-grabbing state. Putin gave up more Russian territory than any other leader except Lenin, who in the Brest-Litovsk peace with the Germans in March 1918 had bought time in exchange for land. Lenin's gamble paid off, and by the end of the year imperial Germany had collapsed, and the great swathes of territory were returned to a Russia now engulfed in civil war. In October 2004 Putin achieved a definitive agreement with China over their 4,400-kilometre-long border, in exchange for the transfer of several major islands in the Ussuri River to Chinese jurisdiction. In September 2010 agreement was finally reached with Norway over the long-contested maritime delineation of the Barents Sea, agreeing to a split down the middle, which turned out to grant Norway the bulk of the energy resources. Under Putin agreement was finally reached over the borders with Estonia and Latvia, although both retained popular aspirations to have part of Russia's neighbouring Pskov region restored to them, which had been part of the interwar republics. Putin even offered to return to the 1956 agreement with Japan and to restore two of the four Kurile Islands (Northern Territories) to that country. Admittedly, these were the two smallest, but in mathematical terms honours would be even.

This was ignored in commentary. Typical of the overheated reaction of the time was that of Jonathan Eyal, of the Royal United Services Institute (RUSI), who argued that Russia sought 'to tear apart the territorial status quo created in Europe after the fall of the Soviet Union'. The evidence for this was not only thin but in fact precisely pointed the other way: Russia under Putin is a profoundly conservative power and its actions are designed to maintain the status quo, hence the effort Moscow put into ratifying its existing borders. It was the West that was perceived to be the revisionist power. Eyal had a point, however, when he argued that

> the events of the last few weeks are not just a blip in East–West relations. They mark the end of an era, the end of the hope that Russia could be incorporated into a united and peaceful European continent.[27]

Framing the argument in this way, of course, excludes Russia's attempts to create a 'united and peaceful continent' on the basis of a Greater European agenda.

Others adopted a more balanced perspective. In Russia, Gorbachev, the architect of perestroika and the end of the Cold War, had long condemned the way that the mutual victory had been distorted into a one-sided declaration of victory. He now endorsed Russia's takeover of Crimea:

> Whereas previously the Crimea was joined to Ukraine by Soviet laws, to be more exact by the Communist Party's laws, which disregarded the opinion of the people, now the people have made up their mind to correct the mistake. This should be welcomed instead of declaring sanctions.[28]

Eduard Limonov and other nationalists who had been in opposition to Putin also welcomed reunification. Abroad, two former German chancellors were also prepared to condone the move. Helmut Schmidt in *Die Zeit* argued that it was not quite legitimate but certainly 'understandable', while Gerhard Schröder was rather more enthusiastic. The former Czech president Václav Klaus argued that Russia's annexation was prompted by the increasing concerns of the Crimean population, and that the movement for independence reflected the genuine aspirations of the people. He condemned the radicalisation of the Maidan and stressed that Yanukovych had granted notable concessions and had not seriously cracked down on what was, after all, the illegal occupation of the central square in a major European city. Equally, he excoriated Western support for the demonstrations, while placing the events in the context of long-standing ties with Russia and the long history of different traditions and perspectives of the regions that make up contemporary Ukraine.[29] He condemned the Western elite's hostility towards Russia, and was contemptuous of their behaviour: 'The US/EU propaganda against Russia is really ridiculous and I cannot accept it.'[30]

From the Russian perspective, the country was responding to the behaviour of the West. Alexander Lukin, a professor at the prestigious Moscow State Institute of International Relations (MGIMO), notes the West's pragmatism in international politics:

> It was not Russia but the West that scrapped the idea of a new system of global politics based on international law, which could have been created after the disintegration of the Soviet Union. It was not Russia but the West that, having believed in the 'end of history', took advantage of its temporary omnipotence to create a world where one can grab everything that comes his way, crush any border and violate any agreement for the sake of 'a good goal'. It was not Russia but the West that purposefully destroyed the post-war legal system based on the sovereignty of states, advancing its theory of 'humanitarian interventions' and 'responsibility to protect'. It was not Russia but the West that put pressure on the UN International Court of Justice to make it rule that the unilateral declaration of Kosovo's independence was not in breach of international law.

He summed up unequivocally:

> As a result, the West's position on Crimea, whereby its leaders refer to the territorial integrity and inviolability of borders, is perceived by Russia as no more than utmost hypocrisy. [...] Since the principle of inviolability of borders no longer works, it is the aspirations of the people that must be taken into account.[31]

So, if the Crimean people wanted to live in Russia, then why couldn't they do so?

Noam Chomsky draws the broader implications of Russia's gambit in Crimea. He quotes the columnist Thanassis Cambanis:

> Putin's annexation of the Crimea is a break in the order that America and its allies have come to rely on since the end of the Cold War – namely, one in which major powers only intervene militarily when they have an international consensus on their side, or failing that, when they're not crossing a rival power's red lines.

Thus what Chomsky categorises as 'this era's most extreme international crime', the Anglo-American invasion of Iraq, in this reading was not a break in world order because the aggressors did not cross Russian or Chinese red lines. By contrast, 'Putin's takeover of the Crimea and his ambitions in Ukraine cross American red lines', hence the furious reaction in Washington and the attempt to isolate Russia and curb its regional ambitions. In other words, 'American red lines, in short, are placed at Russia's borders. Therefore Russian ambitions "in its own neighbourhood" violate world order and create crises.' The US, viewing itself as the global hegemon, could not allow such a challenge to its monopoly on deciding when a red line is crossed, accompanied by its determined commitment to the Wolfowitz Doctrine, which sought to prevent any potentially hostile counter-hegemon dominating its region. Putin's bold stroke represented a fundamental challenge to America's hegemonic maintenance of 'peace and stability', defined in Chomsky's words as 'subordination to US demands'.[32]

In light of this pattern of the exercise of American hegemony, only the most obtuse could fail to raise an eyebrow when John Kerry commented: 'You just don't in the 21st century behave in 19th century fashion by invading another country on completely trumped up pre-text[s].' In his 'emotional' address on 18 March Putin had complained that the US and its allies had

> cheated us again and again, made decisions behind our back, presenting us with completed facts, with the expansion of NATO in the east, with the deployment of military infrastructure at our borders. They always told us the same thing: 'Well, this doesn't concern you.'[33]

Putin's incorporation of Crimea represented a statement that these issues do in fact concern Russia, and that it is no longer prepared to retreat. It refuses to accept the logic that if the US is indeed the 'indispensable' country, then by definition other countries are dispensable. As Putin argued at the end of his condemnation of American exceptionalism in September 2013 (to which I will return): 'There are big countries and small countries, rich and poor. [...] We are all different, but when we ask for the Lord's blessings, we must not forget that God created us equal.'[34]

The timing of the confrontation was not of Putin's choice, but developments in Ukraine represented a challenge that Putin felt he could not avoid. For the first time in the post-Cold War era a major power had thrown down the gauntlet to challenge the Atlantic community's definition of world order. The motivation was not the establishment of a 'Greater Russia', let alone the re-establishment of the Soviet empire (although seized on by those who sought these goals), but in defence of the continentalist idea of a 'Greater Europe' and Russia's national interests. In so doing, Putin has questioned the right of the US to define red lines, while challenging Atlanticism in its entirety. In response, the US has declared a new Cold War against Russia, egged on by the political–media elite and followed with greater or less reluctance by its European allies.

CHAPTER 6

WHEN HISTORY
COMES CALLING

The months following the annexation of Crimea proved as traumatic as any in the preceding period. The Ukrainian presidential elections were scheduled for 25 May, and over two dozen candidates declared their hands. The problem of sequencing remained: should the elections take place before constitutional reform, or would the election of a new president, vested with a constitutional and democratic mandate, remove the incentive to conduct fundamental reform? Four issues were pre-eminent: the respective powers of the president and the prime minister; the status of Russian as a second language; federalisation or some other form of decentralisation of the country; and the question of neutrality between what was once again becoming a type of bloc politics in Europe. This was accompanied by unrest in the eastern and southern parts of the country, something that the Western powers ascribed to Russian intervention, provoking increasingly harsh sanctions.

PRESIDENTIAL ELECTION

On 29 April the interim prime minister, Arseniy Yatsenyuk, called on all political forces to agree measures of constitutional reform before the presidential election. He planned to have a new version of the constitution agreed by that time, with the text to be reviewed by the Constitutional Court and the Venice Commission, Council of Europe's advisory body on constitutional law.[1] The timetable appeared to be optimistic since there was very little consensus on the fundamental constitutional questions.

None had been satisfactorily resolved in over two decades of independence, and it was unlikely that they could be dealt with in such short order now.

A testimony to Ukraine's pluralistic and competitive political culture is the number of presidential candidates who registered for the poll. In the end 28 hopefuls entered the lists, but only 21 names actually ended up on the ballot paper, with potential candidates such as Oleg Tsarev withdrawing. The front-runner from an early stage was Petro Poroshenko, the 'chocolate king', who was able to present himself as a 'new' politician even though he had been round the block more than once. One of his potential main rivals was Vitaly Klitschko, but on 29 March the former world heavyweight boxing champion withdrew and threw his support and that of his UDAR party behind Poroshenko. The deal appears to have been brokered by Firtash at a meeting in Vienna two days earlier, attended by Klitschko and Poroshenko. Firtash was confined to Vienna because of American attempts to extradite him for alleged bribery and racketeering offences. The deal was also favoured by Vitaly Kovalchuk, the deputy head of UDAR, who is considered one of the 'grey cardinals' in the new system. Lacking a developed party of his own, the deal with UDAR provided Poroshenko with a ready-made organisational base. This allowed him to establish a commanding lead in the polls from an early stage.

This left only the former prime minister, Yulia Tymoshenko, as a serious challenger candidate, but she carried a lot of political baggage into the campaign. She had been released on 22 February following a vote in the Verkhovna Rada on that day, and was officially rehabilitated on 28 February. Later the Supreme Court quashed the conviction and found that 'no crime was committed'. Nevertheless, it would not be so easy to resume her political career at the top. On the day of her release she rushed straight to the Maidan, but was shocked at the cool reception she received. The crowd feared that the revolution it had made would once again be hijacked by politicians of Tymoshenko's ilk. She had also lost the support of the West, which considered her 'damaged goods'. As a report by Alexander Nekrassov, a former Russian government advisor put it: 'The word on the street is she's trying to avenge some of her enemies who, she thinks, were instrumental in putting her behind bars on charges of fraud.'[2] On 15 April she declared that she would forgo formal campaigning and instead turn her Batkivshchyna party into the political base for the national battle of resistance against 'Russian aggression', a bizarre move by any measure, allowing Poroshenko to appear a moderate in comparison with Tymoshenko's demagogy.

After much controversy, the PoR in the end supported Mykhailo Dobkin, who appeared to be the most malleable in the hands of Akhmetov. This meant that the

PoR MPs Sergei Tigipko and Oleg Tsarev entered the ballot as self-nominated independents, and they were expelled from the party for refusing to support Dobkin. As the political analyst Vladimir Fesenko puts it:

> Of course Tigipko ought to have been named as the sole candidate, but Rinat Akhmetov and Donetsk's other city fathers saw him as too independent and as a contender for the leadership of the party. They could not allow this to happen.[3]

Tigipko's biography is in some ways similar to Poroshenko's. A self-made entrepreneur, he was born in Moldova before moving to Dnepropetrovsk where he developed his TAS finance and business group with interests in banking, insurance, real estate, machine-building and venture-capital enterprises, making him a billionaire. He also entered politics, serving as deputy prime minister, minister of social policy, and head of the NBU. In the 2010 presidential campaign he came third after Yanukovych and Tymoshenko with 13 per cent of the vote, and became deputy prime minister for economic matters. He oversaw the controversial pension reform that saw the pensionable age for women rise by five years and the necessary pensionable service period increased for all. He supports Russian becoming the second state language, as do Dobkin and the leader of the CPU, Petro Symonenko.

Russia initially intimated that it would not recognise the presidential election, arguing that constitutional reform should come first and that, in any case, Yanukovych remained president, and did not recognise the 'coup' that had overthrown him. In his annual *Direct Line with Vladimir Putin* television programme on 17 April Putin argued that Moscow would not recognise the outcome if the safety of candidates could not be secured. He had in mind the brutal attack on Tsarev, the pro-federalisation presidential candidate, by radicals in Kiev following his appearance on television. Tsarev had been expelled from the PoR, and when guaranteed protection he agreed to appear on the show *Freedom of Speech*, but after outlining his views was severely beaten and stripped of his clothes by Ukrainian nationalists outside the television station. His house in Dnepropetrovsk was burned down and in the end he was forced to flee Ukraine. His fate was symbolic of many opponents of the Maidan revolution, including many policemen, who were hunted down as 'enemies of the revolution'. By early May the Kremlin's stance had softened, accepting that the outcome would be legitimate if the elections were conducted in the appropriate manner. At the St Petersburg International Economic Forum Putin rehearsed a range of complaints about Ukrainian behaviour, yet insisted: 'We understand that the people of Ukraine want their country to emerge from this crisis. We will treat their choice with respect.'[4] On the day before the vote Putin stated that Russia would 'cooperate with the authorities that will come to power as a result of the election', but noted that Yanukovych remained the legitimate president of the country.[5]

In the end, Poroshenko was the first president since Kravchuk to win a presidential election by an absolute majority in the first round (see Table 6.1). He came first in every voting region, although Poroshenko and Tymoshenko combined received fewer votes than Yanukovych in 2010. Despite the large number of candidates, Poroshenko's decisive first-round win was a clear indication that the majority voted strategically to guarantee stability and moderation. He was elected president precisely because he appeared to represent a 'third way' between the former government and the Maidan insurgency. He appealed to both stability and change, in particular to middle-class men and people in older age groups in the cities.[6] He promised to sell Roshen and his other assets to cleanse himself of the oligarch tag, but in the end backtracked and decided not to sell his Channel 5 TV station. He declared that his top priority was to bring Ukraine into the EU, with the establishment of a visa-free regime in the first instance. He also argued that Ukraine could do without Russian gas.

Overall, turnout was 60.29 per cent, although touching 78 per cent in Lviv and falling below 50 per cent in pre-eminently Russophone regions such as Odessa and Kharkov. By historical standards, the turnout was low. In the 2004 election over 28 million people voted, whereas now fewer than 18 million participated, and in the

TABLE 6.1 Presidential election of 25 May 2014

CANDIDATE	% OF VOTE	VOTES GAINED
Poroshenko, Petro	54.70	9,857,308
Tymoshenko, Yulia	12.81	2,310,050
Lyashko, Oleg	8.32	1,500,377
Grytsenko, Anatoly	5.48	989,029
Tigipko, Sergei	5.23	943,430
Dobkin, Mykhailo	3.03	546,138
Rabinovich, Vadim	2.25	406,301
Bogomolets, Olga	1.91	345,384
Symonenko, Petro	1.51	272,723
Tyagnybok, Oleg	1.16	210,476

All the other candidates received less than 1% each.

Turnout: 60.29%

Source: Ukrainian Central Elections Commission [website].
Available at http://www.cvk.gov.ua/vp2014/wp300pt001f01=702.html.

February 2010 presidential election there was a 66.7 per cent turnout. However, turnout is calculated on the basis of the overall electorate of 35.5 million, but 1.5 million voters in Crimea did not participate, while the 5 million voters in the Donbas (14 per cent of the country's total electorate) faced difficulties because of the conflict. Turnout was only 15.1 per cent in the Donetsk region (with 3.3 million voters) and 38.9 per cent in Lugansk (with 1.7 million voters). The total population of the Donbas is 6.5 million, a seventh of the total Ukrainian electorate. Only 426 out of 2,430 polling stations were open in Donetsk, according to the region's governor, Sergei Taruta, and none in the city of Donetsk, which has a million inhabitants.[7] Overall, no results were reported from 14 out of 22 electoral districts in Donetsk, from 10 out of 12 in Lugansk, and across the 12 districts in Crimea and Sevastopol. Fighting continued on voting day, which saw the deaths of Italian photojournalist Andrea Rocchelli and his Russian interpreter, the veteran human-rights activist Andrei Mironov. By subtracting the electorate of the troubled regions, overall turnout rises to 68 per cent.

The lack of a credible candidate from the east is sometimes taken as undermining the legitimacy of the process. In fact, this is not entirely the case, since Tigipko fulfilled this role, and won a respectable 5.2 per cent, in addition to the 3 per cent given to Dobkin, the official PoR candidate. Rabinovich was the head of the All-Ukrainian Jewish Congress and out-polled the radicals with a traditional anti-Semitic profile. The Maidan doctor Olga Bogomolets won 1.91 per cent of the vote; the Communist Symonenko, who had withdrawn from the race, received 1.51 per cent. Others, with less than 1 per cent of the vote each, included the businessman Andriy Grynenko, the former MP Valery Konovalyuk, former deputy prime minister Yury Boiko, former head of the foreign intelligence service Mykola Malomuzh, and Ukrainian People's Rukh leader Vasyl Kuibida. The low vote for the Maidan radicals – Svoboda leader Tyagnybok won only 1.16 per cent and Right Sector leader Dmytro Yarosh 0.7 per cent – demonstrated their relative lack of support in the rest of the country. The low vote for the overtly right-wing nationalists is often used to demonstrate the weakness of integral nationalism in Ukraine, but much of this vote clearly went to the militantly nationalist head of the Radical Party, Lyashko. In March he and his supporters abducted a regional MP in eastern Ukraine and posted a video of his demeaning interrogation. In his campaign speeches Lyashko berated the government for its alleged passivity in the face of threats to the country's territorial integrity. He announced that he would lead the fight himself, which as soon as the election was over he did, heading off to the Donbas at the head of his 'Ukraine Battalion'.

The vote was assessed by PACE, part of the election-monitoring consortium headed by the OSCE, as characterised by a high turnout and a clear resolve by the authorities to hold a genuine election largely in line with international commitments and which respected fundamental freedoms in the vast majority of the country, despite the hostile security environment in two eastern regions of the country.[8]

However, the delegation, headed by the Swiss socialist Andreas Gross, went on to stress:

> The extraordinary quality of yesterday's election provides the new president of Ukraine with the legitimacy to establish immediately an inclusive dialogue with all citizens in the eastern regions, to restore their trust and confidence, and to decentralise State power in order to preserve the unity of the country by respecting the diversity of Ukrainian society. There is no military solution to today's crisis.[9]

In the event, instead of engaging the insurgents in dialogue, Poroshenko promised to liquidate them 'in days'. Despite having gained a popular mandate from across the country, he remained a prisoner of the Maidan. Although the revolution was undoubtedly a complex and contradictory phenomenon, at its heart was a monist vision of Ukrainian statehood that denied the pluralist alternative demanded by the Donbas insurgents.

Poroshenko's room for manoeuvre was limited by the continued mobilisation of the Maidan spirit. Batkivshchyna leader Tymoshenko threatened to launch 'another Maidan' if Poroshenko's presidency did not live up to their expectations. By then the Batkivshchyna party had lost much of its erstwhile liberalism and aligned itself with the radical nationalists. Poroshenko inherited a government largely made up of militants. The interior minister Arsen Avakov had served as Yushchenko's head of the NSDC, while the head of Ukraine's security service (SBU), Valentyn Nalyvaichenko, had already served in this post under Yushchenko between 2006 and 2010. Poroshenko compounded this legacy of entrenched Russophobia by appointing Irina Gerashchenko as his 'commissioner for the peaceful settlement of the conflict in the Donetsk and Lugansk regions'. She had served as Yushchenko's press secretary in 2005–6. In the 2010 presidential election Yushchenko had won a miserable 5.5 per cent of the vote and his team was thereafter eclipsed, but they now sought to avenge its defeat.[10]

Although I have with reservation called the events of February 2014 a 'revolution', the presidential election above all signalled continuity. The election of an 'oligarch' to the presidency, and one who had been in the thick of the turbulent and turgid events of the previous years, has demonstrated that those events have not produced new leaders, and that the business heavyweights will continue to exercise substantive political power. Poroshenko, of course, made his fortune *before* assuming political office, and thus will not need to struggle for wealth in office. His election does, though, signal a change of political generations. Kravchuk had been an old party boss, Kuchma a 'red director', Yushchenko a career politician, and Yanukovych a machine politician. Yushchenko and Yanukovych reflected the Orange/Blue divide in Ukrainian politics, although Yushchenko had been far more of an ideologue than Yanukovych. Yanukovych exploited the division, whereas Yushchenko believed in it. Poroshenko is undoubtedly committed to Ukraine's 'European choice', improved governance and economic reform, but the 'revolution' has not magically whisked Ukraine to some other world. He will have to deal with a powerful and angry neighbour, a broken international system, energy dependency, the loss of territory and, in the immediate term, an armed conflict involving that powerful neighbour. He also has to learn how to govern an unruly polity.

THE BUREAUCRATIC–OLIGARCHIC ORDER REFORMS

Oliver Bullough has a point, although greatly exaggerated, when he argues that 'anyone who tells you Ukraine is a battle between Russia and the West is wrong. It is a lazy narrative told by ignorant people, but is helping create a genuine tragedy that we should all be concerned about.' Quite rightly, he finds the roots of the crisis not in Yanukovych's overthrow in February 2014 but in 1991, when, 'desperate to break Communism, privatisers sold state assets as quickly as they could'. Insiders took control of whole industries, with powerful clans established in Donetsk and Dnepropetrovsk. The newly acquired wealth was moved offshore to Austria and various British tax havens, and then: 'They fought for control of the government in Kiev, but they all had the same basic interest: to perpetuate chaos. The longer Ukraine was a mess, the richer they got.'

> Some would have you believe that Yanukovych was a democratic, pro-Russian president driven out by Western spies – yet he held his palaces and hunting estate via British shell companies and his son's assets were owned through the Netherlands and Switzerland. Ukraine was a modern Prometheus, chained to the ground, while vultures of all geopolitical persuasions companionably pecked at its liver.

In his view, 'the East against West story does have one beneficiary: the Kremlin', with Russia in Ukraine allegedly trying to preserve a crooked regime against the wishes of the Ukrainians who want to live with dignity, because the old ways made it money [...] Journalists who grew up in a world when Moscow and the West were equal adversaries feel comfortable in this narrative. It's far easier to sell Ukraine if it's Czechoslovakia 1968, rather than a messy failed state, a European Congo.[11]

Bullough is as guilty as many other commentators in externalising Ukraine's problems, shifting responsibility to Moscow, when in fact Russia was forced to adapt to the realities of a shifting constellation of power within Ukraine. This was as much the case under Yeltsin in the 1990s as it has been in the 2000s under Putin.

The further weakening of state power following the Maidan revolution created new opportunities for non-state actors. Indeed, the weakness of the state forced the new authorities to use the oligarchs to retain power. In a controversial move, the former interior minister Yury Lutsenko proposed the appointment, ostensibly temporarily, of oligarchs as governors of the eastern regions. Both acting president Turchynov and interim prime minister Yatsenyuk opposed the move, but were persuaded by Tymoshenko, to whose party they belonged, to implement the plan. In Donetsk, Taruta, the head of the Donbas Industrial Union, was appointed, although it may have been more logical to appoint Akhmetov, since he employed some 300,000 workers in the region and could decisively have influenced the course of events. However, he was not trusted by the new authorities, since he was considered too 'pro-Russian' and too much of a federalist. Instead, Taruta soon lost control over the course of events. In April he was expelled from the Donetsk regional-government headquarters and decamped to Mariupol, and following the 11 May referendum Alexander Borodai declared himself prime minister.

Oligarchs and Orangists allied against the Blues. Igor Kolomoisky, a Tymoshenko ally, was appointed governor of Dnepropetrovsk by the provisional government on 2 March 2014. The region contains over 400 major plants, including the Makarov Southern Engineering Plant (Yuzhmash), one of the world's leading plants for rocket and space technology. It manufactured and maintained the giant RS-20 (SS-18 Satan in NATO designation) intercontinental rocket for Russia's strategic arsenal, and had planned deep cooperation with Russian partners to develop the Zenit-3SL missile system. There are also plants manufacturing mineral fertilisers, using ammonia from the TogliattiAzot plant in Russia brought in through the Togliatti–Odessa Transammiak pipeline. The region also has enterprises belonging to Viktor Pinchuk's 'Evraz' and 'Interpipe' holdings, as well as Akhmetov's 'Metinvest'. On 23 May Kolomoisky created a committee for investment and strategic development of the region, which was widely interpreted as an attempt to extend his own business empire. Kolomoisky also signalled ambitions to enlarge his Dnepropetrovsk fiefdom by incorporating some of the neighbouring districts of Lugansk and the Donbas. The Maidan revolution represented a major victory of Dnepropetrovsk over the Donbas, and Donetsk in particular, and this helps explain the viciousness of the war. Kolomoisky suppressed any hint of unrest in Dnepropetrovsk, paid $5 million out of his own pocket for fuel to keep the Ukrainian air force flying, and placed a bounty of $10,000 for every 'Russian spy' captured. He sponsored various national-military units, notably the Dnipro battalion in April. These 'men in black' took part in the 'anti-terrorist operation' (ATO) in the Donbas launched by Kiev on 13 April, but they were also used by Kolomoisky to suppress any manifestations of anti-Maidan activity in the regions and acted as his shock forces against rival businesses. Kolomoisky was one of the oligarchs whose presidential ambitions had long been noted, but he now gained enormous influence in running the country as part of the reshaped bureaucratic–oligarchic order.

Nekrassov's study notes that 'Ukraine's oligarchs are jockeying for power and control of assets'. The report observed that Rinat Akhmetov, with his vast interests in the east of Ukraine, 'is under pressure from the government'. On the other hand, Kolomoisky, appointed governor of the Dnepropetrovsk region by the interim government, 'is reaping the rewards of his support for the "revolution", rapidly extending his business empire – and having created a private army'. Nekrassov goes on to make the following pertinent observation:

> The extraordinary thing about Ukrainian oligarchs is that most of them have come out as fervent supporters of the 'people's revolution' that ousted Yanukovych – albeit, you would have expected them to have been on good terms at least with the previous regime, if only to keep their massive assets intact. But no, now they boast about their involvement in bringing down Yanukovych. And that may well be the case. As my sources on the ground in Kiev have told me, the oligarchs quickly figured out that it was unwise to keep their eggs in one basket, i.e. remaining on good terms with Yanukovych and his people.

There was too much at stake and the swirling pressures were too great to stick to one line. For those coming out of the Soviet system and who had prospered in the treacherous pools of Ukrainian politics, consistency could be dangerous. This certainly applies to Poroshenko:

> Ironically, the current president [...] himself an oligarch who made his fortune, apart from other things, by having good relations with Russia, was not exactly a vocal critic of the previous regime before the protests in Kiev started in earnest last year.

But lo and behold, now it turns out that Poroshenko was a devout 'revolutionary' and his greatest wish of all was to see Yanukovych go and Ukraine joining the EU.

The oligarchs had clearly 'played a key role in financing the uprising. It is also clear that these very same people are now trying to benefit from the regime change, jostling for power and influence and, of course, a piece of the action.'[12] Poroshenko's presidency was quickly formed on the basis of an alliance of the security structures spawned by the Maidan with the bureaucratic–oligarchic system. These were the two elements that needed the most urgent restructuring, yet since they provided the foundations of Poroshenko's power, they were the least susceptible to change. The security sector absorbed the militants after February 2014, and they in turn established themselves in these structures as a semi-independent force that exerted veto power over the new president's ability to act autonomously in resolving the security crisis in the Donbas and elsewhere. The former head of the Maidan's self-defence detachments, Parubiy, remained head of the National Security and Defence Council until his surprise resignation on 7 August. He had advocated an even tougher line against the insurgents in the Donbas, and his departure now cleared the way for him to campaign against Poroshenko. Arsen Avakov was the acting minister of the interior, but his performance was at best patchy. Avakov carried out a purge of police officers, with some 600 fired in Donetsk alone by mid-July. While these two remained in office a negotiated settlement with the Donbas insurgency would be problematic. Equally, the acting head of the security service, Valentyn Nalyvaichenko, retained his power base among the radical nationalists.

Poroshenko drew on experienced managers and oligarchs to staff his administration. Boris Lozhkin, the former head of Ukrainian Media Holding, was appointed chief of staff. He had made his fortune in the media business, but in mid-2013 was forced to sell his business to Sergei Kurchenko, who allegedly fronted the Yanukovych clan's business interests in the field. Lozhkin enjoyed good relations with most of the oligarchs, but his connections with Russia aroused the hostility of Maidan militants. This also applies to the new head of the State Affairs Administration, Sergei Berezenko, who was 'tainted' by his previous post as an advisor to the controversial mayor of Kiev, Leonid Chernovetsky. Poroshenko was clearly looking for good managers who would not also be independent politicians, unlike Yanukovych's former chief of staff, Sergei Levochkin.

War is a disaster for some but an opportunity for others. The property of Alexander Yanukovych and his business partner Kurchenko became the target of attack. Kolomoisky was particularly active as he sought to 'raid' the assets of the Yanukovych family. While conspiracy theorists are having a field day over the Ukraine crisis, certainly some lost and some won. Firtash is one of the losers, while Tymoshenko and Kolomoisky are among the winners. As a BBC report put it: 'Under the guise of Russia's military aggression, Ukrainian oligarchs have begun redistributing state resources.' Parliamentary factions controlled by Kolomoisky (named 'Economic Development') and Ihor Yeremeyev ('Sovereign European Ukraine') were allegedly blackmailing the government by refusing to support tabled bills, while attacking each other. The two had managed to divide between themselves the lucrative gasoline and other petrochemicals market. Kolomoisky controls some 1,500 petrol stations under the brands of Avias, Ukrnafta and Sentosa, while Yeremeyev has 500 stations under the WOG brand.

In addition, Kolomoisky retained control over the Ukrnafta oil company, even though the controlling share belongs to the Ukrainian state, while his associate Alexander Lazorko took over the Ukrtransnafta state oil-transport company. The two waged a war over the so-called technical oil pumped long ago into Ukrtransnafta pipelines at a price at most a tenth of the going price today. While Kolomoisky wanted to take the oil for processing at his refinery in Kremenchuk, Yeremeyev wanted it for his refinery in Kherson. A 'raider attack' had forced out the previous owners from Tatneft, and the refinery had stopped working after Russia stopped oil supplies in retaliation. If the oil is taken out and replaced by a water solution, the pipes are in danger of deterioration. The two traded mutual accusations of corruption as, in Yeremeyev's words, 'each case of political confrontation between Russia could be used for the sake of their own economic interests'.[13] As a result of these endless national and international conflicts, Ukraine was left with just one working oil refinery, at Kremenchuk. The incident demonstrates that in many ways Russia was not an external actor but an organic part of Ukraine's political economy, often acting as a 'collective oligarch' in Ukraine's never-ending business wars.

The same applies to Russia's penetration of the Ukrainian state. The security service (SBU) is thought to have become one of the main conduits of Russian influence, while the general weakness of the state is reflected in the parlous condition of the armed forces and the pervasive corruption that has corroded the tax and customs services. This is one reason that the Maidan regime was forced to ally with sympathetic oligarchs, since there were very few other sources of institutional support. Reform of Ukrainian governance will entail a profound cultural revolution, part of which will be the severance of long-standing organic ties with Russia. Even after Yanukovych's fall there remained a so-called 'Russia Group' of some 20 MPs, allied with a number of independents, who sought to maintain these ties. Equally, as I argued earlier, Yanukovych was not so much 'pro-Russian' as someone who played the Moscow and Brussels cards against each other in his own interests, until the whole pack was thrown to the floor. Now the US joined the oligarch struggles. Hunter Biden, the son of the US vice president, on 18 April joined the board of directors of the independent Ukrainian oil and gas holding company Burisma, one of the fastest-growing companies in the field, which sells most of its gas to traders and industrial customers directly with no sales to households. The move inevitably aroused 'accusations that the US establishment is trying to use the Ukrainian crisis to serve its own ends. Primarily because it is namely US vice president Joe Biden who, among his Western colleagues, is the key ideologist of Ukraine's energy independence.'[14] The Maidan revolution, like the Orange Revolution earlier, was in large part an attempt to escape the constraints and political bankruptcy of two decades of 'multi-vectoralism', tacking endlessly between East and West but in the end going nowhere.

Hence the 'European choice' was to a large extent a symbolic statement of intent, a repudiation of the condition of permanent liminality, of being stuck endlessly betwixt and between. By its very essence this entails separation from Russia, although wiser statecraft in Europe and Kiev could have avoided turning it into an anti-Russian crusade. In economic and governance terms, there was nothing to prevent the formulation of a pluralist 'Ukrainian choice', neutral in security terms but committed to good governance and a competitive market economy integrated into natural larger markets. Instead, the necessary attempt to escape the dead end assumed a monist inflexion, and reform assumed the character of geopolitical voluntarism and domestic repression. The inevitable ensuing confrontation with Russia created a powerful negative consensus against the foreign interloper, including the rebuilding of the coercive sinews of the state, but this only aggravated the tension between monism and pluralism. Ultimately, the profound civic impetus for dignity and good governance at the heart of the Maidan revolution was hijacked by the radicals, who followed the monist path to its logical conclusion while allowing oligarch power to be reconstituted.

FEDERALISATION OR DECENTRALISATION?

Federalism is often touted as a means of holding together deeply divided societies. As the Ukraine conflict unrolled into 2014, another society was coming under enormous pressure – Iraq. The future of the country came under threat in June 2014 as the militants of the Islamic State of Iraq and Syria (known as ISIS, an al-Qaeda offshoot of Sunni Islamists, which was later renamed Islamic State), headed by Abu Bakr al-Baghdadi, swept in from strongholds in neighbouring war-torn Syria to occupy Mosul, Iraq's second-largest city, and drove on to Baghdad. The Iraqi prime minister, Nouri al-Maliki, had a resolutely monist vision of Iraqi statehood, favouring the majority Shia community in military and other institutions, and thus the Sunni ISIS had much local support as they took over an 800-kilometre stretch of border between Syria and Iraq. A federal solution to the country's problem had long been advanced, to give constitutional status to the three main communities: Shias, Sunnis and Kurds. Unlike in Ukraine, where Russia strongly supported federalisation (thus discrediting the idea in the eyes of the monists), in Iraq it was the neighbouring states, including Syria and Turkey, who feared the implications of such a move for their borders. Following the Maidan revolution, even Zbigniew Brzezinski, national-security advisor to President Jimmy Carter from 1977 to 1981 and one of the key strategists of the geopolitical containment of post-Communist Russia, spoke in favour of the federalisation of Ukraine. Given the enormous cultural and historical differences, the idea of a Ukrainian confederation on the Swiss model could in ideal conditions have been considered, but in practice this was not an option. In addition, the Bosnian Federation, created in Dayton, Ohio in 1995, was not an example of an effective state. It kept the various communities together, but paralysed policy making and only stoked rather than dissipated hostilities.

In a statement on 19 April, Yatsenyuk asserted that 'the Ukrainian government is ready to conduct a comprehensive constitutional reform that will secure powers of the regions',[15] and on 14 May he acknowledged that Ukraine faced the 'super complicated task' of preserving peace and tranquillity: 'It is very important to start this national dialogue now because we are responsible for the future of a 45-million state in the heart of Europe.'[16] In an interview on 14 May Akhmetov lamented that the Donbas was 'living in a disaster' and argued that the only way out of the crisis was 'to amend the constitution and decentralize government', insisting: 'I strongly believe that the Donbas can be happy only in a united Ukraine.'[17] Such a dialogue and promises to devolve powers to the regions was not a concession to Moscow or even an attempt to ensure that Ukraine conformed to the European Charter of Local Self-government, but a sensible way of giving expression to the diversity of the country.

In the political roadmap for eastern Ukraine to which the German, Swiss and Russian governments agreed on 7 May, there was to be 'national dialogue' accompanied by 'round-table discussions in the regions' – words taken from the OSCE proposal, which was to be taken forward by the German diplomat Wolfgang Ischinger, who was appointed on 10 May to conduct the dialogue and act as a moderator of the round tables. In the event, a series of round tables were held, but they were far from the promised 'national dialogue' called for by Russia and enshrined in the 17 April Geneva agreement regulating the Donbas conflict (see Chapter 7), which would have gone some way towards meeting the concerns of the pluralists. They were held in parallel with the work of a commission of the Verkhovna Rada, and were not coordinated with parliament's discussions. The debate over constitutional reform was very limited and lacked structured input from the Russophone parts of the country, and thus hopes that the debate over constitutional reform would provide a platform for reconciliation were disappointed. By now 'federalisation' had become a dirty word, tantamount to treason. Unfortunately, the new power centres spawned by the revolution, notably Kolomoisky's stronghold in Dnepropetrovsk and the various field commanders, meant that 'feudalism' was now more likely than federalism.

On 6 May the Verkhovna Rada voted against holding a referendum on federalisation, which was to have been held alongside the presidential election on 25 May. The Maidan monists feared that their victory in February would be diluted by the pluralists, and now rowed back on federalisation plans. Pluralist arguments were now tainted by association with the conflict in the Donbas, and the whole 'anti-Maidan' movement retreated in the face of extreme violence. Instead, after a relatively closed process the proposed amendments were forwarded to the EU's Venice Commission on 26 June. If accepted, in future it would be easier to impeach the president, and parliament rather than the president would be responsible for declaring a state of emergency. The other proposed changes will be discussed below. Overall, it was clear that the new leadership would not take advantage of the liminal moment to renew the Ukrainian state on a broader basis. For defenders of the monist tradition, federalisation and giving Russian the status of a second state language were 'contrary to the fundamental principles of Ukraine's state order'.[18]

Opinion polls before the civil war in the Donbas showed strong support for the idea of Ukraine. As Firtash, one of the major employers in the region, put it: 'The people in Donetsk and Lugansk do not want any separatism. Believe me: I speak with the employees in my factories every day. They do not want to leave Ukraine.' He did, however, favour much greater decentralisation. He was head of the employers' federation between 2011 and 2013, and noted: 'The people are opposed to the centralized system. Only 15 per cent of the money remains in the regions; the rest flows to Kyiv. We need to give the regions more autonomy and powers.' As far as he was concerned: 'Our main problems stem from the US and Russia. They play geopolitics, with Ukraine being in the crossfire. The country has become a battleground of the superpowers.'[19] Equally, the oligarchs lined up across the geopolitical divide, with some – notably Akhmetov, Firtash and to a degree Pinchuk – supporting the 'third way',

> putting pressure on the [Maidan] government to get it to restructure itself taking the interests of the south-east into account, to make it reinforce the country's neutral status and announce the start of the federalisation process. While simultaneously

making peace with Russia. But the problem is that there is no political force which is capable of leaning on the government with these demands and putting forward its own presidential candidate to compete with the 'Maidan candidates'.[20]

This is a fundamental point, stressed in this book. The PoR was in disarray, and Tigipko was far from being supported by all the 'regionals'. Pinchuk, Ukraine's second-richest man, with extensive media holdings, had strong links with think tanks in Washington. He now sought to use his funding of civil-society organisations to temper the conflict. Very quickly the 'third way' was squeezed out and Ukraine effectively descended into civil war.

The great-power battleground fed into domestic debates. Federalisation became associated with Russia and the fear of secession. Instead, decentralisation took centre stage. In a plan devised by the minister for regional affairs, Vladimir Groisman, power was to be devolved from Kiev to the two dozen regions. On 21 May the Verkhovna Rada adopted a memorandum that provided for amendments to the constitution to establish a parliamentary–presidential republic, to restore the balance of authority between all branches of power and to embrace judicial reform, and pledged to back the authority of regions with financial resources through a more equitable distribution of budgetary revenues.[21] The draft constitution of 26 June planned to fold the existing four tiers of government into three: central, regional and local communities (*hromady*). The regions would be granted additional powers, including the right to introduce a second local language. This was an alternative to full-scale federalisation, an idea discredited by the traumas of revolution and separatism. The new model drew on the Polish experience of local-government reform. The practice of parachuting regional governors in from Kiev was to be abolished. To guard against separatism and constitutional deviation, the authority of the centre was to be ensured by the system of presidential envoys. This revived the system introduced by Kravchuk in the early 1990s, when he appointed *predstavnyky* (representatives) to the regions, provoking endless conflicts until they were co-opted by the regional authorities and abolished. The president would now appoint representatives to each region, while the powers of the Constitutional Court in Kiev would be enhanced to allow it to rule on the constitutionality of decisions taken by lower-level authorities. The presidential representatives would be responsible for the implementation of these rulings.

The reform of regional and local government had long been delayed, but even now it was not clear that it went far enough to give a political voice to national groups. The Hungarian prime minister Viktor Orbán, re-elected by a landslide in April 2014, called for autonomy for the 200,000 ethnic Hungarians in Zakarpattia. He argued that 'Ukraine can be neither stable, nor democratic if it does not give its minorities, including Hungarians, their due. [...] That is, dual (Hungarian) citizenship, collective rights and autonomy.' The Ukrainian deputy foreign minister, Natalia Galibarenko, accepted that minority languages would be granted equal status with Ukrainian in education and official documents in regions with significant minorities: 'But cultural autonomy based on ethnicity [...] is not on the agenda.' She stressed: 'We are a united state, we need to treat the concept of autonomy very carefully'. For good measure, she urged Ukraine's partners 'to refrain from statements which only play into the hands of Russia'.[22] This was a government of Ukrainisers, ready to make only limited concessions to Malorussian, pluralist and other traditions.

PURGING THE STATE

Although Russia's campaign to label the 'coup-appointed' government as basically 'fascist' was an exaggeration, some of its ministers used language that was highly suggestive of the 'blood and iron' purification through violence of earlier fascist movements. For example, Avakov posted a blog on his Facebook account on 22 June in which he argued:

> War cannot give rise to fine feelings, but it can give birth to cleansing. The false and dirty are quickly burned away in the fire of war [...] through the death of comrades and the need to kill in return [...] this is a cleansing and atonement for all, an essential condition for victory.

He ended with the postscript that he had discovered the 'strange coincidence' that 'in English the word is written as ATOnement'.[23]

The monist conception of Ukrainian statehood is inextricably bound up with the advancement of Ukrainian as the exclusive language of official politics, education and civic life. The language issue was one of the main causes of conflict in the east, but no resolution of the issue was in sight. The triumph of the Maidan, a movement designed to achieve change, in the event became the greatest obstacle to reform. Poroshenko pledged to accept the July 2012 language law that gives official recognition to a second language on the regional level where the other language group wants it. Even this is a major achievement. The monists feared that granting a special status to other languages would

> lead to the Russification of a number of regions in South-East Ukraine. [...] None of them [the leading presidential candidates] is prepared to take steps to protect

Ukrainian-speakers from Russification in Southern, Eastern and partly Central Ukraine, let alone facilitate the actual rather than formal use of Ukrainian as the state language. Eye-witnesses claim that both Tymoshenko, Poroshenko as well as their families, speak Russian at home and in private life while switching to Ukrainian in public or to talk to the people they find useful.[24]

Russian is a state language in Belarus, and even though it is the most common language used in daily life it is not perceived as a threat to Belarusian identity. Only 10 per cent of the population are ethnic Russians, not so much lower than the 17 per cent who are considered ethnic Russians in Ukraine. This national self-confidence is borne out by statistics, which show that at least half the population opposes Belarus merging in one way or another with Russia, a figure that is comparable to those favouring membership in the EU. As noted, Belarus looks both ways, and it was clearly understood that the EaP was a strategy to pull the country out of Russia's orbit. The Ukrainian crisis intensified uncertainty over the fate of the Eurasian integration, but at the same time it did not make Belarus more pro-EU; in fact, while 45 per cent favoured European integration in December 2013, by the following April this had fallen to 33 per cent, while 70 per cent opposed a Belarusian Maidan.[25] The Ukrainian events proved a salutary shock, making Lukashenko's authoritarian stability look rather more attractive.

Revolutions by definition create governments of war, initially against enemies within but then typically turning outwards. The Maidan government was no exception, although formally committed precisely to end the state of exceptional politics and to return to a condition of normality and the rule of law. However, with the war in the east the martial features of the regime were intensified. An email account was set up in the occupied areas of Lugansk and Donetsk regions for anonymous denunciations of citizens suspected of participating in rebel activity. Keith Gessen, who as we shall see in the next chapter wrote a moving account of the conflict, was shown an order from the ministry of defence, but not repudiated by the ministry of education (headed by the monist nationalist Sergei Kvit)

> demanding that all senior university officials take part in mobilising staff for the ATO. Those who 'sabotaged' the process would be found guilty of 'separatist tendencies' [...] 'This language,' he [the professor at Kharkov University who showed Gessen the order] said. 'It's straight out of the 1930s.'[26]

Gessen goes on to quote the sociologist Vladimir Ishchenko:

It was the liberals' tolerance of the nationalists on Maidan that led to this. If they had rejected them right away, things might have turned out differently. It might have led to the collapse of Maidan. It might even have meant that Yanukovych remained president. But at least there would have been peace.[27]

A whole raft of repressive legislation was adopted to 'combat Russian aggression', including the banning of some Russian films for 'distorting historical facts' and the investigation for 'treason' of dissenting voices. Even Sergei Kivalov (the co-author of the language law), a long-time voice of moderation and inclusivity and an MP from Odessa, was investigated.[28] In early March 2014 the prosecutor general instituted four proceedings against Yanukovych, including one for calling on the public to overthrow the new government. By April he was accused of abusing power because he had refused to declare that the Holodomor famine of 1932–3 was genocide, and of creating a 'terrorist organisation' with former state secretary SBU head Alexander Yakimenko and former interior minister Vitaly Zakharchenko.[29] A tax-evasion case was opened against Yanukovych's son, Alexander, who was also wanted on charges of forgery, fraud and the issuance of knowingly false documents. Alexander was estimated to have a fortune of some $367 to $510 million held in the MAKO corporation.[30] Kiev claimed to have identified some $3 billion in assets allegedly looted by Yanukovych, a sum reported by Ukraine's prosecutor general, Oleg Makhnitsky, to an international conference, the Ukraine Forum for Asset Recovery (UFAR), convened in London on 29–30 April.

On 19 May Turchynov accused the CPU of supporting the separatist violence in the east. He accused the party's leader, Petro Symonenko, of personally taking 'part in the separatist rallies in the south-eastern regions' and of 'openly supporting the separatists'. A week earlier Symonenko condemned the military campaign in the east as 'fascist'.[31] On 8 July Ukraine's justice minister, Pavlo Petrenko, moved to ban the CPU, charging it with supporting and financing 'terrorism' by providing monetary, political and military support to the insurgents. Two weeks later Yatsenyuk dissolved the party in parliament and over 300 criminal cases were opened against members. The disenfranchisement of the 13 per cent of the electorate that had voted for the party in 2012 could hardly be considered democratic. This was on top of the ban imposed in March on the major cable companies carrying the four major Russian television channels (Rossiya-1, Channel One, NTV and Rossiya-24), while on 11 September the Kiev-based newspaper *Vesti* was closed down by the SBU for allegedly 'violating Ukraine's territorial integrity'. On 4 August the security service asked the internet Association of Ukraine to block sites that allegedly supported violent changes to the constitutional order and the territorial integrity of Ukraine. On 19 August, Ukrainian authorities banned 14 Russian television stations for 'broadcasting propaganda of war and violence'. In many cities a lockdown was in place, as in Zaporozhe, where a self-organised pro-Kiev armed militia of 800 men maintained order. The defence minister Valery Heletey announced the creation of a Special Service to root out the Russian 'fifth column' in the Ukrainian armed forces.[32] Instead of developing a more inclusive and competitive political system, monism became more deeply entrenched.

The CPU was not the only group to feel the force of the new regime. Tetyana Chornovil, the journalist at the head of the government's anti-corruption efforts, claimed that former members of Yanukovych's inner circle were 'still having an impact on the situation in Ukraine'. In August she resigned, complaining that her presence in government was 'useless'. She insisted: 'There is no political will in Ukraine for an uncompromising, wide-scale war on corruption', asserting that all her initiatives had drowned in a 'bureaucratic swamp'. Her alienation was exacerbated by the death of her husband, Nikolai Berezovoi, killed in action near Donetsk.[33] Yegor Sobolev, the former journalist and Maidan activist, went on to head the government's Lustration Committee, responsible for checking public officials for past links to corruption and misgovernance. He argued that Yanukovych and other top officials should be banned from Ukrainian politics for life. At a 12 March press conference he listed a number of people who could also face lustration: former prosecutor general Viktor Pshonka, former interior minister Vitaly Zakharchenko, former head of the SBU Alexander Yakymenko, first deputy head of the presidential administration Andriy Portnov and former justice minister Olena Lukash. In addition, he said that 8,500 judges and several hundred thousand police officers would also be investigated and possibly lustrated.[34] An Interim Special Commission of the High Council of Judges was established to evaluate the performance of judges within a year. Plenty of other names were mentioned on other occasions, including Alexander Popov, the mayor of Kiev at the time of the Maidan protests.

There were also scapegoats among the oligarchs, notably the 'Ukrainian Berezovsky', Dmytro Firtash. On 14 March 2014 Firtash was arrested in Austria on a provisional warrant following a request by the US three days earlier. Firtash was released on provisional bail on 21 March on harsh terms, including a bond of €125 million, the highest in Austrian history, and he was pledged to remain in Austria until the end of the extradition proceedings. The indictment reflects investigations conducted since 2008 by the FBI into planned investments in uranium mines in India. Firtash argues that the US government distorted and fabricated the factual case against him for political reasons, to advance its political and economic interests in the region. By having him arrested outside Ukraine he was removed from active engagement with political developments. It was openly bruited in the media that Firtash had made 'a fateful mistake' in not supporting 'the Ukrainian revolution' from the start, and instead his Inter television channel remained a 'Yanukovych mouthpiece practically until the day he fled'. He explained his position as follows: 'I support Poroshenko; I do not have any other choice. I'm ready to support anyone other than Tymoshenko.' The same report noted that

> the authorities in Kiev are currently being constrained in their actions by Yulia's people. The talk behind the scenes in the Ukrainian Cabinet of Ministers is that Firtash's arrest in Vienna was 'cleared' with the acting president of Ukraine, Alexander Turchynov, a long-standing Tymoshenko associate. Nor is there any reason for the oligarch to hope for support from the future government: the businessman has spoken openly in favour of the federalisation of Ukraine, thereby essentially supporting the Kremlin's line on this matter.[35]

Firtash himself argued that the US wanted him out of circulation because he was a 'powerful player' in Ukraine's political struggles. His offer to 'act as a negotiator between Russia and Ukraine' enraged his opponents, as did his argument that 'imposing sanctions against Russia [is] a bad idea'. 'It's better not to pressure him [Putin] because that will only make things worse. America provoked Putin into this situation.'[36]

For many, Poroshenko should have led by personal example. In 2013 Forbes estimated his wealth at $1.3 billion, making him the seventh-richest man in Ukraine. To demonstrate that it was not business as usual in politics, he was urged to sell off his factories and Channel 5. After all, one of the key drivers of the Maidan events was condemnation of oligarch power, and, after all the deaths and disruption, an oligarch was elected to the presidency. The anti-corruption legislation introduced to the Rada in October 2014 required top officials in government, the judiciary and law-enforcement bodies to declare their own and their families' assets and financial transactions. More broadly, by invoking lustration laws to purge the bureaucracy of old-regime officials, the administration raised the spectre of McCarthyism. In condemning the 'fifth column' in parliament, Poroshenko used the language of his opponents in Russia and his precursor in 1950s America. The new lustration law was finally passed on 16 September, although the prosecutor general, Vitaly Yarema, condemned it as being in conformity with neither the Ukrainian constitution nor international law. Lustration by definition limits the rights of certain categories defined not by law but by political criteria, above all restricting the right to work in public administration. All senior civil servants, numbering about half a million, came under threat, barring them from being rehired for a decade, while the police, tax administration and the prosecutor's office were all to be purged, a total of some

1 million people. The mechanism of dismissal was unclear, as were appeal procedures, and it was also unclear where the new generation of competent and politically loyal officials would come from. Poroshenko's Reform Strategy announced on 25 September consisted of 62 points, including anti-corruption measures, tax and court reforms, decentralisation of power, and reforms of the law-enforcement authorities, national security, defence and health care.

ON THE ROAD TO EUROPE

The new government has inherited a disastrous legacy. The Ukrainian economy had already been hit hard by the great recession, with its GDP declining by some 9 per cent in 2009. The economy had not yet recovered before the new crisis hit, with the economy shrinking by 0.3 per cent in 2013, followed by a steeper fall in 2014. The economy as a whole is heavily indebted, owing Gazprom at least $5.3 billion in October 2014. Ukraine is Gazprom's second-largest market, delivering 32.9 billion cubic metres (bcm) in 2012. In 2013 Gazprom supplied 161.5 bcm of gas to Europe, of which 86 bcm transited through Ukraine, accounting for some 30 per cent of Europe's total gas imports. Households enjoy heavily subsidised pricing and government-controlled producers are forced to fulfil household sales quotas.

The financial position was exacerbated by Yanukovych and his 'family' allegedly stripping government coffers of billions. The new government claimed that it needed $35 billion to pay its way over the next two years. Russia quickly put an end to its $15 billion drawing facility, having disbursed only the first tranche in the form of a $3 billion bond in December 2013. On 27 March the IMF agreed to a $17.1 billion loan over two years, supplemented by another $10 billion from the EU and €8 billion from the EBRD. Fears that Ukraine would default on its debts receded, but the fiscal capacities of the state were perilously low. Twice before Ukraine had received IMF support in return for promised reforms. The first $16.4 billion loan came in November 2008, when Tymoshenko was prime minister, but it was frozen after a year and then cancelled because of the lack of reform. In July 2010 another $15.2 billion package was agreed with Yanukovych, but once again payments were stopped after a year because of the country's failure to meet the conditions.

This time the first $3.2 billion tranche was disbursed in May to keep Ukraine afloat, but the conditions were stringent. The budget deficit was to be reduced by cutting public spending, which astonishingly equalled half of GDP, including reductions in pension payments accompanied by deep cuts in the corrupting and distorting energy and other subsidies. The price of household gas was immediately increased by

56 per cent, although even this was still far below cost-recovery levels. In addition, the decade-long pro-family programme that sought to counter the sharp demographic decline by awarding benefits for each child born (which had also sharply decreased the number of abortions) was drastically cut back. The loan opened Ukraine up to the use of genetically modified organisms (GMOs) in agriculture, something that had hitherto been banned. This only confirmed a little-known item in the Association Agreement (Article 404), which called on both parties to cooperate to extend the use of biotechnologies. Ukraine, long known as the breadbasket of Europe, was to be opened up to American agribusiness.

Liberals had long argued that some fundamental problems needed to be addressed. Consumers only paid a quarter of the cost of imported gas, with the difference made up by government subsidies. Yanukovych refused to undertake reforms in this area, knowing how deeply unpopular they would be. The new government raised gas prices by 56 per cent from 1 May, accompanied by a wage freeze and the dismissal of some 24,000 civil servants, a tenth of the total. Taxes were to rise, state assets privatised and corruption tackled. The national currency, the hryvnia, was to be allowed to float against the dollar. To avoid immediate shocks, the worst of the austerity pro-gramme was to fall in 2015–16. The situation inexorably deteriorated, and by July the IMF anticipated that Ukraine's economy would shrink by 6.5 per cent in 2014. The government was spending far more than anticipated in battling the insurgency in the east, revenue collection fell sharply, and Naftogaz was finding it increasingly difficult to get domestic and industrial consumers to pay their debts. It looked like Ukraine would need a new bailout.

A change of regime did not change the structure of the economy, dominated by coal-mining and ageing industries in Donetsk, including shipbuilding, steel and armaments, mostly relying on the Russian market. Many of the country's industries were enormously energy-inefficient. Ukraine has more arable land than any other country in Europe, and its grain and sunflower exports had been beginning to pick up. This was a sector that greatly interested the Chinese, and they had begun to buy up significant tracts of land. The whole economy, however, was distorted by corruption, with one study in 2012 suggesting that the shadow economy made up 44 per cent of Ukraine's economic output.[37] In 2013 Ukraine was ranked 144 out of 177 in Berlin-based Transparency International's 'Corruption Perceptions Index', ranked alongside Papua New Guinea, Nigeria and the Central African Republic.[38] In 2005 it had been 107. The entwining of politics and business fostered a culture of corruption.

The February revolution promised a renewal of Ukrainian society, and despite the war in the east a programme of change was launched. The new regime feared repeating the experience of earlier colour revolutions, which had at most achieved a circulation of elites rather than systemic change. A commission in July examined ways in which structural changes could reduce corruption, above all through the increased use of e-governance systems and simplifying the tax system. On 31 July a new education law came into effect, drafted by the minister of education Sergei Kvit and other Maidan activists, which granted universities more autonomy and introduced a new style of graduate degrees. Kvit is the rector of the Kyiv-Mohyla Academy, a thinker in the Dontsov tradition who espouses the characteristic Russophobia. He was appointed minister of education on 27 February, and stressed that the Maidan revolution was far deeper than the Orange events a decade earlier. The new revolution was not just about a contested election, but about 'the reformation of the entire political system'.[39] He was right to stress the need to reform the system of education and research. As his deputy, Inna Sovsun, argued, 'Only 6 to 7 per cent of research funding went to universities', with the bulk going to Soviet-style research centres, while only 0.29 per cent of GDP was spent on research, low by any standards.[40] This was just one measure that sought to modernise Ukrainian society, but reforming the polity and the economy would be no less of a challenge.

Ukraine finally signed the Association Agreement with the EU on 27 June, at a ceremony at which Georgia and Moldova also signed up. The 'Wider Europe' project ploughed on, regardless of the havoc it had already caused. Instead of negotiating a free-trade agreement with both the CIS and the EU, the fateful choice was made. It was accompanied by disclaimers that the EU was not ready to offer membership to Ukraine. The existing union was not ready to integrate a country such as Ukraine, while Ukraine was not ready to join the EU either.

Moscow warned that signing a free-trade agreement would open the door to 'grey' re-exports of what would now become duty-free European goods to the CIS free-trade zone. If tariffs were raised there was the risk that Ukraine would lose its traditional CIS markets, threatening much of its $23 billion of annual exports to Russia. Responding to the fear that Ukraine would be the conduit for duty-free imports, Russia responded by threatening to treat Ukrainian products as European. Much of Ukraine's heavy industry would be threatened by the imposition of tariffs, notably the plants located in the south-east producing rolling stock, heavy machinery, steel and pipeline goods and military hardware. From 30 June suppliers of goods to Russia already had to present proof of Ukrainian manufacture. These 'country of origin' certificates are a normal practice in international trade, but now added another bureaucratic layer to what were already onerous procedures. On 22 October Russia imposed a ban on the import of fruit and vegetables, claiming that the goods were being imported through Ukraine to evade Russian measures against the EU. The status of Ukrainian guest workers in Russia, of whom there were at least 3 million (with some estimates as high as 5–6 million), was also threatened. Like other workers from the CIS, Ukrainians can stay in Russia for 90 days without registering.

Even Poroshenko's own business was threatened. Up to mid-2013 his Roshen confectionery business exported 40 per cent of its output to Russia, and there was little reason to believe that it would remain competitive in Western markets when pitched against the likes of Nestlé, Unilever or Cadbury. As James Carden notes:

> Poroshenko is basically choosing to cut off trading ties with Russia in favour of joining a bloc that has no appetite for the country's products. That, in addition to the usually disastrous effects IMF austerity measures have on underwater economies, is a recipe for capital flight, stagnation and long-term unemployment.

The unemployed, moreover, would not enjoy visa-free travel for work purposes to the EU, while it would become more difficult to join the Russian labour market. Carden argues that the underlying premise of the EU Association Agreement, the assumption that in the early twenty-first century economics trumps politics, is flawed:

> This line of thinking – call it a version of the Democratic Domino Theory – posits that as Ukraine and the other former states integrate their economies into the larger European markets they will adapt Europe's political and cultural norms. This transformation will, in turn, influence Russia's internal political development and it too (somehow) will Westernise through the power of example. This, it should go without saying, is a remarkably foolish way to see the world. Yet the longer American policy makers adhere to this premise, the more they will end up endangering the long-term viability of the EU.[41]

Not only this, but the agreement was liable to exacerbate the divisions within Ukraine. A Gallup poll released in early June highlighted how majorities in the east expressed distrust of the US, opposition to economic integration with the EU and a reluctance to make sacrifices for the sake of 'reform', and regarded the interim government in Kiev as 'illegitimate'. As the Gallup pollster Neli Esipova noted:

> In the last eight, nine years when we collect data in Ukraine, we see it all the time on most of the aspects of life actually. Any political situation we ask of the country, even economics, the split between different regions and between different ethnic groups existed for years, and the government didn't pay attention to it.[42]

Signing the Association Agreement was only the beginning of a long and traumatic process. It was ratified by the Ukrainian and European parliaments on 16 September, but still needed the approval of EU member states. In a concession to Russia, the application of the DCFTA was postponed until 31 December 2015, allowing negotiations to continue on how the two free-trade zones could be rendered more compatible. Ukrainian goods were allowed into the EU duty-free, but European goods were taxed as normal on their way into Ukraine, a useful source of revenue for the cash-strapped Ukrainian budget. Putin still feared the dumping of Ukrainian goods on the Russian market, and in a letter to Poroshenko dated 17 September he argued:

> We still believe that only systemic adjustments of the Association Agreement, which take into account the full range of risks to Russian–Ukrainian economic ties and to the whole Russian economy, will allow to retain existing trade and economic cooperation between the Russian Federation and Ukraine.[43]

Five problem areas were identified: tariffs; standards and technical regulation; phytosanitary and veterinary norms; energy; and customs administration. Štefan Füle, the commissioner for enlargement and European neighbourhood policy, now accepted that there would have to be negotiations with the EEU, and even possibly a free-trade agreement with it.

Poroshenko's 25 September Reform Strategy envisaged Ukraine submitting a full application for EU membership in 2020. More immediately, signing the Association Agreement was an important symbolic moment, but it resolved none of the immediate issues facing Ukraine. The West was in no position to underwrite the painful reform to which the country was now committed. The acute financial and other problems would be exacerbated by the loss of the 'hidden rents' that Russia had provided in the form of relatively cheap gas and its associated dependent trading patterns. With the reincorporation of Crimea, Russia ended Ukraine's discounted gas price from 1 April 2014, provoking yet another gas conflict between the two countries. More broadly, Gaddy and Ickes outline the dilemmas:

> It is clear to most observers that the West would not be able to defend Ukraine economically from a hostile Russia. [...] The simple fact is that Russia today supports the Ukrainian economy to the tune of at least $5 billion, perhaps as much as $10 billion, each year [...] When we talk of subsidies we usually think of Russia's ability to offer Ukraine cheap gas – which it does when it wants to. But there are many more ways Russia supports Ukraine, only they are hidden. The main support comes in the form of Russian orders to Ukrainian heavy manufacturing enterprises. This

part of Ukrainian industry depends almost entirely on demand from Russia. They wouldn't be able to sell to anyone else.

They go on to speculate how much it would cost for the West to support eastern Ukraine, if they managed to wrest 'full control of Ukraine from Russia'. The only other comparable case is German federal support for the former German Democratic Republic after unification, which amounted to $2.76 trillion over 20 years. With Ukraine's per capita income a tenth of Germany's it would cost a minimum of $276 billion 'to buy off the east. [...] It is unthinkable that the West would pay this amount'.[44]

REGIME CONTRADICTIONS

Even at the height of the Maidan movement only half of the country supported the protesters. Yet on one thing there was almost universal agreement, namely the revolution of dignity, the attempt to forge a new relationship between citizens and government.[45] The executive was to be transformed from a racketeering gang into a representative body that would bring transparency and the rule of law into society. However, if this meant simply a takeover of political posts by the now triumphant opposition, the sense of being excluded would only be aggravated and do little to create a more inclusive and just governmental order. The first wave of Maidan protesters called not just for a rotation of old faces but a complete renewal. This soon came into contradiction with the demands of the second-wave militants for a specific type of state renewal that would consolidate the monist vision of a Ukrainian state cleansed of 'imperial' accretions and distortions. The expulsion of a legitimately elected president, however odious he may have been, was hardly likely to foster the rule of law and the consolidation of the constitutional state. Instead, it fostered lawlessness and violence against political opponents.

The contradiction between the aspirations of the Maidan for a 'civilisational' turn to Europe and the deeply 'un-European' pattern of revolutionary behaviour, as the monists considered themselves the new masters of Ukraine, is obvious. More pressingly, the contradiction between the square (the pressure for democratic renewal) and the castle, the technocratic imperatives imposed by the IMF as a condition of its loans (hikes in utility bills, job losses and much more), moreover, allowed the third force, the bureaucratic–oligarchic order, to emerge as the arbiter and in a reconfigured format to consolidate its power. This in turn provoked the anger of the Maidan idealists, who condemned Poroshenko for cutting deals with the oligarchs rather than launching real reforms. The threat of a new Maidan, a 'third revolution', was ever-present.

Thus the new president faced not only high demands but contradictory pressures. Expectations of state renewal were tempered by the failures of the Orange administration, now exacerbated by a decade of conflict and accompanied by economic decline and war. The February events were at most a partial revolution, with the old elite structures largely intact and the same old faces once again in power. Worse, the power of some of the regional oligarchs was consolidated as they were given executive authority, and they proceeded to extend their business empires while creating warlord regimes, notably in Dnepropetrovsk. It was unlikely that that such a government would 'dismantle the energy rent regime – the one thing that holds the political class together'.[46] At the top of the list of thorny issues facing the new administration was the question of the country's territorial status. Fearing that centrifugal forces could tear the country apart, the 1996 constitution rendered Ukraine a severely unitary state, accompanied by the central appointment of governors. This stymied the political expression of the country's diversity, and also meant that whoever assumed office in Kiev imposed their will on the country. A change of presidency was typically followed by the wholesale firing of governors.

Such a system was conducive neither to good governance nor to consensual nation-building. It was symptomatic of the many problems that pre-dated the Maidan revolution and would challenge Ukrainian leaders long into the future. The immediate challenge was constitutional reform, but even here there were no simple answers. The devolution of power to the regions threatened to reproduce authoritarian systems at the lower level (as Russia had discovered in the 1990s) and could foster fragmentation, if not the break-up, of the country. Reform had to be accompanied by the strengthening of the rule of law, an independent Constitutional Court to ensure compliance with the constitution at all levels, and the genuine separation of powers to ensure that the executive was held accountable while avoiding the heady populism of irresponsible parliamentary majorities. This would be a tough challenge in the best of circumstances, let alone in a country polarised by revolution and war.

The internationalisation of Ukraine's domestic divisions demonstrates how elusive and problematic concepts of sovereignty can be in conditions of geopolitical polarisation. The concept of 'Finlandisation' was anathema to most Ukrainians, and no country likes to be thought of as a 'buffer zone'. Whatever term is used, there are certain fundamental realities facing a country neighbouring a great power or caught between two powerful blocs. As early as 1920 the Irish leader Éamon de Valera assured Britain that a future independent state would be neutral but respect British security interests, the foundation stone for fruitful cooperation.[47] Finland's non-aligned status following World War II did not prevent it taking bold actions to reinvent itself as a multinational community in which Swedish was made the second state language, the mass of refugees from the territories annexed by the Soviet Union in Karelia were successfully integrated, and a democratic political system was created. The only prohibition was on joining military alliances (Finland is still not a member of NATO), and instead Finland played a key role as an intermediary between the East and West. Helsinki hosted the final conference of the Conference on Security and Cooperation in Europe in August 1975, which on 1 January 1995 was transformed into the OSCE. The OSCE remains a core element of the European security architecture to this day, although it failed to become the inclusive and predominant body that Russia favoured.

None of the leading candidates in the 25 May presidential election called for immediate NATO membership, fearing the loss of votes in regions where the population was adamantly opposed to joining the Western bloc. This applies not only to the Donbas, but also Odessa and Kharkov. Instead, there appeared to be a public consensus that Ukraine should be independent and neutral. As Firtash put it:

> I am proud to be a citizen of Ukraine. This is a country that geographically and psychologically is a bridge between Europe, Russia and Asia. I believe we can and should be a strong, independent, and neutral nation. We should be viewed as the 'Switzerland of Eurasia', allied with none, but friends and traders with all.

He warned: 'I believe it serves no nation's interest, either European, or American, and certainly not that of Ukraine, if events in our country lead to a tragic replay of the Cold War.'[48]

CHAPTER 7

THE NOVOROSSIYA REBELLION

Just as the Crimean crisis began to ebb, attention shifted to Ukraine's south-east (see Map 6). The Crimean events provoked what is sometimes called the 'Russian spring', an outburst of Russian self-expression in Ukraine, but just like the 'Arab Spring', it soon turned into the deepest midwinter. On 1 March a 7,000-strong crowd gathered in the central square in Donetsk carrying Russian flags and the flag of a hitherto unknown organisation known as the 'Donetsk Republic'. There were further demonstrations across cities in eastern Ukraine, warning against attack by radical nationalists from Kiev but more immediately fearing that their language and other rights would be abrogated. The movement was fired by alarmist reports in the Russian and regional media, which for weeks had been condemning the radicalisation of the Maidan. The protests, with justification, were suspected of being sponsored in part by Yanukovych, especially since his network of mayors and officialdom remained in place, yet it also had deep local roots. While the degree of separatist feeling in the region is contested, the rebellion gradually turned into a full-scale war. Ukraine's domestic contradictions have been internationalised, with Russia supporting the insurgents on the one side, while the Western powers have lined up in support of the Ukrainian authorities. Instead of snatching Crimea and withdrawing to allow the storm to pass, Russia has been sucked into a new and far more intense conflict, drawing upon it the wrath of the West.

THE DONBAS RISES

The 'other' Ukraine sought to be part of the dialogue about what it means to be Ukrainian. A poll by the Pew Research Center in May 2014 found that 70 per cent of eastern Ukrainians wanted to keep the country intact, including 58 per cent of Russian-speakers, although they expressed plenty of grievances against Kiev, including the over-centralised state that took all tax revenues before redistributing them to the regions. Both Donetsk and Lugansk were heavily subsidised by Kiev, receiving far more from the budget than they contributed, to keep the loss-making mines and mills working.[1] Nevertheless, the Donbas represented the country's economic powerhouse, accounting for 16 per cent of GDP and 27 per cent of industrial production.

Above all, some 60 per cent of Donetsk residents feared 'Banderovtsy' and 50 per cent dreaded the Kiev authorities, while 71 per cent of Donetsk and 60 per cent of Lugansk residents believed that the Maidan events represented an armed coup organised by the opposition and the West. Majorities in other regions in the southeast agreed that the protests were an uprising 'against the corruption and tyranny of the Yanukovych dictatorship'.[2] Gessen describes how one future rebel in the east was shocked to see how

> young men in masks and the insignia of old Ukrainian fascist movements attacked riot police [in the Maidan] – some of them from the Donetsk area – with Molotov cocktails. He saw governors in the western provinces pulled out of their offices and roughed up by furious crowds. It seemed that the country was descending into chaos. When he heard a rumour that some of the young men from Maidan were headed for Donetsk, he believed it.[3]

Any simplistic division of the country into a nationalistic west, a 'pro-Russian' east and a patriotic centre does not begin to capture the complex pattern of responses to the breakdown of Ukrainian statehood. What is clear is that a new relationship was required with the Donbas, but it was not forthcoming. The Ukrainian parliament's attempt to remove Russian as a second regional language was blocked, but the damage was done. As one respondent noted: 'Is there any other country on earth where a language understood by 100% of the population is not a language of state?'[4]

A grass-roots protest movement welled up throughout March 2014, clearly enjoying popular support. Whereas the Maidan protesters were 'middle class and nationalistic', the anti-Maidan movement in the Donbas was 'lower class and anti-oligarchic (and Russian nationalist)'. When the acting minister of the interior, Avakov, visited Donetsk in mid-March, 'he met with civic leaders, but most of all he met with the football ultras, and demanded that they arm themselves and prepare for battle against the pro-Russian forces in the city'.[5] The ultras are hard-core football fans whose far-right views and violent hooliganism were now turned in support of the Kiev regime, as was seen in Odessa on 2 May, and their terrace chant of '*Putin khuilo!*' ('Putin is a dickhead!') was repeated on 14 June by the acting foreign minister, Andriy Deshchytsia, when the Russian embassy in Kiev was besieged by an angry mob. Fighter jets flew low over the pro-Donbas protests, and it appeared that 'from the very start, Kiev had been prepared to use force'.[6] On 10 March the former governor of Kharkov, Mikhail Dobkin, was arrested on charges of leading a separatist movement. From 6 April insurgents occupied government buildings in Donetsk, Gorlovka and Kramatorsk. In Kharkov on 8 April some 70 anti-Maidan protesters were arrested and faced politically charged trials, and this was enough to pre-empt further action in Ukraine's second city. In the Donbas, however, the insurgency continued to spread. These were not the professional 'little green men' seen earlier in Crimea, but ramshackle forces made up overwhelmingly in the first instance by local volunteers. However, on 12 April the administration, police and other buildings in Slavyansk were occupied by what appeared to be highly trained professional armed forces without insignia. As Gessen puts it: 'At that moment, what had been a people's uprising turned into an armed revolt, and some would say a covert invasion.'[7]

One of the first acts of the insurgents was to take over regional television stations to restore the broadcast of Russian television, cut by order of the central authorities in many regions on 11 March. The insurgents set up checkpoints and established an armed presence in the major towns. Supporters of federalisation refused to recognise the legitimacy of the new Ukrainian authorities and called on the government to allow referendums similar to the one in Crimea. In Donetsk protesters occupied the regional administration buildings and on 7 April proclaimed the Donetsk People's Republic (DPR), and next door a Lugansk People's Republic (LPR) was formed on 27 April. The 'people's governor' of Lugansk, Valery Bolotov, announced the formation of the Donetsk People's Army, whose leader soon became Igor Girkin, whose *nom de guerre* is Strelkov ('the shooter'). A former colonel in the Russian army (some accounts say he served in the main intelligence directorate, the GRU, of the General Staff), he fought in Chechnya, in Transnistria and with the Serbs in Bosnia, and was one of the leaders of the takeover in Crimea. He came to the Donbas in May with around two dozen men but soon built up one of the most formidable rebel units of some 2,000 men.[8] He later claimed to have been 'the one who pulled the trigger on this war'.[9] The Donbas was in revolt, and on 24 May the two entities established a *de jure* union known as the 'Novorossiya Republic'. They sought to capitalise on the emotional power of the concept.

Avakov accused Moscow and the ousted president Yanukovych of 'ordering and paying for another wave of separatist turmoil in the country's east'. Using his characteristic form of communication, his Facebook page, he insisted that 'a firm approach will be used against all who attack government buildings, law enforcement officers and other citizens'.[10] The storming of government offices in the west of the country in the final months of Yanukovych's rule was considered something entirely different – part of the revolutionary surge in support of monist nationalism – whereas now the 'anti-Maidan' insurgency using the same tactics in support of pluralism was called a terrorist movement. In mid-April the Ukrainian security service (SBU) took control of what was called the 'anti-terrorist operation' (ATO) – the constitution allows only this designation for an internal counter-insurgency operation, although that does not render the designation any less forbidding. Government forces re-established control over several major towns, including Mariupol, Kirovsk and Yampol, and the insurgency in the end was limited to parts of the Donbas.

The leadership of the insurgency was a motley crew. They included Denys Pushilin, one of the organisers of the MMM pyramid scheme in Donetsk in the 1990s, while Nikolai Solntsev, a technologist at a meat-processing plant, became the DPR's ideology minister. Most leaders were blue-collar workers with limited outside experience. They drew on the experience of Crimea to plan their actions and were deeply imbued with Soviet values, looking to Russia to provide support for their alternative to Maidan-style Europeanism. This applied in particular to Girkin, who soon became one of the most effective rebel commanders in the Donbas. In mid-May he assumed command of all insurgent forces and called on Russia to intervene. It is far from clear how much direct control Moscow could exert over a man who described himself as a monarchist and condemned the USSR and the post-Communist Kremlin authorities. His hobby was dressing up in costume to re-enact historical battles, part of the Russian paramilitary subculture, and he now donned a real uniform and proved himself a ruthless and capable guerrilla leader until he 'disappeared' in August.

The OSCE had created a 'special monitoring mission' to the region in March, but on 25 April a group of seven foreign military monitors from the OSCE and five Ukrainian military observers were detained in Slavyansk. The 'people's mayor' of the city offered to swap the observers in exchange for the release of his supporters detained by the Kiev authorities. Russia, as an OSCE member, condemned the capture, and soon after the observers were released. On 28 April the shooting of Gennady Kernes, the pro-Kiev mayor of Kharkov, Ukraine's second city, demonstrated how far events in the east were spiralling out of control. Kernes had opposed the Maidan, but he reversed his position following Yanukovych's ouster, and he was wounded shortly afterwards.

The conflict became a struggle between west and east Ukraine, with endless shades between. The physical and rhetorical violence of the Maidan was generalised to the rest of the country. The language of the Kiev forces is quite shocking in its brutality. Already in March, in a conversation about Putin, probably recorded by Russian intelligence, Tymoshenko declared: 'I'm willing to take a Kalashnikov and shoot the bastard in the head.'[11] The Orangist demonisation of Putin soon entered the bloodstream of discourse in the Western world, poisoning sensible discussion. Tymoshenko was equally bloodthirsty in her condemnation of the insurgency in the east and no less extreme in her evaluation of the larger geopolitical situation: 'Putin is attempting to uproot the world's security system, established as a result of [the] Second World War, and turn the global[...] order into chaos. Redrawing world maps by wars, mass murders and blood is becoming his *Mein Kampf*.'[12] The new Kiev authorities were fighting for their survival, but their 'Orange' vision of Ukraine was rejected by the insurgents in the Donbas and, in part, by Moscow. Anger and resentment would be laid down for generations.

The ferocity of the ATO can in part be explained by the view of many in western Ukraine that the people of the Donbas were not 'real Ukrainians', but Russians who had come to replace those who had died in the Holodomor and to staff the industrialisation of the region from the 1930s. They were often denigrated by monists as lacking intellect and 'national identity', and could thus be considered a Russian incubus that needed to be cut out to ensure the healthy development of the Ukrainian nation. When asked in a famous YouTube interview 'What should we do now with the 8 million Russians that stayed in Ukraine? They are outcasts?' Tymoshenko responded: 'They must be killed with nuclear weapons.' To which the man answered: 'I won't argue with you here because what happened is absolutely unacceptable.'[13] This reflected the restitutive model of Ukrainian statehood with a vengeance, the idea that there was some Platonic ideal statehood to which the country should return. Where the actual population differed from the ideal, it was to be subject to special measures to bring it into conformity with the ideologically appropriate format.

When Putin in his *Direct Line* session of 17 April brought up the notion of Novorossiya, it was not clear what he had in mind. His assessment of the situation was vivid and clear:

> Regarding the question of what should come first: a constitutional referendum followed by elections, or elections first to stabilise the situation and then a referendum. The essential issue is how to ensure the legitimate rights and interests of ethnic Russians and Russian-speakers in the south-east of Ukraine. I would like to remind you that what was called Novorossiya [New Russia] back in the tsarist days – Kharkov,

Lugansk, Donetsk, Kherson, Nikolaev and Odessa – were not part of Ukraine back then. These territories were given to Ukraine in the 1920s by the Soviet government. Why? Who knows. They were won by Potemkin and Catherine the Great in a series of well-known wars. The centre of that territory was Novorossiisk, so the region is called Novorossiya. Russia lost these territories for various reasons, but the people remained. Today, they live in Ukraine, and they should be full citizens of their country. That's what this is all about.[14]

Was this a reference to his comment to US President George W. Bush in Bucharest in 2008 that 'Ukraine is not really a state', and thus a call for the dismemberment of the country? Novorossiya was a special tsarist administrative arrangement for a broad swath of territory running along the Black Sea as far as Moldova, and its incorporation into the new Ukrainian SSR in 1922 was as controversial then as it has once again become now. Or was it simply an attempt to stress that Ukraine was made up of many traditions, and thus a call to give institutional form to pluralism, diversity and different identities? Either way, it galvanised those who sought to exploit Ukrainian state weakness for their own ends.

The extent of Moscow's materiel and personnel support is far from clear. A welter of volunteers spilled across the border, drawn from the old opposition that had fought against Yeltsin in 1993, Cossack groups, Chechen militants, and a range of Russian nationalist and neo-Soviet imperialists. The danger, as with volunteer militants in Syria, is that these battle-hardened and radicalised fighters would gain experience and then 'blow back' into Russia, and potentially pose a threat to Putin himself if he failed to meet their expectations about supporting the rebellion in Ukraine. In his 17 April *Direct Line* programme he noted:

> Refusing to see that something was badly wrong in the Ukrainian state and to start
> a dialogue, the government threatened to use military force and even sent tanks and
> aircraft against civilians. It was one more serious crime committed by the current
> Kiev rulers.[15]

In this broadcast Putin acknowledged that the 'green men' in Crimea were in fact Russian forces.

Separatist aspirations were not supported by the majority of the population, and the insurgents rejected the 'separatist' label, while the mainstream Western view that the insurgency consisted of 'terrorists' backed by Moscow is equally false. A well-known survey by the Kyiv International Institute of Sociology (KIIS) from 29 April to 11 May 2014 revealed that only 20–30 per cent of the population of the Donbas supported outright separatism, slightly fewer supported Kiev, while about half were in the middle.[16] Various types of autonomy were supported by 54 per cent, but in the Donbas only 8 per cent favoured independence, 23 per cent supported joining Russia, while a further 23 per cent favoured greater autonomy within Ukraine. The majority of the insurgent leadership came from the Donbas, with some from other regions of Ukraine, including Crimea.[17] This demonstrates that there was no overwhelming desire to leave Ukraine, but it also shows a high level of alienation. Serhiy Kudelia's study confirms this finding, arguing that despite Western accusations that the insurgency was provoked and sponsored by Russia, it was in fact 'primarily a homegrown phenomenon': 'political factors – state fragmentation, violent regime change, and the government's low coercive capacity – combined with popular emotions specific to the region – resentment and fear – played a crucial role in launching the armed secessionist movement there'.[18] It would take skilful political management to bring these people back into the fold of Ukrainian state-building. Instead, aspirations for federalism were considered tantamount to separatism, provoking military action and a devastating civil war.

The insurgents announced a referendum on the self-determination of the Donbas for 11 May. On 7 May Putin urged the referendums to be postponed, but they went ahead anyway with a very simple wording: 'Do you support the creation of the Donetsk People's Republic?' and a similar question in Lugansk. Turnout in both regions was reported to be 75 per cent, with 89 and 96 per cent, respectively, voting for independence. Neither Kiev nor the West recognised the ballot as legitimate, with Poroshenko resolutely condemning the vote, although Firtash on 12 May argued that federalisation was the only acceptable option and that Ukraine should be a neutral state, and he personally was ready to step in to act as an intermediary between Russia and Ukraine.[19] The vote can at best be taken as indicative of widespread 'separatist' sentiment at that time and should be tempered by the results of opinion surveys which, as noted, show a strong commitment to Ukrainian integrity. Nevertheless, the high level of dissatisfaction among the Blues is hardly surprising since for the second time in a decade a leadership that reflected their concerns was removed in contentious circumstances. On this occasion the interim administration formed after 22 February lacked representation from the Donbas and propounded a virulently monist ideology. This certainly does not justify armed rebellion, but helps explain the logic of developments.

The agreement between the DPR and the LPR establishing Novorossiya on 24 May was a propaganda move designed to rally support within Ukraine and volunteers from Russia proper. This was accompanied by accusations that Russia was massing a 40,000-strong army on its western border, ready for a possible invasion, and that

Russian undercover operatives were fomenting the occupations and blockade. The troops were ordered back and forth to follow the various diplomatic contortions, while NATO and Western leaders repeatedly claimed that Russia had invaded or was on the verge of doing so, a crying of wolf that in the end rather discredited them. Instead, Russia trained and filtered in some genuine volunteers, as well as regular forces as 'advisors', a category well known from the early stages of US interventions, and only in August did Russian 'volunteer' paratroopers apparently take part in regular battles. The insurgents came to be dubbed 'pro-Russian separatists', and while this may be accurate for some of them, the rebellion reflected broader concern about the lack of constitutional and political defence for their way of life and historical economic and cultural links with Russia.

The pluralists in the Donbas and other Russophone regions seized the opportunity to institutionalise their long-term aspirations for Russian to be made a second state language and for genuine power-sharing of the regions in a more federal state. This was a quite legitimate democratic aspiration, and could have transformed the agenda of the Maidan into a genuinely national movement. The interim government in Kiev was resistant to such a broadening, given its deep roots in the monist tradition. At the same time, the pluralists in the Donbas and more widely in 'Novorossiya' lacked democratic and civil-society organisational capacity. The years of polarisation and corruption had deeply eroded the bases of civic activism. The PoR had become little more than a claque of the Yanukovych regime, and was deeply factionalised between the various oligarchs. It was discredited and in disarray following Yanukovych's ouster. The CPU remained a bastion of neo-Soviet sentiment, winning some 13 per cent of the vote in the 2012 parliamentary election, but was largely discredited because of its failure to condemn Yanukovych's excesses. All that was left were a few individual politicians who could give voice to pluralist sentiments, while oligarchs like Akhmetov hedged their bets. Firtash added his voice in support of the pluralists, but, isolated in Vienna, he was unable to bolster the cause of compromise.

Although it became axiomatic in much of the West that the insurgency was financed and sponsored by Russia, evidence of this before August is far from conclusive. The provenance of the insurgents who emerged in April 2014 to take over administrative buildings in Slavyansk, Kramatorsk and Donetsk is unclear, but they were certainly not the 'little green men' who had operated so effectively and clinically in taking over Crimea. The story of Artur Gasparyan, an Armenian from Spitak, is a moving tale of how he volunteered to fight for the resistance in Ukraine and was given assistance and training in Russia by shadowy organisations and then transferred to the Donbas. He was part of the chaotic attempt to take over Prokofiev International Airport in Donetsk on 26 May. The fighters simply did not believe that the Ukrainian military would bomb the gleaming new terminal, built for the Euro 2012 football championship, and hence left their anti-aircraft missiles back at base. In their chaotic flight one of the trucks was destroyed by 'friendly fire'. After several weeks Gasparyan was transferred back to Russia and home. Asked why he, an Armenian, volunteered, he stated: 'I don't consider Russia a foreign country. I have the mentality of a Soviet person. My grandfathers fought for the Soviet Union and I am fighting for it.'[20]

There is no more controversial issue than the extent to which Russia was implicated in inciting and supporting the insurgency. What is incontrovertible is that two elements developed in parallel: a genuine regional revolt adopting the tactics of the Maidan against the 'Ukrainising' and anti-Russian policies pursued by the Kiev authorities; and the strategic political considerations of Moscow, which exploited the insurgency to exercise leverage against the Kiev government to achieve defined goals – above all a degree of regional devolution, initially called federalisation – as well as to ensure that the strategic neutrality of the country was maintained. These goals, as well as the establishment of Russian as a second state language, may well have been in the best interests of Ukraine itself, but the method was catastrophic for the region and the country. Russia may well have stirred the pot at the beginning, and thereafter held regular consultations with resistance leaders, but the scale of its initial materiel support was greatly exaggerated by the Kiev government and its Western supporters. Moscow did allow a stream of volunteers to join the resistance, and some military equipment found its way across the border. But a constant refrain of the resistance movement was the lack of supplies and support; they repeatedly called on Russia to be more assertive in its backing, including direct military intervention, although this would only ever be a desperate measure. Moscow had learned the lessons of Afghanistan and the West's own ill-advised interventions in that country, Iraq and Libya. Nevertheless, already in April NATO foreign ministers announced that they would suspend practical cooperation and military ties with Russia because of its actions in Ukraine, while once again (as in August 2008) the NATO–Russia Council proved itself to be useless.

PEACE AND WAR

A meeting in Geneva between Ukraine, Russia, the US and the EU on 17 April sought to start a process of 'de-escalation', the term used in this crisis to try to create an 'off-ramp' from the internationalised civil conflict. The brief joint statement by the countries involved called for 'initial concrete steps to de-escalate tensions and restore security for all citizens', and stipulated a number of measures:

All sides must refrain from any violence, intimidation or provocative actions. The participants strongly condemned and rejected all expressions of extremism, racism and religious intolerance, including anti-semitism.

All illegal armed groups must be disarmed; all illegally seized buildings must be returned to legitimate owners; all illegally occupied streets, squares and other public places in Ukrainian cities and towns must be vacated.

Amnesty will be granted to protestors and to those who have left buildings and other public places and surrendered weapons, with the exception of those found guilty of capital crimes.

It was agreed that the OSCE Special Monitoring Mission should play a leading role in assisting Ukrainian authorities and local communities in the immediate implementation of these de-escalation measures wherever they are needed most, beginning in the coming days. The U.S., E.U. and Russia commit to support this mission, including by providing monitors.

The announced constitutional process will be inclusive, transparent and account-able. It will include the immediate establishment of a broad national dialogue, with outreach to all of Ukraine's regions and political constituencies, and allow for the consideration of public comments and proposed amendments.

The participants underlined the importance of economic and financial stability in Ukraine and would be ready to discuss additional support as the above steps are implemented.[21]

The onus was placed on the Ukrainians to take the initiative, with the international community to assist in the implementation of the de-escalation measures. The signatories agreed that that all armed formations should be disbanded, but it was not clear who would be able to do this, or the scope of the provision – would it include the armed battalions spawned by the Maidan? While the Western powers held Russia responsible for controlling the insurgents in the east and getting them to leave occupied buildings and installations, as we have seen they were mostly not under the direct control of a single authority. The situation was exacerbated by the lack of eastern representation at Geneva. Moscow's attempts to get the supporters for regional autonomy invited had been blocked by Kiev, but now the eastern insurgents were held responsible for fulfilling decisions in whose adoption they were not involved.

The Geneva deal was ignored by both sides, although its principles were to be at the core of all subsequent ceasefires. On 5 May, government forces attacked checkpoints around Slavyansk, with the two sides exchanging mortar fire, and the insurgents were able to down a helicopter using a hand-held air-defence system. On 9 May government forces using tanks and heavy weaponry retook the interior ministry building in Mariupol, in which at least seven 'separatists' were killed and 40 wounded. In another action in Mariupol on 16 May insurgents attacked a local military base. The insurgents had taken over Prokofiev International Airport in Donetsk on 26 May, but in a ferocious counter-attack it was retaken by government forces, at great cost in lives and damage. On 28 May insurgents in Slavyansk shot down a military helicopter, killing all 14 servicemen on board, and on 14 June in Lugansk insurgents shot down a Ukrainian military aircraft, killing all 49 servicemen on board (of whom nine were crew). And so the fighting went on. Both sides were subject to international humanitarian law (the laws of war), and both sides egregiously disregarded them, above all in targeting civilian populations, using disproportionate force, not respecting the rights of journalists and abusing the rights of prisoners. Neither Ukraine nor Russia is a signatory party to the Rome Statute establishing the International Criminal Court, with the mandate to try people suspected of genocide, crimes against humanity or war crimes, so it would take a UN Security Council referral to activate an investigation.

Right Sector turned itself into a political party but retained its armed battalions, allied with the football 'ultras', and went to war in the south-east. In April the Donbas battalion was created, while the Aidar battalion was drawn from the mainstream Maidan self-defence units. The Azov battalion drew particular attention for the ferocity of its commitment, taking the Donetsk suburb of Marinka in late July and thereby opening the path for regular forces to attack the city. Azov flew the neo-Nazi *Wolfsangel* (Wolf's Hook) on the background of the *Schwarze Sonne* (Black Sun) on their banner. The battalion was founded by Andriy Biletsky, the head of the extremist Social–National Assembly, who argued: 'The historic mission of our nation in this critical moment is to lead the White Races of the world in a final crusade for their survival [...] A crusade against the Semite-led Untermenschen.'[22] Their ideology harked back to the integral nationalism of the 1930s and 1940s, aiming to create a '*natsiokratiya*' (ethnocracy) based on syndicates representing the different classes of the population. They appealed to Ukraine's European identity, but their Europe was one of corporatism and traditionalism: 'We consider the present tendency of Europe leads to the destruction of civilisation, with no control of immigration, the destruction of the family, of religious identity and of everything that made Europe Europe.'[23] This was accompanied by an assertive foreign policy that included the nuclear rearmament of Ukraine. On 23 July Svoboda registered a motion with the Rada's secretariat to restore Ukraine's status as a nuclear power. Rather surprisingly, this evoked no response from the Atlantic security community. In the end some three dozen volunteer battalions were created, with the number of fighters swelling to around 8,000. While formally subordinate to the Ukrainian Ministry of Internal Affairs (MVD), they were in effect private armies. These proto-Freikorps forces attracted all sorts of malcontents and radicals from across Ukraine, and represented a substantial threat to Poroshenko's ability to pursue an independent policy. He was constantly threatened by a 'third Maidan' when he suggested compromises, and these forces would take control if the government fell.

The fighting became increasingly vicious, with significant casualties on both sides, accompanied by the exodus of citizens who now became refugees if they crossed into Russia, or 'internally displaced persons' (IDPs) if they moved elsewhere in Ukraine. Unleashed against the insurgency was a crew no less motley than the insurgents themselves. The new National Guard absorbed most of the Maidan militants, among whom, as we have seen, right-wing nationalists figured prominently, and their indiscipline and cruelty in the Donbas became infamous. The volunteer detachments organised by 'warlords' such as Kolomoisky added to the volatile mix, as did the worker detachments raised by regional oligarchs such as Akhmetov. There were also volunteer units created by politicians. The most famous of these was Oleg Lyashko, who led volunteer battalions to the region. In a famous incident in mid-May he was seen humiliating a captured insurgent and the self-proclaimed defence minister of the DPR, Igor Kakidzyanov, who appeared in his underwear and with his hands bound. The trademark signature of his black-clad paramilitaries was to strip captives to their underwear, put bags on their heads, and lecture them on camera for their treacherous behaviour. His popularity soared, turning him into a serious political force and winning him over 8 per cent of the vote in the presidential election. Only later did the regular army take the initiative and lead the offensive.

The armed forces had been starved of funds for two decades, and under Yanukovych their resources had been pillaged.[24] As Parubiy, secretary of the NSDC, put it:

> Unfortunately, we now realize that our defense forces were deliberately sabotaged and weakened by the previous government in Kiev, in collaboration with Moscow, to subordinate Ukraine to Russia's imperialist policies. We inherited a dilapidated army, a security and intelligence service awash with Russian agents, a demoralized law-enforcement system and corrupt courts and prosecutors.[25]

The poor state of the Ukraine armed forces was soon exposed. Much of its weaponry and other materiel had been allowed to decay or been sold off, and there were not many more than 6,000 combat-ready troops in an army numbering some 80,000. The regular armed forces lacked training, intelligence equipment and geo-referencing systems. Once launched into combat, the army suffered from defections and desertions. Attempts by the Ukrainian military to dislodge the militants, including the use of air power and later Grad missile-launchers in civilian areas, did little more than harden local sentiment against Kiev. The creation of the National Guard, consisting largely of far right militants and others from the Maidan self-defence forces, had the advantage of removing these militants from the centre of Kiev and other western Ukrainian towns, but they often lacked discipline and treated south-east Ukraine as occupied territory, regularly committing atrocities against civilians and captured 'terrorists'. In addition, the 'third force' of oligarch-sponsored irregular militias, notably those funded by Kolomoisky, added to the volatile mix.

In his speech at West Point on 28 May, Obama boasted of American success in isolating Russia. He dismissed those who suggest that 'America is in decline, or has seen its global leadership slip away – [they] are either misreading history or engaged in partisan politics', and insisted that 'America must always lead on the world stage'. As for the current crisis:

> In Ukraine, Russia's recent actions recall the days when Soviet tanks rolled into Eastern Europe. But this isn't the Cold War. Our ability to shape world opinion helped isolate Russia right away. Because of American leadership, the world immediately condemned Russian actions. Europe and the G-7 joined with us to impose sanctions. NATO reinforced our commitment to Eastern European allies. The IMF is helping to stabilize Ukraine's economy. OSCE monitors brought the eyes of the world to unstable parts of Ukraine. This mobilization of world opinion and institutions served as a counterweight to Russian propaganda, Russian troops on the border, and armed militias.[26]

Soon after, Obama's visit to Europe, including Poland, to commemorate the sixtieth anniversary of the D-Day landings in Normandy, was once again used as an occasion to isolate Russia. The French president, François Hollande, however, took the opportunity to engineer a meeting between Putin and the newly elected Poroshenko, establishing what was to become a pragmatic period of interaction. In all of this, the EU as an institution was redundant and could not be taken as a serious, positive independent player in European – let alone world – politics.

NO WAY OUT

On coming to office, Poroshenko outlined three main challenges: the preservation of a 'unified Ukraine', including stability in eastern Ukraine; the European choice for closer ties to the West; and the return of Crimea. The latter goal, he stressed, would be pursued through diplomatic methods and excluded the military option. As for maintaining the unity of Ukraine, this was obviously a priority and one that had a solid basis. Numerous opinion polls in early 2014 repeatedly showed sizeable majorities in the east and the south supporting Ukrainian unity and only small minorities in favour of secession or accession to Russia. In the event, Poroshenko was unable to build on what was clearly a strong sense of membership of the Ukrainian state, although favouring a pluralist interpretation. Instead, his initial comments were far from conciliatory: 'The first steps of our entire team at the beginning of the presidency will concentrate on ending the war, ending the chaos, ending the disorder and bringing peace to Ukrainian soil, to a united, single Ukraine.'[27] His promise to wrap up the ATO 'in a matter of hours' entrenched the hardliners on both sides, and the irreconcilable tone was repeated in his inaugural speech on 7 June.

The insurgents in the south-east were characterised as 'terrorists', and thus their demands and concerns were rendered null and void. The resolution of the long-standing Ukrainian identity, it appeared, would be settled on the battlefield. The ATO was intensified, with the regular army reinforced by volunteers in the National Guard. On 5 June the Verkhovna Rada adopted changes to the law on terrorism, signed into law by the president on 18 June, giving greater powers to the security forces and legalising the use of the regular army in 'counter-terrorism' operations. Commanders gained the power 'to temporarily restrict the rights of local populations' as well as to 'shut down business entities – fully or partially'. On the other side, the Russian foreign minister Sergei Lavrov proposed a resolution to the UN, but stressed that it would not include the introduction of Russian peacekeepers to the region, a demand repeatedly made by the rebels.[28] A genuine peacekeeping force could only be introduced if sanctioned by the UN Security Council, otherwise it would be another term for occupation.

After several false starts, on 20 June Poroshenko announced a unilateral ceasefire to last a week, while outlining a 15-point peace plan. Building on the Geneva deal, he proposed an amnesty for rebel fighters who had not committed serious crimes, as well as safe passage for volunteers seeking to return to Russia. It also called for decentralisation that would allow a greater degree of self-rule in the east, the fundamental demand of the militants. The insurgents were to surrender and a 10-kilometre-wide security zone would be established along the border with Russia, while the decentralisation excluded federalisation or official status for the Russian language. On 23 June talks were held in Donetsk involving Poroshenko's representative, the former Ukrainian president Leonid Kuchma, and the militant leaders. Also in attendance was an OSCE representative, the Russian ambassador to Ukraine, the pro-Russian politician Viktor Medvedchuk (on the US sanctions list for his part in the annexation of Crimea). The fact that he was trusted in Moscow rendered him suspicious to the new Ukrainian authorities. Following the meeting, the self-declared prime minister of DPR, Alexander Borodai, announced that the militants also agreed to the ceasefire. It was soon threatened when on 24 June the insurgents shot down the helicopter that was carrying equipment and specialists to monitor the ceasefire near Slavyansk, killing nine personnel.

On that day the Russian Federation Council revoked the ruling of 1 March, adopted before the annexation of Crimea, that authorised Russia to deploy troops on Ukrainian territory, 'in order to normalise and regulate the situation in the eastern regions of Ukraine, and due to the start of the three-way talks on the issue', as Putin's spokesman Dmitry Peskov put it.[29] In 2009 the Russian president had been granted a 'universal mandate' allowing him to deploy troops abroad, so this act was meant to signal that Moscow was set on the path of conciliation. Throughout, Russian actions lacked consistency and even coherence. There was no response to the first wave of sanctions imposed in April, whereas retaliation in the form, for example, of stopping cooperation over Afghanistan and blocking the Northern Distribution Network, the rail route for the removal of American forces and materiel, or even withdrawal from the Comprehensive Test Ban Treaty (CTBT), would have signalled Russia's readiness for confrontation. Instead, the repeal signalled Russia's openness for rapprochement and that the country would not intervene militarily, but this allowed the full force of the Ukrainian armed forces to be unleashed against the Donbas militants. Despite the virulence of the anti-Western campaign, Putin clearly did not want to burn all the bridges back to a normal relationship with the EU and the US. Nevertheless, the exploitation of unrest in the south-east to exercise leverage over the rest of Ukraine to achieve desired policy outcomes – notably federalisation and neutralisation – remained.

The insurgents had earlier insisted that there could be no talks until Ukraine withdrew its forces, but, after consultations in Moscow, Borodai (who is a Russian citizen) softened his stance. His security advisor was Sergei Kavtaradze, a military historian and an expert on the conduct of civil wars. This was another example of the eclectic character of the rebel leadership. Borodai compared the fighting in the Donbas with the Spanish Civil War, as it drew in volunteers (notably from Serbia) to join the new international brigades, now united around the ideology of anti-Americanism and geopolitical pluralism.[30] The negotiations were also attended by Alexander Khodakovsky, the commander of the Vostok battalion (no connection with the body of the same name in the Chechen wars), and Valery Bolotov, the leader of the insurgent forces in Lugansk. Notably absent was Girkin, also a Russian citizen, who commanded the insurgent forces in Slavyansk. Speaking in Vienna on 24 June,

Putin warned that a ceasefire and calling on the rebels to disarm without addressing their long-term political grievances would come to nothing.[31] He qualified his support for Poroshenko's plan by insisting:

> It is important that this ceasefire open the way to a dialogue between all of the parties to the combat, so as to find solutions that will be acceptable to all sides, in order to ensure that people in south-east Ukraine have no doubt that they are an integral part of the country.[32]

The talks gave no immediate breakthrough, and Poroshenko's peace plan was condemned at a four-hour extended meeting with the hawkish NSDC on 30 June. Poroshenko's proposal to extend the ceasefire was now dropped, and on 1 July he announced the resumption of hostilities: 'We will attack and we will liberate our land. The end of the ceasefire is our response to terrorists, rebels, looters, all those who mock civilians, who paralyze the economy of the region.'[33] The ceasefire was perceived to have given the insurgents a chance to rearm and regroup. There was not a word here about reaching out to his citizens in the south-east; and, indeed, in the words of one *Moscow Times* journalist, the lack of compassion 'by residents of both Moscow and Kiev over the conflict in eastern Ukraine and the future of Ukraine as a whole ought to give us serious pause'.[34] A hate-filled generation was being nurtured. Poroshenko had come under enormous pressure from the 'war party' in Kiev to continue the attack, with the NSDC urging him to take active measures. Lyashko reported that he had heard from the president 'what he had wanted to hear from him', and, satisfied, he returned to continue his vigilante activities on the eastern front.

There was also a 'war party' in Washington, although both US vice president Joe Biden and Secretary of State John Kerry urged Kiev to exercise restraint. It was not clear that Kerry was able to control his subordinates. Equally, the relationship with Kiev assumed some classic Cold War features, in which the 'client' tail was able to wag the 'patron' dog. There was very little at stake for the US in renewed conflict, whereas the burden of the Ukraine crisis would be borne by Russia and its European partners. Although Poroshenko was responding to the demands for a military victory coming from radical nationalists, in the end his position was weakened by revulsion at the heavy death toll and the destruction of the Donbas. There were many cases in which Kiev's forces refused orders to fire on their compatriots. In the end over 90 per cent of Ukrainian armed forces were deployed in the south-east, accompanied by successive waves of call-up reservists. The Ukrainian armed forces had learned to avoid infantry combat, and instead launched air strikes and long-range artillery bombardments against apartment blocks and villages. This rained down indiscriminate fire on heavily populated areas, causing numerous civilian casualties. This was justified by alleging that the rebels placed their own ordinance next to civilian objects. There are documented cases of this, although in heavily built areas almost any position would be next to a hospital or school; and, as the UN stressed during the Israeli bombardment of Gaza in July and August, the laws of war state that there is no excuse for killing civilians. It looked as if the tide of war was turning to Kiev's advantage.

Stephen Cohen notes how on 2 May at the UN Security Council the US ambassador, Samantha Power, suspended

> her revered 'Responsibility to Protect' doctrine, [and] gave Kiev's leaders a US license to kill. Lauding their 'remarkable, almost unimaginable, restraint', as Obama himself did after Odessa, she continued, 'Their response is reasonable, it is proportional, and frankly it is what any one of our countries would have done.'

Cohen notes that on 26 June Kerry demanded that the Russian president 'in the next few hours [...] help disarm' the resistance in the south-east, 'as though they are not motivated by any of Ukraine's indigenous conflicts but are merely Putin's private militias'. In sum:

> We may honourably disagree about the causes and resolution of the Ukrainian crisis, the worst US–Russian confrontation in decades, but not about the deeds that are rising to the level of war crimes, if they have not already done so.[35]

In early July an intensive round of diplomacy was led by the German and French foreign ministers, Frank-Walter Steinmeier and Laurent Fabius respectively. A hastily convened meeting in Berlin on 2 July brought them together with Lavrov and the new Ukrainian foreign minister, Pavlo Klimkin. As far as the Russians were concerned, the absence of the Americans increased the chances of the peaceful regulation of the conflict. As Lavrov put it in a television interview on 28 June: 'Peace within the warring country [Ukraine] is more likely if negotiations were left to Russia and Europe', and he noted: 'Our American colleagues still favour pushing the Ukrainian leadership towards confrontation.' The hawks in Washington warned the Europeans against 'craven surrender' to Russian aggression (in the words of a *Washington Post* editorial on 2 July), but European leaders were beginning, surprisingly, to show some independent resolve. The provisional deal of 2 July was far-reaching, and included not only a ceasefire and further talks involving the OSCE but also strengthened control over the Russo-Ukrainian border, which would stop the supply of personnel and materiel to the insurgents. The Donbas resistance movement now turned into fierce critics of Putin, accusing him of betrayal and worse. Such nuances were lost on the hawks, with the *Washington Post* thundering: 'A failure by the West to act following such explicit rhetoric would be a craven surrender that would provoke only more Russian aggression'.[36]

On 5 July the insurgent forces under Girkin retreated from Slavyansk and regrouped in Donetsk. By that time over 100,000 refugees had fled the region. Clearly, no help was officially going to come from Russia, despite Girkin's appeals for military aid. The rebels now faced almost certain defeat as the Ukrainian army advanced on all sides. As Pavel Gubarev, the former advertising executive and extreme Russian nationalist who became one of the founders of the DPR, put it on 9 July: 'We are surrounded – we will defend our city to the end, there is no room to move back – we have a situation where we must win or die.'[37] The imposition of a new round of American sanctions on 16 July further narrowed Putin's room for manoeuvre. What could have been the quiet withdrawal of support to groups who had never entirely been controllable proxies would now look like capitulation to hostile Western powers, and that was simply politically impossible in the febrile atmosphere in Russia that the regime had done so much to provoke. Intensified sanctions at this point were entirely counterproductive.

By July 2014 the combined interior-ministry forces, including the National Guard, had swelled to 35,000, including some from abroad, reinforcing the 77,000 regular troops. On 31 July the Ukrainian parliament authorised an additional $743 million for the army, to be financed by a mandatory 'war tax' of 1.5 per cent on all incomes. Already Ukraine was the second-worst-performing economy in the world, with the hryvnia losing 70 per cent of its value by September, when it was trading at 14 to the dollar, a deep recession that the European Bank for Reconstruction and Development (EBRD) expected would see a 9 per cent year-on-year fall in GDP. Prices and unemployment were rising fast. The Donbas had provided a sixth of Ukrainian GDP, but war had removed much of that. Nevertheless, money could still be found to strengthen the frontier. The head of the NSDC, Parubiy, announced on 16 June that Ukraine planned to build a wall along its border with Russia to 'avoid any future provocations from the Russian side'.[38] On 5 September Yatsenyuk announced the plan to build what was later called the 'European Rampart' (*Evropeisky val*) along the border with Russia. In the first instance there would be a four-metre-wide and two-metre-deep ditch equipped with electronic systems. On the 25th anniversary of the fall of the Berlin Wall, there can be no better symbol of the failure of European politics in our era.

The conflict provoked a humanitarian catastrophe. The generation whose grandparents had suffered so much during collectivisation and World War II looked forward to living in peace in a Europe, 'whole and free', but once again they were visited by war. By June some 250 hotels, summer camps and other sites were converted into centres housing up to 30,000 refugees, while another 70,000 escaped across the border into Russia.[39] By late August the UN refugee agency (UNHCR) reported that at least 285,000 people had fled their homes because of the conflict, with some 190,000 IDPs in Ukraine and 17,000 in Crimea. In addition, 25,000 had gone to Belarus, 1,250 to Poland, and 207,000 to Russia, of whom 88,000 asked for temporary refuge and 119,000 applied either for temporary residence or citizenship.[40] The authorities reported that over 800,000 Ukrainians had entered Russia without registering. In July Amnesty International issued a report detailing kidnapping and torture in eastern Ukraine, and in September a further report criticised the 'non-selective' shooting, as a result of which over 1,000 civilians died. The report condemned the lack of oversight over the volunteer units, condemning in particular the Aidar battalion for 'abductions, unlawful detention, ill-treatment, theft, extortion and possible executions'.[41]

From the very beginning Russian policy was caught between bad and very bad options. It was clear that 'Novorossiya' was not Crimea, where there had long been a powerful irredentist movement calling for reunification with Russia. There was nothing of the sort in the Donbas, where the overwhelming majority sought a new settlement *within* Ukraine. Separatist aspirations only came later, after Yanukovych fled and the new authorities made several ill-judged moves in the absence of effective representation from the east, and then launched an all-out war against 'terrorists'. The fragmented and questionable nature of the resistance, moreover, meant that Moscow lacked a credible interlocutor in Ukraine. The only serious politician who could have fulfilled this role was Medvedchuk, Kuchma's former chief of staff, but he was unpopular and was associated with too many failed projects. Above all, the political programme advanced by Moscow lacked substantive popularity in Ukraine. Only 13 per cent, for example, supported the idea of federalisation. This helps explain Moscow's more conciliatory approach, reinforced by the fear of 'level-three' sanctions that would be designed to blast whole sectors of the Russian economy. Russia and Europe sought to avoid moving to that stage, which would immeasurably damage both.

In his speech to diplomats on 1 July Putin adopted a regretful tone. He put the conflict in a broader context:

> We need to understand clearly that the events provoked in Ukraine are the con-
> centrated outcome of the notorious containment policy. As you know, its roots lie
> deep in history and it is clear that unfortunately this policy did not stop with the
> end of the Cold War. [...] I would like to stress that what happened in Ukraine was
> the culmination of the negative tendencies in international affairs that had been
> building up for years. We have long been warning about this, and unfortunately,
> our predictions came true.

He outlined Russia's main concerns:

> What did our partners expect from us as the developments in Ukraine unfolded? We clearly had no right to abandon the residents of Crimea and Sevastopol to the mercy of nationalist and radical militants; we could not allow our access to the Black Sea to be significantly limited; we could not allow NATO forces to eventually come to the land of Crimea and Sevastopol, the land of Russian military glory, and cardinally change the balance of forces in the Black Sea area. This would mean giving up practically everything that Russia had fought for since the times of Peter the Great, or maybe even earlier – historians should know.

As for the latest peace attempts, he stressed the active part played by Russian diplomats, but:

> Unfortunately, President Poroshenko has resolved to resume military action, and we failed – when I say 'we', I mean my colleagues in Europe and myself – we failed to convince him that the road to a secure, stable and inviolable peace cannot lie through war. So far, Mr Poroshenko was not directly linked to the order to begin military action, and only now did he take full responsibility, and not only military, but political as well, which is much more important.[42]

The four-party Berlin talks had offered a genuine chance of stopping the violence, but it appeared that the hawks preferred war rather than a deal in which Russia was involved. Putin had prevented the US from launching a bombing campaign in Syria in September 2013, and Washington sought at all costs to avoid Russia once again garnering the laurels of peace. The Ukrainian offensive breached several international treaties on the conduct of war, and in due course the Kiev regime would have to answer for its actions to international war crimes tribunals.

Putin was coming under enormous pressure to offer succour to the Donbas insurgents and to stop the killing of civilians. As Putin put it in his 1 July speech, he 'would like to make clear' that Moscow would be compelled to protect 'Russians and Russian-speaking citizens of Ukraine [...] I am referring to people who consider themselves part of the broad Russian community; they may not necessarily be ethnic Russians, but they consider themselves Russian people.' There had been a powerful upwelling of domestic support for the resistance movement in the Donbas, to which Putin's fate now became effectively tied – a situation of dependency that he had devoted his whole presidency to avoiding. Already insurgent leaders, such as Girkin, were loudly accusing the Kremlin of betrayal in not providing adequate support. Radicals and nationalists, such as Alexander Dugin, Sergei Kurginyan and Alexander Barkashov (head of the ultra-nationalist Russian National Unity), were raising money, recruiting volunteers and using their extensive influence in Russia's security establishment to provide support for the Donbas rebels.

There was much talk of Russia mimicking the West and imposing a no-fly zone over the Donbas, although in the end Russia appears to have decided to remove Ukraine's control of the air by covertly supplying anti-aircraft missiles. There was increasing pressure for some sort of 'humanitarian' intervention to assist the suffering population, but which would also block Kiev's military victory. There was a full-scale war and a massive humanitarian disaster on Russia's doorstep, but a military intervention threatened to draw Russia into a direct conflict with Ukraine and its Western backers, a conflict that Russia could not hope to win. Like the Afghanistan war in the 1980s, the outcome could in the end be the fall of the government in Moscow. Unlike the Soviet Union, however, Putin faced powerful domestic pressures.

In his study of the Ukraine crisis, the well-known Russian publicist Nikolai Starikov argued that in 2013 Russia moved from its long-term defensive posture to a more activist diplomacy. In Syria, for example, 'Russia did not allow Syrian statehood to be destroyed by the [United] States'; in Ukraine the EU's 'blitzkrieg' was repulsed, and in general Russia found itself on the frontline against the aggressive world politics of the US.[43] Starikov is only one of a vast 'nationalist' civil society that long pre-dates Putin, and towards which after 2012 Putin tacked (having lost the support of the liberal intelligentsia), but which was certainly far from satisfied with his characteristic caution. Indeed, disappointed nationalists began to compare him to Slobodan Milošević, who had fuelled intense Serbian nationalism against Croats and others, only to back down under Western pressure and betray the Serbian diaspora.[44] Although Putin presides over an all-encompassing power system, there are domestic constraints that deprive him of the total 'agency' powers assumed by his critics.

DEATH IN THE AIR

A bad situation became much worse with the shooting down of Malaysia Airlines Flight MH17 from Amsterdam to Kuala Lumpur on 17 July, with the loss of the lives of all 298 people on board, including 15 crew members. Of these, 193 were Dutch, a national calamity of the first order. The plane had been flying at some 33,000 feet and was apparently brought down by a ground-to-air missile fired from near Torez (Snizhne) in the eastern part of the Donetsk region, territory in the hands of the insurgents. The debris was scattered over a large area near the village of Grabovo. The tragedy was followed by an intense period of accusations and recriminations between Washington, Moscow and other European capitals. Shrillest of all was Samantha Power, 'who loses no opportunity to rehearse her trademark denunciations of Russia'.[45] The US imposed intensified sanctions even before the details were clear, while the EU prepared some tougher measures but held off applying them until at least preliminary investigations were complete. There was considerable controversy over whether the insurgents had access to an SA-11 Buk missile-launcher, the system with the capacity to bring down an aircraft at that height. There are plenty of eyewitness accounts, as well as US intelligence sources, indicating that a convoy of vehicles, including a heavy vehicle carrying the Buk system, had crossed the Russian border in the vicinity of Torez shortly before the crash. However, the self-styled prime minister of the DPR, Borodai, insisted that the rebels had nothing to do with the crash.[46]

This was contradicted by Khodakovsky, the head of the Vostok battalion. He is reported to have told Reuters: 'That Buk I know about. I heard about it. I think they sent it back. [...] They probably sent it back in order to remove proof of its presence.' He later denied that he had made this admission.[47] Equally, the Kiev government's attempts to categorise the awful event as a terrorist act were mistaken. A terrorist act is the deliberate targeting of civilians, and in this case it was almost certainly a dreadful mistake. No one had planned to shoot down a civilian airliner, just as the USS *Vincennes* had not deliberately shot down an Iranian airliner in 1988. However, at the least, Russia was irresponsible to have given lethal weapons to forces who did not know how to use them, and, even worse, to have operated them without adequate means of identifying targets. Broader culpability lay with all sides, reaching as far as Kiev, Moscow and Washington, who stoked the fires of war. Hundreds of civilians had died in the Donbas; their homes were relentlessly pounded by Ukrainian aircraft and shelled by cannon and mortars, and tens of thousands had fled to Russia and the rest of Ukraine.

The breakdown of the ceasefire and the accompanying talks, as well as the Berlin negotiations, had clearly enraged Putin. From Moscow's perspective, peace had been on offer and it was sabotaged by those who backed Ukraine's militants. This is why in his response Putin stressed the ambient conditions that had provoked the tragedy. Nevertheless, although notoriously risk-averse, in this case he allowed armaments to be supplied to groups over which he had little control. This meant that effectively the Kremlin became hostage to these forces, a position that Putin had dedicated his whole presidency to avoiding. What had appeared to be a logical response to the threat of an alien security bloc coming right up against Russia's borders was becoming not only a security challenge but a fundamental political threat to the Kremlin regime.

The US imposed a new round of sanctions on 16 July, despite Russia's conciliatory stance. This time some of Russia's major energy companies and banks were targeted as punishment for Moscow's alleged continued support for the insurgency. The sanctions included the freezing of assets belonging to defence companies and a number of senior Russian officials. The new measures were reinforced in milder form by the EU, including restrictions on lending for investment. Obama insisted that the sanctions were intended to remind Russia 'that its actions in Ukraine have consequences', and called for the flow of fighters and weapons across the border to be halted.[48] A UN report released on 28 July stated that more than 1,000 civilians had been killed since the conflict had begun in earnest in early April. The advance of the Ukrainian forces was accompanied by the indiscriminate bombardment of residential areas with Grad missiles, shells and airborne missiles. Although denied by Kiev, who accused the insurgents of shelling their own territory, a report by Human Rights Watch detailed the human-rights and international-law violations by Ukrainian forces. The report also condemned attacks by the insurgents on medical units and personnel. It noted at least five cases where hospitals were hit by explosives, and, since they were in insurgent territory, it is assumed that the Kiev authorities were responsible. Grad, Uragan and other projectiles killed many in the urban centres of Lugansk and Donetsk. Both sides, the report insisted, violated the laws of war.[49]

The rebel campaign was marred by egregious acts of violence, arbitrary killings, hostage-taking, kidnapping (particularly of women), beatings and generalised intimidation. Igor Bezler, known as 'the Demon', was one of the most feared and brutal of the insurgent leaders (and on this basis was criticised by Girkin), using his headquarters in Gorlovka to dispense summary 'justice'. The town was subjected to a merciless pounding with Grad rockets before it was taken by government forces in early August.[50] By the end of July 363 Ukrainian troops had been killed and 1,434 wounded in the 'anti-terrorist' operation. Kiev's forces by then had pinned the insurgents back into their strongholds of the cities of Donetsk and Lugansk. The self-proclaimed governor of the Donetsk region, Pavel Gubarev, called on Russia to send troops: 'Of course it would be great to see Russian peacekeepers here: strong artillery units, tank brigades', he said. 'This war would be over in a day, maybe two.'[51] The onset of street-fighting promised yet more civilian casualties, although by then tens of thousands had fled. By mid-August the violence had escalated, and the UN estimated that the death toll had risen to 2,086, with about 5,000 injured.

By this time the first generation of insurgent leaders, motivated by a romantic separatism, gave way to the professionalism of Girkin, the overall rebel military commander. Later he was flanked by Vladimir Antyufeyev, who became deputy prime minister but acted as security chief. Antyufeyev was a Russian citizen who had previously headed internal security in Transnistria. This was accompanied by the 'Ukrainisation' of the insurgent leadership. Borodai was replaced as the prime minister of the DPR by Alexander Zakharchenko, who had led a police advocacy group before the war. In Lugansk Valery Bolotov, a Russian citizen, 'temporarily' resigned and was replaced by Igor Plotnitsky. Girkin himself resigned as DPR defence minister on 14 August and was replaced by Vladimir Kononov, a local resident. Girkin had become a cult figure, respected for his military skill and his attempt to fight the war in an honourable manner, insisting in particular that prisoners be treated in accordance with the Geneva Convention. Much is made of his Russian security-service affiliation, but far more significant were his political views. He was certainly an old-style conservative and quite possibly a monarchist, and soon became a rallying point of the nationalist opposition in Russia.

The preliminary report of 9 September 2014 on the MH17 disaster by the Dutch Safety Board revealed that the cockpit and other parts of the fuselage were hit by 'a large number of high-energy objects', causing the plane to fall apart over eastern Ukraine. This is consistent with the plane's having been brought down by an anti-aircraft missile, but does not exclude the possibility that an air-to-air missile was used. The final report is due to be published by July 2015, and the Dutch prime minister, Mark Rutte, noted: 'We have to guard against drawing premature conclusions. The case is still open.'[52]

TIDES OF WAR

Kiev's main concern was to prevent Russia establishing a protectorate or some other form of permanent influence in the form of a 'frozen conflict' in the region. The rebels' defeat would remove Moscow's remaining leverage over Ukrainian policy. On the other side, the defeat of the insurgents would humiliate Putin and demonstrate that his Ukraine policy had been ill-advised and poorly executed: he had supported a hopeless insurrection with just enough to keep it going for several months, provoking a storm of sanctions, while not providing enough assistance to give the insurgency a realistic chance of defeating the Ukrainian forces. Putin is not someone who would allow this to happen, so once committed he doggedly fought on.

Meanwhile, the attempt to find a diplomatic solution to the crisis was pursued bilaterally in negotiations between German chancellor Angela Merkel and Putin. She remained one of the few Western leaders with whom Putin remained on relatively good terms, with each fluently speaking the language of the other. The key issues were the stabilisation of Ukraine's border, establishing a framework for Ukraine's economic recovery, and an equitable and enduring energy agreement. Crimea's incorporation into Russia would have to be regulated, something to which Ukraine of course would object, as would a number of UN members. In return for a guarantee of Ukraine's territorial integrity (in other words, withdrawal of support for the Donbas insurgency), Crimea would be granted devolved powers and the deal would be underwritten by a multi-billion-dollar compensation package for the loss of the rent it used to receive for the Sevastopol base.[53] Putin devoted his leadership to insulating the regime from formal political pressure, but he was highly sensitive to popular moods. His high ratings would swiftly evaporate if Russia's policy was seen to have driven the country into a dead end. The anti-intervention movement was weak, but would grow if the pain was seen to outweigh the gain. Already Alexei Kudrin, the finance minister between 2000 and 2011, warned that the Ukraine crisis would drive Russia into a 'historic confrontation' that would hold back the country's development in all spheres.[54]

The foreign ministers of France, Germany, Russia and Ukraine continued to try to hammer out a deal in negotiations in Berlin. The Ukrainian foreign minister, Pavlo Klimkin, insisted that before serious talks could begin, the insurgent militia would have to disarm and Kiev to establish full control over the borders. The demand effectively meant unilateral surrender, which was hardly an acceptable starting point for dialogue. Despite the setbacks, the insurgents still considered themselves a military force that could take on Kiev. It is not clear who would be able to convince the insurgent forces to compromise. The West assumed that was Moscow's role; but then who would try to convince Kiev to sit down with the rebels? Both Fabius and Steinmeier were ready to do this, but ultimately their voices counted for little. US vice president Joe Biden was in frequent communication with Poroshenko, and although he may not have been urging him on to victory, he certainly did not publicly call on him to find a negotiated settlement. European security was hostage to a faraway country with little stake in ending the conflict. The impasse was complete.

The crisis has had a devastating effect, with Donbas exports to Russia in the first half of 2014 falling by a third, driving down living standards and exacerbating unemployment and political discontent. The country's largest chemicals producer, Stirol, halted production in early May for fear of an environmental disaster, according to the owner Ostchem, part of Firtash's Group DF. In August the Enakievo Metallurgy Plant, owned by Metinvest, was severely damaged by shelling. Worse, war damage had stopped half of Ukraine's 115 coal mines and the country was running low on supplies. Ukraine had been Europe's second-largest coal-producer, but output had fallen by 22 per cent year-on-year in July to 5.6 million tonnes. The use of thermal coal had been ramped up to save gas in electricity generation, and there was even talk of importing supplies. On 1 August Gazprom announced that Ukraine's outstanding debt for gas supplies now stood at $5.3 billion.

Instead of using the IMF loan to underwrite economic reform, funds had been diverted to fund military operations in the east. There were increasing fears that the $17 billion IMF package would fall apart, forcing the country to default and restructure its debts. An added piquancy is added to the situation by the fact that if Ukraine's debt-to-GDP ratio rose above 60 per cent, as became inevitable, Moscow could demand immediate repayment of the $3 billion bond it had issued in December 2013 as the first tranche of the $15 billion loan. The hryvnia remained in free fall, and the country was on the verge of bankruptcy. Ukraine ranked one hundred and ninth in the world in terms of per capita GDP ($3,920), but in terms of government spending it was eighteenth, at 48 per cent of GDP, an imbalance that was unsustainable. Conflicts between the oligarchs continued, the fate of constitutional reform unclear, and, as the commentator Arkady Moshes says, there remained 'strong doubts whether Ukraine will be able to successfully transform, to separate business and politics, to become a functioning economy and liberal democracy'. Moshes stresses that 'there seems to be an assumption that Russia will not allow Kiev a military victory in eastern Ukraine, whatever the costs', and makes the sensible point that 'Russia's demands do not look excessive or exorbitant from the point of view of realpolitik: the recognition of Crimea's annexation and keeping Ukraine outside the EU and NATO.'[55] It was not so much EU membership that was at issue but the terms on which the Association Agreement would be implemented.

By mid-August it looked as if the Ukrainian military offensive was close to victory, with the cities of Lugansk and Donetsk effectively encircled. Russia had underestimated the determination of the new Ukrainian government to retake the territory that had slipped from its control, but in the event Kiev overextended its forces. By that time one estimate suggested that 11,000 soldiers had been killed and another 19,000 lost and injured.[56] This was an exaggeration, but Kiev's official statement on 7 September that 864 soldiers had been killed was on the low side, especially since three drafts to the army had sent thousands of reluctant conscripts to the 'front'. By that time the war had taken over 3,000 lives and driven over a million from their homes.

The only way to explain the losses was to blame direct Russian intervention. An interview with Mark Franchetti of the *Sunday Times* on the Savik Shuster show on Ukrainian television on 22 June ended in disorder. A veteran reporter, having visited the Chechnya war zone many times, Franchetti tried to provide an honest appraisal of what he saw in the Donbas, including when travelling with the Vostok battalion. He stressed that most of the insurgents were Ukrainians, with a few Russian volunteers, most without military experience, basically fighting to defend their homes from 'fascists', especially after the Maidan and Odessa events. They hoped for support from Russia, which was simply not forthcoming. Indeed, if the border was crossed, the insurgents were interned by Russian border forces. He could find no 'Chechens' among the Vostok forces, despite repeated reports to that effect in the Ukrainian media. After a few minutes he was shouted down by the studio panel, which included Mikheil Saakashvili.[57] The OSCE observer mission found no evidence of weapons or military personnel pouring in from Russia. On 16 August Alexander Zakharchenko apparently admitted at an official meeting that Russia had contributed 150 armoured vehicles and 1,200 'fighters trained for four months in the Russian Federation'. It is claimed that a company of Pskov paratroopers (from the elite Seventy-sixth Airborne Division) were destroyed on 19 August in a battle for the road to Lugansk, and the Russian press reported on their funerals. In the Duma, Dmitry Gudkov presented a list of 39 soldiers who were buried in Pskov in late August.[58]

The tide of war once again turned, and the rebels broke out of the encirclement around Donetsk to seize the port of Novoazovsk and threatened to retake Mariupol. This prompted a renewed spate of reports claiming that Russian forces were involved in the fighting, although Putin and the Russian authorities continued with their denials. The insurgent forces scored a major victory at Ilovaisk, just south of the city of Donetsk. The 50,000-strong Ukrainian forces suffered a crushing defeat, leaving much of their heavy equipment behind in the rout.[59] If the insurgent forces captured Mariupol, the way would be open to create a land bridge to Crimea. The bloodbath at Ilovaisk exacerbated the breakdown of trust between the volunteer battalions and the regular army command. By now the 'Novorossiya' rebel forces had established a single command structure over their 15,000 personnel, with a general staff deploying brigades and battalions. They had also learned from strategic manuals how to conduct encircling operations, creating so-called 'cauldrons', and to cut off advancing hostile forces from supplies and reinforcements, all of this no doubt with Russian support. There was widespread war-weariness at home, and with winter coming, power shortages and rising unemployment, it was now clear to the Kiev authorities that there would be no military victory.

Russia's demand for the federalisation of Ukraine had fallen into abeyance, but its core demand for an inclusive and representative national government remained. With peace talks in prospect and the Ukrainian military position crumbling, the US once again stepped up accusations that Russian forces were directly involved in combat operations – how otherwise to explain the success of the insurgents? At the same time, in mid-August the Ukrainian parliament adopted legislation that would potentially allow Kiev to impose over 20 different types of sanctions against Russia, including stopping the transit of Russian gas to Europe. The EU seemed remarkably insouciant about this threat to Europe's energy supplies, just as it was to the humanitarian disaster in Lugansk. On 12 August Russia had sent a convoy of some 200 trucks with aid, but this was then held up at the border by the Ukrainian authorities, and only arrived in Lugansk on 22 August, after having unilaterally crossed over into Ukraine.

As for technical proof of a Russian 'invasion', NATO and the State Department had cried wolf so many times that it was natural that observers would be sceptical about the claims, and evidence for a stealth invasion was mixed. In late August Putin had made precisely this point to José Manuel Barroso, when, in response to discussion of troop movements in Ukraine, he responded: 'That's not the problem but […] if I wanted to, I could take Kiev in two weeks.'[60] Barroso, rather shabbily, leaked this as a threat, when in fact Putin's point had been the opposite: if there really were to be an invasion, the world would soon know it. What was not in doubt was the suffering in the Donbas. For Washington and Moscow the conflict was just collateral damage in their geopolitical confrontation. As the anecdote of the time put it, 'America is fighting Russia down to the very last Ukrainian.'

MINSK AND PEACE

On 26 August the Eurasian Customs Union (ECU), Ukraine and the EU met in Minsk on Belarusian president Alexander Lukashenko's initiative to discuss issues associated with the overlapping free-trade areas. The three leaders of the nascent Eurasian Economic Union (EEU) were in attendance, namely Putin, Lukashenko (the host) and President Nursultan Nazarbaev of Kazakhstan. The three had signed the ECU treaty on 29 May, which was to enter force on 1 January 2015 to create the EEU. The Minsk meeting discussed Ukraine's European integration, energy security and the stabilisation of the conflict in the Donbas. Moscow had three main concerns: first, for Ukraine's duties on European goods to be lowered more slowly than envisaged in the current arrangements; second, that more stringent EU regulations would block Russian access to the Ukrainian market; and third, it sought assurances that Russian and European phytosanitary requirements would either be unified or mutually recognised within Ukraine. The European Commission now recognised that the Association Agreement, which was due to be ratified by the Ukrainian parliament in September, would carry risks for Russo-Ukrainian economic relations.

A trilateral working group of Russia, Ukraine and the EU was to work out a strategy by 12 September for managing mutual trade in the new conditions. Putin repeated his concerns about the planned nullification of Ukraine's customs tariffs, technical regulations and phytosanitary standards, noting that the standards in Russia and Europe were incompatible.[61] In his speech at the summit he repeated his now standard complaint that higher-quality EU goods would force Ukrainian items to be dumped onto the Russian market, and at the same time that the re-export of European goods to Russia, after relabelling, via Ukraine could destabilise the Russian market, causing losses of upwards of $3 billion. He once again stressed: 'No one has talked to us about these issues', and that Russia had been told that relations with Ukraine were 'none of our business'.[62] At last the EU started work on ways to find an accommodation with the ECU to prevent the zero-sum options for Ukraine. Moscow drew up a 60-page list of amendments it sought to the Association Agreement, including sections covering tariffs and energy liberalisation. In all, it was looking for 2,376 items out of 11,600 to be modified or excluded. If this trilateral process had begun earlier, as suggested by Putin on innumerable occasions and by Yanukovych in November 2013 but brusquely rejected by Brussels, it could have averted the Ukrainian revolution and civil war in the Donbas. Even now, the talks represented a major concession to Russia, with the EU abandoning its 'us-or-them' strategy which had brought Ukraine to its knees.

In the evening after the multilateral talks Putin and Poroshenko met for two hours to discuss the crisis. This was the first encounter since the two had met in Normandy in early June. Merkel had visited Kiev on 23 August and urged Poroshenko to accept a ceasefire, while in general offering support to the regime.[63] Putin insisted that stopping the fighting was a matter for Ukraine itself – in other words, Russia would not place pressure on the Novorossiya Armed Forces (NAF), as they now called themselves, but Kiev would have to negotiate directly with the rebels if it wanted a ceasefire. Poroshenko announced that a roadmap would be prepared to stop the fighting as soon as possible, but he insisted on a 'ceasefire regime which absolutely must be bilateral in character', recalling the earlier ceasefire in June, which the Ukrainian side believed had allowed the insurgent forces to regroup. Poroshenko argued: 'Our main goal is peace. We are demanding decisive actions which will bring peace on Ukrainian soil', while Putin insisted that it was up to the government in Kiev and separatist leaders to work out conditions for a truce.[64] Poroshenko returned to his 'peace plan', first outlined on 20 June. The fundamental problem was that the plan required the insurgents to lay down their arms and for the border to be secured before negotiations could begin, which was the equivalent of asking for surrender and then to discuss concessions from a position of strength. There was no immediate breakthrough at Minsk, although Poroshenko promised a 'roadmap' that would allow a ceasefire that 'absolutely must be bilateral in character'. Putin insisted that Russia was ready to help build the trust necessary for negotiations, but repeated that it was not for Russia to discuss the specific ceasefire terms between Kiev and the eastern regions.[65] A contact group for Ukrainian reconciliation was established, involving Russia, Ukraine and the OSCE, and a deadline of 12 September was set to outline a peace plan.

On 5 September, following a meeting in Minsk of the 'contact group', Alexander Zakharchenko and the Lugansk prime minister Igor Plotnitsky signed a peace deal, with former president Kuchma acting on behalf of the Ukrainian leadership. Heidi Tagliavini represented the OSCE, while the Russian ambassador to Kiev, Mikhail Zurabov, represented Russia. The rebel forces had stopped the Ukrainian advance, and were recapturing territory around Donetsk and Lugansk and pushing into Mariupol (see Map 6). It was clear that Russia would not allow an unequivocal military victory for Kiev, while the West would not give full-scale support to the Ukrainian military endeavour, hence the ceasefire. It was not sanctions that encouraged the ceasefire but the changing situation on the ground. The core of the 12-point 'Minsk Protocol' had been drafted by Putin two days earlier in the form of a seven-point plan, and agreed with Poroshenko. It included an immediate ceasefire, a full prisoner exchange, the decentralisation of power to the Donetsk and Lugansk regions based on the implicit assumption that they would remain part of Ukraine, permanent monitoring of the Russo-Ukrainian border supervised by the OSCE, a ban on prosecution or persecution of people involved in the events, an 'inclusive national dialogue', measures to improve the humanitarian conditions in the Donbas, the staging of early local elections in the region, the removal of all 'unlawful military formations, military hardware, as well as militants and mercenaries from the territory of Ukraine', and an economic recovery plan for the Donbas.[66]

The OSCE Monitoring Mission increased the number of monitors to 500 to oversee the ceasefire. It was at this time, perhaps not accidentally, that Kolomoisky's assets in Crimea and Moscow were sequestered – he was now perceived as a threat to both Moscow and Kiev. Meanwhile Poroshenko's assets in Russia and Crimea (notably the Sevastopol Marine Plant) remained intact, and he was even allowed to consolidate his chocolate plants preparatory to their sale as a single unit. For the first time the autonomous political agency of the rebels was recognised, something that Putin had insisted on from the outset. With some 10 per cent of its territory given special status, Ukraine's road to NATO membership was indefinitely blocked – an irreducible Russian goal that could have been achieved months earlier without war. Equally, with the advance of Islamic State in Syria and Iraq, the US realised that it would be wiser to fight real enemies rather than conjure them out of the mists of the Donbas. In his speech to Congress on 18 September Poroshenko appealed for 'lethal and non-lethal weapons', warning: 'One cannot win the war with blankets', but instead the US offered a $53 million package, of which only $7 million was (non-lethal) military aid. The danger of a direct confrontation with Russia receded.

The goals of the insurgents were never entirely clear. Putin in April had talked about 'Novorossiya', and this was the name used by the rebels to describe their entity. Oleg Tsarev remained the speaker of the Novorossiya parliament, whose flag has a striking resemblance to that of the Confederacy, but unlike the southern states in the American Civil War his goal was not secession but autonomy within Ukraine. Autonomy was also the goal of Khodakovsky, the head of the Vostok battalion. The 'Ukrainisation' of the rebel leadership entailed the dismissal of first-generation commanders, opening up space for a negotiated compromise. Girkin had entertained far more grandiose ambitions. He represented a powerful brand of romantic-nationalist conservatism, harking back to Russian Civil War generals such as Baron Petr Wrangel, who led the evacuation of the White Army from Crimea in November 1920. Putin's turn to conservatism was of a far more pragmatic sort and combined elements of the 'red' Soviet tradition, which was anathema to nationalists like Girkin. For them a renewed Russia would have to be purged of its residual Communist features, whereas Putin epitomised precisely those characteristics. Like the endless bickering of the White generals at the time of the Russian Civil War, allowing the Bolsheviks victory, divisions between Novorossiya leaders weakened their resolve. At the time of the deal Alexander Zakharchenko told journalists that only complete independence from Ukraine would now be acceptable to the rebels: 'We have all the mineral resources, resort zones, we are a self-sufficient region', he insisted.[67] This was not the view of the Donbas oligarchs, who well understood that if the region were to secede, much stronger Russian corporations would soon 'raid' their assets. However, the war had greatly weakened the political clout of Donbas capital, and it would now be easy prey for hostile takeovers.

Both sides breached the ceasefire, in particular around Donetsk airport, but there was now the political will for peace, especially with winter coming and no military resolution of the crisis in prospect. The UN reported that as of 11 September at least 3,171 people, including 27 children, had been killed and another 8,000 wounded. Those opposed to the ceasefire argued that it would create a 'frozen' conflict that would allow Russia to influence the development of Ukrainian policy. It would ensure that NATO membership for the country would have to be indefinitely postponed. The West would have to recognise the Kremlin's security interest in keeping Ukraine as a 'buffer state' to prevent Russia's encirclement by the Atlantic alliance. At the same time, Russia was opposed to the collapse of Ukraine, and hence Moscow repeatedly called on the leadership of the insurgency to respect the territorial integrity of the country. By keeping the Russophone regions within Ukraine, Moscow would be able to shape policies in not only foreign but also domestic policy. The strategy was to maintain the voice of the pluralists from within, rather than risk the disintegration of the Ukrainian state – although the latter outcome could not be dismissed. With the provisional end of the conflict, the sheer magnitude of Ukraine's problems began to hit home, with widespread poverty, rampant corruption, bankrupt finances, economic decline and continued oligarch power accompanied by the imposition of harsh austerity. The battle-hardened units returning from the unsuccessful campaign in the Donbas would look for a scapegoat for the disasters that had befallen the country.

The same session of the Ukrainian parliament on 16 September 2014 that ratified the EU Association Agreement also adopted 'special status' legislation granting wide-ranging autonomy for the rebel-occupied parts of the Donbas, about a third of the territory, but only for three years. Local authorities were allowed to set up their own police forces and appoint judges and prosecutors, and would be able to make agreements with central state bodies on economic, social and cultural development. The regions would be granted special economic status to encourage the restoration of industry and infrastructure and to create new jobs. Early elections were to be held on 7 December to new councils in those districts. Russian would be allowed to be spoken in state institutions, and the authorities were authorised to establish close relations with neighbouring regions of Russia.[68] A separate law adopted in the same closed session granted an amnesty to participants in the fighting, except those who had committed 'serious crimes'. Thus the law built on the 5 September deal to bring an end to the conflict, which itself was not too far from the deal that Putin and Poroshenko were approaching, brokered by the Germans, before the downing of MH17. Putin showed little sign of wanting a Crimean-style takeover of the region, repeatedly rejecting requests to accept the territory as part of Russia. He certainly did not view the war as a liberation struggle on the Vietnamese model. The purpose of 'Russian aggression' was not territory but strategic space.

Repeated violations of the ceasefire were reported by both sides, with a particularly vicious battle for control of Donetsk airport, which represented a government-held enclave in territory otherwise held by the insurgents. Prisoner exchanges went ahead amid charges that the Kiev forces had so few prisoners to exchange that they kidnapped civilians to make up the numbers. Mass graves of insurgent fighters were discovered. For a Ukrainian population that had been gripped by war fever for months, this was inevitably seen as a capitulation, especially when accompanied an amnesty for those who fought against Kiev, but Poroshenko was right to claim that the law guaranteed 'the sovereignty, territorial integrity, and independence of Ukraine'.[69] He had finally overridden the war party in Kiev headed by Yatsenyuk, who was still calling for NATO backing for an all-out war against Russia. For an army that had lost at least 65 per cent of its military hardware, only foreign intervention could allow it to continue the fight. Poroshenko went on to stress that the creation of the special zone in the Donbas did not mean federalisation, only the delegation of powers for three years.

On the other side, the insurgents felt that victory was snatched from their grasp as they headed for Mariupol and, in their dreams, to Melitopol and Kakhovka, the scene of a legendary battle during the civil war, and on to the liberation of all of historical Novorossiya. The time limitation made the deal a hard one to swallow for the insurgents, but in the end it was accepted, although matters were not helped by the declaration of the DPR and LPR that they would hold simultaneous votes on 2 November for their leaders and 'supreme soviets'. Follow-up talks under the aegis of the contact group resulted in the Minsk Memorandum of 20 September, which stipulated that the ceasefire was to be considered bilateral (point 1); all military formations were to be stopped at the contact line as of 19 September; all heavy weaponry was to be pulled back by at least 15 kilometres from the contact line; mines were to removed from the borders of the buffer zone; operational flights were to be banned apart from those of the OSCE; and, crucially, all foreign fighters and military equipment were to be removed from Ukrainian territory, to be overseen by the OSCE (point 9). There was no agreement over the region's final status, while the demarcation line froze arbitrary battle positions.

Poroshenko and Putin were now united on the need for peace, although for different reasons. They both faced strong opposition at home to what was considered capitulation and betrayal. There were plenty in Kiev and Washington who wished to continue the military offensive to clear the region of insurgents, while hawks in Moscow spoke of resolving the Ukraine problem once and for all by dismembering what they considered to be an artificial creation. They certainly would not allow the insurgency to be defeated. On all sides the nationalist genies would not easily be returned to the bottle. For the ceasefire to turn into peace the status of the Donbas would have to be resolved, the geopolitical role of Ukraine decided, and the structural division of Europe overcome. A pan-European peace conference was the only way this could be achieved.

A PROXY CONFLICT

During the Cold War the main protagonists, the USA and the USSR, avoided direct confrontation and instead fought a number of proxy wars in Africa, Afghanistan and elsewhere. In the new era of the cold peace the Ukraine crisis became one of these proxy wars. The Atlantic powers consistently underestimated the autonomous character of the Donbas rebellion and instead placed all responsibility on Russia. Undoubtedly it was assisted by Russia, although the extent of direct military support is contested. The intelligence at NATO's disposal appeared to be astonishingly primitive, too often relying on 'social media and common sense', as the State Department spokesperson Marie Harf famously put it. The rebellion was deeply contradictory, since its ultimate goals were probably unclear even to the participants – veering between demands for greater autonomy, federalisation, independence, all the way up to unification with Russia. The depth of popular support is also unclear. Certainly, for civilians caught up in the fighting, peace was the greatest good, yet the rebellion did have deep local roots. The fundamental inability of Kiev and its Western allies to understand that this was not simply an 'invasion' but a genuine revolt against a particular type of statehood that had long been unpopular in the south-east, and that the Ukrainian revolution only intensified, meant that they could not recognise the political subjectivity of the rebellion as a force with which there should be dialogue. Instead, labelling the insurgents 'terrorists' meant not only that their political identity was negated but also that their very humanity was dismissed, allowing untold cruelties to be inflicted upon the region. Many of the rebel leaders were indeed unsavoury characters, and even Putin distanced himself from them, but that does not mean that the political question was removed. And that question was fundamentally about equality for the Russian language and some sort of constitutional status for Donbas autonomy.

Putin's deep alienation from the West was once again on display in his speech at the Seliger youth forum on 29 August: 'Anything the US touches turns into Libya or Iraq.'[70] In an interview on 31 August Putin argued that the talks between the Kiev authorities and the rebel leaders should be 'not just [about] technical issues but on the political organisation of society and statehood in south-eastern Ukraine'. Later his spokesman clarified that by 'statehood' he meant greater autonomy within Ukraine – the Russian word *gosudarstvennost* can also mean 'governance' or 'governmental organisation'. Putin was being pushed by the 'peace party' in the Kremlin, represented notably by Vladislav Surkov, to come to a negotiated solution that would avoid the too-obvious defeat of the rebels. This path was constantly stymied by the war party in Washington and its acolytes in Europe. The chair of the Senate Foreign Relations Committee, Robert Menendez, for example now called on the US to arm the Ukrainian military. Speaking in Kiev, he insisted: 'Thousands of Russian troops are here and are directly engaged in what is clearly an invasion.'[71] This was accompanied by threats from the EU even after the peace deal to impose a new round of sanctions. The Western powers feared that the Donbas would become another 'frozen conflict' for Moscow to exert leverage against Kiev.

Equally, Poroshenko in his address to both houses of Congress on 18 September 2014 emotionally called on the US to provide weapons for his country to fight Russia, and claimed that the world was on the verge of a new Cold War. Poroshenko knew how to play to the gallery, and his insistence that the struggle for Ukraine's territorial integrity was 'Europe's and America's war too; it is a war for the free world' was greeted with rapturous applause. He claimed that the world faced the worst security threat since the 1962 Cuban missile crisis and faced a 'choice between civilisation and barbarism'.[72] As Montaigne commented: 'Everyone calls barbarity that to which they are not accustomed.' The White House was reluctant to supply Ukraine with heavy weapons since it knew that it could not match Russian forces and risked escalation into a wider conflict. The Ukrainian leadership sought to catalyse what had long been little better than a rerun of the 'peaceful coexistence' of the post-Stalin years, arising out of the asymmetrical end of the Cold War, into a full-blown new Cold War. Obama sought to avoid this by minimising Russia's status in the world, claiming that it was no more than a regional power. He was correct to the degree that Russia had no coherent or attractive alternative ideological programme to offer the world, other than some inchoate conservative traditionalism. Putin's challenge is not to the system of international politics but only to what he considers its skewed and selective operation in favour of the Atlantic system. This is at most neo-revisionism, but full-scale revisionism and the creation of counter-hegemonic alliances could well be the next step if the confrontation with the Atlantic powers continues.

Russia used proxies in the Donbas to achieve its goals within Ukraine, but this was not an attempted 'land-grab' or even a challenge to the international system. The corollary is clear, and is well put by Angus Roxburgh. He notes that never before has an 'invasion' been so deniable, but stresses: 'Those who see Putin as the cause of the problem refuse to concede that he might also be part of the solution. Those who regard resistance as the only option dismiss negotiations with Putin as "appeasement".' Roxburgh dismisses the consensus in favour of sanctions, stressing this was the West's biggest mistake: 'Sanctions against Russia are worthless. They hurt Western companies and are of no avail in changing Putin's policies.'[73] Sanctions could certainly damage the Russian economy, but as all studies of Putin have demonstrated, when he believes that he is right – as he certainly does in the Ukraine case – external pressure only makes him dig in his heels. One does not need to justify Russian policy to note that the rebellion in the Donbas was a complex phenomenon – as this book has argued – and cannot be reduced to simplistic analogies with Hitlerite Germany or Russian pathologies. The Ukrainian revolution of February 2014 and the Donbas rebellion fed off each other, and were then exacerbated by geopolitical tensions.

CHAPTER 8

WORLDS IN COLLISION

In the period before the Sochi Olympics the Putin administration had been portrayed in harshly dark colours, greatly exaggerating the undoubted governance deficits in Russia. As the crisis unfurled in Ukraine, this cultural 'othering' was ramped up to extraordinary levels, fought over the terrain of defining contemporary political reality. Angela Merkel talked of Putin being 'in another world', while Kerry was at a complete loss to understand what motivated the Russian leader: 'You almost feel that he's creating his own reality, and his own sort of world, divorced from a lot of what's real on the ground for all those people, including people in his own country'. These comments came on the day, 28 April, when new sanctions were imposed on Russia. The precursor to the Ukraine crisis and its attendant economic sanctions was the ideological and political delegitimation of the Russian authorities. What had long been implicit in the relationship as a result of the asymmetrical end of the Cold War became overt. The structural pressure of this asymmetry destroyed the traditional manners of international politics, further degrading what had long been apparent as the decline of diplomacy as the practice of dialogue between equal interlocutors. The ready recourse to sanctions was already evident in relations with other states, and reflected the structural pre-eminence of the West, which resulted in the hubristic application of the instruments of hegemonic power. The West and Russia operated in parallel worlds, each failing to understand the logic that motivated the other.

LEGITIMACY AND REALITY

Kerry went on to argue that the Ukraine crisis was 'obviously very personally driven in ways that I think are uniquely inappropriate to 21st century leadership'. He noted:

It's an amazing display of a kind of personal reaction to something that just doesn't fit into the lessons learned for the last 60 years or 70 years. It's so divorced that it leaves you feeling badly for the consequences. I think the Russian people are going to pay a price for this. It's unfortunate for the Russian people, who clearly don't fit into the costs that are being attached to this, because it appears to be so personal to President Putin.[1]

Kerry noted in particular the dangers of Putin's appeals to nationalism, while discounting the idea that Russia's actions in Crimea had developed in reaction to a perceived security threat: 'Obviously there's a plan. And it's being carried out with a singular resolve.' This was a situation far more dangerous than anything during the Cold War, during which the enemy was at least comprehensible. Ideological opposition gave intellectual structure and coherence to the conflict, whereas this renewed era of global competition lay outside the mental compass of the combatants. Kerry admitted that the situation 'could deteriorate into hot confrontation', but absolved the West of responsibility. The enormity of the epistemological gulf between the protagonists during the cold peace was now exposed.

The basic US case was that Russia manufactured and manipulated the protest movement in eastern Ukraine. At a private meeting in Washington on 25 April of the Trilateral Commission – the body formed in 1973 to bring together experienced leaders to discuss world problems – Kerry argued that US intelligence had recordings of 'pro-Russian forces' being managed by handlers in Moscow: 'We know exactly who's giving those orders, we know where they are coming from.' He did not mince his words:

It's not an accident that you have some of the people identified who were in Crimea and in Georgia and who are now in east Ukraine. This is insulting to everybody's intelligence, let alone to our notions about how we ought to be behaving in the 21st century. It's thuggism, it's rogue state-ism. It's the worst order of behaviour.[2]

There had been widespread recriminations about the fact that the US had not picked up military communications before the Crimean intervention, and now Kerry was making up for it by arguing, on evidence that proved to be far from incontrovertible, that Russian intelligence officers were the catalysts behind the disturbances and the takeover of government buildings. The US framed the events as a shadow invasion, a slow-motion stealth takeover of neighbouring territory on the Crimean model, even though the circumstances were very different. In Crimea there was a long-standing Russian troop presence, and the peninsula had a long history of difficult relations with Kiev.

The US stance was the mirror image of the Russian view that Western forces had been behind the radicalisation of the Maidan and the takeover of government institutions in the west of the country. The American case is backed by the deployment of awesome intelligence-gathering facilities. The US European Command uses the RC-135 Rivet Joint, a modified Boeing 707 equipped with advanced sensor and intercept software, to soak up electronic communications. This is buttressed by the EP3, based in the US naval stations in Rota, Spain, and Sigonella, Italy. It was an EP3 that had been grounded by the Chinese at the beginning of the George W. Bush administration in 2001, provoking a major international crisis. The Russians, of course, are no slouches when it comes to eavesdropping. The spate of telephone intercepts has been mentioned earlier, while at the strategic level the Russians use the Beriev A-50 surveillance and early-warning aircraft to spy on the communications of adversaries.[3]

As the insurrection in the south-east gained traction, Moscow was blamed for arming and directing the rebels. Evidence for this was not always forthcoming. Certainly, the insurgency was useful to Russia as a means of exerting pressure on Kiev to adapt to Russian policy preferences, but motive cannot establish guilt. The goals, as we have seen, included a shift from the integrated-nationalism model of state development to the pluralist one, which in concrete terms meant elements of federalisation, elevating Russian to a second state language, continued economic links and, in foreign policy, guaranteed neutrality. These were issues that exercised Moscow, but were also deeply grounded in the long-term concerns of the Donbas. Just as in Crimea, the ill-advised actions of the revolutionary government after Yanukovych's fall threatened the region in several ways. These fears were certainly exaggerated by the Russian media, but that does not mean that substantive issues were not at stake. The portrayal of the insurgency as purely an external intervention was at best partial, and ignored the domestic roots of discontent – just as it would be inappropriate to deny a degree of external support.

For defenders of Ukrainian integrated nationalism, the insurrection was simply incomprehensible and thus its causes were externalised. On 18 June Poroshenko argued that Ukraine was caught up in a 'new type of war': 'This is a war [...] using professional diversionary groups, mercenaries, volunteers and the local population. The volunteers and the local populations have been brainwashed by the information war.'[4] In describing the insurgents in this way, not only was the legitimacy (or otherwise) of their arguments nullified and their political subjectivity denigrated, but as individuals they were dehumanised, validating the use of extreme force. The 'information war' undoubtedly existed, with Moscow pitted against the Kiev authorities, but both propounded equally partial accounts. The information war ultimately reflected the struggle between the monist and pluralist models of Ukrainian state-building as refracted through the struggle between Atlanticist and continental visions. The revolutionary seizure of power by the monists provoked the resistance of the pluralists, which soon turned to violence. Moscow and Donbas had common cause to that degree, but ultimately these were two separate processes, and this was revealed in the various tensions and contradictions that emerged as the insurgency unrolled across the region. Unlike in Crimea, Moscow's goal was not territorial adjustment (unless the Ukrainian state collapsed in its entirety, at which point Poland, Hungary and Romania would also have territorial pretensions). The Kremlin sought to ensure the constitutional entrenchment of the pluralist model of Ukrainian statehood and an embargo on NATO enlargement, while the insurgents sought greater autonomy for the Donbas.

Washington took an active part in the information war. The State Department repeatedly departed from hallowed traditions of diplomacy. The political autonomy of Russia as a whole was delegitimated, its arguments portrayed as little more than the ravings of an oriental despotism, and curtly dismissed in the manner of an impatient parent with a child. The partisan views of the official and Kiev media were accepted uncritically, just as the slick output and polished media strategy of the Saakashvili regime had been in 2008, only to be repudiated once the truth came out later. In 2014 much of the news came from 'Euromaidan PR', allegedly generously funded by sympathetic oligarchs, which described itself as 'the site of the official public-relations secretariat for the headquarters of the national resistance in Kyiv' and proclaimed in banner headlines that 'Ukraine is united' while reporting on the exact opposite from the conflict on 'the eastern front'.

There was also a 'war' over whose human-rights violations were worst. The Russian foreign ministry brought out an 80-page *White Book* detailing the 'widespread and gross human-rights violations' perpetrated by the Maidan government, with a supplement issued in June 2014. The credibility of the material is weakened by the absence of sources, but even so, the litany of abuses represents a powerful indictment of the interim authorities in Kiev. It covers everything from suggestions that the anti-Yanukovych forces were responsible for the sniper shootings and foreign 'interference' in the form of visits to the Maidan protesters by Western officials, to the demolition of statues of Lenin.[5] In turn, the Institute for Mass Information in Kiev published a report outlining the 'violation of journalists' rights and freedom of speech since Russian aggression started'. It reported that, of 368 human-rights violations between 1 March and 10 June 2014, 'almost 80% are related to actions of terrorists and to Russian aggression, which has been taking place in the east and in Crimea'. These included 88 cases of the disconnection of Ukrainian channels in the 'occupied territories', 87 cases of attacks against journalists, and 46 cases of the abduction of journalists.[6]

SANCTIONS

On 6 March the EU and the US agreed on a staged approach to sanctions. In the first instance, plans for closer economic cooperation between the EU and Russia, including talks on the successor to the Partnership and Cooperation Agreement (PCA) that had lapsed in 2008, were suspended, as were preparations for the G8 summit planned for June 2014 in Sochi. On 6 March Obama issued an executive order imposing sanctions on officials of the Russian government for their alleged role in Ukrainian events. Following the Crimean referendum of 16 March and the region's subsequent incorporation into Russia, the threat to target individual Russians and Ukrainians was implemented. On 17 March America imposed asset freezes and travel bans on 11 individuals, including Vladislav Surkov, Sergei Glazyev, Dmitry Rogozin and Valentina Matvienko in Russia, and Sergei Aksenev, Vladimir Konstantinov (speaker of the Crimean parliament), Viktor Medvedchuk and Viktor Yanukovych. The EU likewise sanctioned 21 people, adding another 12 soon after, and the US also expanded the list and added Bank Rossiya. A group of European business leaders on 13 March pleaded with Vygaudas Ušackas, the EU's envoy to Moscow, to find alternatives to EU plans to impose sanctions on Russia, which they warned were unintelligent and damaging. Not surprisingly, he was totally unresponsive, which led a Finnish businessman to expostulate: 'Europe is dead'.[7]

Two more rounds of sanctions in April 2014 focused on individuals who were considered to have been directly involved in Ukrainian policy or the annexation of Crimea, as well as companies linked to those individuals. Some technology companies related to Russia's military–industrial complex were targeted as well as the natural-gas pipeline construction firms Stroigazmontazh and Volga Group, as well as the latter's Stroitransgaz subsidiaries. There was a grimly personal element, trying to damage people close to Putin. On 28 April, the Obama administration announced sanctions against seven Russian officials and 17 Russian companies. None of the latter was publicly listed and most were relatively minor. All the companies were owned by Gennady Timchenko, Arkady and Boris Rotenberg, or Bank Rossiya, who were the targets in the second round. The sanctioned banks included SMP Bank, Russia's thirty-sixth-largest in terms of assets, Sobinbank, the country's ninetieth-largest, and InvestCapitalBank, number 197. Following the announcement, the US-based payment systems MasterCard and Visa, which together process about 90 per cent of payments in Russia, suspended their services to the two banks, setting off a movement to end Russia's dependence on foreign payment systems.

The second round of sanctions followed the failure of the Geneva agreement and the new spiral of violence within Ukraine, echoed by escalating international tension. The Western powers insisted that Kiev was abiding by the agreement, including disarming the militias and amnestying protesters who vacated buildings and surrendered their weapons, while Moscow allegedly did nothing to meet its Geneva commitments, hence the new sanctions. In fact, the various 'hundreds' that had defended the Maidan and its analogues were incorporated into the armed forces, into the private militias of the warlord oligarchs, and above all into the National Guard. Far from disarming, they became part of the coercive apparatus of the monist state and were unleashed against the pluralists. The sanctioned individuals included Igor Sechin, one of Putin's closest long-term allies, who had served as a deputy prime minister before going on to head Rosneft in 2012, as well as Vyacheslav Volodin, the first deputy head of staff in the Kremlin administration, who had taken over the management of domestic political affairs from Surkov. Volodin was the architect of the domestic political 'reset', allowing a degree of greater competitiveness in elections and encouraging the opposition to enter the formal political process. Another notable individual sanctioned this time was Sergei Chemezov, the head of the wholly state-owned giant Russian Technologies State Corporation (Rostekh, formerly Rostekhnologii), who had not only served in the KGB with Putin in East Germany but also lived in the same apartment complex in Dresden. The companies were faced with asset freezes and banned export licences for high-technology items that could contribute to Russia's military potential.

The list also included Dmitry Kozak, a deputy prime minister with a reputation as a troubleshooter. He had been sent as presidential envoy to the North Caucasus in late 2004 to help pacify the region, and had then overseen the successful delivery of the Sochi Olympics. In March 2014 he was sent to Crimea to oversee its incorporation into Russia. He was joined by Alexei Pushkov, the outspoken head of the Duma's international-affairs committee and a pugnacious regime loyalist. The Kremlin envoy to the new Crimean Federal District was Oleg Belaventsev, and he is considered close to the defence minister Sergei Shoigu. The final member of the list was Yevgeny Murov, the head of Russia's powerful Federal Protection Service (FSO). Soon after, the EU blacklisted another 15 Russian and Ukrainian officials in addition to the 33 already named. The list revealed on 29 April also included Kozak and Belaventsev, as well as Denis Pushilin, one of the leaders of the DPR, Igor Girkin and an assistant to Aksenev, the Crimean prime minister. Western hardliners had lobbied for the list to include Alexei Miller, the head of Gazprom.

The Russian foreign ministry was scathing of the new round of EU sanctions: 'Instead of forcing the Kiev clique to sit down with south-eastern Ukraine to negotiate the country's future political system, our partners are toeing Washington's line to take more unfriendly gestures towards Russia.' The statement went on to argue:

> If somebody in Brussels hopes to stabilize the situation in Ukraine by this, it is evidence of a total lack of understanding of the internal political situation in that country and invites local neo-Nazis to continue their lawlessness and thuggery towards the peaceful civilians of the south-east. Are you not ashamed?[8]

Most countries in the EU were reluctant to broaden the sanctions to encompass the energy sector. European countries take 84 per cent of Russia's oil and about 76 per cent of its natural-gas exports. Russia produces some 10 million of the world's daily output of 90 million barrels. Not only are Western companies deeply engaged in partnership relationships with Russian companies, but ultimately genuine elements of 'interdependence' have emerged. This is not something to be regretted, as it has been by Western hawks, but something to be recognised as signalling the emergence of genuine elements of 'globalisation' independent of geopolitical contestation. The sanctions certainly damaged an economy that was already slowing down, contributing to the weakening of the rouble and accelerating capital flight reaching $128 billion in 2014. While the impact of the sanctions in the end turned out to be quite severe, there is no evidence that they achieved the desired effect. In fact, sanctions only impeded the path of dialogue and the emergence of mutually satisfactory outcomes.

Hawks in the US Congress urged that measures be taken against major companies such as Gazprom, and against whole sectors, notably finance. In the words of Senator Dan Coats, a Republican from Indiana: 'To date, the lack of a forceful, effective response by the administration and Western leaders has given this bully on the playground little reason to expect that further aggression will be punished.'[9] The aggressive lead was taken, typically, by John McCain (Republican senator for Arizona), who, in a statement with Lindsey Graham (Republican senator for South Carolina), lambasted the weak response:

> The Obama Administration's latest round of sanctions is days late and dollars short. While a unified U.S. and European response to Russia's aggression is ideal, the current policy has become a reduction to the lowest common denominator. This has led to a gradual escalation of pressure that, at best, is failing to deter Russian aggression and, at worst, may actually be inviting it. If we are now forced to choose between alliance unity or meaningful action, we must choose action, and America must lead it.[10]

The Obama team adopted a cautious strategy, in part to avoid disruptions to European economies and harming the global economy, while McCain and his fellow militants had no bounds to the damage they were ready to inflict on Russia and its European partners. The cheerleader for this tough approach was the *Washington Post*, using a slew of editorials to condemn Russia's 'first forcible change of borders in Europe since World War II':

> By choosing not to use the economic weapons at his disposal and broadcasting that restraint to the world, Mr. Obama is telling Mr. Putin as well as other potential aggressors that they continue to have little to fear from the United States.[11]

It is hardly surprising that those with less exposure to the Russian economy were the keenest on sanctions, accompanied inevitably by high-minded moralising and condemnation of the pusillanimity of those arguing for a more measured response. Biden later admitted that America, and Obama personally, forced EU members to impose sanctions, against their better judgement.[12] Trade between the EU and Russia in 2012 reached almost $370 billion, while American trade with Russia in that year was a measly $26 billion. About a third of the EU's gas supplies come from Russia, some 40 per cent of which is pumped via Ukraine. In general, about half of Russia's exports go to the EU, while 45 per cent of its imports came from there. Gas supplies had been disrupted in both 2006 and 2009 when Russia and Ukraine engaged in a dispute over prices, but in both cases it had been Ukrainian domestic conflicts, mostly provoked by Tymoshenko, that led to the cut-offs. European customers endured supply shortfalls, which Gazprom argued were provoked by Ukraine siphoning off supplies that were intended for markets further downstream for domestic needs. In other words, the problem was not with Russian supplies but Ukraine's unreliability as a transit country, hence Russia's investment in pipelines bypassing the country. Countries such as France and Italy had developed ramified economic relationships with Russia, with the former selling two Mistral-class amphibious landing ships to Russia, while the Italian energy giant ENI was Gazprom's key partner in building the €17 billion South Stream pipeline under the Black Sea and up through the Balkans.

Although US global engagement in the Russian economy was relatively small, this does not mean that it was insignificant. In 2011 ExxonMobil signed up to wide-ranging strategic cooperation with Rosneft, which included plans for the joint exploration of the Arctic Kara, Chukchi and Laptev seas, pilot projects in the Bazhenov and Achimov shales of western Siberia, and possibly a liquefied-natural-gas (LNG) plant in the Russian Far East. Exxon holds a third of the arctic licences, carrying Rosneft's exploration and development costs, which would be recouped once production starts.

After the fourth round of sanctions, announced on 12 September, Exxon suspended operations at nine out of the ten joint ventures with Rosneft. The US company was in the decidedly odd position of doing business with an organisation, Rosneft, whose boss was not allowed into the US. The farm-equipment-manufacturing corporation John Deere has two factories in Russia, and saw its share price take a severe knock as sanctions began to bite, cutting off credit for purchases in Russia, Ukraine and other ex-Soviet republics. In partnership with Rostekh, Boeing partly owned a joint venture that manufactured about half of the titanium parts fitted in Boeing aircraft.

Rosneft is the world's largest listed oil company, and had also developed a close partnership with BP, having bought out TNK-BP in 2012. As part of the deal, BP ended up with a 19.75 per cent stake in Rosneft and two seats on the board. Bob Dudley, the head of BP, which is Europe's second-largest oil company, had long and harsh experience of working in Russia, yet remained committed to the partnership. BP issued a statement stressing that the company was 'committed to our investment in Rosneft, and we intend to remain a successful long-term investor in Russia'.[13] Shell was a partner in a large LNG plant on Sakhalin. Clearly, the sanctions threatened capital investments in the oil sector, which could damage future output. Gazprom alone invested $24.4 billion in 2013, a sizeable proportion of which included equipment from Western suppliers. The EU imports 15 per cent of its crude oil from Russia. Not surprisingly, Moscow warned of the 'boomerang effect' of the sanctions damaging the West's own interests and the business networks that were so profitable for all sides.

German business leaders and energy companies were in the vanguard of those calling for moderation. Germany is by far Russia's biggest economic partner in Europe, taking some €38 billion in imports and exporting €36 billion. Over 6,000 German companies have established branches in Russia, notably in motor-manufacturing, engineering, electronics and chemicals, accompanied by an intense energy relationship. Joe Kaeser, the head of Siemens, met Putin in late March and was with Rainer Seele, the chairman of Wintershall, a subsidiary of the giant BASF chemical company, which had invested heavily in Russia's oil and natural-gas trade, when he urged caution: 'Neither in energy terms, nor politically, should we turn away from Russia.'[14] He went on to argue: 'Sanctions will not help anybody, they would not just hurt Russia, but also Germany and Europe as a whole.' This view was shared by Gerhard Roiss, the chief executive of the Austrian oil and gas supplier OMV, which had worked with Gazprom for over five decades. On 25 April 2014 he warned: 'You cannot talk about sanctions if you don't know the outcome of sanctions.' He went on to argue:

Europe has developed over the last 50 years into a region where we have a division of labour and a division of resources, and this means in concrete terms that energy is imported from Russia and products – automotive or machinery – are exported from European countries into Russia.

He noted that there had been several earlier political crises, beginning with the Soviet invasion of Czechoslovakia in 1968, the year that Russian gas first started flowing into Austria: 'We've had a crisis situation several times, but if you see it over the 50 years, natural gas was not used as a weapon, and we should not use gas as a weapon.'[15]

The sentiment was reflected by Gazprom executives, who travelled across Europe arguing that Russia and Europe were long-term economic partners. Alexander Medvedev, the deputy head of Gazprom, insisted that the company had done everything possible to keep the gas flowing, but a time of 'financial reckoning' was near, referring to the $18.5 billion allegedly owed by Ukraine. As a publicly traded company (with half owned by the state), how could Gazprom maintain contractual promises and make needed investments when faced by such a 'slippery customer'? Medvedev suggested that Ukraine's Western friends should step up to the plate and help meet the bills. The Kremlin called for three-party talks on Russian gas supplies to Europe through Ukraine. Medvedev insisted: 'We are not planning to cut gas to Ukraine. We just would like to receive payment for the gas that we are going to deliver.'[16] After months of bickering over the price, Russia cut supplies to Ukraine on 16 June. A provisional solution was brokered by the EU in late September, although it would be 30 October before the deal was agreed. Ukraine would pay $1.45 billion to cover part of its outstanding debt to Gazprom, as well as $760 million in pre-payments for November, and another tranche of $1.65 billion was to be paid by the end of the year. Ukraine would pay $378 per tcm until the end of the year, and $365 in the first quarter of 2015. Ukraine had some 17 bcm in storage, but would need some 3–5 bcm by March 2015, depending on the weather. The deal was referred to as the 'winter package' to stress its provisional seasonal character. Gazprom had offered a $100 per tcm discount in the form of an export-duty exemption, but Ukraine sought a long-term revision of the contract price. A more permanent settlement would only come after the Stockholm Arbitration Court gave its judgment on the dispute. Ukraine is reliant on Russia for at least 60 per cent of its supplies. Up to October 2014 Poland, Hungary and Slovakia re-exported some 1.7 bcm of Russian gas to Ukraine through reverse gas flows, compared to 3.8 bcm between 2012 and 2014, but Gazprom questioned the legality of the practice. As noted, about 15 per cent of Europe's gas needs transit through Ukrainian pipelines, and the EU now understood that 'the energy risk is not from Russia but the transit route across Ukraine.'[17]

The Ukraine crisis once again intensified calls for a common energy policy for the 28 countries in the EU. Equally, Russia accelerated efforts to bypass Ukraine as a transit country. Already it had built the Nord Stream pipeline, from the Gulf of Finland to Greifswald in Germany. By early 2014 Russia had just about everything in place to build South Stream, the 2,446-kilometre-long pipeline designed to circumvent Ukraine. It is planned to leave the Russian mainland just south of Novorossiisk, track through the depths of the Black Sea and make landfall in Bulgaria, and then work its way through several countries to join the main European gas distribution network at Baumgarten in Austria, with a line through Hungary. The plan had been for South Stream to come into operation in 2015, and that, when running at full capacity, it would supply Europe with up to 63 bcm of natural gas annually. The project had been introduced in 2007 as an alternative to the EU's planned Nabucco pipeline intended to bring Azerbaijani gas to Europe via Turkey. Nabucco had fallen by the wayside, but the EU still sought to find ways to block South Stream. The 'Third Energy Package' (TEP) was a series of legislative acts designed to reduce monopolies in the energy market, including a provision that prohibits gas-producers from owning primary gas pipelines. Russia argues that the South Stream agreements had been signed in 2008, a year before TEP came into force, and thus could not have retrospective effect, and on that basis in April 2014 filed an appeal with the World Trade Organization (WTO) claiming discrimination in market access.

Bulgaria had long resisted attempts to block construction, but in June 2014 it finally succumbed to pressure from the EU and a group of US senators, including McCain, to stop work on the project. The US had long taken the lead in opposing Russian pipeline projects and sponsoring alternatives, but in this case there was an added interest. The Ukrainian authorities were discussing transferring the Ukrainian gas transmission system (UGTS) to a consortium of American and European investors, but if South Stream were built these assets would become virtually worthless. In early June, Yatsenyuk announced the restructuring of Naftogaz to divest it of its natural-gas pipelines and gas storage facilities, which would then be used 'jointly with the US and the EU'. In August the Rada passed a law that allows foreign companies – from the US and the EU – to co-manage UGTS, with Ukraine retaining 51 per cent of the shares, while foreign partners would be offered 49 per cent. In the event, with Putin present, in late June Austria signed up to create South Stream Austria to manage construction of the pipeline across that country.

The attempt to block South Stream was a type of ersatz sanction. The EU was fundamentally mistaken in trying to block South Stream, since it not only guaranteed supplies to downstream countries but also provided energy security for the countries on its route. The EU's handling of energy relations with Russia was criticised by Andrei Yermolaev, the director of Kirishi-2, Russia's first waste-oil refinery, which was planned to launch in 2017: 'The European Union's pressure on Gazprom's South

Stream pipeline misinterprets both Russian energy initiatives and certain business decisions – such as Gazprom's refusal to export gas to Ukraine – that would seem highly innocuous in other settings.' In his view, these attacks reflect the views of those who remain intent on viewing Russia through a Cold War lens, whereas Russia is a trustworthy partner with enormous scope for future EU–Russian cooperation, notably in the Arctic, all of which are jeopardised by the retrogressive stance adopted by the EU. In particular:

> the EU narrative that Gazprom's decision to halt natural-gas exports to Ukraine is 'political blackmail' is wholly inaccurate and coincides with the mistaken portrayal of Russia as a 'Soviet Union reborn' that is so very prevalent in international media coverage of business and politics in Russia today. In actuality, Gazprom is acting as any sound business. If anything, it has gone to great lengths to try to accommodate Ukraine despite its ballooning debt, which has now reached about \$4.5 billion.[18]

From this perspective, building South Stream is a perfectly rational strategy. Gordon Hahn reiterates this view, arguing:

> In reality, by obstructing South Stream [...] Europe will only cut off its nose to spite its face, for reliance on Gazprom supplies through Ukraine has again proven to be fraught with difficulty, with the latest cutoff of supplies caused by the Russian–Ukrainian conflict.[19]

Even worse, it was not so much that the EU was cutting off its nose but that it was demonstrating its lack of autonomy in acceding to pressure from its meddlesome Atlantic partner, now enjoying energy independence by exploiting tight oil and shale gas.

MORE SANCTIONS AND COUNTER-SANCTIONS

The downing of Malaysia Airlines Flight MH17 on 17 July was followed by an accelerated set of sanctions, imposed by the US and then Europe. The US appeared 'trigger-happy', issuing the ultimatum that Russia should ensure access to independent investigators to the crash site, but then imposing sanctions before local forces or Russia could respond. On 29 July Obama imposed a broad range of economic sanctions, adding three banks to the list of sectoral sanctions and sanctioning one shipbuilding company, the United Shipbuilding Corporation of St Petersburg. The Bank of Moscow, the Russian Agricultural Bank and VTB Bank were added to the list. American persons and firms were barred from providing them with financing for more than 90 days or issuing new equity. Restrictions were also placed on export licences on new technologies for deep-water or Arctic shale-drilling in Russia. As for the EU, on 31 July eight individuals and three entities were added to the list of 87 individuals and 20 entities already sanctioned. An arms embargo was imposed but without retrospective effect, hence theoretically allowing the sale of the two Mistral ships to go ahead. Financial restrictions were imposed on businesses, access to European capital markets was restricted for Russian state-owned banks, and the export of dual-use goods and technologies, including in the petroleum sector, was limited. The EU sought to avoid damaging the dense networks of industrial and commercial contracts with Russia, since this would have a negative effect on its economies, which already as a result of earlier sanctions were dropping back into recession. Equally, there remained a group of EU states who questioned piling on the pressure without an accompanying strategy to resolve the crisis.

At the St Petersburg Economic Forum in May Putin warned: 'In today's interdependent world economic sanctions used as an instrument of political pressure have a boomerang effect that ultimately has consequences for business and the economy in the countries that impose them.'[20] Disproportionate sanctions threatened to provoke Russian retaliation, possibly in the form of oil and gas cut-offs, which could drive the whole continent into recession. As Larry Elliott pointed out at the time: 'Every global downturn since 1973 has been associated with a sharp rise in the price of energy. Russia is one of the world's biggest energy suppliers and is responsible for about one-third of Europe's gas.' He went on to note: 'It is the potential for Russia to damage the West and for the West to cause even more damage to Russia that explains the belief that the crisis will not escalate into a full-scale economic war.' This was only a 'belief', and Elliott was well aware that it was only in the last week of July 1914, once Austria–Hungary had delivered its ultimatum to Serbia, that the financial markets 'woke up to the fact that the assassination in Sarajevo had the potential to lead to a war involving all the great European powers'.[21]

Russia did indeed retaliate. On 7 August a ban was imposed on the import of agricultural goods from countries that had placed sanctions on Russia – the EU, the US, Norway, Australia and Japan – and a ban on European airlines from flying to Asia over Siberia was threatened. Russia's failure to coordinate its actions with its ECU partners meant that Belarus and Kazakhstan failed to follow suit and impose restrictions on the import of foodstuffs. Russia is Europe's second-largest consumer market for food and drink, importing some €12.2 billion of goods in 2013, following years of double-digit growth. Russia had banned imports of US beef in 2013 because of health concerns, but 7 per cent of US poultry exports went to Russia, down from the 40 per cent of the mid-1990s. European producers were harder hit, and demanded compensation from the European Commission. Already Russia's state-owned banks had been cut off from European capital markets, and Russian defence and energy firms were unable to import hi-tech equipment for military purposes, fracking or Arctic oil exploration.[22] Russia's retaliatory measures were announced after a month of 'indiscriminate brutality' in Gaza, in which over 2,000 Palestinians, of whom at least 430 were children, and 67 Israelis were killed. The loudest in calling for sanctions in Russia were the quietest on this question, prompting the realisation of 'how loaded are the scales of Western moral outrage and selective the appetite for action'.[23]

Despite the 5 September ceasefire, on 12 September the EU imposed a fourth round of sanctions in actions coordinated with the US, this time targeting the Russian oil industry's ability to raise money on European capital markets. Rosneft, Transneft and Gazprom Neft were placed on the list of Russian state-owned firms that would not be allowed to raise capital or borrow on European markets, while existing 90-day lending bans affecting six top Russian banks were tightened to 30 days. This drastically increased borrowing costs and access to dollar-denominated funding sources. A further 24 people were added to the list of those barred from entry and whose assets in the EU were frozen. It was clear that the Western powers were attempting to shut down the important new exploration projects in Siberia and the Arctic by banning foreign companies from providing equipment, technology or assistance to deep-water, offshore and shale projects. Companies such as Exxon and Shell would now find dealings with their partners – such as Gazprom, Gazprom Neft, Rosneft, Lukoil and Surgutneftegaz – problematic. This represented a major Western escalation, just at the time when peace was on the table.

The new sanctions were probably part of a deal with the hawks – Poland, the Baltic republics and the UK, and their backers in Washington – as their price to agree to the peace process.[24] This was a bizarre and of course entirely counterproductive approach by any measure. Although Germany's criticism of Moscow had become more vocal, it remained in the pragmatist group, and even the other members of the Visegrád group (an informal alliance formed in 1991 that also included the Czech Republic, Hungary and Slovakia) distanced themselves from Poland's militancy. There was little evidence that the sanctions had in any way tempered Putin's stance, even with Russia's economic woes exacerbated by the fall in the price of oil to below $100 a barrel. Every $1 fall in the oil price wipes about $1.4 billion off Russia's federal tax receipts while reducing the resources available for energy companies to invest. By mid-2014 Rosneft was asking the government for $40.5 billion to repay its enormous debts. Just as a fall in oil prices in the mid-1980s heralded the fall of the Soviet Union, so today a smaller pie will undoubtedly weaken Putin's rule.

Most of the companies targeted had nothing to do with the events in Ukraine, demonstrating the political character of the sanctions. Restrictions on financing and technology exports to the Russian oil industry undoubtedly had a deleterious effect. Some of the Russian responses only exacerbated the problems, as with the hastily adopted law in May requiring Visa and MasterCard to deposit the equivalent of two days' worth of transactions processed in Russia with the Central Bank, on pain of losing their licences to operate in Russia. The measure was later modified to allow the companies to avoid the deposit if they found a domestic partner to process the transactions. The prime minister, Medvedev, argued that the unilateral sanctions against Russia were illegitimate according to international law and WTO rules, and on 20 June he warned that Russia intended to appeal to the WTO.[25] The appeal was still being discussed in September, as well as a new set of retaliatory measures, including an embargo on the import of second-hand cars and textile products. A law was drafted that would allow Russia to seize foreign assets. The sanctions encouraged greater Russian self-reliance, and boosted its manufacturing and service industries, as well as agriculture, although quality would fall behind that of the West. While the exploitation of oil reserves in the Arctic would slow down, there was now an added incentive to exploit stranded fields in Siberia and to improve the efficiency of production in existing fields. Any positive effect would have to be accompanied by improvements in the business climate and the rule of law. The 'fortress Russia' mentality was reinforced, viewing the sanctions as having little to do with Ukraine but reflecting a broader political attack on Russia, especially since a new round of 'economic warfare' was imposed after the ceasefire. From Russia's perspective, it simply made no sense.

ISOLATION AND DAMAGE

The sanctions against Russia were unprecedented in their scale and reach against a major power. Attempts were made to isolate the country and to damage its interests. US ministers roved the globe to bring in new partners in the endeavour, but with little success. On 23 September China announced that it would never support sanctions against Russia and would continue an economic partnership that could make up for losses inflicted by Western economic warfare. What was perceived to be the abuse of the global financial system saw the BRICS countries and their allies accelerate plans to create new financial centres, settlements in national currencies and new reserve currencies to displace American pre-eminence. Critics of globalisation had long argued that it served the interests of the dominant powers, and their views were now reinforced.

The US also put pressure on France to halt the sale of two Mistral assault ships to Russia. Each ship is twice the length of a football pitch and can carry 700 troops, 60 armoured vehicles, four landing craft and 16 helicopters. The contract for the ships, each costing €1.12 billion and to be furnished with navigation and technological equipment, including the licence documentation, was signed in June 2011. This was Russia's first major arms purchase abroad since the end of the Cold War, and encountered significant domestic opposition. On the eve of the NATO summit in Wales, on 3 September France suspended delivery of the completed Mistral *Vladivostok*. It was due to be delivered by 1 November 2014, while the second, ironically called the *Sevastopol*, was due by 1 November 2015. France insisted that the deal had not been cancelled, a move that would result in severe fines for breach of contract. Overall, there is no doubt that the sanctions impeded Russia's programme of military modernisation.[26] There were other creative ways in which Russia could be damaged, including giving Iran unrestricted access to energy markets to offset Moscow's position, as well as the right to enrich uranium. As the respected Russian journalist Georgy Bovt noted:

> The most absurd part is that the United States and the West continue to portray Russia as its [sic] main enemy, an exporter of terrorism in Ukraine. After all, Putin is not some Abu Bakr. And in many respects Ukraine has become part of the 'big chess game' that Brussels and Washington are playing against Moscow. The chessboard spans Eastern Europe and the entire post-Soviet space, and the game has continued in defiance of common sense since the end of the Cold War.[27]

Iraq continues to play an important part in Russian politics. The 2003 invasion, as Fyodor Lukyanov notes, marked

> a turning point in [...] Putin's assessment of the United States, the West and the possibility of full and equal co-operation with them [...] Iraq, in his opinion, proved that the United States is doing and will do what they [sic] want and see fit, even if it is contrary to the rule of law and requires the manipulation of evidence.

Iraq was seen as a test case for the global promotion of democracy, the process that we call 'democratism', and was 'a harbinger of the "colour revolutions" in the former Soviet Union, especially in Georgia and Ukraine'. The idea of the 'democratic peace' postulates that more democratic countries will lead to fewer conflicts and threats to the West. Despite the serious US–Russian confrontation over Ukraine, Lukyanov was convinced that 'Moscow will definitely not try to play the role of spoiler and exacerbate the problems the United States faces in the region', since a collapse of the state system in the Middle East would in the end threaten Russia as well.[28]

By the end of May, Bank Rossiya had already lost at least $1 billion because of the sanctions, while there was a general freeze on inward investment. Car sales declined by a quarter, and the Russian airline Aeroflot lost more than $50 million in the first half of the year. The sanctions, while perhaps not initially punitive in themselves, exacerbated an already worsening economic situation. The economy registered only 1.3 per cent growth in 2013, the weakest performance since 1999 (excluding the recession year of 2009), and the 1.1 per cent growth in the first half of 2014 was reversed thereafter. Instead of the planned 6 per cent inflation, by July it had risen to 7.8 per cent. In the early months of 2014 the rouble lost a fifth of its value against major currencies, while capital flight was anticipated to reach $100 billion, compared to the average annual outflow of $57 billion in the previous five years. The economy was showing signs of 'stagflation': low growth accompanied by high inflation.

The government's macroeconomic probity once again stood it in good stead, with foreign-currency reserves estimated at some $450 billion, but it is estimated that in March 2014 Russian companies had some $653 billion in foreign debt.[29] According to the *Financial Times* on 30 July, Russian state banks had $33 billion in external debt due over the next 12 months, Russian non-financial external debt of $41 billion was due over the same period, while private banks and companies owed $87 billion. This was a major factor in the rouble's weakness, reinforced by falling oil prices and the restrictions on foreign investment. In addition, Russian citizens held 21 per cent of their deposits in foreign currencies, and all payments for imports were carried out in foreign currencies. Since the onset of the Ukraine crisis in mid-March, the Russian Central Bank had raised its benchmark key rate from 5.5 to 8 per cent and spent $26 billion in support of the rouble. This was much less than the $200 billion spent between August 2008 and August 2009, but still a significant sum. The Central Bank's reserves of $440 billion were drawn on to keep the rouble within the floating nine-rouble-wide corridor against the dollar–euro basket. As always, the ratings agencies put the boot in, with Standard & Poor's downgrading Russia's sovereign debt rating to near junk status, cutting it by one notch from BBB to BBB–, the lowest investment-grade level. With the threat of further Western measures to damage the Russian economy, debt markets were closed to Russian companies, with an effective freeze on Eurobond placements and earlier bonds forced to be repaid before time. With $115 billion in foreign debt due by the end of the year, companies were forced to reduce dividends and rely on domestic capital markets to tide them over. One positive effect of the great recession after 2008 was that most companies had sufficient liquidity to survive the closure of the refinancing market.

With an economy that was already slowing down, sanctions were driving Russia into recession. In a sober assessment of the economy, the economic-development minister Alexei Ulyukaev noted that 'we have entered a negative stage of the economic cycle', and admitted that it would be very hard significantly to improve the 'business climate and interest investors given the quality of institutions that we have', and he outlined the tough options facing the country.[30] The government veered between measures to stimulate growth, before the imposition of a more hawkish policy devised by the Russian Central Bank to dampen inflation. Plans to reduce interest rates gave way to a series of rises to encourage rouble savings and to slow capital flight. Western businesses were deterred from developing new contracts with Russian firms, even if they were not directly sanctioned. The Central Bank insisted that it would stick to the plan to allow the rouble to float freely in 2015.

The sanctions could be used as an excuse to explain declining Russian economic performance and thus impede necessary reforms. They certainly strengthened the voice of those within Russia calling for greater self-sufficient development, if not outright autarchy. Already under Putin the shift to greater privatisation had been reversed, and now about half of the economy is in state hands, a high proportion by contemporary standards. The Yukos affair from 2003 had deprivatised what had been Russia's biggest oil company and returned it to the state in the form of Rosneft, while Gazprom had absorbed Sibneft to create Gazprom Neft. In 2008 Putin sponsored 'economic security' laws that restricted the access of international companies to mineral licences and large-scale investment projects. The sanctions now damaged international energy partnerships, notably Rosneft's plan to build an LNG plant on Sakhalin and the exploitation of Arctic resources with ExxonMobil, and various projects with Shell, Statoil and Total. China or Brazil could not make up the loss of technical expertise in the short term, although China has an extraordinarily dynamic petroleum industry, making it the world's fourth-largest oil producer after the US, Saudi Arabia and Russia. Its two major state-owned companies, CNPC and Sinopec, have very advanced secondary and tertiary recovery techniques to reverse declining output from ageing oil fields, and the country is graduating ten times more qualified petroleum engineers each year than the US. In general, import substitution has repeatedly failed as a developmental strategy, leaving economies uncompetitive and bloated with rent-seekers. However, this could become necessary if corporations, threatened with draconian penalties (as they had been over Iran) for breaches in the sanctions regime, prefer to be risk-averse and cut their Russian losses.

On the political front, the regime had long felt threatened by the West, and now the overtly anti-Russian measures, accompanied by the demonisation of Putin himself, provoked a further clampdown at home. Officials explicitly warned that the development of a Ukrainian scenario in Russia would not be permitted. On 24 April Putin expressed the view that the internet was a tool of the CIA. A few days earlier, Pavel Durov, the founder of the most popular Russian social-networking site VKontakte (the equivalent of Facebook), had already revealed that political pressure had forced him to leave Russia. Although Crimea's return boosted Putin's popularity, an extended period of sanctions would undoubtedly damage society and test elite cohesion. Sanctions are easier to impose than they are to lift. In the US they were imposed by presidential executive orders and not Congress, and thus could be repealed relatively easily. In Europe the original plan had been for the sanctions to lapse automatically after one year unless a consensus could be found for them to be renewed. However, Barroso managed to have this inverted, and now after a year it would require agreement to have them lifted, a much more difficult task.

THE PHILOSOPHY OF SANCTIONS

Sanctions are seldom an effective foreign-policy tool, and so it proved in this case. Such measures had a potentially devastating impact, but on their own would not lead to a Russian 'surrender'. They embodied the scapegoat philosophy, allowing policy makers to avoid facing hard questions about how the structure of post-Cold War international politics could have allowed the crisis of Ukrainian statehood to become an international crisis of the first order. The sanctions would certainly not force Russia to become part of the extended Western order, but would shape the future international landscape as Russia and other putative great powers considered their responses. It is quite likely that Russia will be alienated from the West for a generation, accompanied by intensified efforts to create alternative international systems of economic and political power to insulate the non-West from Western pressure.

The sanctions sapped the strength of all sides and undermined the whole structure of international law that had been so laboriously built up in the post-war era. Russia had become one of the most open large economies outside the Organisation for Economic Cooperation and Development (OECD), with its trade-to-GDP ratio of 52 per cent: equal to China's, double that of Brazil, and far higher than Indonesia's and India's. Sanctions made a mockery of the WTO system, returning the world to the free-for-all that it had been established to regulate. Putin insisted that by imposing economic restrictions on Russia, Western countries ignored basic WTO norms and repudiated the principles of fair trade and competition.[31] It proved remarkably easy to roll back on 'globalisation' when geopolitical interests were at stake. Not only did they violate WTO rules, but the EU sanctions were probably illegal since they lacked the sanction of the UN Security Council, quite apart from randomly sanctioning Russian businesses and individuals who had nothing to do with shaping Russian policy.

In the post-Cold War era the West has become 'sanctions-happy', applying them with increasing abandon against regimes of which it disapproves despite the considerable evidence that they are at best a blunt instrument to achieve desired outcomes. The idea is to change the behaviour of the target state, and therefore they have to be of sufficient intensity to cause pain. At the same time, they must not be so intense as to provoke a violent reaction from the sanctioned party. A classic case of the latter were the sanctions imposed on Japan in July 1941 following the latter's invasion of Indochina. America froze all Japanese assets, followed by the UK and the Dutch East Indies (today's Indonesia). The sanctions were devastatingly effective, cutting off the bulk of Japan's international trade and 90 per cent of its oil imports. They did not achieve the desired effect, however – withdrawal from Indochina – and instead Japan attacked Pearl Harbor in December 1941. Acceptance of the terms would effectively have meant subordination to American hegemony. Japan feared that they would have been followed by new demands; hence, although well aware of the risks, the country felt it had no choice but to go to war. Sanctions work better when the capacity of the target state to retaliate is weak, as was the case with Iraq in the 1990s, even though the measures had a devastating impact on health and infant mortality. In South Africa sanctions helped isolate the apartheid regime and prepared the way for the peaceful transfer of power. The efficacy of sanctions against Iran is more finely balanced, but did not do much to discourage its nuclear ambitions or stop its support for various allies in the Middle East.

Russia not only has the potential for a devastating military response, but could also retaliate by seizing economic assets and putting an energy squeeze on Europe. This is the reason that the sanctions were not placed on Russia as a whole but on certain individuals and a select group of companies. The assumption was that the regime cared more for money than the national interest, a questionable view at best. The targeted individuals were only reinforced in their view that Ukraine was but a proxy for deep-seated resentment against Russia's refusal to 'embrace defeat'. They certainly will not rise to depose Putin, and instead rallied to the flag and the leader. The same applies to the people at large, as demonstrated by Putin's extraordinarily high popularity ratings and the further marginalisation of the liberal opposition. Economic interdependency makes the intensification of sanctions problematic. In short, as George Friedman puts it:

> The US sanctions strategy is therefore not designed to change Russian policies; it is designed to make it look like the United States is trying to change Russian policy.

And it is aimed at those in Congress who have made this a major issue and at those parts of the State Department that want to orient US national security around the issue of human rights. Both can be told that something is being done – and both can pretend that something is being done – when in fact nothing can be done. In a world clamouring for action, prudent leaders sometimes prefer the appearance of doing something to actually doing something.[32]

This does not explain why the EU followed so meekly in the wake of the US, especially since its economic interests were so much greater. The answer lies in the broader development of the philosophy of sanctions in the post-Cold War era. They have been practised against countries such as Cuba for several generations, but have now become generalised. They have become the weapon of choice of the hegemonic powers against regimes they do not like, such as that led by Hugo Chávez and his successors in Venezuela, and above all Iran. As with so much Western policy, it is the selective nature of the countries targeted that renders them less an instrument for the consistent defence of human rights than a political weapon against obstreperous countries that refuse to buckle down to Anglo-American leadership. The Russian deputy foreign minister Sergei Ryabkov argued that the US had turned sanctions into a new kind of offensive weapon, used as an alternative to traditional military power that politicised market relations: 'We know for a fact that the American administration pressured its allies and top businesspeople to avoid forums and events that were important for Russia' – he had in mind the St Petersburg Economic Forum of May 2014. There was only one reason for Washington's aggressive behaviour:

America believes that it won the Cold War and Russia, which is the continuation of the Soviet Union, lost it. From this they deduce that Moscow must now obey and behave as a younger partner in international affairs, as well as its interactions with the US. Essentially, this annuls the possibility of us having our own national interests. It annuls the possibility of us having a value system that is different from America's or that of other Western countries.

He stressed that Russia had the right to seek ways to protect itself: 'For every offensive weapon, there must be a defensive one.'[33] In other words, Russia would devise appropriate counter-measures. At root, the Western philosophy of sanctions is based on the inability to recognise the political subjectivity of others and to engage in a genuine dialogue of equals.

This was reflected in comments made by Sergei Lavrov to a group of CIS diplomats in Moscow on 25 April. He argued that the West was engaged in its own propaganda war against Russia, part of which was the charge that Russia was engaging in a propaganda war of its own. Lavrov noted:

> Our Western partners, without batting an eyelid, keep demanding that Russia cease interfering in Ukraine. To withdraw troops and pull out agents allegedly caught in the south-east commanding the whole process. […] I have spoken with John Kerry on this subject over the past two weeks now, and many times I have told him that if the Ukrainians have Russian agents in custody, show them to the people on TV.

He went on to complain that 'we are being addressed with slogans':

> If you think that when I get a call from John Kerry, William Hague, or Laurent Fabius, they express themselves differently on the phone and explain their reasoning, then you don't realize that they use exactly the same slogans even without an audience: 'Sergei, you need to withdraw your troops, pull out your agents – no one in the world believes that this is not Russia's doing in the south-east.' It's very difficult to respond to that.[34]

Former prime minister Sergei Stepashin argued that US actions are

> a consequence of [Obama's] hurt ambitions, which have remained hurt since the Russian president saved the US president from public loss of face in front of the whole world by suggesting the introduction of international control over chemical weapons to prevent military intervention in Syria.[35]

The aim appeared not to be to reduce the suffering of Ukraine but to punish Russia and in particular Putin for his impudent assertion of independence, however ill-advised. The aim had thus become to lever Putin out of power and to isolate Russia on the international stage. If the sanctions had been intended to change Putin's policies, force regime change or alienate popular support, then on all counts they were a spectacular failure. Indeed, many commented that 'the country feels more united than it has done for many years'.[36] But these issues are the least of it. Europe demonstrated that it had not vanquished its demons of war. It was incapable of mastering the very basic principle of modern statecraft – the independent solution of problems. Worse, by simply laying all responsibility on Russia – the classic externalisation of responsibility – recognition that the roots of the conflict lay in Europe's own contradictions was avoided. As a result, the response to the Ukraine crisis saw the intensification of policies that had provoked the conflict in the first place.

CHAPTER 9

FRONTLINE POLITICS

The Ukraine crisis threw the deeper patterns of Russo-Western interaction into sharp relief. The misperceptions and alternative representations of reality on display will keep scholars busy for decades to come. As the two worlds moved apart, the divisions within Ukraine were sorely exposed. External interventions in the affairs of Ukraine became part of the currency of internal debate, including the fierce media war to advance particularistic perspectives. The struggle in the information sphere used to be called propaganda, and it is appropriate to use the term to describe much of the partisan reporting on both sides. This was already in evidence at the time of the Russo-Georgian war in 2008, and if anything intensified in this new round of the same confrontation. At the same time, one of the novelties of great-power conflict in the early twenty-first century is the intensity with which political leaders of countries are demonised. An unholy alliance of opportunist politicians and subservient media traduce their opponents, ignoring the views of experts and scholars, to portray them as mendacious and untrustworthy. The basis for treating the other as a legitimate political subject is undermined and in the end justifies political and military intervention. The Ukraine crisis once again demonstrated the decay of contemporary diplomacy. Abusive and condemnatory rhetoric took the place of rational debate.

RUSSIAN LOGIC AND RATIONALITY

One of the most contentious issues is assessing Russia's motives and ambitions in the Ukraine crisis. The task is made all the harder since the goals have undoubtedly shifted over time, and there was no unity within the Russian elite on what, fundamentally, it was trying to achieve in Ukraine. Policy has changed and evolved in response to the dramatic events. Nevertheless, a number of entrenched views – some would call them myths – need to be examined. The idea that Russia opposed Ukraine's association with the EU needs to be modified by an understanding that the struggle prior to the planned signing of the Association Agreement sought to align Ukraine with the EEU, but not necessarily to force Ukraine to join it. In part, the campaign was an attempt to get the EU to engage in a genuine dialogue about the conditions on which Ukraine would sign up to association with the EU, including security issues. This campaign was conducted in a typically heavy-handed and alienating manner, with bans, boycotts and the like accompanied by some ferocious rhetoric from Sergei Glazyev and others, but some genuine issues were raised. Above all, Russia repeatedly warned that it would take measures to stop poor-quality Ukrainian and relabelled EU goods flooding into the Russian market once better-quality EU goods had free access to Ukraine. The compatibility of two free-trade areas is a matter that should, and could, have been sorted out calmly by technocrats on both sides but instead became politicised.

Further, there is the view that Putin's policy reflected 'Russia's imperialist ambitions and aspirations to restore the former Soviet empire'. These 'assessments are quite simplistic and often erroneous regarding the interpretation of the sources of Russia's behaviour and intentions'.[1] There is a pervasive myth that Russia from the first sought to place Ukraine under its direct control, rather than merely trying to influence its decisions. If this were indeed the goal, then the moment following Yanukovych's ouster on 22 February would have been ideal. The Ukrainian military reforms between 2010 and 2012 left the armed forces in a state of disarray, and defence of a legitimately elected president could have acted as the rallying call. On 22 February, at a meeting in Kharkov, the PoR called on local councils to take power. Yanukovych had rather unwisely left Kiev to attend the conference, and soon after fled to Rostov, from whence he urged intervention to crush the Maidan revolution.[2] If Russia really did want to place Ukraine under Russian control, then there could have been no better time than this.

Third, there is little evidence that the annexation of Crimea followed by unrest in the east and the south was part of a long-established plan to separate 'Novorossiya' from Ukraine. Russia undoubtedly probed and exploited Ukrainian vulnerabilities, but its end goals were not clear. Once Crimea was taken, there was every incentive to stop there, but the movement within Ukraine for 'federalisation' gathered pace, raising genuine concerns about the imposition of a narrow form of monist nationhood on the rest of the country. There had already been the aggressive, and incompetent, Ukrainisation experience of the Yushchenko period following the Orange Revolution, and the early acts of the February regime raised fears, intensified after the 2 May Odessa massacre, of an even more militant version coming to power. As Andranik Migranyan argues: 'if Russia preserved Crimea and the rest of Ukraine fell under the control of anti-Russian nationalists in Kiev, under the command of Washington, the outcome of the fight for Ukraine would obviously be serious defeat for Russia.' The Russians would be forced out of the country, and the rest would be 'forcefully "ukrainianized"'. No one has any illusions about the national-linguistic policy of the incumbent powers in Ukraine, should they prevail in the South and East of the country.'[3]

The terrible point was that Russia was not a challenger at all. It was certainly an awkward neighbour, a difficult friend, testy and insecure, and beset by myriad internal difficulties and dreadfully unsure of its place in the world. But it was not a challenger in anything like the way that the Wilhelmine Reich had become in 1914, let alone Hitler's Third Reich in 1939. It was a conservative and defensive power, in thrall to an increasingly traditionalist domestic ideology and certainly not challenging the bases of international law. Indeed, the very essence of its neo-revisionism was the proclaimed defence of the international law that it believed the Western powers regularly flouted. In his *Direct Line* session of 17 April, Putin insisted that Russia 'had never intended to annex any territories. [...] Quite the contrary, we were going to build our relations with Ukraine based on current geopolitical realities.' It was only when the situation changed that the Russian Security Council agreed to support the 'self-determination' of the Crimean people. Putin insisted that the Crimean takeover had not been 'pre-planned or prepared', but he now admitted that 'Russian servicemen did back the Crimean self-defence forces', drawn from the 'more than 20,000 well-armed soldiers stationed in Crimea'. He also noted that in addition to the strategic importance of the Sevastopol base, there were '38 S-300 missile-launchers, weapons depots and rounds of ammunition. It was imperative to prevent even the possibility of someone using these weapons against civilians.' In broad terms, he argued: 'The intention to split Russia and Ukraine, to separate what is essentially a single nation in many ways, has been an issue of international politics for centuries.'[4] Of course, it was precisely this sort of 'Malorussian' thinking that so enraged the 'Ukrainisers', and one can see why.

On the other side, as Dmitry Trenin puts it:

> The Kremlin absolutely could not ignore the developments in Ukraine, a country of utmost importance to Russia. The armed uprising in Kiev brought to power a coalition of ultranationalists and pro-Western politicians: the worst possible combination Moscow could think of.

Responding to the challenge entailed long-term conflict with the US, with Ukraine 'the main battleground of that struggle. The main goal is to bar Ukraine from NATO, and the US military from Ukraine. Other goals include keeping the Russian cultural identity of Ukraine's south and east, and keeping Crimea Russian.'[5] Putin repeatedly returned to the strategic challenge posed by developments in Ukraine. Meeting the press on 24 May, for example, he stressed:

> Some of the events in Ukraine directly threaten our interests, first of all with regard to security. I'm talking about Ukraine's potential accession to NATO. As I said earlier, such an accession could be followed by the deployment of missile strike systems in Ukraine, including Crimea. Should this happen, it would have serious geopolitical consequences for our country. In fact, Russia would be forced out of the Black Sea territory, a region for legitimate presence in which Russia has fought for centuries. And those who started the coup in Kiev – if they are indeed experts – should have thought about the consequences of their unlawful ambitions.

He rejected the notion that the breach over Ukraine represented the beginning of a new Cold War, arguing: 'No one is interested in that and I don't think it will happen.'[6]

Addressing the Russian Security Council on 22 July, Putin reprised the standard Russian account:

> Today we hear of ultimatums and sanctions. The very notion of state sovereignty is being washed out. Undesirable regimes, countries that conduct an independent policy or that simply stand in the way of somebody's interests get destabilised. Tools used for this purpose are the so-called colour revolutions, or, in simple terms – takeovers instigated and financed from outside.

In his view, this was the case with Ukraine: 'People came to power through the use of armed force and by unconstitutional means.' He admitted that an election was held, but,

> for some strange reason, power ended up again in the hands of those who either funded or carried out this takeover. Meanwhile, without any attempt at negotiations, they are trying to suppress by force that part of the population that does not agree with such a turn of events. At the same time they present Russia with an ultimatum: either you let us destroy the part of the population that is ethnically, culturally and historically close to Russia, or we introduce sanctions against you. This is a strange logic, and absolutely unacceptable, of course.[7]

There is little to suggest that there would be an attempt to 'destroy' the Russophone population, but after the ill-fated first acts of the February regime and the Odessa massacre there were undoubtedly increased concerns that, at the minimum, political and cultural marginalisation would be intensified.

By mid-May 2014 it looked as if the Ukrainian state was on the verge of collapse. At that point there was a clear retrenchment in the Russian position, usually attributed to the sanctions but more likely reflecting domestic struggles within Russia. Putin denounced the independence referendums in Donetsk and Lugansk held on 11 May, and Russia withdrew its forces from the Ukrainian border, then went on, albeit grudgingly, to accept the legitimacy of the presidential election on 25 May. Moscow had a clear strategic objective in taking over Crimea, above all the retention of the Sevastopol naval base, but this was lacking in the Donbas. Although Putin mentioned Novorossiya in his televised dialogue with Russian citizens on 17 April, he recognised the complexities of Ukrainian society, where even the predominantly Russian-speaking parts maintained an allegiance to Ukrainian statehood (although of a more pluralist sort), while the mixed Russo-Ukrainian Surzhyk-speaking regions had their own traditions that were distinct from Russia's. If there had been a plan to create a Novorossiya dependency, then it would have appeared in speeches and policy statements earlier, if only to gather support for such a project among the relevant Ukrainian and Russian publics. Russia, quite simply, lacked any official plans to create such an entity, although of course it was part of the rhetoric of the roiling mass of domestic nationalist movements.

The federalisation of Ukraine was certainly a Russian goal, to temper the monism of the Ukrainisers, but breaking up the state was not part of the agenda. General Philip Breedlove, the Supreme Allied Commander in Europe (SACEUR) suggested that Russia's strategy was to re-establish parts of the pre-revolutionary Novorossiya territories arching across from the Donbas to Odessa, and then to link up with Transnistria, which would be definitively torn from Moldova. Fantasies of dismembering Ukraine and gaining either a friendly protectorate state on its borders or even the outright annexation of territories were certainly played out in the Russian media, but did not gain official support. If indeed Ukraine had collapsed, then Russia would undoubtedly have moved in, as would other states, to protect civilians, installations (especially nuclear power plants) and to re-establish order. Instead, Russian actions were an angry and ad hoc response to Yanukovych's overthrow and the installation of an anti-Russian nationalistic government in Kiev, but rooted in a swelling tide of neo-revisionist sentiment. Cost considerations alone would have deterred all but the most intrepid of imperial expansionists. Russia could have done more to calm the situation in the Donbas, but the early actions of the Maidan government were no less inflammatory, and indeed genuinely threatening to many of Ukraine's pluralists. The killings in Odessa on 2 May and Mariupol on 9 May stand as a stark warning of what could have happened elsewhere. As Mary Dejevsky points out, fear rather than aggression was the most plausible driver of Russian actions. Even Obama after the annexation of Crimea noted that the move reflected weakness rather than strength, accompanied by Russia's 'centuries-old fear of encirclement'.[8]

In the longer term, Russia's strategic goals have been remarkably consistent, reaching back into the 1990s and certainly encompassing the Orange Revolution. The aim was to keep Ukraine out of Western security structures, above all NATO. The promises made at Bucharest in April 2008 were not rescinded but only placed on hold, despite the war in Georgia that summer. In the Medvedev years there was plenty of cooperation with Obama within the framework of the 'reset', and the issue of NATO enlargement was barely mentioned, although it simmered away in the background as more immediate contentious issues, notably missile defence, occupied the centre ground. Equally, from at least 2008 Russia became more suspicious of EU enlargement. All the new EU members were also members of NATO, and, at the same time, the Association Agreements had a profound security dimension. On the purely economic front, the Wider European agenda repudiated the model of mutually negotiated and compatible free-trade areas, and instead sought to reorient partner countries firmly to the West. There were some good reasons to frame the associations in this way, since the aim was to achieve genuine transformations in governance relations that would establish more competitive market economies compatible with the EU's own system. This model had worked well in Eastern Europe, but the incentive structure there had been much stronger – namely the promise of EU membership. Accession was not even part of the medium-term agenda for the EaP countries, so a more gradual approach would have been wiser, building on existing bilateral links to the east while supporting the transformation of regulatory and governance structures. A free and prosperous Ukraine was certainly not something opposed by Russia, but Moscow simply did not understand why this had to be couched in anti-Russian terms and threaten its economic interests.

Hence Moscow fought long and hard to convince the EU and Ukraine to change the Wider European model, and then in the months before November 2013 it applied all the crude tools in its armoury to convince Yanukovych to step back from the brink. He is typically portrayed as 'pro-Russian' in the Western media, but, as I have argued earlier, Yanukovych was neither pro-Russian nor pro-Western, but a rather degenerate representative of the bureaucratic–oligarchic order, largely concerned with his personal aggrandisement. He did receive support from Moscow, but personal relations with Putin were very poor. Putin found it more congenial to do business with Tymoshenko, but he was forced to deal with Yanukovych as the democratically elected leader of Ukraine. The argument that Putin and Yanukovych united in defence of kleptocratic regimes is a thin one, although greatly peddled by Russian liberals and the Western media.[9] The argument that the example of a free and genuinely democratic Ukraine would destabilise the Putinite system in Russia is also unconvincing. Putin was obsessive in his attempts to block Western 'democracy promotion' in Russia, and it was clear that he had a bad case of Orange-phobia, but as I have argued in numerous works, Russian politics is rather more complex than the simple model of 'autocratic' consolidation would suggest. If Ukraine could overcome corruption, oligarchic predominance and the decay of institutions, that was fine, as long as these were not accompanied by a geostrategic shift towards NATO. Equally, association with the EU in and of itself was not considered a threat, and possibly even beneficial if it could resolve Ukraine's governance problems, but not at Russia's expense. Of course, the more passionate supporters of Eurasian integration (notably Glazyev) wanted Ukraine to be part of the new Eurasian Union (EaU), but this was just one faction among many, although since 2012 an increasingly vocal one. The Medvedevite wing of the Russian elite, which still runs the bulk of the government, supports a successful and prosperous Ukraine as long it respects Russia's legitimate concerns.

The geostrategic issue is stressed by Migranyan: 'The unification of Crimea with Russia was a huge achievement; yet the loss of the rest of Ukraine would mean allowing a new frenzied anti-Russian country to be created on the borders of Russia – in line with Poland and the Baltic states – with very grave consequences for Russia.' As far as Migranyan was concerned, Russia's goals were consistent: 'out-of-bloc status, federalization and a friendly state between Russia and Europe', while America's alleged goals were also consistent: 'the consolidation of state power on an anti-Russian basis and making the country a major forefront for Washington's pressure on Moscow'. Any concession by Moscow would lead to yet more demands from Washington, including the return of Crimea, 'until the complete capitulation of Moscow'. The stakes could not be higher: 'the fight for Ukraine is not to decide Ukraine's fate – it is to decide the future of Russia and the United States as well, and therefore, the future of the world'. The US certainly would not in the long run accept Ukraine's permanent non-bloc status.[10] The big picture was the creation of a consolidated Euro-Atlantic alliance to meet global challenges, and as Brzezinski argued, Russia needed to be incorporated into that system – obviously not as an equal but as a subaltern element.[11] This recalled the so-called 'Wolfowitz Doctrine' of 1992, effectively outlining the strategy for containing Russia. The doctrine asserted that the US should prevent 'any country from dominating any region of the world that might be a springboard to threaten unipolar and exclusive US global dominance'.[12] In one form or another, this has been the strategy pursued by the US since the fall of Communism, and is a vivid expression of the asymmetry embedded in Western policy since that time.

Sergei Karaganov argues that the West failed 'to give up the "velvet-gloved Versailles" policy towards Russia, i.e. abandon its policy of systemic encroachment on spheres of Russia's vital interests'. He notes that a similar policy against Germany earlier provoked a predictable surge of revanchist sentiments and ultimately led to World War II, and: 'Now we have the tragedy of the Ukrainian people whom this policy has turned into the cannon fodder of geopolitical strife.'[13] It was precisely Russia's refusal to accept subordination and its advancement of the 'greater Eurasia' plans for integration that provoked the Ukraine crisis. America's refusal to accept Russia's 'alterity' and independence, in Migranyan's view, is the essence of the Ukraine crisis. It made no difference who ruled Russia or what views they had on Ukraine:

If US strategy seeks to limit Russia's sovereignty and subordinate it to Washington's diktat, use Russia's resources in the future collision with China and not allow any closer cooperation between Russia and China, then this strategy will continue no matter what compromises Russia is ready to make on the current stage of the Ukraine crisis.[14]

Thus, in addition to Russia's goals of keeping Crimea, achieving international agreement that NATO would not enlarge to Ukraine, and ensuring that adequate pressure was placed on Kiev to create a more inclusive political order, including genuine decentralisation, there was the global issue of a rising power seeking to find its place in the sun. Quite how much Russia was 'rising' is another matter.

Both Ukraine and Russia face the challenge of creating pluralist democracies and establishing the rule of law, and it is not clear that the 'revolutionary' path pursued by Ukraine is any more effective than the 'evolutionary' one asserted by Putin. One of the dominant monist narratives is that Putin's aggressive actions, in the words of Alexander Motyl, one of the most ardent exponents of this line,

forced Ukraine to become independent, democratic, and pro-Western. He's forced it to develop an army and security apparatus. He's forced the population to take sides and discover its Ukrainian identity – and pride. He's forced the government to streamline the state apparatus. He's forced the elites to embrace democracy. And he's forcing them to embark on radical economic reform and administrative decentralization.[15]

If Putin did indeed force Ukraine to democratise, modernise its bureaucracy and genuinely devolve power to the regions, then he would really deserve to be called father of the Ukrainian state. Instead, a negative consolidation had taken place – against Russia, against Eurasian integration, against 'separatists' – which fanned a virulent monism that assumed some of the hues of the integral nationalism of the interwar years.

Although the Donbas insurgents were portrayed as Putin's puppets, this was far from the case. They were mostly drawn from the local communities, although support did come from across the border, most of which was spontaneous and voluntary. While the crisis may have forged a new Ukrainian identity, its pluralist and civic elements were balanced by darker features. The crisis also strengthened the nationalist wing in Russian politics, and Putin's soaring popularity suggested a no less strong wave of patriotic consolidation. The opposition leader Boris Nemtsov warned that 'a Russian Maidan is inevitable', but there was little evidence of this.[16] On 15 March over 30,000 people joined the 'Peace March' ('*Marsh mira*') through the centre of Moscow in protest against the deployment of Russian forces in Crimea, and a second demonstration on 21 September gathered much the same number, but liberal opposition to Putin's Ukraine policy was remarkably weak. The main danger instead came from the nationalist right. The failure to give concrete form to the Greater European project inspired the advocates of one form or another of 'Greater Russia'. At the head of the reinvigorated traditionalists were ideologues such as Alexander Dugin and Alexander Prokhanov, and field commanders such as Igor Girkin. Their spiritual home was the *Zavtra* newspaper and the Izborsky Club, which brought out a glossy monthly journal. Their ideal of an authoritarian Eurasian state was very different from the relatively liberal model of integration instantiated in Putin's EEU. Prokhanov asserted that his 15-year long dream of a return to the Cold War had now been fulfilled.[17]

Putin's leadership acted as the regulator of factional and institutional conflict, guaranteeing elite interests while managing relations between the state oligarchy and society. He was the supreme arbitrator, drawing strength from all the factions and society but remaining independent of all. This system satisfied all to some degree, but none to the full. It delivered significant public goods in the short term, but was unable to guarantee a strategy for long-term development, increasing the modernisation blockage and political stalemate. It was vulnerable to external shocks and internal disintegration.[18] This does not mean that Ukraine would be Putin's undoing. His return to power in 2012 alienated the liberal intelligentsia, but Crimean reunification brought back some of the radical nationalists to his camp. Putin's mention of 'Novorossiya' in his broadcast on 17 April raised expectations and inspired many to believe that he supported separatism, but soon after he distanced himself from the independence referendums of 11 May. The perceived betrayal of the insurgency in the Donbas threatened once again to alienate the nationalists and the Eurasianists, splitting Putin from his 'patriotic' base, but the regime by now was well practised in the art of societal management. Already in June 2014 Dugin, the ideologist of neo-Eurasianism, was dismissed from his post as director of the International Sociology department of Moscow State University, a move that he described as 'political repression.'[19] Dugin was undoubtedly disappointed: 'Before, we could have an illusion that Putin himself is a Eurasian patriot. [...] His hesitation now is a sign that he has followed this line by some pragmatic calculations, by some realistic understanding of the politics.'[20] Despite the disappointment of the patriots, there were few organised challenges to Putin's regime internally, while his foreign-policy stance was supported at home.

The ethno-nationalists call for solidarity with the ethnic Russian diaspora of some 25 million people, who suddenly found themselves 'abroad' when the Soviet Union broke up in 1991. In his 18 March Crimea speech Putin appealed to this community, with over 20 references to '*Russkii*' (which carries an ethnic connotation, unlike the more inclusive '*Rossiiskii*'). Putin referred to the Russians as a divided people, appealing to national values, but there was no consistent programme to 'reunite' these compatriots with Russia by making claims on such areas as northern Kazakhstan or Narva in Estonia. Putin was even hesitant to recognise the entities in eastern Ukraine that appealed to Russia for help. Thus Andrei Tsygankov is right to argue that

> Putin is not a nationalist. While appropriating key concepts from the nationalist vocabulary, he alternates them with ideas that nationalists may find objectionable. [...] By doing so he preserves the flexibility that he needs to preserve the power of the state, which is his true priority.[21]

Equally, the Ukraine crisis only reinforced Putin's turn away from what used to be called the First World, the West, towards a vague new Second Worldism, comprising countries that were also critical of the existing distribution of world power. The sanctions accelerated Russia's own pivot to the east, and intensified the strategic partnership with China. However, this shift should be kept in perspective. In his speech to the biannual gathering of ambassadors and diplomats on 1 July, Putin called on them to improve the relationship with Europe, despite American attempts to destabilise that relationship.[22] In other words, Ukraine was not such a game-changer after all, and Russia had certainly not turned its back on Europe, although it did seek to strengthen its more enduring relationships in Asia.

Putin, whatever his failings, is not an ideologue. Although passionate in his views and loud in his condemnation of the failings of other states, he remains rational and pragmatic. He was well aware that the US had lured the Soviet Union into the Afghan quagmire, precipitating its collapse. The architect of that strategy was Zbigniew Brzezinski, who even before the Soviet invasion of December 1979 had talked President Carter into arming the mujahideen. Later, drawing on Halford

Mackinder's heartland theory, Brzezinski argued that it was essential to prevent a single power dominating the Eurasian land mass and thus challenging America's global pre-eminence. His formulation of America's Eurasian geostrategy entailed keeping Russia weak, preferably, as he notoriously argued, divided into a number of smaller states, and certainly prevented from exerting any influence on Ukraine. His book *The Grand Chessboard* has been translated into Russian and is part of everyday political discussion.[23] Flushed with the 'success' of his Afghanistan strategy, he now argued in favour of the West arming forces within Ukraine capable of resisting the Russian 'occupation'. Putin was well aware of the dangers of being sucked into a war over Ukraine, which would be unwinnable and disastrous. The costs of maintaining even the two regions of the Donbas would be far beyond Russia's limited capacities, while a full-scale occupation of Ukraine was inconceivable. In short, a 'hybrid war' was one thing, but the dangers of escalation and 'mission creep' were well known. Although the Kremlin could only wonder at how it could be accused of acting in a nineteenth-century manner when the US has been ruthless in the exercise of authority, it understood the limitations of its own power.

THE TWO UNITED STATES

US global policy remains at war with itself. On the one side, it is the arch-exponent of a liberal trading order and with it the whole ramified architecture of liberal internationalism. This is a vision of world order that has predominated since World War II and triumphed with the dissolution of its main ideological competitor, the Soviet Union, in 1989–91. It is a system based on competitive and open economies, stable borders, open seas, free trade and sound money. It is a model of 'globalisation' that most countries of the world have accepted, including Russia and China, although with their own specific caveats. This system has brought unprecedented peace and prosperity to large parts of the world. The US has worked hard to expand that order – for example, by supporting Russia's accession to the WTO, which was finally achieved in August 2012. However, on the other side, the US remains the centre of a vast geopolitical power system in which its claims to lead are challenged today by the so-called rising powers.[24] We have noted some of Brzezinski's thinking, which is ruthlessly realist and geopolitical and has little time for the niceties of dialogue and compromise unless they serve the cause of Atlanticism. Ukraine was to act as the eastern anchor of an Atlanticist Europe.[25] For liberal universalists and geopolitical realists alike, the Ukrainian crisis of 2013 offered an opportunity to complete the 'unfinished revolution' of the Orange administration from 2004, pushing aside the more cautious Europeans to consolidate US hegemony ('leadership') and to punish Russia – for its temerity in upstaging the US over the Syrian chemical weapons crisis in mid-2013, for giving refuge to the whistle-blower Edward Snowden (reluctantly, since the US had cancelled his passport), and in general for its refusal to kowtow in the appropriate manner. Glazyev reflected what had effectively become the orthodoxy in Moscow when he argued that the US 'is essentially provoking an international conflict to salvage its geopolitical, financial and economic authority', and he advocated a 'global anti-war coalition' with Russia at its head.[26] Above all, those with a strategic sense argued that the US had to challenge Russia over Ukraine as a warning to China over its possible ambitions in the South China Sea and Taiwan.

As argued above, Russia's neo-revisionism does not challenge the fundamentals of liberal internationalism (what we can call the 'first' US), but its striving for parity of esteem and diplomatic equality inevitably brought it into conflict with the security order centred on the US (that is, the 'second' US). The genius of this US global dualism is that it can pursue traditional geopolitical goals of great-power maximisation (the nineteenth-century model) while claiming to be serving the dispassionate interests of the liberal-internationalist order (the claimed post-Westphalian, twenty-first-century globalised system).[27] To outsiders, and to Putin's great chagrin, this looks like a double standard. Hence the endless imprecations by Moscow of *tu quoque* ('look at yourself'), otherwise known as 'whataboutism', whenever Russia was criticised, but this rather misses the point. Hegemonic powers will always couch their global goals in the language of a civilising mission, and apply selectively the international law that they impose on others.[28] Equally, rising powers will invoke the universalism of international law to constrain the dominant state.

Russia cooperated with the US in Afghanistan and to prevent Iran from acquiring nuclear weapons, but its criticism of the Iraq war of 2003 and its support for the Syrian regime of Bashar al-Assad increasingly alienated the Western power, and in particular the most aggressive exponents of US leadership, many of whom were found in the State Department. On coming to power in 2009, Obama had favoured Medvedev over Putin, and Putin's return to the presidency in 2012 soured their personal relations further, exacerbated by the Snowden affair. On the other side, Russia was alarmed by the relentless advance of the 'second' US, with its ideology of democratism that implied regime change through subversive political intervention rather than allowing the transformative power of liberal internationalism to do its work. Relations were further strained by the installation of missile defence systems in Eastern Europe, within a rocket's throw from Moscow, and NATO enlargement, urged on by militant 'new Europe' states. As with the US, there was a growing gulf between the first Europe of peace and genuine economic interdependence, and the second Europe of swelling, although inchoate, geopolitical ambitions. This set the scene for a perfect storm of mutual recrimination and distrust over the Ukraine crisis.

Perceptions are everything in international politics, as are the mental maps of the participants. Obama himself was a remarkably disengaged president: 'Absent and *not* accounted for was the general view of him as the crisis in Ukraine built up in January and February.'[29] Hillary Clinton packed the State Department with 'Democrat' neoconservatives with a messianic and Manichean view of the world. Clinton herself had few achievements in her four years as the American foreign minister, and has since concentrated on positioning herself as a potential candidate in the US presidential election of 2016 by scoring easy points – and there are no easier points than Russiabashing. Obama's second-term Secretary of State, John Kerry, has already run once for the presidency, in 2004, when he lost to George W. Bush, and clearly is not going to try again. He showed notable commitment to pushing forward the 'peace process' in Palestine, but he had a clearly articulated, hostile stance towards Russia, although on occasion accepted that Russia had some legitimate interests in Ukraine.

Kerry made little attempt to create his own team in the State Department. The president was 'disengaged' and Kerry was still smarting from Russia's démarche over Syria in September 2013, allowing policy to be made by relatively junior officials: 'The overthrow of Yanukovych and seizure of power by a provisional government in Kiev had been anticipated and indeed encouraged by the European and Eurasian desk of the State Department.'[30] The department is headed by Assistant Secretary of State Victoria Nuland, who as we have seen was an active and engaged participant on the Maidan. She has successfully made the passage from Dick Cheney's staff to Hillary Clinton's team, and now boasted, as mentioned, that the State Department had invested some $5 billion in civil society and democracy promotion in Ukraine, an enormous sum by the standards of the United States Agency for International Development (USAID). Cheney had been Bush's vice president from 2001 to 2009 and a noted advocate of US interventionism in Iraq. Nuland's husband is Robert Kagan, a co-founder of the think tank Project for a New American Century and one of the leading advocates of the 2003 Iraq war. At the heart of Kagan's extraordinary notion that 'Americans are from Mars, Europeans are from Venus' is the idea that the former stand above international law and the normativity that the latter endlessly proclaim.[31] This is an exceptionalist ideology that riled Putin, notably in his op-ed piece in the *New York Times* in September 2013:

> I would rather disagree with a case he [Obama] made on American exceptionalism,
> stating that the United States' policy is 'what makes America different. It's what makes

us exceptional.' It is extremely dangerous to encourage people to see themselves as exceptional, whatever the motivation.[32]

Thus, in the words of David Bromwich:

Obama ceded control of America's public stance to his Secretary of State, John Kerry. The result with Ukraine in 2014, as with Syria in 2013, was to render a critical situation more confused, and bristling with opportunities for hostility between the US and Russia. Eventually, in late March, Obama gave a speech to the EU in Brussels that dressed up the debacle as policy.[33]

The study goes on to note: 'His [Obama's] obliviousness to the Cheney weeds in his policy garden is characteristic and revealing.' Nuland was not the only one. Samantha Power represented Obama in the UN and was a persuasive advocate of humanitarian interventionism who advised Obama on the whole range of foreign-policy issues. The State Department now funded not only peaceful but also coercive foreign engagement, although the latter was traditionally the preserve of the Department of Defence. The advocacy of humanitarian war, combining normative and realist assumptions, created a powerful dynamic in favour of intervention in the domestic affairs of other states. Traditional Westphalian respect for state sovereignty was eroded. This would prove a combustible mix in Ukraine.

American dualism is evident at the operational level. The Ukraine crisis demonstrated a division between what F. B. Ali calls the 'war party' and the 'resolution party'.[34] There is in addition a third category, those who lacked an intellectual compass to navigate the complexity of Ukrainian events; into this 'clueless' group Ali places John Kerry, Catherine Ashton, and even Susan Rice and Samantha Power, whose 'ideological mindset causes them to seriously misjudge the situation'. The 'resolvers' were unable to impose a sensible policy, and instead the running was left to warriors: 'The real reason behind the West's policies in Ukraine and Eastern Europe is that there is a strong faction among its policymakers that fully understands what is going on but has deliberately chosen this course of action.' This was certainly the case with Senate bill S.2277, the 'Russian Aggression Prevention Act 2014', which outlined a frighteningly comprehensive and detailed range of actions against Russia. It included a military component (the strengthening and advancement of NATO to Russia's borders); the full-scale deployment of a missile defence system in Europe; full-scale military cooperation with Russia's non-NATO neighbours; the end of space, defence and intelligence cooperation with Russia; the mobilisation of the whole gamut of global financial institutions to suffocate Russia financially; rapid development of an energy-pipeline system bypassing Russia, and support for the end of the energy dependence of countries such as Ukraine on Russia; the abrogation of all arms-control treaties with Russia; full-scale personal sanctions against Russian officials; the launching of an intense information war, including beefing up media instruments beaming into Russia; and massive support for activists and dissidents within Russia. It prohibited any federal department or agency from doing anything that could be interpreted as recognition of Russian sovereignty over Crimea or approval of the 'illegal annexation' of the region.[35]

According to the bill's sponsors, all this would cost a mere $200 million a year, which undoubtedly is a small price to pay to save the world from the Russian threat. Such militancy is hardly surprising from a Congress that had prevaricated for decades over repealing the 1974 Jackson–Vanik amendment imposing trade sanctions on the Soviet Union because of its restrictions on Jewish emigration. Following its repeal Congress promptly adopted the Magnitsky Rule of Law Accountability Act in December 2012. The new Senate bill authorises the US to grant Ukraine the status of an 'allied nation' independently of NATO membership. Washington would be empowered to send troops to Ukraine, thus committing NATO to war with Russia. It is unlikely that the bill will be passed into law, even with a 'bipartisan' majority comfortable with scapegoating Russia, but it demonstrates that the US is ready to position itself for the long-term containment, if not destruction, of Russia as an independent and alternative pole in world politics. This ambition will not change even when Putin leaves office; hence confrontation is likely to continue until a new generation comes of age. Russia has fallen out of love with the West, accompanied by mutual distrust. The battle against the West has now given Russia a new purpose that will be enduring.[36] Stabilisation of the situation over Ukraine represents a truce with the West, not peace.[37]

There is undoubtedly a powerful Wilsonian strain of liberal interventionism in Washington today, ready to ally with the hawks to advance a genuinely idealist programme of democratic advancement. This is the ideology of democratism, advanced by such figures as the US ambassador to Moscow, Michael McFaul. His residency in January 2012 began with a scandal, when he met oppositionists at a time of intense political tension in the city following the mass demonstrations in protest against the flawed parliamentary elections, and ended in tears two years later amid the Ukraine crisis.[38] McFaul has a deep understanding of Russian politics, albeit filtered through a thick ideological lens, and his resignation in February 2014 left America without an ambassador in Moscow at a crucial time. For others in the hawkish camp the explanation of the Ukraine crisis was reduced to a single proposition: Putin's 'aggression'; and this in turn was located in the narrative, assiduously amplified by the mainstream media, of Russia's inherent proclivity for expansionism, which was now buttressed by an inferiority complex and *ressentiment* against the West. This was the line predominant in Saakashvili's Georgia, which in 2008 had provoked war, and was now the predominant narrative of the February revolution. As Stephen Cohen warns: 'The new cold war may be more perilous because, also unlike during its forty-year predecessor, there is no effective American opposition – not in the administration, Congress, establishment media, universities, think tanks, or in society.'[39] Alternative voices are silenced or discredited, provoking a dangerous cycle of reinforcement of what is at best a partial view of a complex situation.

Thus the future of Ukraine and of relations between Russia and the West depends on the struggle between these two groups. The war party (the 'second' US) believes that the West won the Cold War, and that its victory should not be challenged. This is precisely what Russia is considered to have done by advancing the idea of 'Greater Europe', and intervening in world politics, notably in Syria in September 2013, as an independent actor. Russia needed to be taught its place. At the head of this faction are the neocons and right-wingers, deeply entrenched in the State Department (led by Nuland), reinforced by the virulent Russophobes in Congress (notably John McCain and Lindsey Graham), the think tanks and the media. The *Washington Post* made little attempt to maintain journalistic integrity and balance in the Ukraine crisis; *The Economist* gave free rein to its 'New Cold War' agenda, and even the *New York Times* faltered. On 21 April, for example, a front-page story in the latter argued that 'photos link masked men in East Ukraine to Russia', but in fact the blurred photographs of some bearded individuals were taken in Russia, and three days later the story had been thoroughly discredited, shaming the paper for failing the basic test of checking the facts. In years to come the unabashed militancy of these papers will undoubtedly become the subject of many an intriguing academic study. Their partisanship and profound lack of historical understanding would demean a Third World dictatorship, let alone a country that claims to be the 'essential nation'. This irresponsibility reached the highest echelons of power. In an extraordinary interview with the *Wall Street Journal* on 28 April 2014, Kerry admitted that the Obama administration and security establishment were 'fully aware' that the escalation of the crisis in Ukraine could lead to nuclear war, but he was remarkably insouciant about humanity's imminent destruction. There was no limit to the 'impassioned lunacy' in Washington during the crisis.[40]

The domestic basis of the war party is reinforced by other groups. At their head is the NATO lobby, led by militant Atlanticists like Bruce Jackson, the founder and president of the Project on Transitional Democracies. For them, in both the US and Europe, the Ukraine crisis was a heaven-sent opportunity to revive the organisation and to give it a new mission for the twenty-first century. The summit in Newport, Wales, on 4–5 September 2014 was a festival of the war party. The invitation to Poroshenko to attend ensured that the rhetoric remained at a high level. There was much chest-thumping by the British and Americans about the Russian threat, but in the end the European nations refused to ramp up the threat of war. Anders Fogh Rasmussen, typically, made a range of unsubstantiated assertions, but the rise of Islamic State in the Levant served to divert attention from what ultimately at the international level was an artificial conflict over Ukraine to what was an immediate and genuine threat. The Newport meeting signalled the remilitarisation of world politics but only the partial repudiation of the informal commitments given to Gorbachev at the end of the Cold War and of the 1997 agreement not to station forces permanently in Eastern Europe, although that pledge was conditional as long as there was no security threat to the region. The summit adopted a 'Readiness Action Plan' to establish 'spearhead' military bases in the eastern marches and create a rapid-reaction force headquartered in Poland, although the 4,000 troops assigned to it would be based elsewhere. Military bases would be created in Poland, the Baltic republics and Romania with a permanent deployment of 600 servicemen each. Despite Yatsenyuk's announcement on 29 August that Ukraine would scrap its non-aligned status and resume his country's course for NATO membership, the 2008 Bucharest declaration was not revived. Tymoshenko announced that her Batkivshchyna party would initiate a national referendum on Ukraine joining NATO, but the summit leaders agreed that membership was not on the cards. Even they understood that it would only pour fuel on an already raging fire.

Rather than turning itself into a collective security institution encompassing Russia after the Cold War, NATO had given itself a new 'out of area' mandate to wage 'expeditionary' wars in Afghanistan and Libya. By contrast, the new post-Communist member states wanted NATO to retain its traditional role as a territorial defence organisation, committed to its core Article 5 collective defence mission. As Eric Kraus puts it: 'No sane person truly believes that Russia is about to invade the Baltics, neutralise Finland, or retake Poland. It is, however, convenient to publicly pretend to fear these eventualities.' After listing the economic and other woes in Europe, Kraus makes the crucial argument that underlies much of the thinking in this book:

With no vital interests at stake in Ukraine, in a rational world the Europeans would be even-handed, leaning on both sides to find an accommodation – federalisation, independence or unification with Russia – probably on the basis of an internationally supervised referendum in the Eastern provinces. Instead, the diplomacy of the founding EU states has been hijacked by Washington and the ex-Soviet Republics. It is Europe, not Washington, which stands to pay the price.

This was not a 'new Cold War', a war of ideologies, but a 'classical, 19th-century-style war for imperial domination'.[41] The US urged its allies to increase defence spending, while Russia's $700 billion defence build-up continued, to be completed in 2020. In September Russia successfully tested its Bulava SLBM, a long-range nuclear missile designed to hit targets in the US. At that time the defence minister, Sergei Shoigu, warned about the increased presence of foreign military forces along Russia's borders, and deployed the first of six stealth submarines to the now-permanent home of the Black Sea Fleet in Sevastopol. George Kennan's warning that NATO expansion would herald a new Cold War was on the optimistic side, and a hot war is no longer inconceivable.

As one commentary put it:

> It's not necessary to have any sympathy for Putin's oligarchic authoritarianism to recognise that Nato and the EU, not Russia, sparked this crisis – and that it's the Western powers that are resisting the negotiated settlement that is the only way out, for fear of appearing weak.[42]

Military spending had been declining across the NATO alliance, and apart from the US only three states met the 2 per cent of GDP defence-spending goal: Britain, Estonia and Greece. On the other side, Russian defence spending had increased by 14 per cent in 2012 and 16 per cent in 2013, while Chinese defence spending in those years rose by 14 and 9 per cent respectively. At Newport, the voice of the wiser generation of leaders, like the former NATO Secretary General Lord George Robertson, was signally absent. As if to rub salt in the wounds, NATO staged the Rapid Trident military exercise on Ukrainian territory on 15–26 September. In anticipation of NATO's stance, Russia on 2 September announced that it would amend its military doctrine to address the 'external threats' created by the advance of NATO's infrastructure to Russia's borders. Too involved in locking horns, Russia and the West were unable to work together to deal with the growing challenges in the Middle East, including the bioterrorism threat from Islamic State. Rather than focusing on Article 5 of the 4 April 1949 North Atlantic Treaty, guaranteeing collective defence, all sides would have benefited from revisiting Article 1:

> The Parties undertake, as set forth in the Charter of the United Nations, to settle any international dispute in which they may be involved by peaceful means in such a manner that international peace and security and justice are not endangered, and to refrain in their international relations from the threat or use of force in any manner inconsistent with the purposes of the United Nations.

The US war party is reinforced by the former Soviet bloc members in the EU and NATO. They are far from united in their views, but as we have seen there is a group of militantly revanchist powers, with Lithuania and Poland in the van, for whom Russia's strategic expurgation from the map of Europe would barely be enough. In a rather vulgar leaked recording of an alleged conversation between Polish foreign minister Radosław Sikorski and the former Polish finance minister Jacek Rostowski, published in the Polish magazine *Wprost* on 23 June, the former warned: 'The Polish–American alliance is not worth anything: it's even damaging, because it creates a false sense of security for Poland', suggesting that Washington had been too weak in the conflict with Russia.[43] This scaremongering creates precisely the effect it is ostensibly intended to avert, amplified by the new militant regime in Kiev just as it had been earlier by the Saakashvili leadership in Georgia. These representatives of the 'new Europe', allied with traditional British suspicion of European integration, inhibited the EU's ability to moderate and mediate in world politics. They were far from a united group, however, and also changed policy over time. The elevation of the Polish prime minister Donald Tusk to the presidency of the European Council in October 2014 meant that the new prime minister, Ewa Kopacz, was able swiftly to distance herself from the aggressive policy of her predecessor, while the replacement of foreign minister Sikorski by Grzegorz Schetyna brought an end to a divisive period in Polish, and European, history.

Militancy is further fostered by a range of politicians and public activists who continue the 'Russophobe' tradition of the nineteenth century, when the Polish question after the failed uprising of 1830 allowed Russia to be framed as an irredeemable despotism. The role played by Poland in the nineteenth century now looks set to be taken by Ukraine in the twenty-first. Let Saakashvili speak for this group, since he distils the essence of the axiology of the war party. In an article in the *Wall Street Journal* he argued:

> He [Poroshenko] can deal with Russia only with Western help. What we have observed recently is a major international discrepancy: Russia is weak, but it has a strong will to pursue adventurist policies. The West is much stronger but cannot agree on a unified response, and thereby is projecting weakness. Mr. Putin knows he is vulnerable, and that makes him even more willing to exploit to the max his window of opportunity. The West knows well what Mr. Putin's vulnerabilities are, but the European Union and the US have been unwilling to endure even a minimum of pain to exploit them.[44]

Here is the voice of war to the end of time to bring Russia to heel, irrespective of the cost. Such a policy, whose discourse is redolent of the dangers of appeasement, standing up to bullies and other anachronisms, threatens to turn the eastern part of Europe into the wastelands already created in the Middle East and North Africa.

Countering the fears, phobias and global ambitions of the war party is the 'resolution' party, trying to resolve the Ukraine crisis through sensible discussion, dialogue and engagement, all words that the war party seeks to discredit. Instead of the ceaseless escalation of the crisis, the resolvers look to international mediation and a halt to military action. For them, Russia can undoubtedly be part of the solution, although many understand it is also part of the problem. Thus the resolvers are not necessarily willing to give the pass to Russia, but at least they seek to provide honest information. Even General Breedlove, whose comments on the crisis at the beginning were characterised by wild surmise and exaggerated threats, soon came to temper his views, unlike his NATO boss. Rasmussen, who left office on 1 October 2014, consistently ramped up the tension based on often flawed information. He accused Russia of waging 'hybrid warfare, a combination of military action, covert operations and a media campaign of disinformation'. His language was described as 'blunt', while others would call it aggressive.[45] Even the American intelligence community, embarrassed earlier by Colin Powell's presentation to the UN based on obviously fake information about Iraq's alleged possession of WMD, sought to distance itself from the irresponsibility of the war party. Martin Dempsey, chair of the Joint Chiefs of Staff, called for objectivity in the crisis.[46] Assessment of responsibility for the MH17 disaster by American intelligence officials were more measured than those coming from the State Department. The veteran CIA officer Robert Baer, who had earlier served in Tajikistan and thus knew the region well, conceded to John Humphrys on the BBC's *Today* programme on 28 July that Washington in the person of Nuland was inflaming the conflict and failed to take Russian perspectives into account. The US business community also sought to restrain the war party. The classic realist Henry Kissinger warned from the very beginning that discussion over Ukraine was unnecessarily polarised:

> Far too often the Ukrainian issue is posed as a showdown: whether Ukraine joins the East or the West. But if Ukraine is to survive and thrive, it must not be either side's outpost against the other – it should function as a bridge between them. […] The West must understand that, to Russia, Ukraine can never be just a foreign country. […] For its part, the United States needs to avoid treating Russia as an aberrant to be patiently taught rules of conduct established by Washington. Putin is a serious strategist – on the premises of Russian history. […] For the West, the demonization of Vladimir Putin is not a policy; it is an alibi for the absence of one.[47]

The diplomatic skills that Kissinger had deployed during the Cold War were sadly lacking in this crisis.

In Europe, the position of the resolvers was greatly weakened by the MH17 disaster. The European war party used the tragedy to advance its goals, including the intemperate imposition of sanctions. Whereas the Lithuanian president Dalia Grybauskaitė argued that 'the sanctions are necessary, but long overdue and inadequate', the German foreign minister Frank-Walter Steinmeier worked tirelessly to moderate the response, arguing that 'sanctions are not a policy, that's why we still need to look for ways to defuse the political conflict'.[48] Merkel as usual sought pragmatic policies within the framework of domestic political realities, but as the crisis developed German policy as a whole lost some of its independence and swung behind Washington. Merkel, nevertheless, was one of the few European leaders who maintained a dialogue with Putin. The outgoing president of the European Commission, Barroso, had urged demonstrators to 'have the courage and go out and fight' in December 2013,[49] and throughout only exacerbated tensions. Putin had long shunned his telephone calls, and with good reason.

In all of this Obama appeared to be little more than a referee, laying down red lines and issuing vacuous statements that helped neither war nor peace. His presidency began in anticipation of a continued shift towards a post-Atlanticist stance, marked by the 'pivot to Asia' and global concerns, but the Ukraine crisis returned European issues to the forefront of US policy. Obama's natural instincts were clearly aligned with a traditional US pragmatism and realism, with a turn away from messianic conceptions of US world leadership, but his more ideological stance in the Ukraine crisis was prepared by disappointment over the failure of the 'reset'. His personal relations with Putin were very poor, in part because of his misjudged partisanship for Medvedev earlier, accompanied by some ill-judged personal comments about Putin and Russia. He had won the 2008 nomination because of his criticism of the 'dumb war' in Iraq, but he was now excoriated for his alleged passivity: 'Every advance by Islamists in Iraq, and every missile fired by Russian separatists in Ukraine, is taken as an indictment of his caution. A window may well be closing on the brief era of US restraint.'[50] Obama began as one of the least interventionist US leaders in decades, yet was forced to intervene in the Middle East and Europe.

Obama resisted the extremism of the war party, but his 'restraint' was at best relative. It was his administration that encouraged the overthrow of a democratically elected president, launched an economic war against Russia and impeded the peaceful resolution of the civil conflict in the Donbas – these would not be classified as examples of 'restraint' in normal language, but for the war party this was only the beginning. Edward Luce, the author of the above quotation, for example, goes on to argue: 'In recent months it would have been smart to beef up the US presence in the Baltic states and other NATO members bordering Russia. Instead, he kept them to a minimum. That may have only emboldened Vladimir Putin.'[51] In other words, the recipe of advancing the Euro-Atlantic security system to Russia's borders that provoked the crisis was now advocated as the response to the crisis. Of course, the US could with relatively little effort bring Russia to its knees – if the economic sanctions really did go for the jugular and destroy whole sectors of the economy while encircling the country with US forces. There is very little that Russia could do in response, but it would have made almost no difference to events in the Donbas, which as we have seen were not something simply directed from Moscow nor easily resolved by external interventions. In short, the war party exploited the Ukraine crisis to cut Russia down to size and to achieve its strategic isolation and diplomatic marginalisation. Russia certainly will not succumb to the pressure, since it is operating within the rationality of a very different paradigm. This is the road not so much to a new Cold War as to Armageddon.

In an important analysis, Stephen Cohen asks a fundamental question about the goals of the US. He succinctly sums up the ambiguities in US behaviour:

> In fact, from the onset of the crisis, the administration's actual goal has been unclear, and not only to Moscow. Is it a negotiated compromise, which would have to include a Ukraine with a significantly federalized or decentralized state free to maintain long-standing economic relations with Russia and banned from NATO membership? Is it to bring the entire country exclusively into the West, including into NATO? Is it a vendetta against Putin for all the things he purportedly has and has not done over the years? (Some behavior of Obama and Kerry, seemingly intended to demean and humiliate Putin, suggest [sic] an element of this.) Or is it to provoke Russia into a war with the United States and NATO in Ukraine?[52]

The last of these possible motives is unlikely, given the threat of nuclear escalation, although the US was closely involved in the ATO. The CIA director John Brennan visited Kiev in secret in mid-April, just as the military campaign was beginning. Biden also visited on at least two occasions, followed apparently by a steady flow of senior US defence officials. However, despite pleading from Kiev, Washington refused to supply heavy weaponry.

David Bromwich notes that an accord in US politics has developed 'which unites the liberal left and the authoritarian right [...] The state apparatus which supports wars and the weapons industry for Republicans yields welfare and expanded entitlements for Democrats.'[53] In his West Point commencement address on 28 May, Obama asserted that the US would engage in more military actions than ever before, but with fewer US casualties.

> Here's my bottom line: America must always lead on the world stage. If we don't, no one else will. The military that you have joined is and always will be the backbone of that leadership. But US military action cannot be the only – or even primary – component of our leadership in every instance. Just because we have the best hammer does not mean that every problem is a nail.[54]

America would lead the world but not necessarily police it to defend 'international norms', a key concept of the Obama administration. In Bromwich's words: 'International norms split the difference between international law, which the US reserves the right to violate, and the new "world order" of which the US was the maker and must remain the guardian.' This is a perfect statement of the ambiguities generated by the interplay between the two versions of the US. The spirit of the speech was in keeping with that of Madeleine Albright, the Secretary of State in Bill Clinton's second administration and a noted proponent of NATO enlargement: 'If we have to use force it is because we are America; we are the indispensable nation. We stand tall and see further than other countries into the future.'[55]

THE NEW SUICIDE OF EUROPE

On hearing of the outbreak of World War I, Pope Benedict XV declared that it represented 'the suicide of Europe'. One hundred years later we can talk of a 'new suicide', as the idealism associated with a whole era of European integration has been revealed as nugatory and an illusion. At the heart of the EU is a peace project, and it delivered on this promise in Western Europe before 1989. However, when faced with a no less demanding challenge in the post-Communist era – to heal the Cold War divisions and to build the foundations for a united continent – the EU has spectacularly failed. Instead of a vision embracing the whole continent, it has become little more than the civilian wing of the Atlantic security alliance. Even its increasingly limited commitment to social and cross-national solidarity is jeopardised by the putative Transatlantic Trade and Investment Partnership (TTIP). Atlanticism is becoming increasingly ramified, while Russia is increasingly left out in the cold.

Ukraine exposed the crisis in the EU's development. As an institution, it struggled to make itself relevant in devising policies that could provide solutions to fundamental international problems. The drift towards a merger with the Atlantic security system left it bereft of autonomy and policy instruments when it really mattered – maintaining peace on the European continent. As Lukyanov puts it, the EU was preoccupied with its own survival and

> internal disagreements caused by the conflict over Russia constitute no less of a risk than the losses Europe will suffer as a result of downgrading its ties with Moscow. The question of which risk is more dangerous will be answered by the EU in due course.[56]

It is easy to argue that the EU as an institution was marginalised as the crisis developed, and this was indeed the case, but its performance was even worse: it failed to restrain the war party in Washington or to articulate a strategy that was more nuanced and in keeping with its proclaimed normative values. The EU proved desperately inept as a conflict regulator.

More than that, its lack of strategic perspective and dismissive attitude to Russian concerns reflected the absorption of the US culture of hegemonism. As David Habakkuk, drawing on the work of Hew Strachan, notes regarding British policy on the eve of the Great War, instead of committing to a strategy of 'containment' of Germany in alliance with France and Russia it may have been wise to seek some sort of compromise with Germany. Habakkuk goes on:

> If [...] one looks at recent Western policy, what is evident is a complete lack of any serious attempt to 'calculate at least a step ahead'. That an attempt to wrest the whole of Ukraine away from Russia, and incorporate it in 'the West' would produce essentially the kind of crisis that has developed was obvious to any reasonably rational being years ago. We have here, not simply a crisis of Western foreign policy, but a crisis of our whole system of government, and faith in 'democracy'.[57]

Critics of the failure of the EU to adopt severe sanctions more swiftly complained that this was because of the high level of dependency on Russian energy imports and the intense ties in some countries between their corporations and Russia. This is undoubtedly a factor shaping national policy making and the EU leadership as a whole, but there is also another explanation – there were still a few leaders in the EU who realised that the Ukraine crisis was not simply the outcome of Putinite Russia's alleged malevolence, but was born out of a complex set of interactions, perceptions and fears. Critics of the rush to sanctions and other coercive measures understood that sooner or later a negotiated exit from the crisis would have to be found, and condemned the failure to seize the opportunities as they emerged, for example after Poroshenko's election and after the MH17 tragedy.

The EU of course is not a state but an ensemble of complex institutions, processes and member states, and thus the expectation that it can act with the purpose of a state is ill-founded. Nevertheless, the Ukraine crisis posed a fundamental existential choice before the EU, the answer to which would determine its fate. On the one hand, the EU could try to refine its continental vocation and find mechanisms and means to avoid the imposition of a new Iron Curtain that would doom the continent to a renewed period of militarisation and confrontation. The economic platform for renewed continentalism, whether called 'Greater Europe' or something else, has already been laid. The opportunities offered by interdependence could be used to shape behaviour on all sides. Russia is highly sensitive to threats to its valuable economic partnerships with countries such as Germany, France, Italy and Holland, and throughout the Ukraine crisis sought to protect them. The politics of Greater European interdependence are based on diplomacy and negotiation, and seek to find ways in which contesting parties can retreat with dignity and compromise in an environment where the language of threats is constrained.

On the other hand, although elements of this approach were not entirely stilled, the predominant stance was drawn from the playlist of the hawks, the path of sanctions and confrontation. For a number of 'new' European states, although not all of them, the Ukraine crisis was used to vindicate their stance of irreconcilable hostility to Russia, arguing that the country was a threat to be countered rather than an opportunity to be exploited. In the Ukraine crisis it was the turn of Lithuania to be in the vanguard of anti-Russian sentiments. The ferocity of President Dalia Grybauskaitė's onslaught on Russia was matched only by that of Georgia under Saakashvili. The Polish president, Bronisław Komorowski, even called for Russia to be deprived of its veto power in the UN Security Council:

> We know this is not the right time to reset relations with Russia. This is not the right time to limit any commitment to Euro-Atlantic relations. No, just the reverse. This is an important moment to contain Russia from any dangerous expansion in order to pursue its neo-imperial vision.[58]

This is not a policy but an attitude. It is immune to rational argument or the practices of diplomacy. Based on an essentialist reading of history, it treats Russia as the eternal enemy. This is a stance that in its very essence is axiological – assuming that certain postulates are axiomatic and unquestionable – and anyone who raises questions is condemned as a 'Putin apologist', a 'useful idiot', a 'stooge', and worse. This is a dangerous fundamentalism, masquerading as the defence of the 'European choice' and the avoidance of 'another Munich'.

In practice, relatively normal relations were soon established between Russia and Georgia when the axiological stance of Saakashvili gave way to the more measured and intelligent policies of his successor, Bidzina Ivanishvili, demonstrating that there is no 'eternal essence' to Russian policy but pragmatic (although in the late Putin years increasingly emotional) responses to changing circumstances. Any state in Russia's position has certain security and other concerns, and as long as they are respected, normal business can be conducted. Instead, it appeared that the war party sought to provoke and exploit conflicts between Russia and its neighbours, threatening to lay waste the whole post-Soviet region. Ukraine was in danger of becoming another Afghanistan, Iraq or Libya. This was certainly not the intention of Obama, but the failure to rein in the inflammatory statement of Kerry and his team in the State Department had that effect. In all of this, the independent voice of the EU was missing, and instead Catherine Ashton effectively became little more than Nuland's accessory.

The crisis did provoke some rethinking of EU management. There had already been attempts to improve the EU's foreign-policy efficacy, above all by the creation of the post of 'high representative' at the head of the EEAS and the establishment of a permanent president of the European Council. There were also new procedures, including the introduction of the 'constructive abstention' mechanism, the introduction of qualified majority voting (QMV) and the intensification of cooperation within the CFSP by the Lisbon Treaty. None of these mechanisms prevented what has often been perceived to be a 'race to the bottom for the lowest common denominator' in policy making during the Ukraine events. The crisis provoked an extensive discussion of remedial actions but lacked strategic depth, and hence assumed an axiological character. In the words of Steven Blockmans:

> After the illegal annexation of Crimea and Russia's indirect responsibility for the downing of Malaysia Airlines flight MH17 in eastern Ukraine, what will it take before the EU can confront a conflict on its borders and prove to both its own citizens and third countries that it has a meaningful role to play in foreign policy?[59]

Blockmans argues that the EU needed to enhance its ability for collective action by the better use of existing institutions, above all by activating the 'Crisis Platform' of the EEAS, and in general the EEAS should have the authority to coordinate better the actions of individual member states. Above all, he proposed that strategy towards Russia should be adopted by a European Council decision taken by QMV, although allowing that when national interests are considered to be important but not vital, the constructive abstention mechanism should be invoked by those member states that, for diplomatic reasons, object to the partial or full interruption or reduction of economic and financial relations with Russia, but that at the same time do not wish to derail consensus in the Council on the adoption of a CFSP decision.

In other words, the council would adopt policy by majority voting, and it was assumed that in the case of Russia these would be 'restrictive measures'. It would be the task of the high representative, as chair of the Foreign Affairs Council (made up of member states ministers responsible for foreign affairs, defence and development), to

> remind individual member states of their duty of loyal cooperation under the CFSP and nudge them towards constructive abstention from decision-making. This would allow solidarity among member states and collective action by the EU to prevail over internal divisions.[60]

In the past these measures may have been considered no more than sensible adjustments to improve the efficacy of foreign-policy making. But the Ukraine crisis demonstrated that ultimately the EU was not an instrument to unite the continent and to overcome the logic of conflict in its community of nations, but another institution born in the Cold War that in the end was destined to perpetuate the Cold War in new forms. It was unable to act as an interlocutor between the contending parties or even to act as 'honest broker' between Washington and Moscow, and encouraged a conflict to cancerate into war in its heartlands. Uncritical alignment with the 'Atlantic' community, in other words with Washington's policies, deprived it of credibility with Moscow. Instead, the honest-broker role was taken by Germany, although even here the Atlanticists used the Ukraine crisis to attack the traditional moderation of the Social Democrats (see below).

The continued crucial role of the member states in conducting their own foreign policy has been accentuated. The divergence of national views in the EU remains one of its characteristic features, and while calls for more centralisation are understandable, given the experience of the Ukrainian crisis it is now clear that this would be extremely dangerous. Better to have 28 voices pulling in different directions than one voice making crucial and dangerous mistakes. The Poles and the Lithuanians did little except to amplify the crisis, while the British only added fuel to an already raging fire. As for France, under Sarkozy the country had swung into alignment with US global positions, and this trend was reinforced by his successor. Nevertheless, echoes of the proud tradition of Gaullist independence remained, as in President Hollande's invitation to Putin to attend the D-Day commemorations in June 2014, at which time he facilitated the meeting with the newly elected Poroshenko.

The Ukraine crisis divided Germany like few other international issues. With its deep involvement in the Russian market, the business community was obviously leery of imposing damaging sanctions. As I argued earlier, this was not a matter of venality trumping principle, but the very idea of sanctions as a mode of regulating international conflict was contested. The new foreign minister of Angela Merkel's restructured Christian Democrat–Social Democratic coalition government, formed in late 2013, was the veteran Frank-Walter Steinmeier, who helped broker the 21 February deal. He was under no illusion about the dangers facing Europe, arguing that it was 'the worst crisis since the end of the Cold War'. He warned that Russia was 'playing a dangerous game with potentially dramatic consequences', not least for Russia itself. When asked about the need for NATO to revisit its strategic defence planning, he insisted: 'There is no military solution to the conflict in Ukraine. Even if it can sometimes be frustrating, I am firmly convinced that only tenacious diplomatic work can bring us any closer to a solution.'[61]

The long-term 'special relationship' between Russia and Germany faced unprecedented strain, especially since much of the discourse hit a sensitive spot by drawing the false analogy between pre-war Nazi German behaviour and Putin's alleged 'expansionist' ambitions. A three-page letter to parliamentarians on 18 August revealed how the Ukraine crisis forced Germany to make a choice between Atlanticist – including Wider European – commitments, and its traditional role as mediator between Russia and Europe. Sigmar Gabriel, leader of the Social Democratic Party and minister for economic affairs and energy, Wolfgang Schäuble, federal minister of finance, and Christian Schmidt, food and agriculture minister, repeated the State Department line that Putin was in full control of the 'separatists', and that he failed 'to use his clearly existing influence [...] to convince them of moderation and to secure the borders in Europe that are accepted through international law'. The letter exposed the tension between Germany's commitment to 'European' positions and its ability to act as an independent arbitrator:

> From the very beginning, we pursued a common European position in order to meet this challenge. It is also thanks to our efforts that Europe has found a clear, common position. We want a political solution to the conflict in Ukraine. Yet this also means that we are ready to take all necessary steps, together and in solidarity – including all sectors and member states – to lend weight to our position.[62]

Germany's special understanding of and responsibility to temper conflict in the East through intelligent engagement and dialogue was questioned. The German Atlanticists used the Ukraine crisis to consolidate their position, not only attacking the pragmatism of the Steinmeier line but more fundamentally repudiating the long German tradition of 'special relations' with Russia, in a line from Bismarck through Ostpolitik, the peace movement of the 1970s and 1980s, and on to the contemporary business leaders for whom Russia is not just a market but an active partner in a European developmental project.

The Poles also demonstrated their distrust of European institutions in their desire to gain US security guarantees. As a perceptive commentary noted:

> I have no doubt that Polish foreign minister Radek Sikorski's recent lament that the alliance with the United States is 'worthless' is driven by his despondency that the United States is not sending greater quantities of men and materiel to further his pet project, the [...] Eastern Partnership. Sikorski has many admirable qualities, not least his willingness to act as the EU's principal booster [...] but his perhaps entirely understandable Russophobia has caused him to act in ways that are contrary to the [European] Union's well-being, to say nothing of its longevity.[63]

The destructive Russophobia of new Europe undermined the credibility and coherence of the EU as a whole. It had been anticipated that the new members would be 'socialised' in the ways of the EU, but, instead, the EU was in danger of reverse socialisation – incorporating the axiological dynamics and virulent neo-liberal free marketism of some new members, accompanied by their prioritisation of Atlantic security over EU social solidarity.

The Ukraine crisis has created a new and irreparable dividing line across the heart of the continent. In the words of a recent study: 'The idea of co-operation in the region is dead – at least for the foreseeable future.'[64] What had once been described as the 'common neighbourhood' now became the 'contested neighbourhood'. Almost universally the proposed remedies only deepen the tensions that provoked the crisis. The EaP had indeed been 'an exercise in ambiguity', a relatively low-cost effort that was 'neither a substitute for EU membership nor a prelude to it', condemned as being too technocratic and failing to 'do enough to protect the countries caught between Brussels and Moscow'.[65] More accurately, the EaP was both too bureaucratic and too axiological, setting up a structure of competition with Moscow grounded in the belief that it was axiomatic that the advance of EU governance and trade to the East was of unquestionably benign and progressive purport, irrespective of historical context. The ENP now needed to be rethought to create stronger bilateral political partnerships combined with functionalist multilateral strategies to cover sectoral issues, such as energy security, visa-free travel and judicial reform.

Compromise and balancing are the essence of EU politics, but the Ukraine crisis undermined its credibility as an international actor. It failed to enunciate a European perspective and instead was reduced to no more than a junior partner of the Atlantic alliance, which in turn had become little more than an extended platform for the Washington hawks. The EU's normative agenda was inverted, and instead of bringing peoples and nations together, it acted as yet another instrument of discord. The EU is all about dialogue or else it is nothing, yet as the Ukraine crisis dragged on the EU simply imported the language of sanctions, threats and warnings, even after a ceasefire was agreed on 5 September 2014. The EU allowed the very notion of 'dialogue' to be discredited and, indeed, to become a dirty word. Critics of the EU who had considered it to be just another expression of Cold War politics were vindicated, while those who believed that it could pursue a transformative agenda for continental peace were left disappointed.

THE COLD PEACE

Norman Angell in *The Great Illusion* (1909) argued that war between the industrial powers would be futile and economically disruptive, although he did not argue that such conflict was impossible. On all counts he was proved right. In the post-Cold War era the highly contested 'democratic peace' thesis has gone one step further to argue that *democratic* states do not go to war with each other, an argument that hinges on how one defines a democratic state. In short, a great range of literature suggests that in one way or another classical geopolitics and the realist appreciation of world politics as the endless struggle for power, status and recognition have given way to a liberal-internationalist system in which institutions will mediate conflict and trade will temper national rivalries. This was another great illusion, but it would be a mistake to suggest that the Ukraine crisis signalled the 'return' of geopolitics: that had never gone away. The reality of great-power politics is at the very heart of Atlanticism, although couched in the language of universalism and cloaked in the benign practices of global governance. For its allies and associates the *pax Americana* delivered massive public goods in the form of peace and trade (the 'first' US), albeit riven by inequality and policing operations to avoid defections from within and to pacify outliers (the 'second' US).

Ultimately, the Ukraine crisis was about Russia's refusal to submit itself to Atlanticist hegemony and global dominance. As I argued earlier, the challenge was at most partial, and certainly not intended as a frontal challenge. Russia's neo-revisionism sought to negotiate a path between classical notions of sovereignty and great-power status and adaptation to the norms of a globalising world and the realities of the global balance of power. This balancing act has catastrophically failed in 2014. Russia's neo-revisionism assumed that there was space in which it could sustain its 'quiet rise', on the Chinese model; but Europe is not Asia, and instead Russia has found itself on the frontline of the Atlantic system. Assuming that the EU could police its own borders, the US had begun to 'pivot to the East' to confront China. Instead, the Ukraine crisis drew it back sharply to confront the challenger on its borderlands in Europe.

However, this is not a second Cold War. Russia is neither a consistent ideological nor strategic foe. Instead, cooperation has continued over Afghanistan – the Northern Distribution Network across Russia continued to channel 40 per cent of supplies and personnel to and from Afghanistan throughout the Ukraine crisis – and in the Middle East, and there have even been signs of cooperation over Syria in the face of the Islamic State threat. But the structural cold peace remains unresolved. A cold peace is an unresolved geopolitical conflict that retains the potential to become a full-scale war or to be resolved through some process of negotiation. The dynamics of the current cold peace are vividly described by John Mearsheimer, an international-relations scholar in the realist tradition. He notes that imposing sanctions and increasing support for the new Kiev government were a mistake and were 'based on the same faulty logic that helped precipitate the crisis. Instead of resolving the dispute, it will lead to more trouble'.

Mearsheimer excoriated Washington's attempts to absolve itself of responsibility for provoking the crisis by placing all the blame on Putin and claiming that his motives were illegitimate: 'This is wrong. Washington played a key role in precipitating this dangerous situation, and Mr. Putin's behaviour is motivated by the same geopolitical considerations that influence all great powers, including the United States.' For Mearsheimer: 'The taproot of the current crisis is NATO expansion and Washington's commitment to move Ukraine out of Moscow's orbit and integrate it into the West.' The US then made the 'fatal mistake' of backing the protesters when Yanukovych had decided to accept the better deal on offer from Russia. Mearsheimer understood Putin's concerns about the new government in Ukraine, which he viewed as

> a direct threat to Russia's core strategic interests. Who can blame him? After all, the United States, which has been unable to leave the Cold War behind, has treated Russia as a potential threat since the early 1990s and ignored its protests about NATO's expansion and its objections to American plans to build missile defense systems in Eastern Europe.

He called on Obama to think more like a strategist than a lawyer, and to acknowledge Russia's security interests by recognising that Georgia and Ukraine would not become NATO members, and that 'Ukraine should become neutral between East and West'.[66]

In a later article, in *Foreign Affairs*, Mearsheimer developed his argument, now including America's European allies in the circle of blame. They were 'blindsided by events' because 'they subscribe to a flawed view of international politics', believing that the logic of realism was no longer relevant and that Europe could be 'kept whole and free on the basis of such liberal principles as the rule of law, economic interdependence, and democracy'.[67] These principles have indeed gained added weight in the era of 'globalisation', but, as I have argued, realpolitik and geopolitics remained relevant and represents the other half of the walnut of American hegemony. With the EU's enlargement to the contested frontier zone of Eastern Europe, it had also inadvertently become an adversarial geopolitical player, even though it lacked the language and the means to manage such a role. Mearsheimer argues that the Ukraine crisis demonstrated that realpolitik remains relevant, but also exposed the contradictions between the two aspects of Western power – liberal universalism and hegemonic geopolitical power – which are particularly acute in the case of the EU. The enlarged EU simply had no way of dealing with the aggressive geopolitical stance adopted by some of its newer members, and this then spectacularly blew back to destroy the credibility of the EU's normative proclamations. The more the contradiction was exposed, the more aggressive it became in advocating sanctions and Russia's punishment.

In Mearsheimer's view, the march to the East of NATO and the EU was perceived as a threat of the first order to Russia's strategic interests. As he puts it: 'The West's triple package of policies – NATO enlargement, EU expansion, and democracy promotion – added fuel to a fire waiting to ignite.'[68] The fundamental point for Mearsheimer is that 'Washington may not like Moscow's position, but it should understand the logic behind it'. As he and so many others argue: 'the United States does not tolerate distant great powers deploying military forces anywhere in the Western hemisphere, much less on its borders'.[69] Washington's rhetoric in favour of 'sovereign' choices of independent countries rings rather hollow in light of the 60 years of sanctions it has imposed on neighbouring Cuba, and the use of the Guantánamo naval base it seized from the country to conduct extra-legal activities. As Mearsheimer remarks, most realists were opposed to NATO expansion, and he recalls George Kennan's strictures on the folly of enlargement.

The standard response is that the West went out of its way to assuage Russian concerns. It denied that enlargement had anything to do with containment, and sought to engage Russia in multiple formats. The Permanent Joint Council of 1997 had been enhanced by the establishment of the NATO–Russia Council (NRC) in 2002. No permanent military forces were deployed in the post-Communist member states, and in 2009 the planned missile defence system was reoriented away from Poland and the Czech Republic to Romania and warships, and its fourth array redeployed to Alaska. In addition, as we have seen, the commitment in early 1990 not to enlarge NATO concerned only the military status of the eastern part of Germany after unification, although it was agreed that the united Germany would be in NATO. It is also argued that any commitments given in 1990, when the USSR and the Warsaw Pact still existed, were somehow voided by their disintegration the following year, but all commitments given by and to Russia, as the 'continuer' state, remained in force. This is tacitly accepted by initial American resistance to accede to the demands of the newly liberated Eastern European countries to join NATO. Thus the West, rather than aggressively expanding, had in fact been remarkably restrained and had resisted some of the more extreme demands of its new Eastern European members. Indeed, they complained long and hard about being neglected, especially when America allegedly adopted a post-Atlanticist stance with its 'pivot' to Asia. In any case, Russia's nuclear weapons gave it a certain security, since, irrespective of how many neighbours joined, a NATO attack is almost inconceivable. None of this was enough to allay Russian fears, to the great frustration of the partisans of the 'reset' and other attempts to 'engage' Russia on Western terms.

However, as Mearsheimer puts it: 'it is the Russians, not the West, who ultimately get to decide what counts as a threat to them'.[70] While indeed there were attempts to mitigate the consequences of the asymmetrical end of the Cold War, the brute fact that one side was consolidating its victory could not be avoided. Engagement ultimately meant co-optation, which in turn meant that to join the victorious alliance Russia would have to lose elements of its autonomy. For two decades Russian appeals to multipolarity were code for the attempt to 'democratise' the structure of hegemonic power. Thus neither side was willing to change in ways that would have allowed a genuinely new cooperative community to emerge. Russia remained distrusted as long as it demanded changes to the system that it was being invited to join; and the West was distrusted as long as the terms of engagement meant a transformation of Russia itself. In the Cold War this had ended in a stable compromise known as 'peaceful coexistence', the uneasy acceptance of difference and the devising of means to manage the conflict. These were dismantled at the end of the Cold War, while the sustainability of difference was questioned. This was the impasse that gave rise to confrontation over Ukraine.

CHAPTER 10

THE FUTURE
OF UKRAINE

What was it all for? This is the question that faced Europe in 1918, and does so once again. One hundred years ago Europe 'sleepwalked' into war, and now a century later comfortable illusions that 'globalisation' would render another major international conflict of that sort impossible were nullified. Instead, the architecture of European and global security was found to be wanting. The obvious response was simply to blame Putin and Russia, and thus obviate the necessity of examining the foundations of a system that had provoked the most dangerous confrontation since the end of the Cold War, if not since the Cuban missile crisis of October 1962. I have argued that the heart of the conflict was the coming together of two major processes: the 'Ukraine' crisis as a particular manifestation of the inadequacies of the structure of international politics; and the 'Ukrainian' crisis, the domestic contradictions that had been bubbling away since independence in 1991 but with roots that go all the way back to the emergence of Rus and the division between its Kievan and Muscovite manifestations, between Ukrainism and Malorussianism. These two crises combined, with devastating effect.

PARLIAMENTARY ELECTION

Poroshenko promised early elections, but with the restoration of the 2004 constitution he no longer has the power to dissolve parliament and has been forced to work with a rump assembly elected in very different circumstances. Filled with former supporters of Yanukovych, the regime has had to fight hard to get its legislation adopted. With the formal resignation of the Yatsenyuk government on 24 July, the constitutional mechanism for the dissolution of parliament came into play. The departure of UDAR and Svoboda broke up the ruling coalition, and if another one was not formed within 30 days then the president had the right to dissolve parliament. Poroshenko welcomed the move, noting that it would open the door to new elections: 'Society wants a full reset of state authorities.'[1] Yatsenyuk's resignation was prompted by parliament's failure to pass legislation to increase military expenditure and to regulate the energy sphere amid the collapse of the governing coalition. In early July parliament had rejected a bill that would have lifted restrictions on the UGTS leasing out its underground gas-storage reservoirs. The cabinet had earlier agreed on the possibility of establishing two public joint-stock companies – 'main gas pipelines of Ukraine' and 'underground storage facilities of Ukraine' – which would be fully owned by the state. The reform also allowed the government to establish a gas-distribution system operator that could be 49 per cent owned by investors from the US or the EU.

On 25 August Poroshenko dissolved the Rada and announced that new parliamentary elections would be held on 26 October, and that local-government elections would be held on the same day (in the event, the latter were postponed to 7 December). Poroshenko argued that the existing Rada was 'Yanukovych's pillar' for a year and a half, and accused the MPs of being responsible for the Euromaidan tragedy and the killing of the 'heavenly hundred'.[2] He insisted that it was 'no secret that there is a fifth column comprising dozens of MPs'. There had been a plan for the election to be held through an open proportional system, but the mixed electoral system was retained since it suited Poroshenko. Half the 450 MPs were elected through a closed-list proportional system with a 5 per cent threshold, and the other half in single-mandate majority seats – a group who would undoubtedly tend to gather behind the president. Poroshenko was clearly looking for a support base in parliament. However, in ridding himself of MPs who were previously loyal to Yanukovych, Poroshenko created a whole new set of problems, above all the election of a bloc of populist nationalists. With the rise of a militant Ukrainian nationalism, the new Verkhovna Rada found itself populated by anti-liberals of various stripes. The almost 8 per cent won by the militant populist Oleg Lyashko in the presidential election was a harbinger of what was to come.

Social tensions were rising as conditions deteriorated. The government was shedding state employees, utility costs were rising, power cuts were becoming more frequent and hot-water supplies were reduced as municipalities tried to save natural gas, and the economy in general was in deep difficulty. The IMF loan of $17 billion was only a drop in the ocean of the support Ukraine needed, but it was clear that the EU would not bail out Ukraine – Germany was not even prepared to fund other Eurozone members. The US planned to spend $1 trillion on modernising its nuclear arsenal in response to the non-existent threat from Russia, although just a small portion of that would make a big difference to Ukraine. Frustration at the slow pace of change prompted the resignation of the economy minister, Pavlo Sheremeta, on 21 August, warning that the government acted 'like a predator towards business'.[3] Successive waves of the mobilisation of army reservists were becoming increasingly unpopular, sparking protests in many regions. The war in the Donbas had ended in stalemate, amid a catastrophic loss of life, widespread destruction and enduring recriminations.

The civil-society bodies spawned by the protest movement, notably the Maidan Public Council, the Maidan All-Ukrainian Union, the Civic Sector of Maidan and the Reanimation Package of Reforms, continued to monitor the work of the new authorities. On the whole they remained aloof from formal politics, and few set up parties themselves. When they did, success was far from guaranteed. The Democratic Alliance won just two seats on the Kiev city council in May.[4] Right Sector continued its struggle with the interior ministry, making demands in August for the ministry to be purged and for all criminal cases against its own members to be closed. Dmytro Yarosh's demands were met in part, and thus he agreed to continue fighting in the east and not to march on Kiev. This was a foretaste of the threat that the armed militias could pose to the Kiev administration. Battle-hardened and angry, a new and more violent 'Maidan' was a permanent threat.

This spilled over into the violence during the parliamentary campaign. On 16 September the MP Vitaly Zhuravsky, a member of the Economic Development Party, was seized as he left parliament and placed in a rubbish bin. In Odessa on 30 September the former PoR MP Nestor Shufrych was beaten by activists carrying the Bandera flag, in an action that was repeated with others and came to be known as 'people's lustration'. The election campaign has been accompanied by an atmosphere of intimidation, but ultimately reflects Ukraine's deeply democratic, although increasingly polarised, culture. The 12 majoritarian seats in Crimea have not been contested, and another 15 (of 32) in the insurgent-controlled parts of the Donbas have also not been represented. The insurgent-controlled part of the Donbas held its own legislative elections on 2 November.

At 52.4 per cent, turnout was lower than for the 2012 parliamentary elections and the presidential elections earlier in the year, with voters from Crimea and Donbas missing. In the event, only six parties of the 29 contesting the election crossed the 5 per cent threshold (Table 10.1), and once again there was clear division in preferences between the west of the country and the south-east. Poroshenko's party, Solidarity, was the core of the Petro Poroshenko Bloc, which allied with Klitschko's UDAR. In an echo of the personal feuds that had torn the Orange government apart in the mid-2000s, Yatsenyuk refused to join Poroshenko's bloc. The president refused to place

TABLE 10.1 Parliamentary election of 26 October 2014

PARTY/ GROUPING	VOTE (% AND TOTAL)	PV SEATS	CONSTITUENCY SEATS	TOTAL SEATS
Narodny Front (People's Front) (Arseniy Yatsenyuk/ Alexander Turchynov)	22.14% (3,488,144)	64	18	82
Blok Petra Poroshenka (Petro Poroshenko Bloc) (Solidarity and UDAR)	21.82% (3,437,521)	63	70	132
Samopomoch/Samopomich (Self-reliance) (Andriy Sadovy)	10.97% (1,729,271)	32	1	33
Blok Oppozitsionyi (Opposition Bloc) (Yury Boiko)	9.43% (1,486,203)	27	2	29
Radikalnaya Partiya (Radical Party) (Oleg Lyashko)	7.44% (1,173,131)	22	—	22
Batkivshchyna (Fatherland) (Yulia Tymoshenko)	5.68% (894,877)	17	2	19
5% THRESHOLD				
Svoboda (Freedom) (Oleg Tyagnybok)	4.71% (742,022)		6	6
Komunistichna Partiya Ukrainy (Communist Party of Ukraine) (Petro Symonenko)	3.88% (611,923)	—	—	—
Sylna Ukraina (Strong Ukraine) (Sergei Tigipko)	3.11% (491,471)	—	—	—
Grazhdanskaya Pozitsiya (Civic Position) (Anatoly Grytsenko)	3.11% (489,523)	—	1	1
Agrarian Party 'Zastup' (Vira Ulianchenko)	2.65% (418,301)	—	1	—
Pravy Sektor (Right Sector) (Dmytro Yarosh)	1.8% (284,943)	—	1	1
Independents	—	—	94	94
Unfilled seats	—	—	27	27
Others	3.91% (506,541)	—	2	4

Source: Ukrainian Central Elections Commission [website]. Available at http://vybory.com.ua/.

him in the number-one spot or to change the name of his bloc to include Yatsenyuk's grouping. Instead, Yatsenyuk, with Alexander Turchynov, campaigned at the head of the People's Front. Reflecting his hard-line position, Yatsenyuk allied with militia leaders and included Andriy Biletsky, leader of the Azov battalion and the far-right Patriots of Ukraine, and soon became known as 'the party of war' because of its criticism of Poroshenko's Donbas peace plan. The Petro Poroshenko Bloc benefited from the presidential effect, but its hopes of being able to govern on its own were disappointed, coming a close second in the poll. The People's Front did remarkably well, winning over a fifth of the vote, reinforced by a sizeable contingent of constituency MPs. This group would be an uncomfortable ally for Poroshenko, and its strong showing forced the president once again to appoint Yatsenyuk as prime minister and accept much of their programme as the basis of the coalition agreement. The Christian Democrat Samopomich (Self-reliance) party, headed by the mayor of Lviv Andriy Sadovy, did remarkably well, coming third with 11 per cent. The party attracted businesspeople and professionals from western and central Ukraine. Tymoshenko had lost much of her political lustre, and her Batkivshchyna party was clearly a waning force. To compensate, Tymoshenko cranked up the populist rhetoric and condemned the Donbas peace plan, arguing that it represented capitulation to Putin. The party now squeaked in with just 5.7 per cent of the vote. These four parties are considered to be 'pro-European', and despite their differences offered a solid bloc in support of pro-European reform.

Lyashko's Radical Party benefited from the polarised atmosphere in the country, and figured prominently on the Inter television channels owned by Firtash and Yanukovych's former chief of staff, Sergei Levochkin. Lyashko absorbed much of the populist vote that would otherwise have gone to Yarosh's Right Sector and Tyagnybok's Svoboda. Several prominent paramilitary commanders entered the lists, including Semen Semenchenko, the commander of the Donbas battalion. Given the plethora of choice on the nationalist wing, Svoboda lost ground and it failed to cross the 5 per cent threshold.

Electoral support for the old governing group, the Party of Regions (PoR) and the Communists (CPU), collapsed. The CPU's faction put up some candidates, despite having lost its status as a faction in parliament, but in the event, the party failed to clear the 5 per cent threshold. More than half of the PoR's former 207 MPs had migrated to various centrist groupings or became independents. The rump PoR, now headed by Mikhail Chechetov, did not run a party list but put up some candidates in individual constituencies. A number of successor parties emerged, including the Economic Development Party, which hoped to pick up the 'pro-Russian' vote in the south and east. There were attempts by Medvedchuk to forge a new 'pro-Russian' party, led by Shufrych, but progress was halting. The Opposition Bloc headed by former fuel and energy minister Yury Boiko, who is considered to be close to Dmytro Firtash, brought together some of these groups and won nearly 10 per cent. The group represented the only real opposition to Orangist forces in the new parliament.

The new Rada had only 423 members, instead of the stipulated 450, because no elections were held in Crimea (10 seats), Sevastopol (2 seats), or the 'special zone' parts of the Donbas (9 from Donetsk and 6 from Lugansk). Over half (55 per cent) of the MPs were new to the Rada, an unprecedented turnover for the house. Parliament as a whole was more pro-European, with an influx of journalists, civil-society activists and commanders of the volunteer battalions. The vote was generally recognised as free and fair, although interpreted in different ways. For Barroso the election was considered a 'victory of democracy' and a vindication of a pro-European agenda, while Lavrov stressed:

> It is very important for us that Ukraine finally will have authorities which do not fight one another, do not drag Ukraine to the West or to the East but which will deal with the real problems facing the country.[5]

No single party could govern on its own, and even before the final tally had been announced, Poroshenko and Yatsenyuk began coalition negotiations. The radical tone of the new assembly rendered it as intractable as the one it replaced, while the influx of a mass of uncontrollable independent MPs from the single-mandate seats added to the fluidity, prompting speculation that the new convocation would be unlikely to see out its four-year term. The prime minister had an extensive range of powers at his disposal, but lacked the legitimacy enjoyed by the president through national direct election. In late November a five-party coalition comprising the Petro Poroshenko Bloc, the Popular Front, Samopomich, the Radical Party and Batkivshchyna was created, controlling 288 of the 423 seats in the Rada. Yatsenyuk was once again appointed prime minister. The coalition agreement was expansive on its geopolitical ambitions, including NATO membership, but short on concrete economic reform plans. The new parliament overwhelmingly reflected the views of western Ukraine, eliminating the prospects for the adoption of a more pluralistic model of state development. Instead, the monist impulse would be strengthened.

The success of the People's Front reduced the chances for a peaceful settlement of the conflict in the south-eastern part of the country or for a decrease in tensions with Russia. On 2 November the breakaway regions of the Donbas held regional elections of their own. At the time of the Minsk accords the two Donbas republics controlled a territory of 16,000 square kilometres with a population of 4.5 million, out of a total population of 6.5 million in the Donbas. Their territory included the two regional centres of Donetsk and Lugansk as well as the important towns of Makeevka, Gorlovka and Novoazovsk (Map 6). The 5 September Minsk agreement had suggested that these elections would be held 'according to Ukrainian legislation', but the Kiev government had then unilaterally decided that they would be held on on 7 December. The insurgent regimes argued that elections needed to be held earlier, to provide them with the necessary popular legitimacy in negotiations. Alexander Zakharchenko easily won the election in Donetsk region with 79 per cent of the vote, while in Lugansk Igor Plotnitsky won over 63 per cent. Russia 'respected' the outcome of the elections, despite protests from the West, which considered the ballot illegitimate. In a furious reaction, Poroshenko denounced the ballot as an 'electoral farce' and announced that he would scrap the law that offered areas in the east, including those controlled by the rebels, 'special status'. Soon after, the government announced that it would withdraw all state services in 'occupied' areas, including social welfare and pension payments and state salaries for teachers and doctors. On 15 November banking services were cut off, accompanied by warnings that gas supplies could also be stopped. The Donetsk and Lugansk People's Republics began to develop the sinews of statehood, although there was little chance of them being recognised. Kiev's refusal to hold direct talks with the separatists, who they called 'terrorists' and 'bandits', stymied the development of the peace process and even the basic normalisation of daily life. Kiev refused to recognise negotiating partners in the Donbas. The ceasefire was looking increasingly shaky, and with the victory of the more militant parties in the national election, the resumption of full-scale hostilities was possible at any time. Neither side was ready to commit to a genuine dialogue.

On 20 November the UN reported that 4,132 civilians and over 1,100 servicemen had been killed and over 9,000 injured since the fighting in the Donbas had begun, with on average 13 killed every day since the ceasefire. The stand-off with Russia would also continue. The sanctions regime institutionalised a pattern of Western pressure that exceeded even the practices of the Cold War. Their implicit goal was not simply to modify Russian policy but to achieve regime change. Russia was held hostage to developments in Ukraine for which it was at most only tangentially responsible. It was clear that Putin sought an end to the conflict in the Donbas, but it was equally clear that the situation had developed to a point where the military defeat of the insurgency was a red line that Russia would not allow to be crossed. Russian nationalists condemned the Minsk accords and viewed Novorossiya as a model for the future of Russia. The EU geared up for a long-term competition with Russia for cultural and geopolitical hegemony over the European 'borderlands', while in Washington pro-war sentiments were further strengthened by the Republican victories in the mid-term Congressional elections in November 2014. The Western leaders refused to accept that the conflict was an internal one and required domestic dialogue to be resolved. Until they did so, Ukraine was doomed to further conflict and economic decline while the world headed towards a period of intensified global confrontation.

UKRAINIAN OPTIONS

The Ukrainian crisis is multifaceted and complex, and is certainly far from over. I have focused on the political aspects, above all the tension between monist and pluralist models of state development, but these were accompanied by deep-rooted economic and social problems. The IMF loan of April 2014 was little more than a sticking plaster on a gaping wound. The country would need at least $35 billion in 2014–15 just to bridge the immediate funding gaps. Ukraine is a country of enormous potential, with a talented, dynamic and educated people and rich natural resources, yet for over two decades, since independence, it has been effectively locked in a developmental stalemate. Both the Orange and February revolutions were attempts to break out of the deadlock, but they only exacerbated the problems and further destabilised what was already a weak state. The economy would need massive external support to survive, let alone to restructure, while the polity was eroded by corruption, arbitrariness and state capture. Rather than acting as an independent adjudicator ruled by law, the state became an instrument in the struggle for the right to determine what it is to be Ukrainian and to redistribute property, resources and rents.

The system of oligarchic power in itself did not prevent development, although plutocratic struggles, which typically assume political coloration, certainly did impede rational economic policy making. The opening up of the Ukrainian market to foreign capital could break the stranglehold of the oligarchs, but would bring in its train a new set of problems, above all associated with equality, inclusion and independence. The 700 pages of the EU Association Agreement outlined a roadmap for economic and social modernisation, but it did not resolve the fundamental question about the nature of the polity. The political crisis could only be resolved through a synthesis of the Ukrainising and Malorussian traditions, taking the best of monism and pluralism to renew the Ukrainian state. For this to be achieved, contradiction would have to give way to dialogue, and everyone would have to give up a little in order to create a lot. Dialogue in this context is not a vacuous word but represents a substantive programme of reconciliation and development. It entails a positive commitment to compromise for the greater good of a country in which everyone could feel comfortable. Various federalist or consociational models have been advanced, but the February revolution only intensified monist paradigms.

This was resolutely impeded by the Ukraine crisis, the endlessly unresolved problem of the country's international status and orientation. The asymmetrical end of the Cold War endowed European international politics with a competitive dynamic, at times hidden and managed, but by the late 2000s assuming an increasingly conflictual character. Ukraine was torn between two increasingly hostile poles, which only exacerbated its internal divisions. The 'multi-vector' policy was one way of managing the tension, but at its heart this approach was a negative one. Equally, the attempt to insulate Ukrainian national capital from Western and Russian corporate interests was insular and short-sighted, and did little to enhance the competitiveness of the country's economy. The Chinese gambit only illustrated how desperate things had become. Both Moscow and Washington sought to align Ukraine with their respective axes, while the failure of Brussels to enunciate a genuinely continental vision meant that ultimately its Wider European policy collapsed into a crude Atlanticism, and thus lost its political and security autonomy. Support for the Greater European vision would have offered Ukraine a way to reconcile its diverging orientations (as it would have for Europe as a whole), accompanied by a greater confidence in asserting a positive vision of neutrality (as Austria and Finland had done earlier). A substantive stance of non-alignment (working with countries such as India and Indonesia) would have enhanced Ukraine's international status as the voice of the developing world. Instead, by 2013 the choice was reduced to the primitive one: between EU-style Atlanticism and a greater Russian inflection of Eurasian integration. Caught between the hammer and the anvil, a new revolution was forged.

Lacking was a genuinely Ukrainian voice in the country's destiny. Its voicelessness derived from the factors just discussed, and the country became a bit player in its own drama. The events of 2013–14 have only made everything worse, and it is not clear if the developmental path outlined above can be retrieved. For the great powers Ukraine was just a pawn on Brzezinski's infamous chessboard, and too many of Ukraine's leaders simply aligned themselves with its simplistic black-and-white arrangement, whereas an infinity of options lay in the field of grey. The internal division between East and West is real, but only one facet of a highly complex pattern of regional, class, ethnic and cultural interactions. The various political traditions were inflamed by the events after November 2013 and exacerbated by the Maidan revolution. The seizure of power by radical nationalists was considered not only unconstitutional but also illegitimate by one group, while for others it represented a new founding moment of the state. Ukraine will only have a stable future if its complex reality is mediated through a domestic constitutional settlement that incorporates diversity within the framework of a viable state aligned with a regulated international status.

Instead, the country was faced with internal disintegration and acted as the spark for a new international conflagration. The chair of the Federation Council, Valentina Matvienko, warned that Ukraine was in danger of turning into a Middle East in Europe, a permanent source of instability.[6] Too many problems were externalised, and thus the path to their resolution blocked. The Ukrainian media came together, if only on one thing – the denunciation of Putin and Russia. Much of this was greatly exaggerated, although in conditions of conflict in part understandable. However, anyone who has followed the Ukrainian media over the years will have noticed a proclivity for blaming Russia for any misfortune, and after the Crimean events this was given free licence. This included a rather crude campaign of personal denigration of Putin, which was demeaning for all concerned and avoided asking hard questions about the country's own failures. Much has been made about the way that Ukraine came together in the face of adversity, and how even many traditionally Russophone Ukrainians now made a point of speaking in Ukrainian to signal their newly reinforced solidarity with the fate of the nation. This, too, is understandable, and in many cases signalled a new sense of civic responsibility and a revived patriotism, as well as engagement in civil-society activism. This activism also took the form of volunteering to join battalions that went to kill other Ukrainians. Once again, this was simply another form of externalisation – blaming some 'other' for the self-inflicted woes of the country. The reinforcement of a monist, Ukrainising vision of nationhood only exacerbated the tensions that provoked the deep crisis of statehood, while the ostensible pluralism of those in the Malorussian tradition increasingly assumed retrograde imperial forms as the idea of Novorossiya took hold.

Equally, Ukraine needed to insulate itself from great-power conflicts: to move from being a pawn to a player. Washington, in thrall to its nineteenth-century geopolitical representations but tempered by twenty-first-century liberal universalism, had consistently impeded the formation of some substantive Ukrainian–Russian alliance, which would have created a powerful market of some 200 million people and harnessed the dynamism of the two countries to purposes that may not always have served the interests of the Atlantic alliance. There were powerful domestic constituencies who also defined Ukraine's future in terms of a negation – the reduction of Russian influence. The consequences of such policies were obviously suicidal, as long recognised by pragmatists and 'resolvers', while ideological representations of democratism posed their own dangers. The triumph of liberal aspirations and Atlanticist orientations now blocked the path of dialogue, reconciliation, neutrality and non-alignment. Instead, the drive was in the opposite direction. On 28 August the NSDC approved the cancellation of Ukraine's non-aligned status, while at the same time restoring conscription across the country. The next day Rasmussen stressed that Ukraine was free to pursue NATO membership, even though polls still showed that a majority, despite all the tribulations and the upsurge in patriotic sentiments, still opposed joining.[7] Although accession was not immediately on the cards, it was clear that territorial disputes would not be an insuperable obstacle.

A minor industry has developed proposing various plans to resolve the crisis. The task of recuperation will involve repairing many damaged relationships, but there appears to be little will to begin the process. Every opening is soon blocked off by the overheated rhetoric from Washington. Two days after the Minsk summit of 26 August Samantha Power argued:

> The mask is coming off. In these acts – these recent acts [the alleged movement of Russian forces into the Donbas] – we see Russian actions for what they are: a deliberate effort to support, and now fight alongside, illegal separatists in another sovereign country.

She warned that 'if unchecked, the damage that Russia's blatant disregard for the international order poses is much, much greater', and insisted: 'How can we tell these countries that border Russia that their peace and sovereignty is [sic] guaranteed if we do not make our message heard on Ukraine?'[8] This was not the voice of a diplomat but that of an ideologue who failed to understand even the very basic elements of what had provoked the crisis, and instead called for a war until the end of time against Russia. It also pushed Ukraine to the brink of political, economic and social collapse.

Kiev sought to reassert its control over the national territory, but the military operation undermined what was already limited trust in the new Kiev authorities in the region. The mayor of Donetsk, Alexander Lukyanchenko, had run the city from Kiev during the war and now assessed the scale of the damage: 'Over 900 buildings in Donetsk have been damaged or destroyed, including 35 schools, 17 kindergartens, and very many enterprises, especially mining [...] and a number of energy facilities – electrical power sub-stations – for good.' It was particularly hard to ensure the regular payment of pensions.[9] Equally, the virulent language applied against the insurgency alienated much of the rest of the country from the region, seeing it as troublesome and in need of pacification. From the other side, the Ukrainian events forced Russia to reassess relations with what had long been considered a 'fraternal' neighbour. Polls suggested that a large proportion now considered Ukrainians as enemies. This was a shocking and tragic outcome. Not only was Europe divided, but relations between two countries that shared a long, although troubled, history had soured in a spectacular manner. This rests on the consciences of the current generation of Atlantic and Eastern European leaders.

There is a wide external consensus on the rudiments of a solution. Anatol Lieven puts it well when he argues: 'Ukraine contains different identities, and cannot be ruled unilaterally by one of them alone, or pulled in a single geopolitical direction, without risking the breakup of the country itself.'[10] He advocated a federal constitution internally and neutrality abroad. Jack Matlock notes the four key elements:

(1) A commitment, embedded in the constitution, by Ukrainian political leaders to power sharing that prevents the domination of one section of the country by the other; (2) A federal structure in function if not necessarily in name; (3) Acceptance of Russian as an official language along with Ukrainian in regions with a significant number of Russian speakers – ideally in the entire country; and (4) A credible assurance that Ukraine will not become a member of a military alliance hostile to Russia, perhaps by requiring the vote of a supermajority as a prerequisite to joining any military alliance.[11]

The last provision should be extended to cover membership in any military alliance, and thus would exclude Ukraine joining the CSTO, in the unlikely event of a group coming to power with that ambition. The popular super-majority (say, two-thirds of all voters) should also be reinforced by two-thirds of all regional legislatures having to vote in favour. Thus Ukraine's two major camps would effectively enjoy veto power against each other, a classic feature of consociationalism. There would also have to be agreements concerning gas transit and energy relations as a whole. As for Crimea, David Owen, a former British Foreign Secretary, came up with the useful idea that the international status of the region could be established 'along the lines of an indefinite international lease of Crimea to Russia along the lines of the US–Cuba agreement over Guantánamo'.[12] Another idea was to hold a second referendum under international supervision after a certain period, say five years, to determine the real aspirations of the Crimean people. This would be in keeping with the UN principle of self-determination and recognise the historical special status of Crimea.

Elements of this were reflected in the recommendation of a group of six leading US and seven Russian experts who worked in private on the Finnish island of Boisto on 'track II diplomacy' to develop a roadmap for a possible international peace deal to resolve the Ukraine crisis. The 24-point plan, published on 26 August, covered an 'enduring, verifiable ceasefire', including an end to hostilities, removal of the National Guard from the Donbas, the imposition of effective border controls and a range of confidence-building measures. This was accompanied by 'humanitarian and legal issues', including compensation for property losses, an investigation into crimes and an amnesty for those not involved in war crimes. The plan went on to present ideas on 'economic relations' and 'social and cultural issues', although its stress on the 'protection of the Russian language' was rather vague. On Crimea the Boisto group was even vaguer, calling for 'discussion of the settlement of legal issues'. The report ended with a call for 'mutual respect for the non-bloc status of Ukraine as stipulated by Ukrainian legislation'.[13] All these were sensible ideas, but failed to address the fundamental question about the nature of the Ukrainian state. The plan had merit in effectively recognising the substance of the grievances that provoked the rebellion, but not only did its recommendations mean that the conflict would be effectively frozen, it offered no ideas on how to provide for the constitutional reconciliation of the monist and pluralist traditions through some form of consociationalism and federalism.

Instead of using these various ideas as the basis for dialogue, the Western powers increasingly intensified the axiology that lay at the root of the Ukraine crisis. The telephone diplomacy that characterised the crisis largely consisted of Western leaders reprimanding Putin from the comfort of their offices. The aim was to make Putin 'see reason', as Obama put it on 29 July when announcing the latest round of sanctions. This approach simply ratcheted up tension, and imposed the burden of change on Russia, as if the West's position were axiomatically correct and above criticism. This is what Samuel Charap calls a 'coercion strategy' that was doomed to fail.[14] The West's desired outcome in Ukraine was neither immutable nor inflexible (for example, NATO enlargement to the country after 2008 was effectively put on hold, although not taken off the table), yet with the consolidation of a Western-backed revolutionary regime after February, it looked as if Russia's historic positions would be irrevocably lost. Russia's fears may well have been exaggerated, but they were not illegitimate. This is why the sanctions strategy was both inept and ineffective, and indeed counterproductive since it only provoked a tougher response from Moscow. The battle between the warriors and the resolvers would continue over the lifting of sanctions. Whereas Obama promised that they could be repealed if Russia followed through on the Donbas peace plan, Yatsenyuk urged them to remain until Kiev's control was restored over the whole territory, including Crimea.

Paul D'Anieri traces the filiation between the Orange Revolution of 2004 and the Maidan revolution of 2014, noting that much the same repertoire of protest activities was employed in both cases, and that the second event was a continuation of the struggle for power that had been first rehearsed in 2004. The battle of the oligarchic clans continued in largely similar forms, although in the second event the EU now emerged as a symbolic rallying cry. The Donetsk group was defeated in 2004, but won in a relatively free and fair election in 2010, and thus from this perspective the protests from 2013 'were another move by western Ukrainian forces, supported by Western governments, to seize control of the country'.[15] By early 2014, D'Anieri notes, no shared view of governmental legitimacy existed in Ukraine, with the constitution a plaything of opposing groups and the outcome of elections denied when they came up with the wrong winner. To compensate, direct action and street mobilisation gained a degree of legitimacy that would be unthinkable in London or New York. This was a genuinely revolutionary situation in which the sinews of state power and the ideological props that sustain them had dissolved. When constituted power tended towards the autocratic and popular power towards the anarchic, the Ukrainian state was in deep crisis. The order associated with the bureaucratic–oligarchic system in that context looked like the best option, and was the one overwhelmingly chosen in the 25 May presidential election. However, this could at best only be a temporary reprieve before the forces unleashed by the revolution once again beat at the gates of the temple of state power.

The Ukrainian crisis raises questions about the coherence of the post-Communist democratic paradigm when faced by a country whose societal, economic and political foundations remain so fundamentally in question. Equally, it is an abnegation to externalise the roots of the Ukraine crisis to the 'rogue' behaviour of Russia, but that crisis stemmed from some of the fundamental contradictions in the liberal-universalist order. If Russia had indeed defected from observance of the rules of that order, then the reasons need to be understood and cannot simply be based on essentialist arguments about the Russian political character or Putin's alleged megalomania. If Russia had not defected but simply wished to be part of a more inclusive understanding and the operation of the order, my argument about Russia's neo-revisionism, then the reasons for this also need to be established. The Ukraine crisis, in this reading, was an aspect of the continuing problems stemming from the asymmetrical end of the Cold War, and it may well not be the last. As for the European context, Slavoj Žižek makes the pertinent point:

> The issue isn't whether Ukraine is worthy of Europe, and good enough to enter the EU, but whether today's Europe can meet the aspirations of the Ukrainians. If Ukraine ends up with a mixture of ethnic fundamentalism and liberal capitalism, with oligarchs pulling the strings, it will be as European as Russia (or Hungary) is today.

Žižek notes that the EU probably had not given Ukraine adequate support in its conflict with Russia:

> But there is another kind of support which has been even more conspicuously absent: the proposal for any feasible strategy for breaking the deadlock. Europe will be in no position to offer such a strategy until it renews its pledge to the emancipatory core of its history.

In Žižek's view, that includes living 'up to the dream that motivated the protesters on the Maidan'.[16]

This 'dream' was a reprise of the aspirations of the anti-Communist revolutions in 1989 – a 'return to Europe', good governance and integration in Atlantic structures – but as in that year there was no substantive emancipatory agenda. The anti-revolutions of 1989 only confirmed the power of capital and neo-liberal governmentality, which in the Ukrainian context could well be considered progressive but in a global context are profoundly retrograde. Žižek was seduced by the neo-Leninist revolutionary romanticism of an armed people seeking to take control of its destiny, but the reality of the Maidan was deeply anti-democratic. This was not another Paris Commune of 1870, but an attempt to wrest the country from one power system to another. It was a popular revolution but not one that had a substantive vision of the empowerment of people at its heart. There was much talk, as there had been in 1989, about the rebirth of civil society, but the notion both then and now was little more than a cipher, an empty signifier – to use a term of Žižek's Lacan – to occupy the intellectual space where more creative thinking could take place. The real struggle was not for society, civil or otherwise, but for the impartiality of law and the probity of strong, just and universal institutions accompanied by dialogism in which all citizens could be included as equals, with their various tongues and manners. The contradictions of the February revolution in the end were those of the whole post-Communist era.

DOG-END OF THE WOLFHOUND CENTURY

Osip Mandelstam described his era as 'this wolfhound century', but the twenty-first is turning out to be the dog-end century, with the chewed-over remnants of the twentieth poisoning international society and the quality of political relationships. The Ukraine crisis has revealed the deep schism between Russia and the West, and exposed the failure of the post-Cold War settlement. International politics was characterised by a number of problems that provoked and exacerbated the Ukraine crisis. First, there was the tension between 'Wider' and 'Greater' representations of Europe. The idea of a Common European Home as presented by Gorbachev may have lacked substance, but it reflected the powerful aspiration of the Soviet leader for his country to join the European political mainstream as part of a shared civilisation and political community. Although in the end Russia and the other CIS countries pursued a '1991' rather than '1989' developmental path, they all shared a dream to be part of this Greater European community. European international society does exist in the form of the Council of Europe, the OSCE and the myriad links between the EU and non-member countries, but this turned out to be a poor substitute for a genuine process of continental unity.

Second, the struggle between continental and Atlanticist approaches to European security and affairs in general once again created a bipolar dynamic that veered between a cold peace and a reprise of the Cold War. Out of this was generated one of the greatest crises of our times. In strategic terms, these different representations of Europe have solidified into two putative new blocs, with a contested territory between them. The Wider European perspective quickly absorbed the bloc of '1989' countries, enlarging the EU to the borders of Russia while raising the stakes with the enlargement of the Euro-Atlantic security system in the form of NATO; meanwhile, the '1991' countries began to integrate in the form of the EEU, along with a number of 'Greater Asian' perspectives in the form of the Shanghai Cooperation Organisation (SCO) and various Silk Roads, and the BRICS countries offered the perspective of a new 'Second World' alliance system that started to create its own financial instruments and institutions of international governance. The sanctions on Russia have exposed the vulnerability of this putative Second World to the geopolitical pressure of the First World, and therefore accelerated attempts to create alternatives less vulnerable to Western manipulation. Globalisation, like so much else, has fizzled out in the contested borderlands of Europe. So too has the belief that rapprochement between Russia and the West is possible on the basis of common values and interests. The gloves are now off and a new period of confrontation will continue until there is a change of either leaders or paradigms, or both.

The Ukraine crisis had deep structural roots. Instead, too often the issue has become personalised in the form of the incomprehensible and 'rogue' behaviour of an individual. Christopher Booker puts the issue well:

> For months the West has been demonising President Putin, with figures such as the Prince of Wales and Hillary Clinton comparing him with Hitler, oblivious to the fact that what set this crisis in motion were those recklessly provocative moves to absorb Ukraine into the EU.[17]

Alexander Lukin outlines the larger picture and the choices facing Russia: 'The post-Soviet consensus was based on mutual understanding with the West that both sides would move towards closer co-operation, respect each other's interests and make mutual compromises. However, these conditions were met only by Russia.' This is in keeping with long-standing concerns about not only the asymmetrical nature of the end of the Cold War, but the continuing imbalance whereby Russia is expected to concede while the West gains ground. Lukin notes that it is the West that is the new ideological power, far more than Russia:

In the West, practically everyone believes its ideology [...] This ideology of 'democratism' [...] is quite simple: Western society, albeit not ideal, is nevertheless more perfect than all the others, it is at the forefront of public progress, and the rest of the world should try to use the Western model as we know it. In principle, this is primitive cultural chauvinism which is characteristic of many nations and countries from small tribes to large civilizations which considered themselves the centre of the universe, and all the others were barbarians. The West's foreign policy is based on this belief.

The monism espoused by the dominant nationalising elites in Ukraine has been accentuated by this monism of the West. More than that, the West's civilising mission, in Lukin's view, has sought to incorporate new territories, even if they did not meet the appropriate democratic standards. Economic and political engagement was anticipated in due course to come up to the required standards under the West's benign influence. This also explains 'why radical nationalists in Ukraine remain unnoticed: they are the ones who are acting towards progress and from the historical point of view they can be justified and some of their crimes can even be overlooked'. Russia has refused to subordinate itself to this civilising imperative and thus cannot be incorporated into the ideal of Western society. Echoing my distinction between the projects of 1989 and 1991, Lukin notes: 'This is what makes Russia different from Eastern Europe.'

This is not because Russia's leaders are congenitally opposed to the West, but Russia's whole history militates against simply adapting to an alternative 'imperial' project, in this case succumbing to the West's ideological expansionism in the form of democratism:

Countries close to Russia are being torn apart by the West's ideologized expansion which has already led to the territorial division of Moldova and Georgia, and now Ukraine is falling apart in front of our eyes. [...] the cultural border was drawn across their territories and they could stay undivided only if their leaders would have taken into account the interests of people living in both the regions that gravitate towards Europe and those that would like to preserve historical ties with Russia.

Russia's proposals to resolve the Ukrainian crisis – including the formation of a coalition government taking into account the interests of the south and east; federalisation and neutrality; and the granting of official status to the Russian language – could not be adopted: 'Accepting these proposals would be interpreted by Western ideologists not as a solution that satisfies all sides but as an attempt by "the bad guys" to slow down Ukraine's movement towards progress, and that is an ideological taboo.'[18] The US has sought to create a regime in its image, while Russia has sought to prevent the creation of one hostile to its perceived interests. In classic realist terms, the borderlands have become a power vacuum, and thus the site of competing geopolitical projects.

Russia became a bone in the throat of the Atlantic community, while the EU struggled to recognise the enduring multipolarity of European politics. The EU demonstratively refused to engage with the various projects for Eurasian integration, which was clearly a major mistake. No one pretends that there are not serious governance and human-rights issues in the countries comprising the EEU, but these are not the bloody despotisms presented in much of the Western media. An intelligent policy would have been to understand that classic EU methods of extending its normative zone of peace had reached their finality in the borderlands between Europe and Eurasia, and that new approaches were required. This would not be at the expense of the 'sovereign choices' of the relevant countries, but these choices would be mediated by the legitimate concerns of the larger geopolitical environment. It is pure hypocrisy to argue that the EU is little more than an extended trading bloc: after Lisbon, it was institutionally a core part of the Atlantic security community, and had thus become geopolitical. The meeting in Minsk on 26 August of the EU, Ukraine and the Eurasian Customs Union (ECU) should have been held before the crisis, not after. Nevertheless, it is to be welcomed as the beginning of an adjustment of European policy.

At the same time, Russia's stance of resentment and self-exclusion, despite having, as argued throughout this book, a rational and empirical basis, needs to be modified to encompass the fact that neither NATO nor the EU is systemically hostile to Russia's interests. Non-negotiated enlargement and missile defence are perceived as threats by Russia, and this should have been enough to modify Western behaviour, yet none of this has been enough to provoke a confrontation. This was provided by the Ukrainian crisis, where domestic contradictions greatly exacerbated the existing tensions in international politics. The tension between the civic and the ethno-nationalist models of Ukraine state-building, between monist and pluralist representations of the political community, and all the shades in between, remain unresolved. Ultimately both the Ukrainian and the Ukraine crises can only be resolved by imaginative political leadership and a willingness to engage in dialogue on all sides. A constituent assembly would provide a forum for debating how to reconcile the monist and pluralist traditions and begin the process of reconciliation. A European peace conference should examine how the new lines of division could be overcome by reconciling the Wider and Greater European projects, accompanied by commitments to support

Ukraine economically and politically. Above all, Moscow needs to show the courage of compassion towards Ukraine. It is a country that in many respects is another side of Russia itself, while Russia is inevitably part of Ukrainian identity. The crises will only be resolved when 'normal' relations are established between the two countries. The reconstruction of the Donbas will cost billions, but a no less onerous task is the rebuilding of trust between the various communities and states. Otherwise, the Ukrainian state will continue to degenerate; there will be a new popular uprising; the country will be in danger of further division; Europe will once again be torn by a new Iron Curtain, and the dogs of war will be unleashed on a global scale.

THE CHALLENGE OF TRANSFORMATION

The crisis in and over Ukraine has reached a stalemate in several respects, each of which will be examined in greater detail below. First, although the post-Maidan leadership of President Petro Poroshenko and the government headed by Prime Minister Arseniy Yatsenyuk have been legitimated in democratic votes, elections alone have not been able to create a liberal democracy. This also requires the rule of law, a state monopoly over the means of coercion, judicial independence, a free media, constraints on corruption and a culture of trust and tolerance. Instead, society has become increasingly polarised, including the intensified demonisation of those who have stood up against the narrow monist vision of Ukrainian statehood pursued by the regime.

Second, although domestic reforms have been pursued by the administration, it is not at all clear that they really offer a path out of economic crisis and social conflict. On 11 March 2015 the IMF approved an Extended Fund Facility (EFF) of $17.5 billion, to supersede the Stand-by Agreement (SBA) of 2014, accompanied by a further $7.5 billion pledged by the US, the EU and the World Bank. This still fell short of the $40 billion funding gap identified by the IMF. The IMF insisted that the remaining $15 billion would have to come from Ukraine's private creditors.[1] The disbursement of $5 billion a month later bought the government precious time, although the programme required deep structural reforms. The economy has continued to decline, accompanied by bank failures, falling real wages, rising unemployment, increased poverty and intensifying social tensions. Ukraine's debt crisis has only worsened as the country veers towards some sort of default on its loans.

Third, this has only deepened the culture war between the radicalised Ukrainian nationalist elites in control of the Verkhovna Rada and government and those favouring a more traditional and pluralistic understanding of Ukrainian identity. The adoption of the 'decommunisation' laws in April 2015 has sought to impose a sharp break with the country's Soviet past by removing monuments of the Soviet era, changing the names of streets and towns, reshaping the way that history is taught and changing archive management. More moderate nationalists and democrats have tried to temper the radicalism of the ultra-nationalists, but they have been countered by pressure from the 'armed Maidan', the various battalions and vigilante groups.

Fourth, the Minsk-1 agreement of September 2014 for a time stabilised the conflict in the Donbas, but did little to address the core issues that had provoked the war. By December a new wave of fighting had broken out, focused on the struggle by the insurgents to take over Donetsk airport and the Debaltsevo salient, a finger of Kiev-held territory reaching deep into the DPR. The Minsk-2 agreement of 12 February 2015, once again brokered by the Normandy four (France, Germany, Russia and Ukraine) and mediated by the OSCE, imposed an uneasy ceasefire accompanied by the stipulated withdrawal of heavy arms from the demarcation line. Point 11 of the agreement is crucial, committing the Kiev government to

> carrying out constitutional reform in Ukraine with a new constitution entering into force by the end of 2015 providing for decentralisation as a key element (including a reference to the specificities of certain areas in the Donetsk and Luhansk regions, agreed with the representatives of these areas), as well as adopting permanent legislation on the special status of certain areas of the Donetsk and Luhansk regions [...] until the end of 2015.[2]

All 'foreign armed formations' were to leave, while all 'illegal groups' were to be disbanded (point 10), accompanied by a discussion of the modalities for the 'full resumption of socio-economic ties, including social transfers such as pension payments and other payments' (point 8). Despite the agreement, radical forces on both sides of the line have sought the resumption of hostilities to achieve a decisive victory, but have been restrained by Moscow and Washington. The whole 'Novorossiya' project has been quietly shelved by Moscow, with the announcement in May 2015 that the parliament of Novorossiya had been suspended. Kiev has sought to avert a 'third Maidan' by bringing the battalions under its control, a project resisted by the groups themselves.[3] The ceasefire was meant to be only the beginning of a peace process in Ukraine, but so far there is little evidence of that.

And finally, the broader international context of the conflict remains as polarised as ever. Sanctions against Russia were extended on 22 June 2015 for another six months to 31 January 2016, while Crimea-related sanctions have been extended to 23 June

2016. There is little evidence that they are achieving their goal of changing Russian behaviour. In fact, it is clear that Moscow is looking for a face-saving formula that would allow it to withdraw from the Donbas conflict without appearing to betray its allies in the region or giving up its broader goal of a neutral if not non-aligned Ukraine. In defending the Minsk-2 agreement, Moscow, paradoxically, has become the most consistent defender of Ukrainian sovereignty within its new borders (that is, minus Crimea, but with the Donbas). The Kremlin has come under sustained critique for its half-hearted support for the Donbas, allegedly sacrificing Novorossiya on the altar of improved relations with the West. Meanwhile, critics of Minsk-2 in the West have argued that its provisions, which include the call for dialogue with the insurgents and constitutional reform that would give them some sort of special devolved status, would create another 'frozen conflict' that Russia could use to exert leverage against Kiev. This is reminiscent of the swift repudiation of the deal signed with Yanukovych on 21 February 2014 – an agreement that offered an evolutionary resolution to the crisis.

In short, there has been no conceptual or practical breakthrough. Instead, each of the five levels of the crisis have reinforced the others, exacerbating the conflicts within Ukraine and in global politics. Vladimir Ishchenko notes that the Maidan revolution 'drew strength from mass popular mobilization but failed to articulate social grievances, allowing itself to be represented politically by oligarchic opposition forces. Ultimately it brought a neoliberal–nationalist government to power in Kiev.' Not surprisingly, the people of the south-eastern regions who had voted for Yanukovych 'were frightened by the Maidan's violence and by the first moves of the Yatsenyuk government against the status of the Russian language'.[4] Just as by the end of 1914 World War I had settled in for the long haul of trench warfare, so by the end of 2014 all sides had dug themselves into a stalemated position, entrenched by the erection of walls, both metaphorical and physical. This chapter will examine the five levels in more detail, and end with some broader reflections.

REVOLUTION AND REFORM

A veritable mountain of challenges confronted the administration created by the Maidan revolution and legitimated by the presidential and parliamentary elections of May and October 2014. Constitutional and governance reform was at the top of the government's agenda, especially since the Minsk-2 agreement called for constitutional reform by December 2015. One of the government's first acts after coming to power in the wake of the Maidan revolution in February 2014 was the restoration of the Orange constitutional amendments, which granted parliament greater powers vis-à-vis the presidency. Soon after, plans were launched to decentralise power to local-government authority, including a reform package introduced to parliament in December 2014 that included extensive fiscal decentralisation. Decentralisation was balanced by replacing governors with the new office of prefect, appointed by the president on the nomination of the Cabinet of Ministers and thus subordinate to both. The prefect exercises executive power at the regional level and thus establishes a 'vertical of power' on the Russian model. In certain circumstances, the president also gained the right to disband regional legislatures.

The bill on constitutional reform was proposed to the Verkhovna Rada on 1 July 2015, but it contained only vague 'transitional provisions' about the status of Donetsk and Lugansk. The official proposals sent by the two republics in May were ignored. However, under US pressure, including the personal intervention of Victoria Nuland who flew to Ukraine on 15 July, Kiev finally moved ahead with implementing the Minsk Accords. The following day Poroshenko tabled a revised version, with paragraph 18 now stating: 'The particulars of local government in certain districts of the Donetsk and Luhansk regions are to be determined by a special law.'[5] The decentralisation amendments to the constitution were then approved by the Constitutional Court. The first reading on 31 August was passed with 265 votes, comfortably exceeding the required simple majority of 226 votes, but the second reading required a majority of 300 votes since the legislation entailed a change to the constitution. The Minsk-2 peace agreement called for a third stage, namely 'special status' entailing substantive devolution to the insurgent regions. The agreement unambiguously stated that these separate arrangements needed to take into account the suggestions put forward by the republics themselves. Point 4 is clear about the need for 'dialogue', and both points 11 and 12 insist that they are 'agreed with the representatives of these areas'. Thus the new constitutional arrangements required consultation with the people's republics of Donetsk and Lugansk. Addressing the question in the form of a special law rather than a constitutional amendment would make it easier to withdraw this status in the future and inhibit other regions from seeking these privileges. The prime candidate was Transcarpathia, with its large Hungarian population.

Nevertheless, the 'special law' formulation provoked the violent opposition of Oleg Tyagnybok's Svoboda and other nationalist groups. Three members of the National Guard – all young draftees – were killed and 130 were injured, ten seriously, in violent clashes accompanied by a grenade attack outside the parliament building at the bill's first reading on 31 August, the worst violence in the capital since Yanukovych's overthrow. The protesters feared that decentralisation would de facto grant the eastern regions too much power and threaten the integrity of the country. The violence was an intimation of what could happen if the war in the south-east ended and the battle-hardened battalions returned to Kiev to act as the shock troops of a 'third Maidan'. Those of a cynical disposition suggest that this is one reason for Kiev's intransigence in coming to terms with its rebellious subjects. Poroshenko had little room for manoeuvre, caught between radicals opposed to concessions to the Donbas and with his own coalition held together by fragile bonds. There was a powerful national anti-Minsk coalition, which in the Rada consisted of Samopomich, Batkivshchyna (Fatherland) and Oleg Lyashko's Radical Party. This only accentuated the role of international mediation in the Donbas crisis, since a domestic solution was clearly impossible. Such mediation was helped by the growing war-weariness in Ukraine. Only 60 per cent of eligible draftees were signed up in the sixth mobilisation in summer 2015, and most Ukrainians (57 per cent) wanted a peaceful resolution to the conflict and were dissatisfied by the lack of progress at the negotiating table.[6]

Constitutional change was accompanied by the governance reforms promised by the Association Agreement with the EU. As we have seen, this was signed on 27 June 2014 but its implementation was postponed, at Moscow's request, until 31 December 2015. Moscow, Kiev and Brussels conducted trilateral discussions over how to implement the agreement in an attempt to allay Russian concerns that the DCFTA could lead to the Russian market being flooded with cheap EU goods. In a deeply corrupt environment, Moscow feared that rules of origin would not be an effective barrier to the abuse through trade deflection of the current arrangements for free trade between the two countries. In May 2015 technical arrangements were agreed to strengthen the management of rules of origin and customs arrangements of the CIS free-trade agreement. By September 2015 22 of the EU's 28 member states had ratified the agreement. In general, Ukraine was committed to adopting 426 EU norms by 2025, and by September 2015 it had fully adopted two and partially adopted nine. A poll in July 2015 found that support for these reforms remained high, but there was frustration over the slow pace of their achievement. An astonishing 72 per cent of Ukrainians felt that the country was heading in the wrong direction, with 67 per cent supporting greater devolution of power to local authorities and communities. Support for EU integration remained strong at 55 per cent, while support for integration into what was dubbed the 'Russia-led Customs Union' had plummeted from 43 per cent in March 2012 to 14 per cent. By contrast, 41 per cent would vote to join NATO while 30 per cent would vote against.[7]

Ukraine has long been recognised as 'one of the most corrupt countries in the world'.[8] On 14 October 2014 Ukraine adopted a package of anti-corruption laws. The National Agency for Prevention of Corruption (NAPC) started work in April 2015 as a special governmental body, while the National Anti-Corruption Bureau, an independent body designed to fight corruption at all levels of the administration, started work in September 2015. The common criticism is that Ukraine has chosen to fight corruption through the creation of more bureaucratic agencies.[9] Amendments in July 2015 to the autumn 2014 law on prosecutors granted them more powers in the struggle against corruption, accompanied by a purge of local prosecutors and their deputies. They were replaced by some 700 new regional prosecutors. At the top, the prosecutor general appointed by the Euromaidan authorities, Vitaly Yarema, was dismissed after a year because of his alleged dilatoriness in tackling corruption and prosecuting members of the Yanukovych regime, and his successor, Viktor Shokin, faced the same fate. Following the Georgian example, the traffic police was gradually replaced by new units. As in Georgia, the traffic police was notoriously corrupt, and thus the general approach was disbandment and the formation of new units rather than reform of the old system. The national police as a whole was the subject of substantive reform, including a change of name from 'militia' to 'police'. A thorough reform of the judiciary was under consideration by parliament, including new criteria for the selection, promotion and powers of judges. The aim was to strengthen the independence of the judiciary and to ensure equal and impartial justice for citizens.

The Maidan revolution had in part been inspired by revulsion against the ostentatious wealth of a small group of well-connected businesspeople. The rampant consolidation of the wealth of the Yanukovych family, especially of his son Alexander, was the proximate cause of the protests, yet in all essentials Ukraine remains an oligarch republic. Although the wealth of some individual magnates has taken a battering, the old oligarchs have been joined by a new generation of wealthy power brokers. The interior minister Arsen Avakov and his colleagues appear to be building their own business empires. The revolution brought to power one of those well-connected billionaire businesspeople, Poroshenko, who had served as a minister in several governments (including Yanukovych's) while accumulating his wealth.[10] Thus Poroshenko's programme of 'de-oligarchisation' would clearly be contradictory and selective, targeting those who threatened his position.

This naturally entailed conflict with Igor Kolomoisky, who had been appointed governor of the Dnepropetrovsk region in March 2014 and who took the lead in the struggle against anti-Maidan insurgency. In March 2015 Kolomoisky sought to assert his power over Ukrnafta, Ukraine's largest oil company. It was 52 per cent owned by Naftogaz, 42 per cent by the Privat Group; the rest was owned by minority shareholders, although Privat Group had been managing Ukrnafta for a dozen years. Following the adoption of a law on the management of joint stock companies on 19 March 2015 that was perceived to threaten his interests, Kolomoisky laid siege to the Ukrnafta offices in Kiev. This represented a blatant attempt to use private armies for personal gain and a challenge to state power. Poroshenko responded to this direct challenge to his authority by forcing Kolomoisky's resignation on 25 March. Kolomoisky remained in control of PrivatBank, Ukraine's largest bank, holding 26 per cent of the country's retail deposits, which is officially owned by the Privat Group of Kolomoisky and others. The Privat Group continued to gain benefits from the revolution, including the contract to supply fuel to the army, as well as winning substantial stabilisation credits for Kolomoisky's assets, including Ukrainian International Airlines (MAU) and a state refinancing deal for PrivatBank. Dnepropetrovsk remained the centre of an autonomous regional power constellation.[11] The US Department of Justice began an investigation into $1.8 billion of IMF emergency liquidity assistance to the NBU, which allegedly disappeared into PrivatBank and related party accounts offshore.[12] In April 2014 $3.2 billion had urgently been disbursed and another $4.5 billion was issued over the following five months to stabilise Ukraine's financial system. Some of the money apparently found its way to a Cyprus bank account controlled by Kolomoisky.[13]

On 29 May 2015 Poroshenko astonished the world by appointing the former Georgian president, Mikheil Saakashvili, to become the governor of the Odessa region, replacing Kolomoisky's ally, Igor Palitsa. The aim was to apply Saakashvili's experience of reforming Georgia to deal with the intractable problems in Ukraine, and this he proceeded to do in his characteristically energetic style. Under his control Georgia became one of the leaders in the region for ease of doing business and reforming property and construction rights, but while everyday corruption decreased, it is alleged to have become concentrated in the top echelons of the elite. He was accused of violently dispersing peaceful demonstrations and forcefully closing opposition television stations, leading to the opening of several criminal cases against him in Georgia. In Odessa, Saakashvili planned to reduce the 8,000-strong regional administrative staff to some 3,000, accompanied by the spectacular dismissal and public humiliation of officials, agency heads and other leaders. In July he was joined by Maria Gaidar, who agreed to serve as deputy governor responsible for social reforms. She is the daughter of the architect of Russia's tumultuous economic reforms of the early 1990s, Yegor Gaidar, and an outspoken critic of Putin, condemning the annexation of Crimea.

In politics, the government was backed by a five-party coalition comprising the People's Front, headed by Yatsenyuk, the Petro Poroshenko Bloc, the Radical Party of Oleg Lyashko, Yulia Tymoshenko's Batkivshchyna and Samopomich. On 28 August 2015 Vitaly Klitschko, the mayor of Kiev, fused his UDAR party with the Petro Poroshenko Bloc under the revived name of Solidarity (Poroshenko's old party). The two fought the local government elections of 25 October together, although the majority of the lists were filled by Poroshenko supporters. There were endless tensions between the partners, notably between the two largest, since Yatsenyuk's presidential ambitions were well known. Although he styled himself as a technocrat, in practice he was an extreme ideologue. His poll ratings took a battering as his irreconcilable style failed to solve any of the fundamental problems facing the country. His People's Front in the end joined Solidarity in the October elections – a deal that effectively allowed him to stay on as premier. Solidarity gradually assumed the features of a classic 'party of power', working to support the incumbent president. Its main challenger was Batkivshchyna, which now regained some of its earlier ratings, although Yulia Tymoshenko, despite her populist rhetoric, retained only a shadow of her former support. The Opposition Bloc, which had won 9.4 per cent in the October 2014 elections, was dominated by deputies from the former Party of Regions (PoR), and now it became the main voice trying to temper the radicalism of the regime. It was headed by former energy minister Yury Boiko and Yanukovych's former chief of staff Sergei Levochkin, both of whom were associated with the so-called 'gas lobby' connected to Dmytro Firtash. On 24 July the Communist Party of Ukraine (CPU) was finally banned by the courts and therefore was excluded from participation in the local elections, further restricting the range of choices open to the public. Right Sector also announced that it would not participate, instead focusing on organising a nationwide referendum.

The election used a closed-list system, and there were run-offs for mayors in larger towns with a population over 90,000 (47 meet that criterion). There had been plans to use an open-list system in which voters select both a party and their preferred candidates from the party list, but the closed-list system allowed the party leaders to decide on candidates. The election was contested by a record 132 parties, and those that gained more than the 5 per cent representation threshold received seats on local councils. The new voting law prohibits candidates from running as independents and bans blocs, whereby parties get together to run a single list (although the run-off rule forces coalition-building in the second round). The law also banned internally displaced persons (IDPs), numbering at least 1.5 million, from voting, and it neglected to place limits on campaign financing. In Kiev Klitschko faced a tough challenge to be re-elected mayor from Batkivshchyna, but in the event won a second term. The mayor of Kharkov, Gennady Kernes, consolidated his position despite his earlier dalliance with separatism, and now enjoyed the support of business leaders and the city's Russophone population and romped to victory with over 60 per cent of the vote. The Opposition Bloc took the lead in six south-eastern regions, but was unable to reproduce anything like the electoral success of the old PoR, and in any case faced a leadership split between Boiko and Levochkin. The 46.5 per cent turnout was only 2 per cent lower than the last local elections, yet in the circumstances it reflected popular disillusionment with the continuation of the oligarchic status quo, especially among young people, who were notably absent from the poll. Hopes that an oligarch (Poroshenko) would lead a campaign to destroy the oligarchs were disappointed, and instead the election was characterised by endless 'old-style deals with oligarchs and local power brokers'.[14]

The Kiev authorities failed to gain control over the 'volunteer battalions', in effect a form of vigilantism that demonstrated the decay of state power in the country. The OSCE Special Monitoring Mission (SMM) noted in July 2015 that Right Sector 'insisted that they had their own orders and did not fall under the command of the Ukrainian Armed Forces'.[15] The CyberBerkut hackers reported an alleged document from the Ukrainian Procurator's Office that admitted that the battalions were out of control and that it 'couldn't cope with the lawlessness of the security forces and the "volunteer" battalions'.[16] Now firmly lodged in a new base in Dnepropetrovsk, a gift of the former governor Kolomoisky, they refused to submit to Kiev and demanded a return to war. The Azov battalion, the subject of international condemnation earlier, remained in its base in Mariupol. On 11 July 2015 an armed confrontation took place in the town of Mukachevo between a private security unit working for a Rada deputy and some Right Sector activists. The incident was triggered by tensions between organised crime groups and corrupt police officials, but reflected the larger breakdown of public order. Nicolai Petro notes:

> Alas, many 'pro-Western' Ukrainian political figures have spent years undermining the legitimacy of every legal and official institution in post-Soviet Ukraine. They have done so not just under Yanukovych, but also under all five presidents, and all five versions of the constitution. The lingering legacy of nihilism now makes it exceedingly difficult for people to put their trust in anything that the government says or does.[17]

ECONOMY AND SOCIETY

The breakdown of the state's monopoly over legal coercion has been accompanied by deteriorating socio-economic conditions. According to the World Bank, in its 24 years of independence (1991–2014) Ukraine's real GDP decreased by 35 per cent. This is absolutely the worst performance in the world and surpasses the falls in Moldova (–29 per cent), Georgia (–15.4 per cent), Zimbabwe (–2.3 per cent) and the Central African Republic (–0.94 per cent). Ukraine never recovered from the catastrophic 60 per cent fall in its GDP in the 1990s, one of the factors rendering the population prone to protest in the 2000s. The UN estimated that a third of the population would be in poverty by the end of 2015. Another UN report on 10 July 2015 stated that at least 5 million Ukrainian citizens were in need of humanitarian aid, 1.4 million of whom were IDPs.[18] The economy decreased by 6.7 per cent in 2014, and fell another 17.2 per cent in the first quarter of 2015 compared to the same period in 2014, and by 14.7 per cent year-on-year in the second quarter, suggesting that the IMF's predicted 9 per cent decline in Ukraine's GDP in 2015 looked rather optimistic. Inflation rose from the 15 per cent registered in 2014 to 55 per cent in 2015. According to the economy ministry, the shadow economy was reckoned to make up 47 per cent of GDP.[19] Property values were collapsing.

Already in 2014 exports fell by 13.5 per cent compared to 2013 – from $63.3 to $54 billion – and in the first six months of 2015 Ukraine sold goods worth only $18.5 billion, compared with $28.62 billion in the same period in 2014, a fall of 35 per cent. In the first half of 2015 imports fell even more sharply, by 38.5 per cent. The precipitous fall in exports was in large part made up by a decline in sales to Russia and CIS countries, still the main export market for Ukraine, and was not compensated by rises elsewhere. According to Ukraine's State Statistics Service, in 2014 the country's exports to Russia fell by 33.7 per cent, and in the first half of 2015 fell by a further 59.4 per cent, with all exports to Russia in the first half of 2015 amounting to a miserly $2.3 billion. Russia remained the leading coal exporter to Ukraine, despite attempts by Kiev to diversify its suppliers. In the first half of 2015 Ukraine's exports to the EU fell by 35.6 per cent compared to the same period the previous year, and even though the EU's trade preferences, removing most quotas, came into effect on 23 April, whereby Ukrainian producers are able to export goods to the EU without paying customs duties, non-tariff barriers remain, such as different quality and regulatory standards. On 1 January 2016 the free-trade area with the EU comes into effect, entailing the abolition or significant reduction of about 95 per cent of tariff duties. The Ukrainian domestic market will be exposed to the full range of EU consumer goods, which in conditions of the lack of credit and modernisation funds will further undermine domestic production.

The major Ukrainian industrial complexes were facing difficulties, if not collapse. The metallurgical complex Metinvest, owned by Rinat Akhmetov, defaulted in April 2015, and others on the brink included the giant Yuzhmash missile plant, the Zaporozhia car factory, the Sumy factory complex, the Antonov plane manufacturer, Turboatom, the Motor Sich helicopter engine plant, the Kharkov tractor plant Electrotyazhmash, and more, many of which had relied on Russia for contracts. Steel production, which provided the country with over 30 per cent of its foreign-currency earnings, fell by a third. Even agriculture was in difficulty, with production costs rising sharply, while the monocultural exploitation of cash crops such as maize (corn) and sunflowers threatened the fertility of even Ukraine's black earth. In July 2015 the economic development minister Aivaras Abromavičius (one of the foreigners brought in to reinforce the expertise and independence of the government) announced that 345 firms (out of the 1,800 owned by the state) would be offered for sale to US and European investors (Russian ones were specifically excluded), hoping to raise billions of dollars to help bolster a leaking budget. It was not clear that there would be great interest in buying the mostly heavily indebted firms, since the profitable companies had long ago been snapped up by the oligarchs, typically seized in what were often rigged auctions. The jewel in the crown of this privatisation round was undoubtedly the Odessa Portside Plant, with 17 per cent of Ukraine's ammonium nitrate and 19 per cent of urea production capacity, exporting 85 per cent of its output.

Privatisation has become an intensely controversial issue in Ukraine, especially when it comes to selling off land. The breakdown of the integrated Soviet market and production complexes began Ukraine's deindustrialisation; this has now accelerated, and it is unlikely that Western 'investors' will in the short term make up for the losses. In the longer term, when the political conditions have stabilised, the highly educated workforce, cheap labour costs and proximity to European markets, as well as abundant natural resources, will make Ukraine an attractive location for investment.

The banking sector was notoriously corrupt, but the attempts by the NBU to clean it up came with its own costs. The NBU itself was granted greater operational independence in June 2015. By that time 53 out of Ukraine's 180 banks had been closed down, but the compensation for depositors proved inadequate, and funds appeared to disappear back into the state treasury.[20] If these claims are true, then this represents a spectacular case of 'taxation by confiscation'. Activists representing aggrieved bank customers estimate that the savings of some 5 million large personal and business depositors were not covered by the national deposit-guarantee scheme and were effectively wiped out. Yatsenyuk's full-frontal revolutionary approach to dealing with issues once again had the counterproductive effect of deepening the problem, in this case destroying what residual faith there had been in Ukraine's banking system, a scandal that Gary Scarrabelotti calls 'Ukraine's great silence'.[21] He notes that a quarter of the funds granted by the IMF went to refinance Ukraine's precarious banks, but despite the support the banks disappeared together with the refinancing funds and the bulk of the assets of depositors. Leading oligarch-controlled banks to be liquidated *after* refinancing include Mykola Lagun's Delta, Oleg Bakhmatyuk's VAB, and Dmytro Firtash's Nadra.[22] Scarrabelotti comments:

> It wouldn't really fit the mantra – would it? – to suggest that the 'good guys' in Ukraine might be fleecing the Ukrainian people far more extensively than Viktor Yanukovych ever dreamed of. He at least was chiefly preoccupied with 'taxing' the oligarchs in his family's interest. The new configuration of oligarchs and their cronies now running

Ukraine have directly attacked the savings of the middle-class people who brought the new government to power.[23]

The middle class, the group intended to be the bedrock of support for the liberal economic reforms, lost their savings. Not surprisingly, trust in the banking system fell dramatically, accompanied by a halving of foreign currency deposits by July 2015 to some $10 billion compared to December 2013 levels. The hryvnia had long been pegged to the dollar, but the introduction of a floating exchange rate saw the value of the national currency fall by half by early 2015. Capital controls were reintroduced in February 2015 in an attempt to staunch capital flight. The government engaged in a long struggle with its creditors to stave off a default. An interest payment in July 2015 gave it some breathing space, helped by the disbursement of a second tranche of $1.7 billion from the IMF.

One of the most intractable problems has been dealing with Ukraine's external debt. After months of often fraught negotiations, in particular with the leading bond-holder Franklin Templeton Investments, on 27 August 2015 the US-born finance minister, Natalie Jaresko (another foreigner), secured a 20 per cent write-down on $19 billion of the country's $72 billion foreign debts. Some $3.8 billion would be written off by the funds holding Ukrainian debt and there would be a four-year extension on repayments, but in return the bondholders would receive securities entitling the holders to a payout from the envisaged Ukrainian growth from 2021, with the government paying a higher interest rate on the remaining debt. Jaresko had originally sought a 40 per cent 'haircut', but even this deal was unlikely to help reduce Ukraine's debt from the current near 100 per cent to the IMF-stipulated 71 per cent of GDP by 2020 (in 2013 Ukraine's sovereign debt had been a comfortable 40 per cent of GDP), one of the key indicators of the financial restructuring operation. The deal represented a relatively minor cut in the total stock of Ukraine's public debt, from about $71 billion to $67 billion, at a time when Ukraine's total GDP (in dollar terms) was no more than $70 billion.

Above all, Russia was not a party to the agreement since it refused to engage in private-sector discussions for what it insisted was a public-sector loan from one government to another. Russia's finance minister Anton Siluanov insisted that Moscow would expect the $3 billion Eurobond issued to Yanukovych in December 2013 to be repaid in full by the redemption date of 20 December 2015. This would make it difficult for Ukraine to find the $5 billion in debt relief assumed in IMF calculations. Jaresko insisted that the bond was a private (commercial) rather than a sovereign (state) debt, but since it had been issued by Russia's sovereign wealth fund she was on shaky ground. The general consensus was that Kiev would be obliged to honour the sovereign debt, and failure to do so would represent a default, with all of the disastrous consequences that entails. IMF rules do not allow it to lend to a country in default to another sovereign, although a variety of fudges were mooted to get round the problem.

Insistence on repayment in full prompted the US vice president Joe Biden to argue that Russia was trying to provoke Ukraine's economic collapse.[24] Ukraine made determined efforts to reduce its dependence on imported Russian gas. In 2015 some 60 per cent of gas came from European sources, including reimported Russian gas through reverse flows from Eastern Europe, and only 40 per cent came directly from Gazprom. This was accompanied by sharp increases in household gas prices, rising between three- and fivefold, although balanced by increased subsidies to Naftogaz. The government introduced legislation to bring Ukraine into conformity with the liberalised gas market envisaged by the EU's Third Energy Package (TEP). The so-called 'winter package' setting prices for imported Russian gas ended in March 2015, and was followed once again by tense negotiations between Kiev and Moscow to set a new tariff. On 1 July Ukraine suspended all gas imports from Russia and relied instead on reverse gas supplies from the EU. Ukraine sought a price of around $200 per tcm and was not ready to pay Russia's asking price of $247 per tcm (although it was paying more for reverse-flow gas), while demanding a fixed price for the entire winter season and a trilateral agreement with the EU, terms that Russia refused to accept. Ukraine continued to buy nuclear fuel, coal and electricity from Russia, without which there would be no hot water or electricity.

Russia also sought to reduce its transit dependency on Ukraine. The launching of the second line of the Nord Stream pipeline in October 2012 allowed Russia to reduce its gas deliveries to Europe via Ukraine, and there are now plans to build a third and fourth line. In 2012, 11 bcm was delivered via Nord Stream and 79 bcm transited through Ukraine. By 2014 these figures were 34 bcm and 53 bcm respectively, thus registering a 23-bcm rise for Nord Stream, and transit through Ukraine fell by 26 bcm. Over the same period, all gas deliveries to Europe rose slightly from 121.8 bcm in 2012 to 123.7 bcm in 2014.[25] Thus there was a clear attempt to reroute rising gas deliveries away from Ukraine. Gazprom's gas-transit contract with Naftogaz expires in 2019, and by that time Nord Stream's capacity will have been doubled by the addition of the new lines. Even after 2019 Gazprom will not be able entirely to stop transiting gas across Ukraine because of long-term contracts with some Eastern European countries. As for South Stream, in response to what had become an increasingly intractable set of regulatory and political issues in the south-east of Europe, Putin in December 2014 abruptly announced the termination of the project, and instead planned to divert the pipeline south into a planned new hub on the Turkish–Greek border. However, getting what is now known as the Turk Stream project off the ground is hardly less complicated than South Stream, especially since new connecting lines will have to be built to take the gas from the new hub to European markets.

CULTURAL CONTRADICTIONS

The newly independent Ukraine in 1991 adopted the generous policy that anyone permanently resident in the country at the time could automatically assume Ukrainian citizenship. Some radical nationalists sought to emulate the example of Estonia and Latvia and limit citizenship to those with adequate knowledge of Ukrainian, but the territorial approach to nationality, irrespective of ethnicity, triumphed. Ukraine developed as a tolerant and pluralistic society, with Russian remaining the pre-eminent language in the capital, in the media and in many other spheres of life. Yet since 1991 the country has developed on the basis of 'one nation, one language'. The Ukrainophone elites have displayed an 'existential perception of threat', provoked in large part by the 'historic proximity between the two main linguistic groups in Ukraine', the Russophones and the Ukrainophones.[26] The failure to institutionalise linguistic pluralism in the constitution remained a sore point, but attempts to remedy the situation only aggravated tensions. The fundamental flaw of the 2012 language law was that in regions where other languages were adopted, Ukrainian thereby suffered and in places was effectively squeezed out – as pointed out by the Council of Europe's Venice Commission in its critique of the law. One form of monism was simply replaced by another rather than creating a new and genuine pluralism. As noted earlier, Ukraine has all the characteristics of what Samuel Huntington called a 'cleft country', and he identified Crimea as a particularly contentious region.[27] The problem is not so much that Ukraine finds itself straddling the boundary between civilisations, but that the whole Intermarium region from the Baltic to the Black Sea finds itself a new borderland between contesting geopolitical ambitions. Ukraine finds itself at the centre of a new shatter zone of contrasting cultural and political expectations. The struggle for the Eurasian borderlands is far from over.[28]

Contemporary Ukraine is often considered to be in a post-colonial situation. In Chapter 1 I noted how Taras Kuzio and others argue on this basis that a programme of anti-colonial rectification is required, to bend back the stick so distorted by centuries of Russian occupation. This includes, in various combinations, linguistic de-Russification, cultural purification and geopolitical distancing. Mykola Riabchuk, a well-known Ukrainian public intellectual, has applied postcolonial theory in a sophisticated way to the language issue. Riabchuk's thinking is located in the classical postcolonial problematic – the hyphen is missing and the issue is the more complex cultural interchanges between imperial power and the subaltern.[29] Riabchuk argues that the continuing predominance of Russian language and culture reflects Ukraine's broader postcolonial condition. He conceptualises this as the Ukrainian Creole state, 'that is, a state that belongs primarily to the descendants of Russian settlers as well as to those indigenes who had eventually assimilated into the dominant (Russophone) culture'. In his view the Ukrainian case is very different from the traditional Creole state in the Americas, Australia and elsewhere, because the culture and language of the settlers is 'unusually proximate to those of indigenes', accompanied by the unusual capacity of the indigenes to compete against the culture of the colonisers in terms of culture, language and various modern arts.

His policy response is not dissimilar to that of the anti-colonialists, namely a gradual but consistent and determined Ukrainianisation, a state-led affirmative-action programme to enhance the status of the Ukrainian language and culture. In his view, 'the Ukrainian state will remain dysfunctional as long as it remains Creole, that is, neither Ukrainian nor Russian but, rather, Soviet.'[30] By contrast with this monist view, the pluralists would argue that the very proximity of the two cultures means that they have grown together and both are legitimate inheritors of the modern Ukrainian state. Pluralists would argue that the very idea of 'indigenes' and 'settlers' are reified concepts, and instead argue that nation-building in post-Communist Ukraine should recognise the diversity of paths that its constituent peoples have taken to join the modern state, and thus the ethnonym 'Ukrainian' should be primarily civic. As Mikhail Pogrebinskiy, a scholar at the Kiev Centre of Political Research and Conflict Studies, argues: 'The idea of Russians in Ukraine being a national minority similar to, for instance, Hungarians in Romania or Slovakia, Swedes in Finland, or even Russians in Estonia, is in fact profoundly fallacious,' and he condemns Western policies derived from this false premise:

> According to that idea, the Ukrainians, with the moral support of the West, are trying to free themselves from the centuries-old Russian colonial oppression, while Moscow resists it in every way, and as soon as it 'lets Ukraine go', European values will triumph in Ukraine.[31]

Ukraine from this perspective is a state of all its peoples, and not the property of so-called 'indigenes'. This unresolved contradiction is at the heart of contemporary struggles.

The Maidan revolution was certainly far more than a struggle of the 'indigenes' for mastery, although clearly some radical nationalist groups took the lead in the final period in the struggle against Yanukovych. Even here there is an ambiguity, since Right

Sector had some sort of secret relationship with the Yanukovych regime.[32] The Maidan brought together citizens of all national and social groups in the struggle against a corrupt and dysfunctional oligarch state. This civic struggle for 'dignity' continues to inspire a multitude of civil-society groups and multifarious forms of civil activism. At the same time, the democratic impulse is tempered by various nationalist inflexions. The anti-colonial narrative in support of some sort of indigenous rebirth and the anathema cast against the 'Creole' character of hybrid social development provoked a radical narrowing of the revolutionary breakthrough. At its worst, this assumed narrow and inflexible forms that alienated those who considered Ukraine a multi-civilisation state. The pressure of external intervention only accentuated the harshly intolerant features, while fostering the unprecedented consolidation of the nation.

Nicolai Petro notes that alternations in the presidency allowed the country to

> preserve national unity while maintaining their often contradictory regional narratives about Ukrainian identity [...] thereby preventing the consolidation of one narrative at the expense of the other. The resulting political gridlock was Ukraine's way of avoiding civil war, which many believed would erupt if one side were to dominate and turn its definition of Ukrainian identity into a test of civic loyalty.

Petro observes that the 'violent ouster ended this delicate balance, and the civil war came'. Drawing on Huntington, he notes that the conflict can end either in 'the separation of Ukraine into two territories corresponding to their predominant cultural identity', or 'the subjugation of one cultural identity by the other'.[33] Neither option in the Ukrainian context could be achieved without intense conflict, while a return to the old pendulum politics would hardly be a solution to the underlying problem. Instead, as Petro argues, the fact that the two populations had been able to avoid civil war for a quarter century 'suggests that they complement each other in important ways'. Above all, he makes the point that is the leitmotiv of this book (and which is the stance adopted by Valentin Yakushik, as noted earlier):

> This suggests that social peace lies in identifying ways that reinforce that complementarity, such as fostering a civic culture that respects Ukraine's bicultural identity. While promoting an inclusive Ukrainian civic culture might seem fanciful today, given the ongoing war, it is the only alternative to separation or suppression.

This would require constitutional reform based on a genuine dialogue between all Ukrainians, and rejection of the post-colonial model of emancipation of an alleged suppressed true character of the nation, which only generates new patterns of oppression and exclusion. In addition, Ukraine's economic recovery requires an international project (including Russia) accompanied by the development of a less polarised international environment.[34] Both require sustained dialogue between Moscow and Washington. The Ukraine crisis has demonstrated, unfortunately, that the aspiration for European solutions to European problems was an unsustainable chimera of the late perestroika years.

A paradox lies at the heart of the present political system. On the one side, the democratic revolution sought good government, honest administration, dignity for all citizens and a competitive and open economy. These goals reflected the deep-seated desire to move away from the compromises, manipulations, dependencies and distorted political economy of oligarch rule of the first post-Communist decades. The 'return to Europe' became a messianic creed, which would inevitably be disappointed by the lukewarm reaction of the object of desire. On the other hand, the anti-colonial features of the nationalist revolution alienated the 'Creoles', notably in the Crimea and the Donbas, and aroused the natural geopolitical hostility of the neighbour against whom so much animus had for so long been directed. The radicalisation of both the democratic and the national revolutions endowed the post-Maidan administration with a peculiar harshness. Supporters described the response of the Kiev administration as resolute, while critics considered its stance irreconcilable. The launching of the 'anti-terrorist operation' (ATO) on 15 April 2014 came as a surprise to the protesters in the Donbas, who considered that they were doing no more than the demonstrators had done in the Maidan – putting forward their vision of Ukraine. Already on 25 January 2014 an umbrella anti-Maidan movement had been created in the Donbas.[35] After a number of raids and occupations of public buildings, the DPR was established on 7 April and the Lugansk People's Republic (LPR) on 28 April. As Anna Matveeva argues: 'Too much focus on Moscow runs a risk of betrayal of an indigenous process going on.'[36] Igor Girkin (Strelkov), who claimed to have inspired the Donbas uprising, only arrived in Slavyansk on 12 April, and thus Gordon Hahn stresses that his role has been greatly exaggerated (not least by himself) and that his activities could not serve as a legitimate *casus belli* for the Kiev authorities. As Hahn puts it:

> Maidan Kiev's civil war or 'ATO' was not a reaction to a Russian invasion or even to Donbas rebel violence. Rather, it was a deliberate policy to refuse to negotiate with, and deny the anti-Maidan forces the very same tactics they, the Maidan forces, had used to seize power in Kiev and much of the rest of Ukraine.[37]

This substantively is the same argument advanced by Keith Gessen, outlined in Chapter 7.

The regime has been intolerant of dissent from the outset. Dissident voices have been suppressed in the country as a whole following the Odessa fire. For example, the education ministry stripped 12 academics of their status for alleged 'separatism' in mid-2015.[38] A Ministry of Information was established to counter 'Russian propaganda', run by one of Poroshenko's friends. Some 554 people were placed on a blacklist of cultural personalities, mostly Russians but also Steven Seagal and Gérard Depardieu. In conformity with a special law of February 2015, the Ukrainian State Cinema committee proudly boasted that whereas earlier it had banned only 161 films, the total had now risen to 384. The law proscribed all films produced in Russian since 1991 dealing with history, the world wars, the army, police, special forces and allied issues. A special presidential decree of June banned all Russian films produced since 2014, including cartoons. At least 30 journalists were kidnapped, 100 Russian journalists deported, 14 Russian television channels were banned and the Russian 'Euronews' lost its licence. Over 20 churches of the Ukrainian Orthodox Church – Moscow Patriarchate (UOC-MP) were seized, and there were over 70 attacks by radicals on priests and parishioners.

There was a spate of unexplained murders and 'suicides' in early 2015. The former Rada deputy and anti-Maidan activist Oleg Kalashnikov was shot to death on 15 April, and eight former high-profile officials committed suicide, some in suspicious circumstances. The independent pro-Russian Ukrainian journalist Oles Buzina was killed in Lviv on 16 April 2015. The radical nationalist groups 'Revansh' and 'Chernyi Komitet' ('Black Committee'), who had carried out various attacks around Kiev, were suspected of carrying out some of these killings. In the end, Andrei Medvedko, one of the radical activists in the Maidan who had hijacked the democratic revolution, a member of the ultra-nationalist group 'C14', was charged with Buzina's killing. Medvedko had fought in the Donbas as part of the ATO, and then worked in the Ukrainian MVD until his dismissal on 8 June, ten days before his arrest.

The adoption of a package of four so-called 'decommunisation' laws on 9 April 2015 sought to shape the new national identity and memory. The measures were signed into law the following month and hence are known as the 'May laws'. They were largely drafted by the 82-year-old Yuri Shukhevich, a legislator in the populist Radical Party, and the son of Roman Shukhevich, one of the most notorious leaders of the Organisation of Ukrainian Nationalists (OUN-UPA). As we saw earlier, this body and its offshoots and collaborators were responsible for mass killings including up to 850,000 Jews, 220,000 Poles, 500,000 Ukrainian and Belarusian civilians and 400,000 Soviet prisoners of war. The law 'on the legal status and honouring of fighters for Ukraine's independence in the twentieth century' warned that 'the public denial of [...] the just cause of the fighters for Ukrainian independence in the twentieth century insults the dignity of the Ukrainian people and is illegal'. This explicitly included the controversial activities of Stepan Bandera and his associates in World War II.[39]

The second law, 'on access to the archives of repressive organisations of the Communist totalitarian regime from 1917 to 1991', placed all secret police archives under the control of the Institute of National Memory (UINP), headed by Volodymyr Viatrovich. As the former head of the archives of the secret police, the SBU, he had exonerated the OUN of complicity in the mass murder of Jews and Poles during World War II, 'presenting the Ukrainian Insurgent Army (UPA) as a democratic organisation open to Jewish members', while stressing Ukrainian suffering in the terrible famine of the early 1930s. He downplayed the role of the head of the UPA, Roman Shukhevich (as noted, the father of the sponsor of the anti-Communism laws), when he worked with the Nazis until 1943 as commander of a mobile police battalion that murdered thousands of civilians in Belarus.[40] This attempt to create a nationalist version of Ukrainian history continued the work begun by Yushchenko, who had established the UINP and made Bandera and Shukhevich 'heroes of Ukraine'. The Orange revolution, like the later Euromaidan events, was democratic in intent but gave an impetus 'to the revival of the radical versions of [the] Ukrainian national movement that first appeared on the historical scene in the course of World War II and a national discourse focused on fighting against the enemy'.[41] Above all, the laws closed down discussion of controversial topics when informed historical discussion was essential.

The third law sought to demythologise the war, reclassifying the Soviet-style 'Great Patriotic War' as 'World War II', thus including the period of the Molotov–Ribbentrop Pact from August 1939 to the start of Operation Barbarossa on 22 June 1941 as part of the war. The fourth law prohibited the 'propaganda of the Communist and/or National Socialist totalitarian regimes' in Ukraine. The line between professing Communist beliefs and engaging in 'propaganda' is unclear, and this law clearly threatened civil liberties and freedom of expression. The law called for the renaming of towns and streets by 21 November 2015, with renaming commissions established in each municipality. Given the prevalent radical populism, this soon moved far beyond decommunisation and became a wholesale project for forceful Ukrainisation. In Dnepropetrovsk, for example, instead of the anticipated 60 street-name changes, 350 were planned. Everywhere 'Lenin Streets' became 'Bandera Avenues' as everything Russian was purged. One set of mass murderers was changed for another. Just as the Soviet regime had changed toponyms to inscribe its power into the physical environment, so now the Euromaidan revolution seeks to remould daily life. In Germany today the names of Nazis and their collaborators are anathema, whereas in Ukraine they are glorified.

Ukraine is not alone in adopting decommunisation laws, but the radicalism of their formulation and the harshness of their implementation is something new. For this reason the laws have been severely criticised by academics, and prompted an open letter signed by 70 leading Western scholars.[42] The various 'lustration' laws adopted after the fall of Communism from 1989 in Eastern Europe were careful to include legal and other safeguards to avoid the struggle against the Communist legacy becoming a witch-hunt against Communists. In 2014 the civil service and the judiciary were subject to strict lustration measures. The selective character of the planned laws was criticised by the Council of Europe's Venice Commission, and they went to review by Ukraine's Constitutional Court. The radicalism of the Ukrainian laws is justified on the grounds that they are necessary to win the struggle against Russia, and this characteristic distinguishes them from comparable processes earlier in Poland, the Czech Republic and elsewhere. They are intended to draw a sharp line from the period when the Ukrainian SSR had been one of the founding and core members of the USSR (December 1922–September 1991). Eastern Galicia, of course, had only been part of the Soviet Union from September 1939 to June 1941, and then from 1944 to 1991. The decommunisation agenda is only part of the goal. The package of laws seeks to reinforce cultural and political separation from Russia, the long-term aspiration of the monist nationalists who insist on the autochthonous character of Ukrainian culture and polity. The argument, so often advanced by Putin, that Russia and Ukraine are part of a single civilisational community is rejected, but it is not clear how they can develop as separate sovereign states unless a new mode of reconciliation is found.

Instead, an important study of post-Maidan Ukraine has argued that 'a distinctive feature of the new Ukrainian concept is the militarization of politics and ideology'.[43] Matthew Rojansky, the director of the Kennan Institute in Washington, DC, and Mykhailo Minakov, an academic at the Kyiv-Mohyla Academy, argue that the predominant philosophy of the Kiev regime has became a 'new Ukrainian exceptionalism' that has 'little tolerance for views that dissent from the dominant party line in Ukraine'. In their opinion, the Russian-backed insurgency in the south-east

> pushed many Ukrainians to adopt a deeply polarized worldview, in which constructive criticism, dissenting views, and even observable facts are rejected out of hand if they are seen as harmful to Ukraine. [The new Ukrainian exceptionalism] is worrisome because it threatens the very democratic values Ukrainians espouse, while weakening Ukraine's case for international support.[44]

This intolerance is not restricted to Ukraine, taints much of the global discussion of Ukrainian issues and now includes bans and prohibitions on artists and thinkers who question Atlanticist orthodoxies. A neo-McCarthyite spirit threatens to undermine the liberal tolerance on which the West so prides itself. Positions in Ukraine and beyond have become polarised, squeezing out the space for genuine dialogue and intensifying the domestic and international stalemate.[45]

The political contradictions have been reinforced by cultural ones. The regime's rhetoric against internal and external enemies has deflected attention from its own shortcomings and inability to create a genuine positive consensus based on pluralism and development. Instead, a negative consensus has excoriated opponents and 'Russian aggression'. Rivalry between political leaders and oligarchs has been accompanied by media campaigns against opponents, and media pluralism has continued to come under attack. Pressure, for example, was exerted on the Vesti news company, with its offices ransacked by officers calling themselves the 'tax police' on 18 June 2015, who impounded all the office's servers, computers and laptops, while the regime's *titushki* (hired thugs) waited outside to finish the job. There are suggestions that the *Vesti* newspaper was closed just prior to its planned publication of an exposé on the banking crisis. As Gordon Hahn notes, 'the Poroshenko administration and/or its neo-fascist allies are employing the same coercive tactics used by the dastardly Yanukovych regime that the West considered needed overthrowing'.[46] Most of the Russian media outlets had been banned in summer 2014, and since then other news agencies and television stations that were not entirely loyal came under attack. These included the television stations 'Inter', '112', 'TVi' and 'ZIK', although, not surprisingly, Channel 5, owned by Poroshenko, thrived.

The official investigation into the sniper killings of 20 February 2014 remained stymied. The International Advisory Panel established by the Council of Europe found that at least three demonstrators were killed by fire from the Maidan-controlled Hotel Ukraina and that at least ten protesters were killed from other occupied buildings. Independent research by Ivan Katchanovski draws on numerous videos, eyewitness reports and other sources to prove that at least 22 protesters were killed in the same area, and that they were shot from the Hotel Ukraina and other Maidan-controlled buildings. He denied that any Russian or 'third force' was involved in the Maidan massacre, despite various fanciful theories generated by the authorities.[47] He concludes that 'the massacre was a false flag operation, which was rationally planned and carried out with a goal of the overthrow of the government and seizure of power'.[48] Although the killings had initially been attributed to Yanukovych's forces, and even to a special unit sent by Moscow, the evidence now overwhelmingly suggests that the violence was initiated by militant nationalist groups, notably Right Sector.[49]

WAR AND PEACE IN THE DONBAS AND BEYOND

The Minsk-2 agreement left the people's republics in control of some 7 per cent of Ukraine's population, in a region that had once produced 17 per cent of Ukraine's GDP. According to the UN Human Rights Mission in Ukraine (HRMU), from mid-April 2014 to 8 September 2015 the fighting between the Ukrainian armed forces and the insurgents claimed the lives of 7,962 military personnel and civilians, and 17,811 had been injured. The conflict destroyed 5,000 houses and public buildings, including 63 hospitals, 150 schools and 135 kindergartens. Over 2.3 million people had fled the Donbas. Some 1.5 million had become IDPs in central and eastern Ukraine.[50] The UNHCR reported that by September 2014 more than 172,000 Ukrainians had applied for asylum in neighbouring countries, including over 168,000 in Russia. A further 149,000 had applied for other forms of stay in Russia.[51] By that time, some 2.6 million Ukrainian citizens were in Russia. Over a million were refugees from the conflict, while the others included those visiting relatives, guest workers and defectors unwilling to participate in the hostilities. About 550,000 had been granted temporary refuge in Russia. The Kiev authorities steadily increased the intensity of the economic and social blockade of the separatist regions. Both the government and rebels placed restrictions on the movement of people and goods across the contact line. Water and electricity supplies to the 3 million-strong population of non-government controlled areas (NGCAs) were sporadic, while basic requirements in food, medicines and shelter were lacking. As a letter, surprisingly enough published in the *Washington Post*, noted: 'These people are not terrorists or Russian collaborators. They are Ukrainian citizens, and their only crime is having the misfortune of living in what became a war zone.'[52]

Both sides interpreted the Minsk-2 agreement selectively. While Kiev emphasised the restoration of its control over the border with Russia and adopted a unilateral approach, Moscow insisted on the devolution of power '*po soglasivaniyu storon*' (by agreement with all parties). The withdrawal of military hardware from the demarcation line was at best partially implemented. Matters were even worse with the political part of the agreement, which stipulated that amendments to the constitution should be coordinated with the Donbas, that the law on elections to local government bodies should also be coordinated with the Donbas, that a law on amnesty was to be adopted, and that a law on the special status of the territories should be enacted. It demanded dialogue with the insurgents in the south-east, yet the Kiev authorities insisted that they would not talk with 'terrorists'. The problem was a real one. With the collapse of the accustomed patterns of interest aggregation and articulation in the region, the new authorities had a contested legitimacy to speak on behalf of the local population. In particular, the PoR, whose heartland was in the Donbas, effectively dissolved in

February 2014, and the Opposition Bloc only had a tenuous base in the separatist area. The official leader of the DPR, Alexander Zakharchenko, and that of the LPR, Igor Plotnitsky, won the regional elections held in November 2014, but the poll was not recognised by Kiev.

There were various civil-society groups active in the region, some of whom remained loyal to a vision of a united Ukraine, but it would be hard to base any durable settlement solely on them. Early on, the new Kiev authorities had missed the opportunity to engage with these moderates to isolate the militants. Under pressure from Moscow the essence of the conflict had changed, and the demand now (at least officially) was for autonomy rather than separation, a stance that was in keeping with the preferences of the population.[53] This was reflected in the proposals sent by Zakharchenko to Kiev in May 2015 with ideas of how autonomy could work. The document was conciliatory in tone, but was ignored by Kiev and soon after it was withdrawn. Instead, the situation was exacerbated by the decision that the DPR would hold local elections on 18 October, a week before the ones staged by Kiev, and that the LPR would hold them a week later, on 1 November. If agreement could be reached on holding the nationally organised elections in the Donbas, then the authorities there would gain a recognised legitimacy to speak on behalf of the territories.

It is clear that the DPR and the LPR are gradually accumulating the attributes of statehood, notably a monopoly on revenues, on the dispensation of justice and on coercion. The two proto-states control tens of thousands of soldiers as well as hundreds of tanks, rocket launchers, artillery and personnel carriers. Both entities have at their disposal an enormous military force to defend their autonomy, although ultimate control is shared with the Moscow authorities and at the local level with an unknown number of Russian officers and specialists. On the other hand, there were persistent rumours that Moscow was taking soundings over some sort of 'grand bargain' in which Russia would withdraw support for the people's republics in exchange for Ukraine's recognition of Russia's sovereignty over Crimea, accompanied by debt forgiveness to the tune of $100 billion, reduced gas tariffs and the possibility of an OSCE-monitored self-determination referendum in Crimea.[54] Although such a 'grand bargain' makes a lot of sense (although of course not to the leaders of the people's republics), such a deal is extremely unlikely in present circumstances of deeply entrenched positions and the utter lack of trust – and respect – by all the parties for each other. In any case, Putin promised that he would not 'surrender' the territories, although he insisted on the full implementation of the Minsk agreements.[55]

Moscow was not ready to see the insurgent states defeated, but neither was it supportive of earlier aspirations to create a broad 'Novorossiya' entity, envisaged initially to encompass not only the two Donbas breakaway regions (small Novorossiya) but also some of the neighbouring south-eastern regions as well – Kharkov, Kherson, Zaporozhia, Nikolaev and Odessa regions (greater Novorossiya). Acceptance of the Minsk agreements by definition negated the greater Novorossiya project, although for many the Donbas remained the base for the possible future advance of Russophone political projects. The Kremlin now became a hostage to the dynamics of conflict in the Donbas. It could not simply walk away without incurring enormous reputational damage as a fickle ally and inconsistent champion of what it had itself proclaimed as the 'Russian world'. Moscow was certainly not interested in a freezing of the conflict until the Minsk-2 stipulations had been implemented, but neither was it ready to underwrite a new military campaign to bring the whole of the Donbas under the control of the peoples' republics. The Kremlin was certainly not ready to write off the rest of Ukraine, and in one way or another sought to retain influence over the whole country. The intensity of Kiev's blockade suggested that it was ready to amputate the rebellious regions, while Moscow wanted them to remain as part of the Kievan polity to dilute the ultra-nationalist fervour.

The grandiose Novorossiya project had clearly been shelved, much to the disappointment of militant neo-Eurasianists such as Alexander Dugin. One of the leading exponents of geopolitical thinking in post-Communist Russia, Dugin was the principal ideologist of the recreation of some sort of post-national Eurasian empire, encompassing the many peoples and nations of the region. He had long argued that Russia was being undermined from within by a 'fifth column' intent on subverting Russian sovereignty, but in summer 2014 he took this a step further in suggesting that a 'sixth column' was to be found in the administration itself that sabotaged plans for the creation of Novorossiya.[56] Paradoxically, in pressing for a revision of post-Soviet borders he ended up running up against the Russian state-building endeavour. In summer 2014 Dugin was dismissed from his post as professor in the department of Sociology at Moscow State University, and he lost whatever marginal influence he had ever had on Russian policy. Putin once again proved himself to be more of a pragmatic great-power statist than a Russian ethno-nationalist or imperial traditionalist.

Crimea has been gradually assimilated into the Russian polity, but at enormous cost, estimated to have reached $3 billion in 2014 alone. This is in addition to the cost of the 19-kilometre bridge across the Kerch Strait to Russia, which is planned to open in 2019. The region has been placed under an effective blockade by Ukraine, cutting off water, power and transport links. At the same time, the US and the EU placed Crimea 'under one of the toughest embargoes in the world', with Western credit cards not working and travel and business links impeded. All this, according to Thomas de Waal, represented a 'new siege of Crimea'.[57] As in the rest of Ukraine, the revolutionary change of power was accompanied by endless struggles for power and redistributed property. The sharpest tensions were in Sevastopol, where the governor, Sergei Menyailo, confronted the popular mayor of the city, Alexei Chaly, a hero of the 2014 change of power.

A census conducted in October 2014 found that the peninsula was home to 175 different ethnic groups. Russians made up the largest community at 68 per cent, followed by Ukrainians at 16 per cent, and Crimean Tatars at 10 per cent. As for language, 84 per cent listed Russian as their native tongue, 8 per cent named Crimean Tatar, 3.7 per cent Tatar, and 3.3 per cent Ukrainian. These figures were given by Putin on a visit to Crimea on 17 August 2015, when he insisted that Ukraine's future was 'together with Russia', and he repeated his long-standing argument that 'I consider Russians and Ukrainians generally to be one people'. He warned that 'any speculation on the notion that people belonging to this or that ethnic group have some particular rights is very dangerous'.[58]

He had in mind the Crimean Tatars, whose television station ATR had been closed down earlier in the year – although in its place a Public Crimean Tatar Television and Radio Company (OKTRK) was established, a pale substitute yet at least some sort of platform for Tatar concerns. Some Crimean Tatar activists had disappeared as the authorities, in their typically heavy-handed way, clamped down on dissent. Although Putin may have been right to argue that no group has 'special rights', given the tragic history of the Crimean Tatars they certainly deserve special consideration, above all in ensuring that promises on the equality of the three languages are translated into concrete opportunities on the ground, above all in education and the media. Apart from some irreconcilable individuals, notably Mustafa Dzhemilev, who was banned from entering Crimea for five years and who rained down imprecations on Russia from Kiev, the bulk of Crimean Tatars are ready to make their peace with the new authorities, as long as their concerns and interests are treated with sensitivity. Crimean Tatars are ready to become loyal citizens of Russia, but clumsy policing and political operations threaten to alienate the community and create the very problem that they seek to avoid.[59]

Although in the early stage of the post-Yanukovych period Putin may have toyed with wholesale changes to Ukraine's borders, given that from his perspective the Ukrainian state had effectively undergone a revolutionary breakdown, he soon backtracked and limited himself to the repatriation of Crimea. Putin after all is the great rhetorical defender of the sovereignty of states, together with the body of international law that enshrines the principles of the Westphalian state system. In the case of Ukraine, Putin's defence of legitimism – the maintenance of legally constituted authorities against revolutionary events of the colour variety – came into contradiction with his defence of state sovereignty. The tension between the two principles was resolved in a forceful manner in Ukraine, but the contradiction remained and threatened in the end to undermine Russia's own sovereignty. Once the principle of territorial rearrangement was accepted in Eurasia, no state could feel entirely safe. The debate in international law continues. In his major study, Thomas Grant is unequivocal in condemning the act of 'territorial aggrandizement': 'For the first time since World War II, a State in Europe invaded a neighbour and forcibly annexed part of its territory.' In his view, a basic condition for the development of international law since 1945 has been 'a basic stability in the relations between States' but that stability has now been undermined.[60] By contrast, there is an extensive literature on secessionism, but no conclusive resolution in international law on the tension between the right of a territorial unit to self-determination and the equally firm right of states to maintain their territorial integrity.[61] Crimea's status is likely to be somewhat akin to that of the Turkish Republic of Northern Cyprus, with the major difference that Crimea is now part of Russia.

Putin undermined Ukrainian sovereignty but, unlike the rhetoric of the radical nationalists in Russia, he did not negate it. The repatriation of Crimea may have been a revisionist act, but it was not part of a revisionist strategy. It does not augur an era of further Russia 'land grabs', but represented a reaction to the claimed breakdown of legitimate government in Ukraine and threats to a Russophone population, as well as perceived security fears, including the loss of the Sevastopol base. Putin insisted, moreover, that the return of Crimea to Russian jurisdiction had been accomplished through a democratic procedure (the referendum) and reflected long-held popular aspirations, and in any case was an exceptional case (the argument advanced by supporters of Kosovo's independence). This is why Putin ended up defending the territorial integrity of Ukraine, as stipulated in the Minsk Accords (with the exception of the Crimea), by calling for the reintegration of the Donbas into a constitutionally revised Ukrainian state. The Donbas was to achieve a degree of self-government, but as part of a more pluralistic Ukrainian state order. The Kiev government advanced wide-ranging plans for decentralisation, but the specific provisions for devolution within the framework of the Minsk peace process remain vague. The government is concerned that granting special status to the separatist entities would only encourage them to advance their influence into adjacent territories, where they would find a ready constituency. The absence of the stipulated dialogue with the self-constituted Donbas authorities means that the deadlock continues. The Minsk process survives because all the alternatives are worse.

This is why a renewed ceasefire from 1 September 2015 has largely put an end to the fighting, accompanied at last by the stipulated withdrawal of heavy weaponry. There have been repeated breaches of the ceasefire provisions by both sides, with civilians coming under shelling attacks. The Donbas leaders Zakharchenko and Plotnitsky have enough forces at their disposal to prevent a military solution to the conflict, although many on the Kiev side believe that the forcible reincorporation of the entities into the Ukrainian state is feasible. Their model is the Croatian destruction of the separatist enclave of Serbian Krajina in 'Operation Storm' in August 1995, provoking a mass exodus of over 150,000 ethnic Serbs, many of whom remain in exile. Others have come to believe that Ukraine would be better off getting rid of the Donbas enclave, with 62 per cent in one poll in May 2015 willing to give up the territory in exchange for peace.[62] With every day of its existence, the demarcation line becomes a more permanent frontier of control.

This is the formula for an extended stalemate. Although Putin is often accused of wanting a 'frozen conflict' in the region to allow him to exert leverage of broader Ukrainian policy, above all to prevent membership of NATO and to hamper the course towards the EU, it is far from self-evident that this is his strategy.[63] As long as the Donbas conflict rumbled on, Russia remained hostage to the situation, with all of the attendant punitive measures from the west. The OSCE undertook courageous and important work in monitoring the ceasefire, but its mandate and resources were clearly too limited to shape events. There were various plans to institutionalise and broaden the Minsk process, above all by expanding the Normandy format to include the US or by raising its status by ensuring the attendance not just of foreign ministers but also of heads of government. Russia's air campaign in Syria from 30 September 2015 has reinforced its attempts to de-escalate the conflict in Ukraine.

A meeting in the Normandy format (the leaders of France, Germany, Russia and Ukraine) in Paris on 1 October was overshadowed by Western concerns about Russia's military intervention in Syria, but reached agreement on the removal of light weapons from the frontline and issued a joint call to postpone local elections in the Donetsk and Lugansk republics. Soon after, the leaders of the republics, undoubtedly under pressure from Moscow, agreed to postpone the elections until early the following year. The Russian side and Putin personally listed four key Minsk-2 provisions that were not addressed by Kiev's constitutional reform proposals: direct negotiations between Kiev and the Donbas leaders on the format of Ukraine's constitutional changes and on the special status of the breakaway regions; mutual agreement on Ukraine's local-election law; a general amnesty by the Ukrainian parliament; and the adoption of a new law on the special status of the republics, again by negotiation with them. Kiev was undoubtedly caught on the horns of an unpalatable dilemma: reincorporation of the separatist entities would undermine the coherence of Ukraine as a unitary state and impose constraints on foreign-policy options, while keeping them out would mean the loss of more territory (in addition to Crimea), the institutionalisation of permanent conflict with Russia and the constant risk of renewed armed conflict.

Although few were committed to the Minsk-2 deal, all the alternatives were palpably worse. If Minsk-2 fails, there will be no Minsk-3, since Moscow would be unlikely to agree to another deal with a government in Kiev that it considered had failed to honour the commitments it had previously made. The root of the problem was the complete lack of trust by all sides at all levels. The Donbas and the Kiev authorities suspected that the other side was ready to escalate the military conflict to gain territory, while both Moscow and Washington suspected that the other side was sponsoring the stand-off. The insurgents wished to capture the remaining parts of Donetsk and Lugansk regions in Kiev's hands, while the various battalions were in the vanguard of attempts to liberate what they considered to be foreign-occupied territory. The Kremlin's overseer of Ukraine policy, Vladislav Surkov, expended considerable efforts to keep the insurgents in line to prevent an escalation, but history demonstrates how hard it is to ensure that 'clients' remain obedient. The American side was keen to ensure bloc discipline to prevent the sanction-sceptical members of the EU peeling away to allow the restoration of normal relations with Moscow, at a time when the US insisted that there could be no return to 'business as usual'. A simple return to the *status quo ante* would not be much of a solution, since it was that status quo which had allowed the European confrontation to take a sharp and dangerous form.

The stalemate is complete. On the one side, it is clear that the political elite in Moscow will not allow the separatists to be defeated, however much damage the continuing confrontation will inflict on the economy. The Kremlin is in danger of repeating the mistakes it made in Afghanistan, being sucked into a conflict where victory was unlikely but defeat was unpalatable as it propped up a 'client' regime that was more nationalistic than the Kremlin itself. Russia certainly does not want to assume full economic and financial responsibility for the region, but the political costs of what would be considered a 'betrayal', certainly by the nationalists in Russia, would be very high, and could even threaten the stability of the Putin system in its entirety. Having unleashed the bear of Russian nationalism and neo-imperial ambitions, the Kremlin now faces the challenge of getting the unruly beast back under control. On the other side, Kiev is adamant that it will not engage in dialogue with what they call 'terrorists' in the south-east. Some voices do argue that it seems rather perverse for the country, facing an economic crisis of the first order itself, to expend so much effort and lives to achieve a reunification with a region that no longer wants to be part of Ukraine, and which would entail yet more financial costs.[64]

INTERNATIONAL STALEMATE

The deadlock over the Donbas conflict is only a symptom of the larger international stalemate. On the one side, as Andrew Wilson puts it:

> Ukraine feels that it has been left without adequate military or diplomatic support to fight war of overwhelming odds in the east. Kyiv has felt that France and Germany, the key EU negotiators in the so-called Normandy format, are so preoccupied with finding peace at any price that they have led Ukraine into a series of one-sided agreements that have only strengthened Russia's hand.[65]

On the other side, the people's republics feel that their populations have been left to endure endless bombardments that took a heavy toll on civilians, with their suffering exacerbated by a ruthless blockade that has cut them off not only from welfare services and pensions, but even from food. The Donbas population became a collective hostage to the breakdown of the European security order and Kiev's refusal to recognise what they considered the legitimate grievances of part of their own population. As for Moscow, the Kremlin has repeatedly complained about the one-sided interpretation of the Minsk agreements, accompanied by the failure by the Western powers to press adequately for Kiev to fulfil its side of those agreements. Western governments blamed the Donbas armed forces for violations of the ceasefire, accompanied by repeated warnings of an imminent Russian invasion. The Minsk peace, as Dmitry Trenin notes, is at best a truce that 'will not end confrontation, but rather recognize it'. In his view, it reflects the breakdown in the largely cooperative European order that endured from 1989 to February 2014. This was not a throwback to the Cold War since the new situation was far more fluid and multi-dimensional, but it did mean that 'the world disorder that so many pundits talked about for years has finally arrived in Europe'.[66]

The G7 summit in Bavaria on 7–8 June 2015 once again met without Russia, and focused on how to maintain the pressure. With bloc discipline once again imposed, on 22 June the EU announced that sanctions would be extended for another six months. At that time the Austrian Institute of Economic Research (WIFO) calculated that the sanctions would cost the EU €34 billion in short-term losses and €92 billion in longer-term losses, as well as 2.2 million jobs. Germany alone faced a loss of 1 per cent of GDP, with its exports of machinery to Russia dropping by 28 per cent in the first three months of 2015.[67] At the same time, in response Russia extended its counter-sanctions, mainly affecting foodstuff imports from the EU and its allies, for another year up to August 2016. Prior to the sanctions the EU had supplied 80 per cent of Russia's dairy market, and this now collapsed, provoking the worst crisis in

40 years in Europe's dairy sector. The Mistral warship deal was cancelled and Paris returned €1.2 billion to Moscow.

Russia's economy was being battered on all sides. GDP growth in 2014 fell to 0.6 per cent, the lowest since the great financial crisis of 2009, and the economy was on track to contract by 3.6 per cent in 2015. The slowdown long pre-dated the sanctions, and the biggest single factor by far was the collapse in the price of oil, which has mostly remained below $50 per barrel in 2015 compared to the glory days of over $100 from which Russia so greatly benefited. The country has now resigned itself to the reality that the US will probably maintain sanctions for years. Prime Minister Dmitry Medvedev noted that it had taken nearly 40 years for the Jackson–Vanik amendment to be rescinded, having turned from an economic lever into a political one. As for the EU measures, he argued that 'exchanging sanctions benefits no one. Europe needs Russia, while Russia needs Europe.'[68] Instead, as a recent study puts it, 'whereas sanctions are designed to compel Russia to solve her ongoing conflict with Ukraine diplomatically, the EU is also undertaking soft balancing measures that allow it to undermine Russia's interests in Ukraine without confronting her directly.'[69] Equally, Russia has been held responsible for the actions of the Donbas republics, even though Russia is not *de jure* a party to the conflict. If the two people's republics do not hold local elections under Ukrainian law, Russia could be subject to new sanctions.

The Western debate has focused not only on the degree to which sanctions should be intensified, but also on calls to provide the Kiev government with more weapons, not only defensive but also lethal (although the line between the two is often blurred). Already in April 2015 some 300 US trainers arrived in Lviv to train National Guard forces. Poroshenko and Yatsenyuk sought to internationalise the conflict by portraying it as a struggle for Western civilisation, and their Washington backers talked in terms of raising the 'battlefield costs to Putin'. However, awareness of the instability in Ukraine led to the House of Representatives on 10 June 2015 unanimously passing amendments to the Defence Spending Bill to block the training of the Azov volunteer battalion, fearing that they could turn their guns against Kiev, and warning of the dangers of supplying shoulder-fired anti-aircraft missiles to Ukraine (and Iraq), in case they fell into the hands of radical groups.[70]

In May 2015 Ukraine adopted a new national-security strategy, stressing the defence of territorial integrity and enhanced military capabilities. The military budget was increased to 2 per cent of GDP, the NATO target. British and American trainers were sent to improve the professionalism of the Ukrainian armed forces. The US committed $200 million in non-lethal military assistance to Ukraine in 2015. This was accompanied by an increase in the funding of the National Guard while at the same time extending its responsibilities. The new Military Doctrine approved by the

NSDC on 2 September 2015 identifies Russia as a military adversary and outlines the terms for the recapture of the 'temporarily occupied territories'. The doctrine abandons Ukraine's non-aligned status and reaffirms its strategic course towards Euro-Atlantic integration. NATO membership is the central goal. A poll in July 2015 found that if a referendum on the question were to be held at that time 64 per cent would vote for joining NATO, while 28.5 per cent would be against, with western Ukraine (77 per cent) more strongly in favour than the Donbas (49 per cent).[71] The doctrine outlines its own version of 'hybrid warfare', shifting the emphasis from the conduct of military operations to the combined use of military and non-military tools, including economic, political, informational and psychological strategies.[72] It effectively condemns Ukraine to endless conflict that it has no chance of winning, but which could drag all of Europe into war.

There can be no enduring solution to Ukraine's domestic and international problems without some sort of global settlement, yet the foundations of that resolution remain fundamentally contested. The issue is often posed in the form of Ukraine's right to self-determination set against Russia's attempts to impose some sort of neo-Brezhnevite limited-sovereignty order. Such a formulation is fundamentally misleading, since Ukraine's sovereignty has long been recognised by Russia, but instead focuses on the quality of the relationship between the two neighbours. Even Zbigniew Brzezinski, while excoriating Russia in his characteristic manner, nevertheless argued that 'Ukraine should be free to choose its political identity, its political philosophy, and institutionalize it by closer links with Europe. But at the same time, Russia should be assured credibly that Ukraine will not become a member of NATO.'[73] On that score, there have been fundamental problems from the first, provoking the breakdown in 2014. When asked how 'the United States can extricate itself from the Ukraine impasse', Henry Kissinger answered in the following manner:

> The issue is not to extricate the US from the Ukrainian impasse but to solve it in a way conducive to international order. A number of things need to be recognized. One, the relationship between Ukraine and Russia will always have a special character in the Russian mind. It can never be limited to a relationship of two traditional sovereign states, not from the Russian point of view, maybe not even from Ukraine's. So, what happens in Ukraine cannot be put in a simple formula of applying principles that worked in Western Europe, not that close to Stalingrad and Moscow. In that context, one has to analyze how the Ukraine crisis occurred. It is not conceivable that Putin spends 60 million euros on turning a summer resort into a winter Olympic village in order to start a military crisis the week after a concluding ceremony that depicted Russia as a part of Western civilisation.[74]

For Kissinger, 'the first mistake was the inadvertent conduct of the European Union. They did not understand the implications of some of their own conditions.' When Yanukovych rejected the terms proposed for signing the Association Agreement in November 2013, 'the Europeans panicked, and Putin became overconfident. He perceived the deadlock as a great opportunity to implement immediately what had heretofore been his long-range goal.' He offered the Ukrainians $15 billion to draw the country towards Eurasian integration. In all of this, according to Kissinger, America was passive: 'There was no significant political discussion with Russia or the EU of what was in the making. Each side acted sort of rationally based on its misconception of the other, while Ukraine slid into the Maidan uprising.'

Crucially, although Kissinger recognises that Germany had an important role to play 'in the construction of European and international order', it was the 'American contribution to Ukrainian diplomacy' that was 'essential to put the issue into a global context'. Instead, 'the United States has put forward no concept of its own except that Russia will one day join the world community by some automatic act of conversion.' In keeping with his realist convictions, Kissinger argues:

> If we treat Russia seriously as a great power, we need at an early stage to determine whether their concerns can be reconciled with our necessities. We should explore the possibilities of a status of non-military grouping on the territory between Russia and the existing frontiers of NATO.

This would mean a 'militarily non-aligned Ukraine', but the Ukraine crisis 'is turning into a tragedy because it is confusing the long-range interests of global order with the immediate need of restoring Ukrainian identity'. He is alarmed by reports that Muslim units are fighting on behalf of Ukraine, which to Kissinger suggests 'that breaking Russia has become an objective; the long-range perspective should be to integrate it'. He agrees with his interlocutor that in Washington the neoconservatives and liberal hawks are 'determined to break the back of the Russian government'; at least, Kissinger warned, 'until they face the consequences'.[75] Reports that Chechen jihadis have been leaving Syria to fight with the pro-Kiev forces reveals the danger that Ukraine might collapse into a welter of competing warlords and warriors.[76]

REFORM, RECONSTRUCTION AND RECONCILIATION

The government's commitment to the radical overhaul of Ukraine's system of governance is long overdue, requiring the creation of a far more professional and independent public administration and judicial system. Above all, given the effective collapse of the political system in February 2014, the entire polity has to be reconstructed. Equally, the economy is in free fall, exacerbated by the rupture of traditional links with Russia. Society is divided, and although nationalist mobilisation is stimulated by the government media, the general tone is divisive and sectarian. Although many needed reforms have been adopted, much of this activity is futile without the resolution of domestic and international political contradictions. Before economic problems can be resolved, the politics must be sorted out. Although Ukraine remains loyal to democratic forms, the various illiberal actions undermine the competitiveness and pluralism that are the hallmarks of a well-functioning democracy. The parliamentary opposition is far too weak to hold the government accountable, while the persistent tension between the presidency and the prime minister introduces a dysfunctional dynamic that undermines the coherence of governance in its entirety. The power of the oligarchs has changed its forms but retains much of its substance.

The struggle has continued over who will decide what it means to be Ukrainian. The monist line had been advanced by Ukrainisers since at least the nineteenth century, drawing on much deeper roots of cultural and communal identity. In the 1930s the struggle in Galicia had been against the Poles, but with incorporation into the Soviet Union the 'Russians' became the main enemy. Alexander Solzhenitsyn in his *The Gulag Archipelago* noted the resilient nationalism of his Ukrainian comrades imprisoned in the camps with him, and it was reproduced by the Ukrainian dissidents of the late Soviet period. Since independence a whole generation has been socialised into accepting the nation-building myths of the Ukrainisers. The use of the word 'myth' is not intended to denote falsehood, but to suggest that narratives of national victimhood and rebirth sustain nation-building. In this case, the Ukrainising narrative, with its own distinctive martyrology and pantheon of heroes and blackguards, replaced not only the Soviet mythology of brave comrades building a more just, modern and developed society, but also the 'Malorussian' tradition of Ukraine as a Russophone polity. This narrative had traditionally been dismissive of autochthonous Ukrainian cultural traditions, but in the post-Soviet era it has been forced to assume a pluralist inflection. Ukrainisers suspected that this belated advocacy of a pluricultural Ukraine was little more than a strategy to weaken the cultural and political resurgence of what they considered to be the authentic Ukrainian nation.

As Marxists of an Althusserian bent would put it, this was not a dialectical process but a question of overdetermination. For the first two decades of independence there was a chance that the interaction of the monist and the pluralist representations of Ukrainian identity would merge to create a new Ukrainian nation drawing on the best of both traditions. This is why opinion surveys up to early 2014 showed that the Donbas remained committed to its Ukrainian identity, and even in the Crimea the majority had reconciled themselves to finding a way of living in Ukraine. This would have allowed the Russia-focused pluralism to broaden into a genuine pluri-cultural phenomenon that recognised that Ukraine is constituted by peoples shaped by different traditions and languages, but that whatever the route into the modern Ukrainian state, they were all part of this national endeavour. This would have entailed recognition that the Ukrainian language is one of the pillars of this modern Ukrainian nation, and therefore that it was incumbent upon all citizens to learn the language to an adequate level. Equally, the institutionalisation of bilingualism on the Canadian, Finnish or Welsh model would have given cultural diversity a political form, and thus reinforced the civic character of nation-building.

On the other side, the Ukrainian monist tradition contained within it a breadth with the capacity to encompass many different peoples, as long as they were ready to become part of the Ukrainising ideal. The most eloquent representative of this more capacious representation of monist nationalism was Vyacheslav Chornovil, one of the leaders of the Rukh national movement during perestroika, who died in suspicious circumstances in March 1999 just when he was preparing to launch what would have undoubtedly been a credible presidential bid. Interestingly, he was a native of Lviv, and his statue still stands in the city, not far from the one commemorating Stepan Bandera.

Thus both the monist and Russophone pluralist traditions have the potential to contribute to forging a modern, inclusive and pluricultural civic nation state. It is here that the problem of overdetermination explains why in the end this path, to which so many in the newly independent Ukraine were committed (and indeed, which retains a strong constituency to this day), has failed so far to become hegemonic. Space does not allow a full exposition, but I will here briefly list the key reasons, most of which in one way or another have been addressed in earlier chapters. First, there is the problem of distorted political articulation of nation-building grievances. Making Russian a second state language was one of the most troubled issues in Ukraine since independence, but the debate over genuine issues of national representation was overshadowed by the struggle for immediate political advantage. Thus in an attempt to appeal to Russophones the question would be raised before elections, but then promptly dropped afterwards as more immediate issues of wealth-redistribution predominated. Even Yanukovych, allegedly a representative of the Russophone south-east, failed to pursue a persistent policy.

Second, party-political representation is overshadowed by oligarch power. The various popular mobilisations against the degraded political system have tended only to aggravate the problems rather than resolve them, as one lot of oligarch-affiliated power brokers replaces another. This exacerbated the long-term failure to achieve anything approaching economic modernisation. The national patrimony was carved up by powerful economic–political clans, who then struggled between themselves for power.

Third, in terms of foreign policy, Leonid Kuchma's vaunted 'multi-vectoralism' was a symptom of the failure to articulate a genuinely autonomous national position in the region and the world, and reduced the country to veering between East and West, where neither pole represents a viable strategy on its own for national development, and tacking between the two even less so. The Euromaidan government chose the so-called 'European' option, but this itself was little more than an accentuated symptom of the perennial failure to enunciate a policy that could take advantage of Ukraine's central position. It was another type of political bankruptcy that differed little from those who sought to return to the Russian embrace. Both positions became ideologies rather than intelligent responses to policy dilemmas. The polarisation was exacerbated and encouraged by the failure to transcend the division within Europe between the wider- and greater-European agendas, leading in the end to the struggle that we see today between Euro-Atlanticism and a revived and reinvigorated agenda of greater Eurasianism, in which Russia and its EEU allies work with China and other BRICS and SCO countries to create the Silk Road Economic Belt and an alternative global economic order. The international divide now feeds back to intensify the divisions within Ukraine, in which each side is not only unwilling to make compromises with the other, but the very existence of the other is denigrated and delegitimated. There is a real danger that Ukraine will become the nemesis of Europe.[77]

So what are the potential trajectories of Ukraine today? There are a number of possible futures, if not scenarios. The first accepts the Maidan revolution at face value, and envisages a Ukraine in which the current Western-backed reforms, against all the odds, achieve a measure of success. The economy is liberalised, corruption is contained, plants are privatised (many of them to Western investors), the back of oligarch power is broken, and the economy becomes more dynamic and competitive. The funds provided by the IMF and other Western institutions are put to good effect, allowing the budget to be balanced and debts to be repaid. The sanctions against Russia force the Kremlin to withdraw from interference in Ukraine's affairs and the rebellious regions in the Donbas are brought back under Kiev's jurisdiction (possibly in the form of a blitzkrieg on the Croatian model); the border with Russia is sealed by the Great Wall of Ukraine, allowing the country to pursue its European destiny. Trade is reoriented to the West and the Association Agreement with the EU becomes ever deeper, entailing also a governance and regulatory revolution that unleashes Ukraine's enormous intellectual and economic potential. Ultimately a security pact is agreed with NATO that makes the country part of the Atlantic security system. Ukraine remains a unitary state and the language concessions are rescinded to ensure the full flowering of Ukraine culture, with Russian-language usage largely extinguished in educational and official institutions, while a cultural revolution finally purges history and culture of Moscow-inspired distortions. This is the ideational framework of the power system created in 2014, and entails a high degree of wishful thinking.

The second scenario also assumes the triumph of the Maidan revolution, but now shorn of its utopian assumptions and giving due weight to its contradictions. A reshaped oligarchy remains at the heart of the power system, and as is traditional for post-Communist Ukraine, formal politics is little more than an epiphenomenon of the struggle between powerful economic and regional magnates. Parties are in the pocket of power brokers, opposed by radicalised nationalist movements who are at the same time also used as instruments in inter-oligarchic struggles. The state fails to restore a monopoly over the means of coercion, and the armed groups and battalions intervene at various points to block accommodation with opponents. With the loss of its Russian market, the economy loses much of its advanced manufacturing capacity and relies increasingly on primary commodities and agriculture. The European market cannot compensate for Russia, and Ukraine enters a sustained period of trade and budget deficits. The attempt to impose the Ukrainising cultural agenda provokes the sullen resistance of a large part of the Russophones, who increasingly endorse the separatist aspirations of the revived Novorossiya project of the Donbas insurgency. Although sanctions exacerbate Russia's economic woes, especially when they are intensified to compensate for the West's disappointment at the failure of the first scenario, the Kremlin helps the Donbas governments to create the institutions of separate, although unrecognised, entities. There is no scenario in which the Kremlin would allow the people's republics to be defeated militarily. Like the Turkish Republic of Northern Cyprus, a state-in-formation takes on enduring qualities that can only be brought back into Ukrainian jurisdiction with wide-ranging powers in a confederated state. The West provides enough arms for Kievan Ukraine to defend itself, but not enough to launch the *reconquista* of the Donbas. This scenario is largely the one that operates at present, reflecting a stalemate that could easily assume a protracted character.

The third scenario entails a change of government in Kiev that allows reconciliation to take place on the basis of a broader pluralistic social consensus. The creation of the Committee for the Salvation of Ukraine in August 2015, headed by Mykola Azarov, was certainly working for such an outcome. Its programme calls for Russian to become an official language alongside Ukrainian and for Ukraine to become a federal state. Because of the disastrous fall in its popularity, Yatsenyuk's People's Front pulled out of contesting the local elections of October 2015, which are also part of the Minsk agreement. Any strategy that banks on the inevitable collapse of the Kiev regime will be disappointed, just as 'waiting for Russia to collapse is a terrible Ukraine policy'.[78] The Kiev administration is torn by contradictions, and there will probably be some sort of radical restructuring. The fundamental question in this scenario is whether the parliament elected in October 2014, which was radically monist, will be able to see out its full term or whether pre-term elections will give political representation to a wider range of views. Poroshenko was clearly a more pragmatic politician than Yatsenyuk, and despite his harsh rhetoric was ready to work with Moscow to deal with Ukraine's problems. In this scenario there are enough internal changes (multilingualism, the genuine devolution of power if not federalisation, and enduring neutrality) that would allow Russia to become part of the solution rather than the source of dysfunctionality and problems. The EU and Washington agree to work with Moscow to devise an economic and social recovery plan for Ukraine.

A fourth scenario is far more apocalyptic, suggesting that Ukraine as presently constituted is beyond saving. From this perspective, the intensity of the internal contradictions and political polarisation in recent years have only worsened, the Maidan government is headed the way of the Orange administration after 2004, the economic collapse and 'reforms' give way to widespread social disturbances, Donbas-style insurgency spreads across historical Novorossiya, and partisans of Galician nationalism organise the existing armed formations in a more systematic way to provoke what effectively becomes a civil war. The next stage of the Ukrainian 'demolution', the term coined by Miquel Puertas to denote demolition and revolution, would be state failure.[79] Warlordism becomes rampant, armed battalions roam the countryside and terrorise the cities, and Europe is faced with another mass influx of refugees. The EU remains a bystander as Washington is confronted by a fundamental dilemma – to work with or against Moscow. The former strategy would mean rowing back on the militant rhetoric that Russia represents the main threat to America, while the latter entails the danger of a military escalation with the potential use of nuclear weapons. Once again, as Kissinger has warned, the militant 'idealists' in Washington are faced with the utter failure of their ill-thought-out and dangerous adventures.

For the Donbas insurgents, the collapse of Ukraine represents the optimistic scenario, allowing the reconstitution of the country as a Federal Social Republic. For them, the pessimistic scenario is the consolidation of a 'fascist dictatorship' along the lines of Salazar's Portugal or Antonescu's Romania, with the Donbas surviving as a new Transnistria. The Moscow authorities are condemned for limiting their ambitions to restoring partnership with the West.[80] Plans for the territorial division of Ukraine are equally problematic. Riabchuk identified 'two Ukraines', with their respective centres in Galicia and the Donbas, and although the identities of these two regions differ, all sorts of other cross-cutting issues (including regional, occupational and socio-cultural identities) blur the picture. The idea of dividing Ukraine into Ukrainian- and Russian-speaking areas does not map onto any actual demographic reality, although as so often in Europe's terrible twentieth century, artificial division can be imposed at terrible human cost. Although Ukraine may be a typical cleft country, separation along ethno-linguistic lines would be no less traumatic than the partition of India. At the international level, all sides want peace, but on their own terms. Matters have not yet matured to the point when the root causes of the Ukraine conflict can be discussed. Instead the most serious confrontation between the West and Russia continues. Only when all sides are ready to reappraise their actions and embrace dialogue and engagement will peace be possible in the Donbas, the road to development and civic accord be opened up for Ukraine as a whole, and one of the gravest international crises of our time be resolved.

LIST OF ABBREVIATIONS

AA	Association Agreement
ATO	Anti-terrorist operation
BRICS	Brazil, Russia, India, China and South Africa
BSF	Black Sea Fleet
BYuT	Bloc Yulia Tymoshenko
CES	Common Economic Space
CFE	Conventional Forces in Europe
CFS	Common Foreign and Security Policy
CIS	Commonwealth of Independent States
CoE	Council of Europe
CPSU	Communist Party of the Soviet Union
CPU	Communist Party of Ukraine
CSCE	Conference on Security and Cooperation in Europe
CSTO	Collective Security Treaty Organisation
DCFTA	Deep and Comprehensive Free Trade Area
DPR	Donetsk People's Republic
EaP	Eastern Partnership
EaU	Eurasian Union
EBRD	European Bank for Reconstruction and Development
ECU	Eurasian Customs Union
EDA	European Defence Agency
EEAS	European External Action Service
EEU	Eurasian Economic Union
ENP	European Neighbourhood Policy
FSB	Russian Federal Security Service
ICJ	International Court of Justice

IDP	Internally displaced person
LDPR	Liberal Democratic Party of Russia
LNG	Liquefied natural gas
LPR	Lugansk People's Republic
MAP	Membership Action Plan
MVD	Ministry of Internal Affairs
NAPC	National Agency for the Prevention of Corruption
NBU	National Bank of Ukraine
NSDC	National Security and Defence Council
ODIHR	Office for Democratic Institutions and Human Rights
OSCE	Organisation for Security and Cooperation in Europe
OUN	Organisation of Ukrainian Nationalists
PACE	Parliamentary Assembly of the Council of Europe
PoR	Party of Regions
QMV	Qualified Majority Voting
RSFSR	Russian Soviet Federated Socialist Republic
RUE	RosUkrEnergo
SBU	Security Service of Ukraine
SCO	Shanghai Cooperation Organisation
SNPU	Social–National Party of Ukraine
SSR	[Ukrainian] Soviet Socialist Republic
SVOP	Council for Foreign and Defence Policy
TTIP	Transatlantic Trade and Investment Partnership
UDAR	Ukrainian Democratic Alliance for Reform party
UESU	United Energy Systems of Ukraine
UGTS	Ukrainian gas transmission system
UNHCR	United Nations High Commission for Refugees
UoM	Union of the Mediterranean
UPA	Ukrainian Insurgent Army
USSR	Union of Soviet Socialist Republics
WTO	World Trade Organization

NOTES

In the following notes the abbreviation *JRL* refers to *Johnson's Russia List*, an English-language email newsletter containing news and analysis relating to Russia.

All URLs given in the notes for Chapters 1–10 and bibliography were accessible as of 29 October 2014 unless otherwise stated, and all URLs given in the notes for the Afterword were accessible as of 5 November 2015 unless otherwise stated.

1. COUNTDOWN TO CONFRONTATION

1   Margaret MacMillan, *The War That Ended Peace: How Europe Abandoned Peace for the First World War* (2013; paperback edn, London: Profile, 2014).

2   Christopher Clark, *The Sleepwalkers: How Europe Went to War in 1914* (London: Penguin, 2013); Sean McMeekin, *July 1914: Countdown to War* (London: Icon, 2014); Geoffrey Wawro, *A Mad Catastrophe: The Outbreak of World War I and the Collapse of the Habsburg Empire* (New York: Basic Books, 2014).

3   Thomas Otte, *July Crisis: The World's Descent into War, Summer 1914* (Cambridge: Cambridge University Press, 2014), p. xi.

4   For an overview, see Richard Sakwa, '"New Cold War" or twenty years' crisis?: Russia and international politics', *International Affairs* lxxxiv/2 (March 2008), pp. 241–67.

5   For Japan, see John W. Dower, *Embracing Defeat: Japan in the Wake of World War II* (New York: Norton, 2000).

6   The distinction is also drawn by Dmitri Trenin, *The Ukraine Crisis and the Resumption of Great-power Rivalry* (Moscow: Carnegie Moscow Center, 9 July 2014). Available at http://carnegie.ru/2014/07/09/ukraine-crisis-and-resumption-of-great-power-rivalry/hfgs.

7   Robert Jervis, *Perception and Misperception in International Politics* (Princeton, NJ: Princeton University Press, 1976).

8   Mikhail Margelov, 'Russia-West-East', *Valdai Discussion Club* [website] (17 July 2014). Available at http://valdaiclub.com/russia_and_the_world/70320.html.

9   Richard Sakwa, 'The cold peace: Russo-Western relations as a mimetic cold war', *Cambridge Review of International Affairs* xxvi/1 (2013), pp. 203–24.

10   Andrew Wilson, *Ukraine Crisis: What It Means for the West* (London and New Haven, CT: Yale University Press, 2014).

11   Richard Sakwa, *Putin and the Oligarch: The Khodorkovsky–Yukos Affair* (London and New York: I.B.Tauris, 2014).

12   Robert Horvath, *Putin's 'Preventive Counter-revolution': Post-Soviet Authoritarianism and the Spectre of Velvet Revolution* (London and New York: Routledge, 2013).

13   Clifford G. Gaddy and Barry W. Ickes, 'Ukraine, NATO enlargement and the Geithner doctrine' (10 June 2014). Available at http://www.brookings.edu/research/articles/2014/06/10-ukraine-nato-geithner-doctrine-gaddy-ickes.

14   For a concise and balanced introduction, see Andrew Wilson, *The Ukrainians: Unexpected Nation* (New Haven, CT: Yale University Press, 2000).

15   For an excellent analysis, see Pietro Shakarian, 'Ukraine: Where nation-building and empire meet', *Reconsidering Russia and the Former Soviet Union* [website] (22 August 2014). Available at http://reconsideringrussia.org/2014/08/22/ukraine-where-nation-building-and-empire-meet/.

16   Alexander Solzhenitsyn, *Rebuilding Russia: Reflections and Tentative Proposals* (London: Harvill, 1991).

17   S. N. Plekhanov (ed.), *Novorossiya: Vosstavshaya iz pepla* (Moscow: Knizhnyi mir, 2014) provides an enthusiastic historical analysis of the term.

18   Wilson, *The Ukrainians*, p. 40.

19   Aleksandr Burakovskiy, 'The Rukh Council of Nationalities, the Jewish Question and Ukrainian independence' [paper delivered at the ASN conference, New York, 24 April 2014]. Later data in my account supplemented by *SSSR v tsifrakh v 1989 godu* (Moscow: Finansy i statistika, 1990), p. 36.

20   Vladimir Fesenko, 'Ukraine: between Europe and Eurasia', in Piotr Dutkiewicz and Richard Sakwa (eds), *Eurasian Integration: The View from Within* (London and New York: Routledge, 2015), p. 127.

21   Pietro Shakarian, 'Putin and Poroshenko: a tale of two presidents', *Reconsidering Russia and the Former Soviet Union* [website] (19 June 2014). Available at http://reconsideringrussia.org/2014/06/19/putin-and-poroshenko-a-tale-of-two-presidents/.

22   Donald Rayfield, 'Songs for survival', *Guardian Review* (21 June 2014), referring to the four-volume history of the Crimean Tatars by Valeri Vozgrin, published in 2013.

23   Fesenko, 'Ukraine: between Europe and Eurasia', p. 128.

24   Oleksandr Zaitsev, *Ukraïns'ky integral'nyi natsionalizm* (Kiev: Krytyka, 2013).

25   Alexander Motyl, *The Turn to the Right: The Ideological Origins and Development of Ukrainian Nationalism, 1919–1929* (New York: Columbia University Press, 1980).

26   Roger Griffin and Matthew Feldman (eds), *Fascism: Critical Concepts* (London: Routledge, 2004), p. 6.

27   David Marples, *Heroes and Villains: Creating National History in Contemporary Ukraine* (Budapest: Central European University Press, 2007), pp. 150, 161.

28   Oleksandr Zaitsev, 'Ukrainian integral nationalism in quest of a "Special Path" (1920s–1930s)', *Russian Politics and Law* li/5 (September–October 2013), p. 13.

29   Ibid., p. 17.

30   For a scholarly analysis of these events and on contemporary radical Ukrainian nationalism, see various works by Per Anders Rudling, for example '"The honor they so clearly deserve": legitimizing the Waffen-SS Galizien', *Journal of Slavic Military Studies* xxvi/1 (Spring 2013), pp. 114–37 [review article of Bohdan Matsiv (ed.), *Ukrains'ka dyviziia 'Halychyna': Istoriia u svitlynakh vid zasnuvannia u 1943 r. do zvil'nennia z polonu 1949 r.* (Lviv: ZUKTs, 2009)].

31   Andreas Umland, 'Starting post-Soviet Ukrainian right-wing extremism studies from scratch', *Russian Politics and Law* li/5 (September–October 2013), p. 7.

32   For an excellent study of the debates of the period, see Andrew Wilson, *Ukrainian Nationalism in the 1990s: A Minority Faith* (Cambridge and New York: Cambridge University Press, 1996).

33   Michael Averko, 'Pro-Bandera sentiment', *Eurasia Review* [website] (23 June 2014). Available at http://www.eurasiareview.com/author/michael-averko/. Averko refers to the infamous and virulently anti-Russian book by Bernadine Bailey, *The Captive Nations: Our First Line of Defense!* (Chicago: Hallberg, 1969).

34   For an excellent overview, see Matthew Kupfer and Thomas de Waal, 'Crying genocide: use and abuse of political rhetoric in Russia and Ukraine' (28 July 2014). Available at http://carnegieendowment.org/2014/07/28/crying-genocide-use-and-abuse-of-political-rhetoric-in-russia-and-ukraine/his9.

35   Taras Kuzio, *Ukraine: State and Nation Building* (London: Routledge, 1998). See also: Taras Kuzio, Paul D'Anieri and Robert Kravchuk (eds), *State and Institution Building in Contemporary Ukraine* (Basingstoke: Macmillan, 1999); Taras Kuzio and Paul D'Anieri (eds), *Dilemmas of State-led Nation Building in Ukraine* (Westport, CT: Praeger, 2002).

36   Michael Ignatieff, *Blood and Belonging: Journeys into the New Nationalism* (New York: Farrar, Straus and Giroux, 1995).

37   Andreas Umland and Anton Shekhovtsov, 'Ultraright parties in post-Soviet Ukraine and the puzzle of the electoral marginalism of Ukrainian ultranationalists in 1994–2009', *Russian Politics and Law* li/5 (September–October 2013), p. 41.

38   Spiegel staff, '"Prepared to die": The right wing's role in Ukrainian protests', *Der Spiegel* (27 January 2014). Available at http://www.spiegel.de/international/europe/ukraine-sliding-towards-civil-war-in-wake-of-tough-new-laws-a-945742.html.

39   Viacheslav Likhachev, 'Right-wing extremism on the rise in Ukraine', *Russian Politics and Law* li/5 (September–October 2013), p. 74.

40   Viacheslav Likhachev, 'Social-nationalists in the Ukrainian parliament', *Russian Politics and Law* li/5 (September–October 2013), p. 83.

41   This was expressed in personal discussions. For some of his ideas, see Valentin Yakushik, 'Revolyutsiya, no ne oranzhevaya', *Den'* 232 (15 December 2005). Available at http://www.day.kiev.ua/154501/.

42   Samuel P. Huntington, 'The clash of civilizations?', *Foreign Affairs* lxxii/3 (summer 1993), pp. 23–49 and *The Clash of Civilizations and the Remaking of World Order* (New York: Simon & Schuster, 1996).

43   Vladimir Golstein, 'Why everything you've read about Ukraine is wrong', *Forbes* (19 May 2014). Available at http://www.forbes.com/sites/forbesleadershipforum/2014/05/19/why-everything-youve-read-about-ukraine-is-wrong/.

2. TWO EUROPES

1   Alexander V. Prusin, *The Lands Between: Conflict in the East European Borderlands, 1870–1992* (Oxford: Oxford University Press, 2010).

2   Timothy Snyder, *Bloodlands: Europe Between Hitler and Stalin* (New York: Basic Books, 2010).

3   Melvin Croan, 'Lands in-between: the politics of cultural identity in contemporary Eastern Europe', *East European Politics and Societies* iii (March 1989), pp. 176–97.

4   Nicolas Sarkozy, 'Déclaration de M. Nicolas Sarkozy, Président de la République, sur l'action de la France en faveur de la construction européenne, à Nîmes le 5 mai 2009'. Available at http://discours.vie-publique.fr/notices/097001329.html.

5   Cited by Leonid Bershidsky, 'No illusions left, I'm leaving Russia', *Moscow Times* (19 June 2014).

6   Speech delivered to the Fourth Berlin Economic Leadership meeting organised by the *Süddeutsche Zeitung*, which the day before was presented as an article in that paper. A summary of the speech is available at at http://premier.gov.ru/events/news/13120/. The article is Wladimir Putin, 'Von Lissabon bis Wladiwostok. Handelspakt zwischen Russland und Europa: Moskau will als Lehre aus der größten Krise der Weltwirtschaft seit acht Jahrzehnten wesentlich enger mit der Europäischen Union zusammenarbeiten', *Süddeutsche Zeitung* (25 November 2010). Available at http://www.sueddeutsche.de/wirtschaft/putin-plaedoyer-fuer-wirtschaftsgemeinschaft-von-lissabon-bis-wladiwostok-1.1027908.

7   Vladimir Putin, 'Novyi integratsionnyi proekt dlya Evrazii: budushchee, kotoroe rozhdaetsya segodnya', *Izvestiya* (4 October 2011). Available at http://premier.gov.ru/events/news/16622.

8   Vladimir Putin, 'Russia–EU summit', *President of Russia* [website] (28 January 2014). Available at http://eng.kremlin.ru/transcripts/6575.

9   Richard Sakwa, *Putin: Russia's Choice* (2nd edn, London and New York: Routledge, 2008), ch. 10.

10 For a discussion of the issue see Hiski Haukkala, 'A norm-maker or a norm-taker? The changing normative parameters of Russia's place in Europe', in Ted Hopf (ed.), *Russia's European Choice* (Basingstoke: Palgrave Macmillan, 2008), pp. 35–56. See also Haukkala's 'The European Union as a regional normative hegemon: the case of European neighbourhood policy', *Europe–Asia Studies* lx/9 (November 2008), pp. 1601–22.

11 Viatcheslav Morozov, *The Forced Choice Between Russia and the West: The Geopolitics of Alienation* [PONARS Policy Memo 327, November 2004].

12 *Nezavisimaya gazeta* (17 November 2004).

13 RIA Novosti [Russian news agency] (26 May 2005).

14 Review of William H. Hill, *Russia, the Near Abroad and the West: Lessons from the Moldova–Transdniestria Conflict* (Washington, DC: Woodrow Wilson Center Press; Baltimore, MD: Johns Hopkins University Press, 2012), by Vsevolod Samokhvalov, in *Europe–Asia Studies* lxvi/6 (August 2014), pp. 1021–2.

15 'Russian President Vladimir Putin's speech at the 2007 Munich conference on security policy' (10 February 2007). Available at http://archive.kremlin.ru/eng/speeches/2007/02/10/0138_type82912type82914type82917type84779_118123.shtml.

16 Robert Gates, *Duty: Memoirs of a Secretary at War* (London: W. H. Allen, 2014), p. 157.

17 Angela Stent, *The Limits of Partnership: US–Russian Relations in the Twenty-first Century* (Princeton, NJ: Princeton University Press, 2014), pp. xi, 265.

18 Hillary Clinton, *Hard Choices* (New York: Simon & Schuster, 2014).

19 Theodore Karasik and Heinrich Matthee, 'Russia's emerging defense and security doctrine', *Real News* [website] (9 June 2014). Available at http://nocache.therealnews.com/t2/component/content/article/371-dr-theodore-karasik-and-dr-heinrich-matthee/2097--russias-emerging-defense-and-security-doctrine-impact-on-europe-and-the-near-east [in *JRL*, 2014-129/39].

20 For a broad overview of the historical context of Russian neo-revisionism, see Andrei P. Tsygankov, *Russia and the West from Alexander to Putin: Honor in International Relations* (Cambridge: Cambridge University Press, 2014).

21 Piotr Dutkiewicz and Richard Sakwa (eds), *Eurasian Integration: The View from Within* (London and New York: Routledge, 2015); Rilka Dragneva and Kataryna Wolczuk (eds), *Eurasian Economic Integration: Law, Policy and Politics* (Cheltenham: Edward Elgar, 2013).

22 Barry Buzan and Ole Waever, *Regions and Powers: The Structure of International Security* (Cambridge: Cambridge University Press, 2003).

23 The report was in the Norwegian paper *Aftenposten*, reported by James Carden, 'Who's really playing a zero-sum game in Ukraine?', *Russia Direct* [website] (1 July 2014). Available at http://www.russia-direct.org/opinion/whos-really-playing-zero-sum-game-ukraine.

24 Ekaterina Furman and Alexander Libman, 'Europeanisation and the Eurasian economic union', in Piotr Dutkiewicz and Richard Sakwa (eds), *Eurasian Integration: The View from Within* (London and New York: Routledge, 2015), pp. 173–92.

25 Nadia Diuk, 'Ukraine: a land in-between', *Journal of Democracy* ix/3 (July 1998), pp. 97–111.

26 Taras Kuzio, 'History, memory and nation building in the post-Soviet colonial space', *Nationalities Papers* xxx/2 (2002), pp. 241–64.

27 Sergei Glazyev, 'Nastoyashchee i budushchee evraziiskoi integratsii', *Izborskii klub: Russkie strategii* iv (2013), pp. 11–39.

28 Stefan Lehne, *Time to Reset the European Neighbourhood Policy* (Brussels: Carnegie Europe, February 2014), p. 3.

29 Nathaniel Copsey and Karolina Pomorska, 'The influence of newer member states in the European Union: the case of Poland and the Eastern Partnership', *Europe–Asia Studies* lxvi/3 (May 2014), p. 430.

30 Copsey and Pomorska, 'The influence of newer member states', p. 435.

31 Ibid.

32 From a comment by David Habakkuk posted under the article 'The rise of Novorossiya', *Sic Semper Tyrannis* [blog] (6 July 2014). Available at http://turcopolier.typepad.com/sic_semper_tyrannis/2014/07/the-rise-of-novorossiya-ttg.html [in *JRL*, 2014-149/18].

33 Dominik Tolksdorf, 'The EU, Russia and the Eastern Partnership: what dynamics under the New German government?', *Russie.Nei.Visions* lxxiv (February 2014). Available at http://www.ifri.org/?page=contribution-detail&id=8000.

34 For a broad analysis, see Christopher Marsh and Nikolas K. Gvosdev, *Russian Foreign Policy: Interests, Vectors and Sectors* (New York: CQ Press, 2013).

35 Andrew Wilson gives the case of 'Russian Deputy Prime Minister Igor Shuvalov's disastrous trip to Brussels in February 2013, when he was basically told that the process had nothing to do with Russia', *Ukraine Crisis*, p. 17.

36 'Novoe bol'shinstvo: mezhdu mifami i real'nostyu', *IISEPS* [website] (9 January 2013). Available at http://iiseps.org/analitica/20.

37 Larissa Titarenko, 'Belarus between the Eurasian Union and the European Union: material and symbolic options' [paper delivered at the ASN conference, New York, 25 April 2014].

38 Lehne, *Time to Reset*, p. 7.

39 Stefan Meister, *EU–Russia Relations and the Common Neighbourhood: The Ball is on the EU's Side*, DGAPanalyse 7 (Berlin: DGAP, August 2013), p. 1. Available at https://dgap.org/en/article/getFullPDF/24250.

40 Sergei Glazyev, 'Who stands to win? Political and economic factors in regional integration', *Russia in Global Affairs* (27 December 2013). Available at http://eng.globalaffairs.ru/number/Who-Stands-to-Win-16288.

41 Samuel Charap and Mikhail Troitskiy, 'Russia, the West and the integration dilemma', *Survival* lv/6 (December 2013–January 2014), p. 50.

42   Mark Kramer, 'The myth of a no-NATO-enlargement pledge to Russia', *Washington Quarterly* xxxii/2 (2009), pp. 41, 47–8.

43   The issue is reviewed by Josh Cohen, 'Don't let Ukraine into NATO', *Moscow Times* (19 September 2014).

44   'Intervyu V. Putina Devidu Frostu', *Kommersant* (7 March 2000), p. 2; Alexander Golts, 'Putin could aim for Europe alliance', *Russia Journal* (20–26 March 2000), p. 8.

45   Thomas Friedman, 'Foreign affairs: now a word from X', *New York Times* (2 May 1998).

46   Martin Walker, 'Cold warrior foils warning about NATO', *Moscow Times* (4 July 1997).

47   Richard Sakwa, 'Conspiracy narratives as a mode of engagement in international politics: the case of the 2008 Russo-Georgian war', *Russian Review* lxxi (October 2012), pp. 2–30.

48   'An open letter to the Obama administration from Central and Eastern Europe', *Gazeta Wyborcza* (15 July 2009). Available at http://wyborcza.pl/1,98817,6825987,An_Open_Letter_to_the_Obama_Administration_from_Central.html.

49   Robert Coalson, 'NATO's Eastern countries fractured over response to Russia', *Radio Free Europe/Radio Liberty* [website] (6 September 2014). Available at http://www.rferl.org/content/russia-europe-divisions-ukraine-czech-hungary-poland-slovakia/26569958.html.

50   Sergei Karaganov, 'Russia needs to defend its interests with an iron fist', *Financial Times* (5 March 2014).

3. UKRAINE CONTESTED

1   Anatol Lieven, *Ukraine and Russia: A Fraternal Rivalry* (Washington, DC: US Institute of Peace Press, 1999).

2   Alexander Lukashenko, speech of 23 March 2013, reported in the Belarusian newspaper *Nasha Niva*. Available at http://nn.by/?c=ar&i=125276&lang=ru.

3   Leonid Kuchma, *Ukraina – ne Rossiya* (Moscow: Vremya, 2003).

4   David Marples, *Belarus: A Denationalized Nation* (London: Routledge, 1999).

5   The various perspectives on the Orange Revolution are covered by the following: Anders Åslund and Michael McFaul (eds), *Revolution in Orange: The Origins of Ukraine's Democratic Breakthrough* (Washington, DC: Carnegie Endowment for International Peace, 2006); Taras Kuzio (ed.), *Democratic Revolution in Ukraine: From Kuchmagate to Orange Revolution*, special issue of the *Journal of Communist Studies and Transition Politics* xxiii/1 (March 2007); also book by the same title (London: Routledge, 2008); Andrew Wilson, *Ukraine's Orange Revolution* (New Haven, CT: Yale University Press, 2006).

6   David Lane, 'The Orange Revolution: "people's revolution" or revolutionary coup?', *British Journal of Politics and International Relations* x/4 (November 2008), pp. 525–49.

7   'Ukraine: Yushchenko discusses energy, Russia, defense reform, domestic politics' (25 January 2006). Available at https://wikileaks.org/plusd/cables/06KIEV333_a.html.

8   'Economic policy and the new GOU' (28 December 2007). Available at http://cablegatesearch.net/cable.php?id=07KYIV3165&q=rosukrenergo.

9   See Simon Pirani, Jonathan Stern and Katja Yafimava, *The Russo-Ukrainian Gas Dispute of January 2009: A Comprehensive Assessment* (Oxford: Oxford Institute for Energy Studies, 2009).

10   See for example 'Turkmenistan: Ukraine stumbles as it seeks to re-engineer the bilateral relationship' (5 February 2008). Available at http://search.wikileaks.org/plusd/cables/08ASHGABAT173_a.html.

11   James Sherr, 'The mortgaging of Ukraine's independence' [briefing paper for Chatham

House, the Royal Institute of International Affairs, August 2010]. Available at http://www.chathamhouse.org/sites/files/chathamhouse/public/Research/Russia%20and%20Eurasia/bp0810_sherr.pdf.

12 'Ukraine: Gazprom again threatens Ukraine over debt, intermediaries' (29 February 2008). Available at http://www.wikileaks.org/plusd/cables/08KYIV461_a.html.

13 'Russia–Ukraine relations: Yushchenko and Tymoshenko in Moscow' (1 March 2008). Available at http://search.wikileaks.org/plusd/cables/08MOSCOW587_a.html.

14 Ibid.

15 'Scenesetter for codel visit to Kyiv' (30 October 2008). Available at http://cablegatesearch.net/cable.php?id=08KYIV2174&q=rosukrenergo.

16 Reported in 'Kuchma: Yanukovych–Kuchma contest a choice between "bad and very bad"', *Kyiv Post* (3 December 2010). Available at http://www.kyivpost.com/content/ukraine/kuchma-yanukovych-tymoshenko-contest-a-choice-betw-92047.html.

17 For example, the 30 April 2013 ECtHR judgment on the case stated that 'Ms Tymoshenko's pre-trial detention had been arbitrary; that the lawfulness of her detention had not been properly reviewed; and, that she had no possibility to seek compensation for her unlawful deprivation of liberty'. The document is available at http://hudoc.echr.coe.int/sites/fra-press/pages/search.aspx?i=003-4343134-5208270.

18 Cited in Justine Doody, 'On a path to decentralisation', *European Voice*, 16 May 2014. Available at http://www.europeanvoice.com/other-voices/on-a-path-to-decentralisation/.

19 Sergei Kudelia, 'The house that Yanukovych built', *Journal of Democracy* xxv/3 (July 2014), pp. 26–7.

20 Nicolai N. Petro, 'Ukraine's ongoing struggle with its Russian identity', *World Politics Review* (6 May 2014), p. 5.

21 Deema Kaneff, paper presented to the annual conference of Centre for Russian, European and Eurasian Studies (CREES), 7 June 2014.

22 One of the best studies of problems of institutional design in Ukraine is Paul D'Anieri, *Understanding Ukrainian Politics: Power, Politics, and Institutional Design* (Armonk, NY: M. E. Sharpe, 2007).

23 Anders Åslund, 'Oligarchs, corruption, and European integration', *Journal of Democracy* xxv/3 (July 2014), p. 64.

24 Sławomir Matuszak, *The Oligarchic Democracy: The Influence of Business Groups on Ukrainian Politics*, OSW Studies 42 (Warsaw: Centre for Eastern Studies, September 2012), p. 5.

25 Sophie Lambroschini, 'Genèse, apogée et métamorphose du présidentialisme clientéliste en Ukraine', *Revue d'études comparatives Est-Ouest* xxxix/2 (2008), pp. 117–48.

26 Andrei Mal'gin, *Ukraina: Sobornost' i regionalism* (Simferopol: Sonat, 2005).

27 'FBI agent on Tymoshenko's role', *Kiev Times* (19 May 2014). Available at http://thekievtimes.ua/politics/375348-agent-fbr-o-roli-Tymoshenko.html.

28 'Ukraine: Tymoshenko runs on populist economic policies' (17 December 2009). Available at http://cablegatesearch.net/cable.php?id=09KYIV2165&q=rosukrenergo.

29 'Presidential election: rhetoric heats up; race Yanukovych's to lose' (15 January 2010). Available at https://wikileaks.org/plusd/cables/10KYIV67_a.html.

30 'Ukraine: IUD's Taruta on regions, elections, and gas deals' (13 September 2007). Available at http://www.wikileaks.org/plusd/cables/07KYIV2286_a.html.

31 A. A. Zotkin, 'Gosudarstvennaya vlast' i politicheskie elity Ukrainy v kontekste otnoshenii mezhdu tsentrom i regionami', in A. V. Duka (ed.), *Vlastnye struktury i gruppy dominirovaniya* (St Petersburg: Intersotsis, 2012), pp. 286–306.

32 Sarah A. Topol, 'The chocolate king who would be president', *Politico Magazine* (22 May 2014). Available at www.politico.com/magazine/story/2014/05/the-chocolate-king-who-would-be-president-106998_Page2.html#.VEzj3eeOiDk.

33 'WikiLeaks show turnaround in US attitude to "discredited" Poroshenko', Itar-Tass [Russian news agency] (29 May 2014). Available at http://en.itar-tass.com/world/733920.

34 'Vladimir Putin answered journalists' questions on the situation in Ukraine', *President of Russia* [website] (4 March 2014). Available at http://eng.kremlin.ru/transcripts/6763.

35 'The gas king of all Ukraine', *Forbes* (12 November 2012). Available at http://forbes.ua/business/1341072-rassledovanie-gazovyj-korol-vseya-ukrainy.

36 'The gas king turned media mogul', *The Economist* (28 June 2013). Available at http://www.economist.com/node/21580347.

37 Graham Stack, 'The edge of darkness', *Business New Europe* [website] (25 May 2011). Available at http://www.bne.eu/content/edge-darkness.

38 Serhii Plokhy, *The Last Empire: The Final Days of the Soviet Union* (New York: Oneworld, 2014), p. 176.

39 Ibid., p. 177.

40 Igor Zevelev, 'The Russian world boundaries', *Russia in Global Affairs* (7 June 2014). Available at http://eng.globalaffairs.ru/number/The-Russian-World-Boundaries-16707.

41 Yuliya Tymoshenko, 'Containing Russia', *Foreign Affairs* lxxxvi/3 (May–June 2007), pp. 69–82.

42 'Scenesetter for the visit of deputy secretary Steinberg and senior director Lipton' (22 April 2009). Available at https://cablegatesearch.wikileaks.org/cable.php?id=09KYIV692&q=%3Dsteinberg.

43 Ibid.

44 'Ukraine: Firtash makes his case to the USG' (10 December 2008). Available at http://cablegatesearch.net/cable.php?id=08KYIV2414&q=rosukrenergo.

45 Stack, 'The edge of darkness'.

46 Oleg Grytsaienko, 'The crisis in Ukraine: an insider's view', *Russie.Nei.Visions* lxxviii (June 2014). Available at http://www.ifri.org/?page=contribution-detail&id=8135.

47 State Statistics Committee of Ukraine, *Energy Balance of Ukraine* (2011).

48 Cited by Robert Parry, 'High costs of bad journalism on Ukraine', *Consortiumnews.com* [website] (22 September 2014). Available at http://consortiumnews.com/2014/09/22/high-cost-of-bad-journalism-on-ukraine/.

49 Mark Adomanis, 'Ukraine, Russia, and the European Union', *Forbes* (27 June 2014). Available at http://www.forbes.com/sites/markadomanis/2014/06/27/ukraine-russia-and-the-european-union-the-end-of-the-beginning/.

50 'Russia remains Ukraine's main trade partner in first quarter of 2014', Itar-Tass [Russian news agency] (20 August 2014). Available at http://en.itar-tass.com/economy/745840.

51 Stefan Lehne, *Time to Reset the European Neighbourhood Policy* (Brussels: Carnegie Europe, February 2014), p. 3.

52 Shaun Walker, 'EU "remaining vigilant" as Ukraine signs on dotted line', *Guardian* (27 June 2014).

53 Štefan Füle, 'Statement on the pressure exercised by Russia on countries of the Eastern Partnership' (11 September 2013). Available at http://europa.eu/rapid/press-release_SPEECH-13-687_en.htm.

54 See Elena Korosteleva, 'The EU, Russia and the eastern region: the analytics of government for a sustainable cohabitation', *Journal of Common Market Studies* [forthcoming].

55 Vladimir Putin, 'St Petersburg International Economic Forum', *President of Russia* [website] (23 May 2014). Available at http://eng.kremlin.ru/news/7230.
56 Dmitry Efremenko, 'Russia, "American Mars" and "European Venus": Ukraine's future', *Russia Direct* [website] (8 July 2014). Available at http://www.russia-direct.org/analysis/russia-'american-mars'-and-'european-venus'-ukraines-future.
57 Tony Wood, 'Back from the edge?', *London Review of Books* xxxvi/11 (5 June 2014), p. 37.

4. THE FEBRUARY REVOLUTION

1   Richard Sakwa, *Putin Redux: Power and Contradiction in Contemporary Russia* (London and New York: Routledge, 2014), pp. 120, 127, 154.
2   Olga Onuch, 'Who were the protesters?', *Journal of Democracy* xxv/3 (July 2014), pp. 14–51.
3   Elena Gerasimova, 'Pozor Ukraine, esli ee spasaet Kolomoiskii', *Pravda.ru* [website] (13 June 2014). Available at http://www.pravda.ru/world/formerussr/ukraine/13-06-2014/1211905.
4   Anton Shekhovtsov and Andreas Umland, 'Ukraine's radical right', *Journal of Democracy* xxv/3 (July 2014), pp. 58–63.
5   Spiegel staff, '"Prepared to die": The right wing's role in Ukrainian protests', *Der Spiegel* (27 January 2014). Available at http://www.spiegel.de/international/europe/ukraine-sliding-towards-civil-war-in-wake-of-tough-new-laws-a-945742.html.
6   This is the broad thrust of the wide-ranging collection E. V. Semenov (ed.), *Evromaidan i Russkaya vesna: sbornik statei* (Moscow: Traditsiya, 2014).
7   For a harshly critical study, see S. O. Byshok and A. V. Kochetkov, *Evromaidan imeni stepana bandery: ot demokratii k diktature* (2nd edn, Moscow: Knizhnyi mir, Narodnaya diplomatiya, 2014).
8   Notes from discussions with Vladimir Kushnirenko, Kyiv-Mohyla Academy, May 2014.
9   Victoia Nuland, 'Remarks at the US–Ukraine Foundation Conference' (13 December 2013). Available at http://iipdigital.usembassy.gov/st/english/texttrans/2013/12/20131216289031.html.
10 'Ukraine crisis: transcript of leaked Nuland–Pyatt call', *BBC News* [website] (7 February 2014). Available at http://www.bbc.co.uk/news/world-europe-26079957.
11 M. S. Grigor'ev, *Evromaidan* (Moscow: Kuchkovo pole, 2014), pp. 417–18.
12 Byshok and Kochetkov, *Evromaidan imeni stepana bandery*, pp. 432–3.
13 Ariadna Theokopoulos, 'Ukraine, Crimea: crimes against truth', *Deliberation* [website] (15 March 2014). Available at http://www.deliberation.info/ukraine-crimea-crimes-truth/.
14 For a 'Maidanite' account of the events, see Andrew Wilson, *Ukraine Crisis: What It Means for the West* (London and New Haven, CT: Yale University Press, 2014), pp. 94–5.
15 According to Ukraine's acting prosecutor general Oleg Makhnitsky in the *Financial Times*, 28 April 2014. Such reports should be taken with a large pinch of salt, especially since Makhnitsky was a member of Svoboda and was clearly interested in exaggerating the crimes of the old regime.
16 Patrick Armstrong, 'Russian Federation sitrep', *Russia: Other Points of View* [blog] (28 August 2014). Available at http://www.russiaotherpointsofview.com/2014/08/russian-federation-sitrep.html.
17 Stephen D. Shenfield, 'On Maidan: democratic movement or nationalist mobilization', *Johnson's Russia List* [website] (20 June 2014). Available at http://russialist.org/stephen-d-shenfield-on-maidan-democratic-movement-or-nationalist-mobilization/ [in *JRL*, 2014-137/14].

18   It appears that the call was intercepted by SBU officers, no friends of the new regime, and made public on 5 March. Available at https://www.youtube.com/watch?v=ZEgJ0oo3OA8.

19   An English translation of key elements of the broadcast was posted on 15 April. Available at https://www.facebook.com/permalink.php?story_fbid=725705100783621&id=161448950542575.

20   Ivan Katchanovski, 'The "Snipers' Massacre" on the Maidan in Ukraine' [paper presented at the Chair of Ukrainian Studies seminar at the University of Ottawa, 1 October 2014].

21   'Kiev takes on far right', *BBC News* [website] (1 April 2014). Available at http://www.bbc.co.uk/news/world-europe-26841732.

22   The MP was Iryna Farion. Instances of Maidan violence are listed in the Russian foreign ministry's *White Book on Violations of Human Rights and the Rule of Law in Ukraine (November 2013–March 2014)* (Moscow: Ministry of Foreign Affairs, April 2014), which documents human-rights abuses in revolutionary Ukraine. The Odessa events are described in the supplement, published in Russian only: *Belaya kniga narushenii prav cheloveka i printsipa verkhovenstva prava na Ukraine (aprel' – seredina iyunya 2014)* (Moscow: Ministry of Foreign Affairs, June 2014), p. 53.

23   Will Stewart, 'Putin wants to "wipe Ukraine off the map" says Kiev', *Daily Mail* (5 May 2014).

24   Andrew E. Kramer, 'In Odessa, home-grown combatants keep pro-Russian forces in check', *New York Times* (9 May 2014).

5. THE CRIMEAN GAMBIT

1   For a clear and balanced analysis, see Vasiliy Kashin, 'Khrushchev's Gift: The Questionable Ownership of Crimea', in Colby Howard and Ruslan Pukhov (eds), *Brothers Armed: Military Aspects of the Crisis in Ukraine* (Minneapolis, East View Press, 2014), pp. 1–21.

2   Andrew Wilson, *The Ukrainians: Unexpected Nation* (New Haven, CT: Yale University Press, 2000), p. 164.

3   For a detailed study, see Gwendolyn Sasse, *The Crimea Question: Identity, Transition, and Conflict* (Cambridge, MA: Harvard University Press, 2007), with pp. 96–126 on the 1954 transfer; and Taras Kuzio, *The Crimea: Europe's Next Flashpoint?* (Washington, DC: Jamestown Foundation, 2011).

4   For an analysis of the military aspect of the Crimea crisis, see in particular Alexey Nikolsky, 'Little, Green and Polite: The Creation of Russian Special Operations Forces' (pp. 124–131) and Anton Lavrov, 'Russian Again: The Military Operation for Crimea' (pp. 157–184), in Colby Howard and Ruslan Pukhov (eds), *Brothers Armed: Military Aspects of the Crisis in Ukraine* (Minneapolis, MN: East View Press, 2014).

5   'Vladimir Putin answered journalists' questions on the situation in Ukraine', *President of Russia* [website] (4 March 2014). Available at http://eng.kremlin.ru/transcripts/6763.

6   Paul Roderick Gregory, 'Putin's "Human Rights Council" accidentally posts real Crimean election results', *Forbes* (5 May 2014). Available at http://www.forbes.com/sites/paulroderickgregory/2014/05/05/putins-human-rights-council-accidentally-posts-real-crimean-election-results-only-15-voted-for-annexation/. For the report itself, see 'Problemy zhitelei Kryma', 21 April 2014, www.president-sovet.ru/structure/gruppa_po_migratsionnoy_politike/materialy/problemy_zhiteley_kryma.php.

7   For a study of the '30 days that shook the world', see Anatoly Belyakov and Oleg Matveichev, *Krymskaya vesna: 30 dnei, kotorye potryasli mir* (Moscow: Knizhnyi mir, 2014).

8   'Address by the president of the Russian Federation', *President of Russia* [website] (18 March 2014). Available at http:/eng.kremlin.ru/news/6889.

9   Ibid.

10 Federal'nyi konstitutsionnyi zakon RF ot 21 marta No. 6-FKZ, 'O prinyatii v RF Respubliki Krym i obrazovanii v sostave RF novykh sub"ektov Respubliki Krym i goroda federal'nogo znacheniya Sevastopolya', *Rossiiskaya gazeta*, 24 March 2014.

11 Angus Roxburgh, 'Russia's revenge: why the West will never understand the Kremlin', *New Statesman* (27 March 2014). Available at http://www.newstatesman.com/politics/2014/03/ russias-revenge-why-west-will-never-understand-kremlin.

12 Thomas Sherlock, 'Putin's public opinion challenge', *National Interest* (21 August 2014). Available at http://nationalinterest.org/feature/putins-public-opinion-challenge-11113?page=2. Sherlock reports a VTsIOM poll in June that saw 94 per cent support reunification.

13 Peter Rutland, 'A paradigm shift in Russia's foreign policy', *Moscow Times* (19 May 2014).

14 For a detailed discussion, see Sergei Baburin, *Krym naveki s rossiei: Istoriko-pravovoe obosnovanie vossoedineniya Respubliki Krym i goroda Sevastopol' s Rossiiskoi Federatsiei* (Moscow: Knizhnyi mir, 2014), pp. 52–6.

15 Diana Kulchitskaya, 'Crimean chemical plants threatened by Ukraine's water war with Russia', *Moscow Times* (15 May 2014).

16 Viktoriya Podolyanets, '"F" time: what is behind Firtash's return to Ukraine?', *Ukrainska Pravda* [website] (23 May 2014). Available at http://www.epravda.com.ua/rus/ publications/2014/05/23/456627.

17 'Crimean Tatar leaders say Kremlin relying on "old Soviet policy"', *Radio Free Europe/ Radio Liberty* [website] (11 June 2014). Available at http://www.rferl.org/content/crimean-tatar-leader-says-kremlin-relying-on-old-soviet-policy/25418707.html.

18 Alexander Winning, 'Resist or cooperate? Crimean Tatars split over Russian rule', Reuters (15 May 2014). Available at http://www.reuters.com/article/2014/05/15/us-ukraine-crisis-crimea-tatars-idUSBREA4E06120140515 [in *JRL*, 2014-108/31].

19 Jeffrey Mankoff, 'Russia's latest land grab: how Putin won Crimea and lost Ukraine', *Foreign Affairs* xciii/3 (May–June 2004), p. 68.

20 Alexander Mikhailenko, a professor at the Presidential Academy of National Economy and Public Administration, quoted in 'BRICS summit decisions may change world economic climate', Itar-Tass [Russian news agency] (16 July 2014). Available at http:// en.itar-tass.com/opinions/1829 [in *JRL*, 2014-155/27].

21 'BRICS summit opens in Brazil', *Radio Free Europe/Radio Liberty* [website] (15 July 2014). Available at http://www.rferl.org/content/brazil-russia-india-china-south-africa-summit-/25457016.html.

22 Dimitar Bechev, *Turkey's Illiberal Turn* [ECFR Policy Brief 108, July 2014], p. 6.

23 V. V. Putin, 'Poslanie Federal'nomu Sobraniyu Rossiiskoi Federatsii', *President of Russia* [website] (25 April 2005). Available at http://www.kremlin.ru/text/appears/2005/04/87049. shtml.

24 'It's all about the money', *Kyiv Post* (17 May 2014). Available at http://www.kyivpost. com/opinion/editorial/weak-resolve-348059.html.

25 'Germany and Russia: how very understanding', *The Economist* (10 May 2014). Available at http://www.economist.com/news/europe/21601897-germanys-ambivalence-towards-russia-reflects-its-conflicted-identity-how-very-understanding.

26 Anders Fogh Rasmussen, 'The future of Euro-Atlantic security', *Carnegie Europe* [website]

(15 September 2014). Available at http://carnegieeurope.eu/2014/09/15/future-of-euro-atlantic-security.

27 'Viewpoint: Russia's Ukraine strategy ends Europe's Dream', *BBC News* [website] (2 April 2014). Available at http://www.bbc.co.uk/news/world-europe-26842065.

28 'People of Crimea amend Soviet-era mistake – Gorbachev', Interfax [Russian news agency] (17 March 2014). Available at http://www.interfax.com/newsinf.asp?id=489110.

29 Václav Klaus and Jiří Weigl, 'Let's start a real Ukrainian debate', *Václav Klaus* [website] (22 April 2014). Available at http://www.klaus.cz/clanky/3553.

30 Neil Clark, 'Václav Klaus: the West's lies about Russia are monstrous', *Spectator* (27 September 2014). Available at http://www.spectator.co.uk/features/9322652/europe-needs-systemic-change/.

31 Alexander Lukin, 'Chauvinism or Chaos?', *Russia in Global Affairs* (7 June 2014). Available at http://eng.globalaffairs.ru/number/Chauvinism-or-Chaos-16709.

32 Noam Chomsky, 'Red lines in Ukraine and elsewhere', *Truthout* [website] (2 May 2014). Available at http://www.truth-out.org/opinion/item/23448-noam-chomsky-red-lines-in-ukraine-and-elsewhere [in *JRL*, 2014-100/32].

33 'Address by the president of the Russian Federation', *President of Russia* [website] (18 March 2014). Available at http:/eng.kremlin.ru/news/6889.

34 Vladimir V. Putin, 'A plea for caution from Russia', *New York Times* (12 September 2013).

6. WHEN HISTORY COMES CALLING

1 'Yatsenyuk urges Ukrainian sides to agree on new constitution', RIA Novosti [Russian news agency] (29 April 2014). Available at http://en.ria.ru/world/20140429/189454872/Yatsenyuk-Urges-Ukrainian-Sides-to-Agree-on-New-Constitution.html.

2 Alexander Nekrassov, 'Ukraine and the battle of the oligarchs', *Al Jazeera* [website] (1 July 2014). Available at http://m.aljazeera.com/story/20147181130186548.

3 Yury Marchenko, 'Ukrainskii pas'yans', *New Times* 16 (19 May 2014). Available at http://www.newtimes.ru/articles/detail/82569.

4 'Peterburgskii mezhdunardodnyi ekonomicheskii forum', *President of Russia* [website] (23 May 2014). Available at http://www.kremlin.ru/news/21080.

5 Michael Birnbaum and Fredrick Kunkle, 'In Ukrainian presidential election, chocolate tycoon Poroshenko claims victory', *Washington Post* (25 May 2014).

6 Yury Marchenko, 'Ukrainskii pas'yans', *New Times* 16 (19 May 2014). Available at http://www.newtimes.ru/articles/detail/82569.

7 Birnbaum and Kunkle, 'Chocolate tycoon Poroshenko claims victory'.

8 Parliamentary Assembly, Council of Europe, *Observation of the Early Presidential Election in Ukraine (25 May 2014)* (23 June 2014), para. 53. Available at http://www.assembly.coe.int/nw/xml/XRef/Xref-DocDetails-EN.asp?fileid=20943&wrqid=0&wrqref=&ref=1&lang=EN.

9 Ibid.

10 Dmitry Babich, 'Ukraine is ruled by Yushchenko's team, with the same result as in 2005–2010', *Voice of Russia* [website] (18 June 2014). Available at http://voiceofrussia.com/2014_06_18/Ukraine-is-ruled-by-Yushchenko-s-team-with-same-result-as-in-2005-2010-0288/.

11 Oliver Bullough, 'Stop forcing Ukraine into a narrative of Moscow versus Washington', *Guardian* (19 May 2004).

12 Nekrassov, 'Ukraine and the battle of the oligarchs'.

13   'Ukrainian website sees "new authorities' first oligarchic war"', *BBC Monitoring Ukraine and Baltics* (19 May 2014).

14   Alexander Golubev, 'What Biden's son and former president of Poland are doing at gas company of Yanukovych's friend', *Slon.ru* [website] (6 May 2014). Available at http://slon.ru/world/gazovoe_uravnenie_baydena_kvasnevskogo-1098956.xhtml.

15   Justine Doody, 'On a path to decentralisation', *European Voice*, 16 May 2014. Available at http://www.europeanvoice.com/other-voices/on-a-path-to-decentralisation/.

16   'Yatsenyuk calls for constitutional amendments and decentralization of power in Ukraine', Itar-Tass [Russian news agency] (14 May 2014). Available at http://en.itar-tass.com/world/731663.

17   'Akhmetov calls for constitutional reform, decentralization', *Kyiv Post* (14 May 2014). Available at http://www.kyivpost.com/content/ukraine/akhmetov-calls-for-constitutional-reform-decentralization-interview-text-347830.html.

18   Words used by the acting Ukrainian foreign minister, Andriy Deshchytsia, in discussion with Sergei Lavrov, Interfax [Russian news agency] (30 March 2014).

19   'Austrian paper interviews Ukrainian tycoon Firtash on crisis', *BBC Monitoring European* (21 May 2014).

20   Taras Kozub, 'Compromising material about Putin's circle: Tymoshenko's revenge or a redistribution of property?', *Reporter: Vesti* x (21–27 March 2014). Available at http://reporter.vesti.ua/43287-firtash-po-kom-zvonit-avstrijskij-kolokol#.U3HVJ3aoXRw.

21   'Ukrainian parliament votes for decentralization of power', RAPSI [Russian legal news agency] (21 May 2014). Available at http://rapsinews.com/legislation_news/20140521/271372313.html.

22   'Ukraine rejects autonomy calls for ethnic Hungarians made by Orban', Reuters (3 June 2014). Available at http://www.reuters.com/article/2014/06/03/us-ukraine-crisis-hungary-autonomy-idUSKBN0EE0N120140603.

23   Available at https://www.facebook.com/arsen.avakov.1/posts/657281451028631.

24   Oles Oleksiyenko, 'Déjà vu? Poroshenko vs Tymoshenko', *Ukrainian Week* (20 May 2014). Available at http://ukrainianweek.com/Politics/110202.

25   Larissa Titarenko, 'Belarus between the Eurasian Union and the European Union: material and symbolic options' [paper delivered at the ASN conference, New York, 25 April 2014].

26   Keith Gessen, 'Why not kill them all?', *London Review of Books* xxxvi/17 (11 September 2014), pp. 19–20.

27   Ibid., p. 21.

28   Nicolai N. Petro, 'Russia has responded to popular aspirations in Eastern Ukraine very differently from the way it responded in Crimea', *National Interest* (3 September 2014). Available at http://nationalinterest.org/feature/eastern-ukraine-the-neverending-crisis-11181.

29   'Ukrainian authorities seek access to ex-prosecutor Pshonka's archives', RAPSI [Russian legal news agency] (20 May 2014). Available at http://rapsinews.com/news/20140520/271361933.html.

30   'Ukraine opens tax evasion case against Yanukovych's son', RAPSI [Russian legal news agency] (3 June 2014). Available at http://rapsinews.com/judicial_news/20140603/271461607.html.

31   'Turchynov seeks ban of Communist Party for support of separatists', AFP [news agency] (19 May 2014).

32   Luke Johnson, 'Ukraine looks to Stalin era to root out spies', *Radio Free Europe/Radio Liberty* [website] (3 September 2014). Available at http://www.rferl.org/content/smersh-ukraine-heletey-counterintelligence/26564677.html.

33   Leonid Bershidsky, 'Ukraine's revolutionaries surrender to corruption', Bloomberg
      [news agency] (18 August 2014). Available at http://www.bloombergview.com/
      articles/2014-08-18/ukraine-s-revolutionaries-surrender-to-corruption.
34   'Turchynov seeks ban of Communist Party for support of separatists'.
35   Valentin Maltsev, 'Beginning of the end for the "Ukrainian Berezovsky"', Rosbalt Ukraine
      [website] (23 May 2014). Available at http://www.rosbalt.ru/ukraina/2014/05/23/1271994.
      html.
36   Irina Reznik and Henry Meyer, 'Magic wand billionaire says Putin secrets safe from
      US', Bloomberg [news agency] (13 May 2014). Available at http://www.bloomberg.com/
      news/2014-05-12/magic-wand-billionaire-says-putin-secrets-safe-from-u-s-.html.
37   'Ukraine economy: how bad is the mess and can it be fixed?', BBC News [website]
      (28 March 2014). Available at http://www.bbc.co.uk/news/world-europe-26767864.
38   Available at http://www.transparency.org/cpi2013/results.
39   Sergei Kvit, 'The ideology of the EuroMaidan revolution', Kyiv Post (24 March 2014).
      Available at http://www.kyivpost.com/opinion/op-ed/serhiy-kvit-the-ideology-of-the-
      euromaidan-revolution-340665.html.
40   Jack Grove, 'Ukraine has a youth problem – there's too little', Times Higher Education
      (10 July 2014), p. 18. Available at http://www.timeshighereducation.co.uk/news/inna-
      sovsun-ukraines-youngest-minister-plans-academy-shake-up/2014360.article.
41   James W. Carden, 'America's Ukraine-policy disaster', National Interest (2 July 2014).
      Available at http://nationalinterest.org/feature/americas-ukraine-policy-disaster-
      10790?page=2.
42   Fred Weir, 'Has Putin reached his limit on his willingness to intervene in Ukraine?',
      Christian Science Monitor (1 July 2014). Available at http://www.csmonitor.com/World/
      Europe/2014/0701/Has-Putin-reached-his-limit-on-his-willingness-to-intervene-in-
      Ukraine-video.
43   Robin Emmott, 'Putin warns Ukraine against implementing EU deal – letter', Reuters
      (23 September 2014). Available at http://www.reuters.com/article/2014/09/23/ukraine-
      crisis-trade-idUSL6N0RO3N220140923.
44   Clifford G. Gaddy and Barry W. Ickes, 'Ukraine: a prize neither Russia nor the West
      can afford to win' (22 May 2014). Available at http://www.brookings.edu/research/
      articles/2014/05/21-ukraine-prize-russia-West-ukraine-gaddy-ickes.
45   For a broad overview, see Vladimir Pastukhov, Ukrainskaya revolyutsiya i Russkaya
      kontrrevolyutsiya (Moscow: OGI, 2014).
46   Margarita Balmaceda and Peter Rutland, 'Ukraine's gas politics', openDemocracy [website]
      (8 May 2014). Available at https://www.opendemocracy.net/od-russia/margarita-
      balmaceda-peter-rutland/ukraines-gas-politics.
47   Neo Loizides, Politics of Majority Nationalism: The Framing of Peace, Stalemates and
      Crises (Stanford, CA: Stanford University Press, 2015), ch. 6.
48   'Dmytro Firtash: Ukraine must be strong, independent and neutral', Kyiv Post (21 May
      2014). Available at http://www.kyivpost.com/opinion/op-ed/dmytro-firtash-ukraine-
      must-be-strong-independent-and-neutral-348768.html.

7. THE NOVOROSSIYA REBELLION

1   Charles Recknagel, 'What are Eastern Ukraine's (legitimate) grievances with Kyiv?', Radio
      Free Europe/Radio Liberty [website] (29 May 2014). Available at http://www.rferl.org/
      content/ukraine-explainer-eastern-greievances/25402922.html.

2   Oleg Grytsaienko, 'The crisis in Ukraine: an insider's view', *Russie.Nei.Visions* lxxviii (June 2014), p. 10. Available at http://www.ifri.org/?page=contribution-detail&id=8135.

3   Keith Gessen, 'Why not kill them all?', *London Review of Books* xxxvi/17 (11 September 2014), p. 18.

4   'Ukraine crisis: a guide to Russia's vision of Crimea', *BBC News* [website] (25 March 2014). Available at http://www.bbc.co.uk/news/world-europe-26695808.

5   Gessen, 'Why not kill them all?', p. 18.

6   Ibid., p. 22.

7   Ibid., p. 19.

8   For a sympathetic portrait, see Mikhail Polikarpov, *Igor' Strelkov: uzhas banderovskoi khunty – oborona Donbassa* (Moscow: Knizhnyi mir, 2014).

9   Aleksandr Prokhanov, 'Kto ty, "Strelok"?', *Zavtra*, 19 November 2014.

10   'Pro-Russians storm offices in Donetsk, Luhansk, Kharkiv', *BBC News* [website] (7 April 2014). Available at http://www.bbc.co.uk/news/world-europe-26910210.

11   Erich Follath and Matthias Schepp, 'Loved and hated: can Tymoshenko still lead Ukraine?', *Der Spiegel* (16 May 2014). Available at http://www.spiegel.de/international/europe/yulia-tymoshenko-divides-ukraine-a-969645.html.

12   'Putin's aggression against Ukraine isn't a local conflict – it threatens the democratic world', *Yulia Tymoshenko* [website] (19 March 2014). Available at http://www.tymoshenko.ua/en/press/yulia_tymoshenko_19_03_2014_1.

13   The conversation is reported in Antony Penaud, 'People from the Donbass seen from other Ukrainians', *Johnson's Russia List* [website] (12 August 2014). Available at http://russialist.org/people-from-the-donbass-seen-from-other-ukrainians/ [in *JRL*, 2014-176/5].

14   'Direct line with Vladimir Putin', *President of Russia* [website] (17 April 2014). Available at http://eng.kremlin.ru/news/7034.

15   Ibid.

16   'Mneniya i vzglyady zhietelei yugo-vostoka Ukrainy: Aprel' 2014', *ZN.ua* [website] (18 April 2014). Available at http://zn.ua/UKRAINE/mneniya-i-vzglyady-zhiteley-yugo-vostoka-ukrainy-aprel-2014-143598_.html.

17   Ivan Katchanovski, 'What do citizens of Ukraine actually think about secession?', *Washington Post* (21 July 2014). For a more extended analysis, including the full results of the KIIS survey on the strength of separatist sentiments, see Ivan Katchanovski, 'The separatist conflict in Donbas: a violent break-up of Ukraine', https://www.academia.edu/9092818/The_Separatist_Conflict_in_Donbas_A_Violent_Break-Up_of_Ukraine.

18   Serhiy Kudelia, 'Domestic Sources of the Donbas Insurgency', PONARD Eurasia Policy Memo No. 351, September 2014, p. 1.

19   'South-eastern Ukraine: new political reality', Fars [news agency] (19 May 2014). Available at http://english.farsnews.com/newstext.aspx?nn=13930225000128.

20   'Interview: I was a separatist fighter in Ukraine', *Radio Free Europe/Radio Liberty* [website] (13 July 2014). Available at http://www.rferl.org/content/ukraine-i-was-a-separatist-fighter/25455466.html.

21   'Geneva statement on Ukraine', *US Department of State* [website] (17 April 2014). Available at http://www.state.gov/r/pa/prs/ps/2014/04/224957.htm.

22   Tom Parfitt, 'The neo-Nazi brigade fighting pro-Russian separatists', *Daily Telegraph* (11 August 2014).

23   Oleg Odnorozhenko, the deputy head of the Azov battalion and its chief ideologue, quoted in Ben Hoyle, 'Neo-Nazis give Kiev a last line of defence in the east', *The Times* (5 September 2014).

24   Anton Lavrov and Alexey Nikolsky, 'Neglect and rot: degradation of Ukraine's military in the interim period', in Howard and Pukhov (eds), *Brothers Armed*, pp. 57–73

25   Andriy Parubiy, 'Ukraine needs immediate US military aid', *Wall Street Journal* (16 May 2014).

26   Catherine A. Traywick, 'President Obama at West Point', *Foreign Policy* [website] (28 May 2014). Available at http://blog.foreignpolicy.com/posts/2014/05/28/watch_now_president_obama_at_West_point.

27   Michael Birnbaum and Fredrick Kunkle, 'In Ukrainian presidential election, chocolate tycoon Poroshenko claims victory', *Washington Post* (25 May 2014).

28   Shaun Walker, 'Kiev claims Russia let tanks across border', *Guardian* (13 June 2014).

29   Shaun Walker and Alec Luhn, 'Putin calls off the troops as rebels agree to ceasefire', *Guardian* (25 June 2014).

30   Alexandr Litoy, 'Putin's international brigades', *openDemocracy* [website] (2 October 2014). Available at https://www.opendemocracy.net/od-russia/alexandr-litoy/putin%E2%80%99s-international-brigades.

31   Neil MacFarquhar, 'Putin calls for extension of shaky Ukraine cease-fire', *International New York Times* (25 June 2014).

32   Shaun Walker, 'Putin backs Kiev's ceasefire plan with call for compromise', *Guardian* (23 June 2014).

33   'English-language translation of Poroshenko's message to Ukraine ending ceasefire against Kremlin-backed separatists', *Kyiv Post* (1 July 2014). Available at http://www.kyivpost.com/content/ukraine/english-language-translation-of-poroshenkos-message-to-ukraine-ending-ceasefire-against-kremlin-backed-separatists-354065.html.

34   Natalia Antonova, 'Kiev must show compassion to eastern Ukraine', *Moscow Times* (18 August 2014). Available at http://www.themoscowtimes.com/opinion/article/kiev-must-show-compassion-to-eastern-ukraine/505310.html.

35   Stephen F. Cohen, 'The silence of American hawks about Kiev's atrocities', *The Nation* (1 July 2014). Available at http://www.thenation.com/article/180466/silence-american-hawks-about-kievs-atrocities.

36   'The West can't afford to make empty threats on Russia sanctions' [editorial], *Washington Post* (2 July 2014).

37   Harriet Salem, Oksana Grytsenko and Shaun Walker, 'Pro-Russia fighters muster for a last stand as Ukrainian troops close in on Donetsk', *Guardian* (11 July 2014).

38   Iana Koretska, 'Changes to terrorism law give Ukraine forces fighting chance to defeat Eastern insurgency', *Kyiv Post* (20 June 2014). Available at http://www.kyivpost.com/content/ukraine/changes-to-terrorism-law-give-ukraine-forces-fighting-chance-to-defeat-eastern-insurgency-352701.html?flavour=mobile.

39   Alec Luhn, 'Ukraine's humanitarian crisis worsens as tens of thousands flee combat in Ukraine', *Guardian* (13 June 2014).

40   'UN says at least 285,000 flee Ukraine crisis', *Radio Free Europe/Radio Liberty* [website] (5 August 2014). Available at http://www.rferl.org/content/ukraine-refugees-285000/26515471.html.

41   'Ukraine: abuses and war crimes by the Aidar volunteer battalion in the North Luhansk region' [Amnesty International briefing] (8 September 2014). Available at http://www.amnesty.org/en/library/asset/EUR50/040/2014/en/e6776c69-fe66-4924-bfc0-d15c9539c667/eur500402014en.pdf.

42   Vladimir Putin, 'Conference of Russian ambassadors and permanent representatives', *President of Russia* [website] (1 July 2014). Available at http://eng.kremlin.ru/news/22586 [translation modified].

43 Nikolai Starikov, *Ukraina: Khaos i revolyutsiya – oruzhie dollar* (Moscow: Piter, 2014), pp. 9, 17, 163–95.

44 Brian Whitmore, 'Slobodan's ghost', *Radio Free Europe/Radio Liberty* [website] (14 July 2014). Available at http://www.rferl.org/content/slobodans-ghost/25456814.html.

45 Mary Dejevsky, 'Europe must learn to deal with Moscow on its own', *Guardian* (24 July 2014).

46 Shaun Walker, 'More cracks appear in rebels' story as witnesses report sightings of launcher', *Guardian* (23 July 2014).

47 Shaun Walker, 'Commander backtracks after saying separatists controlled a Buk missile', *Guardian* (24 July 2014).

48 Paul Lewis, 'Obama steps up Russia sanctions along with EU', *Guardian* (17 July 2014).

49 'Ukraine: unguided rockets killing civilians', *Human Rights Watch* [website] (24 July 2014). Available at http://www.hrw.org/news/2014/07/24/ukraine-unguided-rockets-killing-civilians.

50 Shaun Walker, 'My audience with the Demon of Donetsk', *Guardian* (30 July 2014).

51 'Rebels call for Russia's help as army advances', *Guardian* (4 August 2014).

52 Julian Borger and Gwyn Topham, 'MH17 broken apart by "large number of high-energy objects", experts conclude', *Guardian* (10 September 2014).

53 Margareta Pagano, 'Land for gas: Merkel and Putin discussed secret deal could end Ukraine crisis', *Independent* (31 July 2014).

54 Neil MacFarquhar, 'A sanctions pile up, Russians' alarm grows over Putin's tactics', *New York Times* (30 July 2014).

55 Arkady Moshes, 'EU will likely get a bad deal on Ukraine', *Moscow Times* (25 August 2014).

56 Figures by the MP Viktoria Shilova, 18 August 2014, in *JRL*, 2014-180/18.

57 For a later evaluation, see Mark Franchetti, 'No surrender of the truth from this "Kremlin hero"', *Sunday Times* (29 June 2014).

58 Anna Dolgov, 'Defense Ministry dismisses reports of Russian paratroopers killed in Ukraine', *Moscow Times* (30 September 2014). Available at http://www.themoscowtimes.com/news/article/defense-ministry-dismisses-reports-of-russian-paratroopers-killed-in-ukraine-as-rumors/508089.html.

59 For a moving account of the battle, see Tim Judah, 'Ukraine: a catastrophic defeat', *New York Review of Books* (5 September 2014). Available at http://www.nybooks.com/blogs/nyrblog/2014/sep/05/ukraine-catastrophic-defeat/.

60 Laurence Norman, 'EU moves to temper Putin "two weeks to Kiev" row', *Wall Street Journal* (4 September 2014).

61 'Vladimir Putin, 'Answers to journalists' questions following working visit to Belarus', *President of Russia* [website] (27 August 2014). Available at http://eng.news.kremlin.ru/transcripts/22852.

62 Vladimir Putin, 'Vystuplenie na vstreche glav goudarstv Tamozhnego soyuza s Prezidentom Ukrainy i predstavitelyami Evropeiskogo soyuza', *President of Russia* [website] (26 August 2014). Available at http://kremlin.ru/transcripts/46494.

63 Fred Weir, 'Wide gaps remain as Putin and Poroshenko discuss Ukraine crisis', *Christian Science Monitor* (26 August 2014). Available at http://www.csmonitor.com/World/Europe/2014/0826/Wide-gaps-remain-as-Putin-and-Poroshenko-discuss-Ukraine-crisis-video.

64 'Poroshenko vows "roadmap" for peace', *BBC News* [website], 27 August. Available at http://www.bbc.co.uk/news/world-europe-28940095.

65 'Questions left unanswered at Putin–Poroshenko Minsk talks', RIA Novosti [Russian news agency] (27 August 2014). Available at http://en.ria.ru/world/20140827/192388946/Questions-Left-Unanswered-at-Putin-Poroshenko-Minsk-Talks.html.

66 'Protocol of the Trilateral Contact Group, Minsk, 5 September 2014' (7 September 2014). Available at http://slavyangrad.org/2014/09/07/protocol-of-the-tripartite-contact-group-minsk-september-5-2014/.

67 'Rebel leader in Ukraine says independence is new aim', Interfax [Russian news agency] (24 August 2014). Available at http://russialist.org/interfax-rebel-leader-in-ukraine-says-independence-is-new-aim/.

68 There is confusion about the details of this law, and even whether 'special status' was granted at all. Yatsenyuk characteristically opposed key parts, while parliament's speaker, Turchynov, refused to sign the adopted law.

69 'Ukraine seals EU pact, offers rebel East "special status"', Radio Free Europe/Radio Liberty [website] (16 September 2014). Available at http://www.rferl.org/content/ukraine-european-union-association-agreement-/26586513.html.

70 'Seliger 2014 National Youth Forum', President of Russia [website] (29 August 2014). Available at http://eng.kremlin.ru/news/22864.

71 Shaun Walker and Dan Roberts, 'Putin wants talks for "statehood" in eastern Ukraine', Guardian (1 September 2014).

72 Dan Roberts, 'Ukraine's leader calls on politicians to send arms', Guardian (19 September 2014).

73 Angus Roxburgh, 'Dangerous delusions', Guardian (30 August 2014).

8. WORLDS IN COLLISION

1 Gerald F. Seib, 'Kerry Sees Ukraine crisis as uniquely Putin's', Wall Street Journal (29 April 2014).

2 Josh Rogin and Eli Lake, 'Kerry: US taped Moscow's calls to its Ukraine spies', Daily Beast [website] (29 April 2014). Available at http://www.thedailybeast.com/articles/2014/04/29/kerry-u-s-taped-moscow-s-calls-to-its-ukraine-spies.html [in JRL, 2014-98/18].

3 Ibid.

4 Shaun Walker and Alec Luhn, 'Unilateral ceasefire in Ukraine could begin "in days"', Guardian (19 June 2014).

5 White Book on Violations of Human Rights and the Rule of Law in Ukraine (November 2013–March 2014) (Moscow: Ministry of Foreign Affairs, April 2014).

6 Institute of Mass Information, 'Summary for violation of journalists' rights and freedom of speech since Russian aggression started' (13 June 2014). Available at http://imi.org.ua/en/analytics/44673-summary-for-violation-of-journalists-rights-and-freedom-of-speech-since-russian-aggression-started-imi-infographics.html.

7 Cristina Giuliano and Andrew McChesney, 'European investors say pleas against sanction on Russia ignored', Moscow Times (17 March 2014). Available at http://www.themoscowtimes.com/business/article/european-investors-say-pleas-against-russian-sanctions-ignored/496238.html.

8 'EU "should be ashamed" after sanctions on Russia – Moscow', RT [website] (29 April 2014). Available at http://rt.com/news/155620-eu-japan-sanctions-russia/ [in JRL, 2014-98/13].

9 '"Slap on the wrist": congressional critics slam "tepid" Russian sanctions', Radio Free Europe/Radio Liberty [website] (28 April 2014). Available at http://www.rferl.org/content/russia-sanctions-us-lawmakers-tepid/25365864.html.

10   'Statement by senators McCain and Graham on sanctions against Russia and the situation in Ukraine', *John McCain* [website] (28 April 2014). Available at http://www.mccain.senate.gov/public/index.cfm/2014/4/statement-by-senators-mccain-and-graham-on-sanctions-against-russia-and-the-situation-in-ukraine [in *JRL*, 2014-98/1].

11   'Obama's half-measures give Vladimir Putin little to fear' [editorial], *Washington Post* (29 April 2014).

12   'Biden says US forced EU countries to impose sanctions against Russia', RIA Novosti [Russian news agency] (3 October 2014). Available at http://en.ria.ru/world/20141003/193605738/Biden-Says-US-Forced-EU-Countries-to-Impose-Sanctions-Against.html. Biden was speaking at Harvard, 2 October 2014.

13   Andrew E. Kramer, 'Sanctions over Ukraine cause headaches in energy sector', *New York Times* (29 April 2014).

14   Alison Smale and Danny Hakim, 'European firms seek to minimize Russia sanctions', *New York Times* (26 April 2014).

15   Ibid.

16   Ibid.

17   Chris Weafer, 'Russia has eager new oil and gas customers in Asia', *Business New Europe* [website] (25 September 2014). Available at http://www.bne.eu/content/story/macro-adviser-russia-has-eager-new-oil-and-gas-customers-asia.

18   Andrei Yermolaev, 'European Union is wrong to block South Stream pipeline', *Moscow Times* (14 July 2014). Available at http://www.themoscowtimes.com/opinion/article/european-union-is-wrong-to-block-south-stream-pipeline/503353.html.

19   Gordon M. Hahn, '"Isolating Russia" in the oil and gas sector', *Johnson's Russia List* [website] (14 July 2014). Available at http://russialist.org/isolating-russia-in-the-oil-and-gas-sector/ [in *JRL*, 2014-154/36]. Hahn is an analyst and advisory board member of the Geostrategic Forecasting Corporation, Chicago.

20   Vladimir Putin, 'St Petersburg International Economic Forum', *President of Russia* [website] (23 May 2014). Available at http://eng.kremlin.ru/news/7230.

21   Larry Elliott, 'Fears of economic meltdown put pressure on Russia and the West', *Guardian* (11 July 2014).

22   Jennifer Rankin and Alec Luhn, 'Putin bans food imports in backlash at sanctions', *Guardian* (7 August 2014).

23   Seumas Milne, 'Gaza is a crime made in Washington as well as Israel', *Guardian* (7 August 2014).

24   Pietro Shakarian, 'Sanctions against Russia are dividing Europe more than you think', *Russia Direct* [website] (22 September 2014). Available at http://www.russia-direct.org/opinion/sanctions-against-russia-are-dividing-europe-more-you-think.

25   'Russia to contest West's unilateral sanctions in WTO', RIA Novosti [Russian news agency] (20 June 2014). Available at http://russialist.org/ria-novosti-russia-to-contest-wests-unilateral-economic-sanctions-in-wto/.

26   Julian Cooper, 'How sanctions will hit Russian rearmament plans', *Chatham House* [website] (13 August 2014). Available at http://www.chathamhouse.org/expert/comment/15523.

27   Georgy Bovt, 'Iraq's collapse, or why Putin isn't Abu Bakr', *Valdai Discussion Club* [website] (19 June 2014). Available at http://valdaiclub.com/middle_East/69580.

28   Fyodor Lukyanov, 'Russia will not be a spoiler in Iraq', *Al-Monitor* [website] (15 June 2014). Available at http://www.al-monitor.com/pulse/tr/originals/2014/06/russia-iraq-policy-worldview.html.

29   Andrew E. Kramer and David Jolly, 'Russia raises rate to bolster economy after S.&P. cuts its debt rating', *New York Times* (26 April 2014).

30   'Russian economic development minister Alexei Ulyukaev on growing budget deficit', *Vedomosti* (25 August 2014).

31   'Putin: Western sanctions on Russia contradict WTO norms, fair competition principles', RIA Novosti [Russian news agency] (18 September 2014).

32   George Friedman, 'The US opts for ineffective sanctions on Russia', *Stratfor.com* [website] (29 April 2014). Available at http://www.stratfor.com/weekly/us-opts-ineffective-sanctions-russia. My account is drawn from this article.

33   Sergei Ryabkov, '"My imeem delo s novym nastupatel'nym vidom oruzhiya"', *Kommersant* (4 July 2014), p. 5.

34   Vladimir Kabeev, 'Russian foreign minister Lavrov accuses West of Anti-Russian propaganda', *Russia Direct* [website] (28 April 2014). Available at http://www.russia-direct.org/russian-media/russian-foreign-minister-lavrov-accuses-west-anti-russian-propaganda.

35   'Stepashin: US, its allies are looking to get Putin out of power, isolate Russia', Interfax [Russian news agency] (5 September 2014).

36   Jack Farchy, 'Russians pull together in face of sanctions', *Financial Times* (5 September 2014).

9. FRONTLINE POLITICS

1   Alexander Sergunin, 'Russian views on the Ukrainian crisis', in Thomas Flichy de La Neuville (ed.), *Ukraine: Regards sur la crise* (Lausanne: L'Âge d'Homme, 2014), p. 55.

2   This point is made by Alexey Fenenko, who also examines the various myths, in 'An inside look at Moscow's evolving Ukrainian strategy', *Russia Direct* [website] (29 July 2014). Available at http://www.russia-direct.org/opinion/inside-look-moscows-evolving-ukrainian-strategy.

3   Andranik Migranyan, 'What is at stake in Ukraine', *National Interest* (30 July 2014). Available at http://nationalinterest.org/feature/what-stake-ukraine-10979.

4   'Direct line with Vladimir Putin', *President of Russia* [website] (17 April 2014). Available at http://eng.kremlin.ru/news/7034.

5   Dmitry Trenin, 'Europe's nightmare coming true: America vs. Russia… again', *National Interest* (29 July 2014). Available at http://nationalinterest.org/feature/europes-nightmare-coming-true-america-vs-russiaagain-10971.

6   Vladimir Putin, 'Meetings with heads of leading international news agencies', *President of Russia* [website] (24 May 2014). Available at http://eng.kremlin.ru/news/7237.

7   'Security Council meeting', *President of Russia* [website] (22 July 2014). Available at http://eng.kremlin.ru/news/22714.

8   Mary Dejevsky, 'Fear is what fuels Moscow', *Guardian* (7 July 2014).

9   For an assessment, see Anastassia Obydenkova and Alexander Libman, 'Understanding the foreign policy of autocratic actors: ideology or pragmatism? Russia and the Tymoshenko trial as a case study', *Contemporary Politics* xx/3 (May 2014), pp. 347–64. Available at http://www.tandfonline.com/doi/full/10.1080/13569775.2014.911500#.VDf-ZufY2Dk.

10   Migranyan, 'What is at stake in Ukraine'.

11   Zbigniew Brzezinski, *Strategic Vision* (New York: Basic Books, 2013).

12   Anatol Lieven, 'The spectre of Wolfowitz', *Valdai Discussion Club* [website] (5 May 2014). Available at http://valdaiclub.com/near_abroad/68580.html. Originally published in the *American Review* (August 2014).

13   Sergei Karaganov, 'Towards the great ocean', *Rossiiskaya gazeta* (26 August 2014).

14   Migranyan, 'What is at stake in Ukraine'.

15   Alexander J. Motyl, 'How Putin lost Ukraine', *World Affairs Journal* (19 June 2014). Available at http://www.worldaffairsjournal.org/blog/alexander-j-motyl/how-putin-lost-ukraine.

16   Boris Nemtsov, 'Uroki Maidana' (24 February 2014). Available at http://www.echo.msk.ru/blog/nemtsov_boris/1264336-echo/.

17   Ellen Barry, 'Foes of America in Russia crave rupture in ties', *New York Times* (15 March 2014).

18   The Putin system is described in my *Putin Redux: Power and Contradiction in Contemporary Russia* (London and New York: Routledge, 2014).

19   Fred Weir, 'With Ukraine rebels on the ropes, some Russians ask: where is Putin?', *Christian Science Monitor* (7 July 2014). Available at http://www.csmonitor.com/World/Europe/2014/0707/With-Ukraine-rebels-on-the-ropes-some-Russians-ask-Where-is-Putin-video.

20   Paul Sonne, 'Russian nationalists feel let down by Kremlin, again', *Wall Street Journal* (5 July 2014).

21   Andrei Tsygankov, 'Putin is not a nationalist', *Moscow Times* (24 June 2014). Available at http://www.themoscowtimes.com/opinion/article/putin-is-not-a-nationalist/502466.html.

22   Vladimir Putin, 'Conference of Russian ambassadors and permanent representatives', *President of Russia* [website] (1 July 2014). Available at http://eng.kremlin.ru/news/22586.

23   Zbigniew Brzezinski, *The Grand Chessboard: American Primacy and its Geostrategic Imperatives* (New York: Basic Books, 1997).

24   For a recent sophisticated analysis, see Bruce Jones, *Still Ours to Lead: America, Rising Powers, and the Tension between Rivalry and Restraint* (Washington, DC: Brookings Institution, 2014).

25   Brzezinski, *The Grand Chessboard*, pp. 39, 84–5, 121–2.

26   Sergei Glazyev, 'The threat of war and the Russian response', *Russia in Global Affairs* (25 September 2014). Available at http://eng.globalaffairs.ru/number/The-Threat-of-War-and-the-Russian-Response-16988.

27   For a brilliant analysis of American foreign policy, see Perry Anderson, 'Imperium' and 'Consilium', *New Left Review* 83 (September–October 2013), pp. 5–111, pp. 113–67.

28   For a classic statement of this argument, see E. H. Carr, *The Twenty Years' Crisis, 1919–1939: An Introduction to the Study of International Relations*, reissued with a new introduction and additional material by Michael Cox (London: Palgrave, 2001 [1939]).

29   David Bromwich, 'The world's most important spectator', *London Review of Books* xxxvi/13 (3 July 2014), pp. 3–6.

30   Ibid., pp. 3–6.

31   Robert Kagan, *Of Paradise and Power: America and Europe in the New World Order* (New York: Knopf Doubleday, 2007).

32   Vladimir V. Putin, 'A plea for caution from Russia', *New York Times* (12 September 2013).

33   Bromwich, 'The world's most important spectator', p. 3.

34   This account uses Ali's terminology and some of his information, but is interspersed with my comments. See F. B. Ali, 'The West and Ukraine: and the wars within', *Sic Semper Tyrannis* [blog] (13 May 2014). Available at http://turcopolier.typepad.com/sic_semper_tyrannis/2014/05/the-west-and-ukraine-and-the-wars-within-fb-ali.html [in *JRL*, 2014-108/38].

35   'S.2277 Russian Aggression Prevention Act 2014' [113th Congress (2013–14); introduced

in Senate 1 May 2014], *Congress.gov* [website]. Available at https://beta.congress.gov/bill/113th-congress/senate-bill/2277/text.

36   Fyodor Lukyanov, 'Battle against the West gives Russia new purpose', *Moscow Times* (16 September 2014). Available at http://www.themoscowtimes.com/opinion/article/battle-against-west-gives-russia-new-purpose/507245.html.

37   Georgy Bovt, 'Russia makes truces with the West, not peace', *Moscow Times* (16 September 2014). Available at http://www.themoscowtimes.com/opinion/article/russia-makes-truces-with-the-west-not-peace/507256.html.

38   For a sympathetic account, see David Remnick, 'Watching the eclipse: Ambassador Michael McFaul was there when the promise of democracy came to Russia – and when it began to fade', *New Yorker* (11 August 2014).

39   Stephen F. Cohen, 'The new cold war and the necessity of patriotic heresy', *The Nation* (12 August 2014). Available at http://www.thenation.com/article/180942/new-cold-war-and-necessity-patriotic-heresy.

40   The term is Patrick Armstrong's. See 'Russian Federation sitrep', *Russia: Other Points of View* [blog] (1 May 2014). Available at http://www.russiaotherpointsofview.com/2014/05/russian-federation-sitrep.html.

41   Eric Kraus, 'Stumbling into the apocalypse', *Russia Insider* [website] (4 September 2014). Available at http://russia-insider.com/en/opinion/2014/10/10/06-30-15pm/stumbling_apocalypse [in *JRL*, 2014-195/25].

42   Seumas Milne, 'Far from keeping the peace, Nato is a constant threat to it', *Guardian* (4 September 2014).

43   Ben Smith, 'Polish foreign minister: we gave the US a "blowjob" and got nothing', *BuzzFeed* [website] (22 June 2014). Available at http://www.buzzfeed.com/bensmith/polish-foreign-minister-we-gave-the-us-a-blowjob-got-nothing.

44   Mikheil Saakashvili, 'The tasks ahead for Ukraine's new president', *Wall Street Journal* (29 May 2014).

45   Mark Landler and Michael R. Gordon, 'NATO chief warns of duplicity by Putin on Ukraine', *New York Times* (9 July 2014).

46   Ali, 'The West and Ukraine: and the wars within'.

47   Henry Kissinger, 'To settle the Ukraine crisis, start at the end', *Washington Post* (5 March 2014).

48   'West toughens sanctions on Russia, as fighting intensifies in Eastern Ukraine', *Open Europe* [website] (30 July 2014). Available at http://www.openeurope.org.uk/Article/Page/en/LIVE?id=20429#.

49   Cited by James W. Carden, 'Will the Ukraine crisis tank Europe's fragile economy?', *National Interest* (3 October 2014). Available at http://nationalinterest.org/feature/will-the-ukraine-crisis-tank-europes-fragile-economy-11401.

50   Edward Luce, 'Obama's Hippocratic oath enfeebles his diplomacy', *Financial Times* (18 August 2014).

51   Ibid.

52   Stephen F. Cohen, 'The silence of American hawks about Kiev's atrocities', *The Nation* (1 July 2014). Available at http://www.thenation.com/article/180466/silence-american-hawks-about-kievs-atrocities.

53   Bromwich, 'The world's most important spectator', p. 5.

54   Catherine A. Traywick, 'President Obama at West Point', *Foreign Policy* [website] (28 May 2014). Available at http://blog.foreignpolicy.com/posts/2014/05/28/watch_now_president_obama_at_West_point.

55 Bromwich, 'The world's most important spectator', p. 7.
56 Fyodor Lukyanov, 'Istoriya bol'shaya disgarmonii', *Rossiya v global'noi politike* [website] (27 June 2014). Available at http://www.globalaffairs.ru/redcol/Istoriya-bolshoi-disgarmonii-16751.
57 David Habakkuk, 'Habbakuk on "truth and honor", the MH17 shootdown, and the centenary of World War I', *Sic Semper Tyrannis* [blog] (4 August 2014). Available at http://turcopolier.typepad.com/sic_semper_tyrannis/2014/08/on-truth-and-honor-the-mh17-shootdown-and-the-centenary-of-world-war-i-.html.
58 Rick Lyman, 'Poland says Russian veto should be limited at UN', *New York Times* (18 September 2014).
59 Steven Blockmans, 'Ukraine, Russia and the need for more flexibility in EU foreign policy-making' [CEPS Policy Brief 320, 25 July 2014]. Available at http://www.ceps.be/book/ukraine-russia-and-need-more-flexibility-eu-foreign-policy-making.
60 Ibid.
61 Frank-Walter Steinmeier interviewed by Nikolaus Blome, 'Russia is playing a dangerous game', *Der Spiegel* [website] (28 April 2014). Available at http://www.spiegel.de/international/europe/frank-walter-steinmeier-talks-about-the-ukraine-crisis-and-russia-a-966493.html.
62 Judy Dempsey, 'Russia is losing Germany', *Carnegie Europe* [website] (21 August 2014). Available at http://carnegieeurope.eu/strategiceurope/?fa=56433.
63 James W. Carden, 'America's Ukraine-policy disaster', *National Interest* (2 July 2014). Available at http://nationalinterest.org/feature/americas-ukraine-policy-disaster-10790?page=2.
64 Mark Leonard and Andrew Wilson, 'Introduction: protecting the European choice', in Andrew Wilson (ed.), *Protecting the European Choice* (London: European Council on Foreign Relations, July 2014), p. 5.
65 Ibid., p. 5.
66 John J. Mearsheimer, 'Getting Ukraine wrong', *International New York Times* (14 March 2014).
67 John J. Mearsheimer, 'Why the Ukraine crisis is the West's fault: the liberal delusions that provoked Putin', *Foreign Affairs* xciii/5 (September–October 2014), p. 78.
68 Ibid., p. 80.
69 Ibid., p. 82.
70 Ibid., p. 83.

10. THE FUTURE OF UKRAINE

1 Shaun Walker, 'Prime minister quits as parties pull out of coalition', *Guardian* (25 July 2014).
2 'Poroshenko calls an early election on Oct. 26', *Kyiv Post* (25 August 2014). Available at http://www.kyivpost.com/content/ukraine/president-petro-poroshenko-calls-an-early-election-on-oct-26-362001.html.
3 'Ukraine's economy minister Sheremeta offers resignation', Reuters (21 August 2014). Available at http://uk.reuters.com/article/2014/08/21/ukraine-crisis-sheremeta-idUSL5N0QR1OW20140821.
4 Andrew Wilson, 'Ukraine under Poroshenko', in Andrew Wilson (ed.), *Protecting the European Choice* (London: European Council on Foreign Relations, July 2014), p. 13.
5 'Ukraine elections: pro-Western parties set for victory', *BBC News* [website] (27 October 2014). Available at http://www.bbc.com/news/world-europe-29782513.

6   'Kiev's actions may lead to Ukraine's "disintegration"', RIA Novosti [Russian news agency] (8 May 2014). Available at http://russialist.org/ria-novosti-kievs-actions-may-lead-to-ukraines-disintegration-russian-speaker/.

7   As shown for example in a poll organised by Alexei Navalny in Odessa and Kharkov, showing 26 per cent who thought Ukraine should join NATO while 48 per cent were against. Only 41 per cent supported the demands of the Maidan movement, but enormous majorities wanted to remain part of Ukraine. Reported by Mark Adomanis, 'Ukrainians still don't want to join NATO', *Forbes* (23 September 2014). Available at http://www.forbes.com/sites/markadomanis/2014/09/23/ukrainians-still-dont-want-to-join-nato/ [in *JRL*, 2014-201/11].

8   'Full transcript: remarks by Ambassador Samantha Power, US permanent representative to the United Nations, at a Security Council session on Ukraine', *Washington Post* (28 August 2014).

9   'War did massive damage to Donetsk – city mayor', Interfax [Russian news agency] (8 September 2014). Available at http://www.interfax.com/newsinf.asp?id=534857.

10   Anatol Lieven, 'Ukraine: the only way to peace', *New York Review of Books* (5 May 2014).

11   Jack Matlock, 'Cool the rhetoric; focus on the outcome', *JackMatlock.com* [website] (26 August 2014). Available at http://jackmatlock.com/2014/08/ukraine-cool-the-rhetoric-focus-on-the-outcome/ [in *JRL*, 2014-188/20].

12   David Owen, 'Decoding the Russia riddle', *Guardian* (26 August 2014).

13   'A 24-step plan to resolve the Ukraine crisis', *The Atlantic* (26 August 2014). The absence of Ukrainian participants was criticised in an open letter organised by the head of Freedom House, David Kramer, one of the most virulent hawks in the whole crisis.

14   Samuel Charap, 'Why Obama's coercion strategy in Ukraine will fail', *National Interest* (4 August 2014). Available at http://nationalinterest.org/feature/why-obamas-coercion-strategy-ukraine-will-fail-11006.

15   Paul D'Anieri, 'Legitimacy, force, and the Ukrainian state: the legacy of the Orange Revolution in 2014' [paper delivered at the ASN conference, New York, 26 April 2014], p. 4.

16   Slavoj Žižek, 'Barbarism with a human face', *London Review of Books* xxxvi/9 (8 May 2014), p. 37.

17   Christopher Booker, 'Fresh evidence of how the West lured Ukraine into its orbit', *Telegraph* (8 August 2014).

18   Alexander Lukin, 'Chauvinism or Chaos?', *Russia in Global Affairs* (7 June 2014). Available at http://eng.globalaffairs.ru/number/Chauvinism-or-Chaos-16709.

AFTERWORD

1   Elaine Moore, Roman Olearchyk and Neil Buckley, 'Ukraine: costs of conflict', *Financial Times* (3 September 2015). Available at http://www.ft.com/cms/s/0/22f59e84-4d9a-11e5-9b5d-89a026fda5c9.html#axzz3l2F62xLa.

2   'Ukraine crisis: what is in the Minsk ceasefire agreement?', *Guardian* (12 February 2015). Available at http://www.theguardian.com/world/2015/feb/12/ukraine-crisis-minsk-ceasefire-agreement-details.

3   Rosaria Puglisi, *Heroes or Villains? Volunteer Battalions in Post-Maidan Ukraine* [Istituto Affari Internazionali Working Papers 8, March 2015].

4   Volodymyr Ishchenko, 'Maidan mythologies', *New Left Review* 93 (May–June 2015), p. 156.

5   Brian Whitmore, 'How do you solve a problem like the Donbas?', *Radio Free Europe/ Radio Liberty* [website] (21 July 2015). Available at http://www.rferl.org/content/how-do-you-solve-a-problem-like-the-donbas/27141099.html.

6   Maxim Vikhrov, *Turmoil in Kiev* (Moscow: Carnegie Moscow Center, 4 September 2015). Available at http://carnegie.ru/eurasiaoutlook/?fa=61191.

7   International Republican Institute, 'Public opinion survey: residents of Ukraine' (24 August 2015). Available at http://www.iri.org/sites/default/files/wysiwyg/2015-08-24_survey_of_residents_of_ukraine_july_16-30_2015.pdf.

8   Organized Crime Observatory (OCO), *Ukraine and the EU: Overcoming Criminal Exploitation Toward a Modern Democracy?* (Geneva: OCO, April 2015), p. 15. Available at http://www.o-c-o.net/wp-content/uploads/2013/11/Ukraine-and-the-EU-Overcoming-criminal-exploitation-toward-a-modern-democracy.pdf.

9   Ibid., p. 22.

10 The capture of the state by big business is at the heart of Anders Åslund's study of 'what went wrong in Ukraine', and he considers breaking that power essential if reforms are to be successful. Anders Åslund, *Ukraine: What Went Wrong and How to Fix It* (Washington, DC: Peterson Institute for International Economics, 2015).

11 Andriy Portnov, '"The heart of Ukraine"? Dnipropetrovsk and the Ukrainian revolution', in Andrew Wilson (ed.), *What Does Ukraine Think?* (London: European Council on Foreign Relations, 2015), pp. 62–70.

12 Graham Stack, 'Ukraine's largest lender PrivatBank investigated for diverting $1.8bn of IMF funds', *Business New Europe* [website] (24 August 2015). Available at http://www.bne.eu/content/story/ukraines-largest-lender-PrivatBank-investigated-diverting-18bn-imf-funds. See also Andrew Cockburn, 'Undelivered goods: how $1.8 billion in aid to Ukraine was funneled to the outposts of the international financial galaxy', *Harper's* [blog] (13 August 2015). Available at http://harpers.org/blog/2015/08/undelivered-goods/.

13 For a good analysis, see John Helmer, 'IMF officials implicated in theft', *Dances with Bears* [blog] (3 September 2015). Available at http://johnhelmer.net/?p=14017.

14 Andrew Wilson, 'Five lessons from the local elections in Ukraine', European Council on Foreign Relations [website] (29 October 2015). Available at http://www.ecfr.eu/article/commentary_five_lessons_from_the_local_elections_in_ukraine4087.

15 'Latest from OSCE Special Monitoring Mission (SMM) to Ukraine based on information received as of 19:30 (Kyiv time), 5 July 2015', OSCE [website] (6 July 2015). Available at http://www.osce.org/ukraine-smm/170456.

16 See http://www.cyber-berkut.net/en/.

17 Nicolai Petro, 'From Maidan to Mukachevo: evolution of the Ukraine crisis', *Russia Direct* [website] (21 July 2015). Available at http://www.russia-direct.org/opinion/maidan-mukachevo-evolution-ukraine-crisis.

18 'At least 5 million Ukrainian citizens in need of humanitarian aid – UN', *Kyiv Post* (10 July 2015). Available at http://www.kyivpost.com/content/ukraine/at-least-5-million-ukrainian-citizens-in-need-of-humanitarian-aid-un-393161.html.

19 Leonid Bershidsky, 'Ukraine is too corrupt for debt deal to work', Bloomberg [news agency] (25 August 2015). Available at http://www.bloombergview.com/articles/2015-08-25/ukraine-is-too-corrupt-for-debt-deal-to-work.

20 A. V. Luponosov, 'Bankrotstvo ukrainskikh bankov – uzakonennaya natsionalizatsiya depozitov grazhdan' (27 June 2015). Available at http://ua-banker.com.ua/articles-and-analytics/deposits/23843.

21 Gary Scarrabelotti, 'Toughest job in the world', *Scarra Blog* (7 September 2015). Available at http://www.scarrablog.com.au/2015/09/07/toughest-job-in-the-world/.

22 Gary Scarrabelotti, 'Despoiling Ukraine's middle class', *Scarra Blog* (9 April 2015). Available at http://www.scarrablog.com.au/2015/04/09/despoiling-ukraines-middle-class/.

23 Gary Scarrabelotti, 'Saving an imagined Ukraine', *Strata Forum* [website] (27 July 2015). Available at http://strataforum.org/saving-an-imagined-ukraine/.

24 'Russia seeking Ukraine's economic "collapse", Biden says', *Radio Free Europe/Radio Liberty* [website] (14 July 2015). Available at http://www.rferl.org/content/ukraine-biden-russia-seeks-economic-collapse/27125993.html.

25 Jack Sharples, *EGF Gazprom Monitor* 49 (June 2015), p. 4.

26 Egor Fedotov, 'Weak language norm(s) versus domestic interests: why Ukraine behaves the way it does', *Review of International Studies* xli/4 (October 2014), pp. 739–55. Available at http://journals.cambridge.org/action/displayAbstract?fromPage=online&aid=99520 79&fileId=S0260210514000448.

27 Samuel P. Huntington, *The Clash of Civilizations and the Remaking of World Order* (New York: Simon & Schuster, 1996), p. 138.

28 Alfred J. Rieber, *The Struggle for the Eurasian Borderlands: From the Rise of the Early Modern Empires to the End of the First World War* (Cambridge: Cambridge University Press, 2014).

29 For a more extended discussion, from which these paragraphs draw, see Richard Sakwa, 'Ukraine and the postcolonial condition', *openDemocracy* [website] (18 September 2015). Available at https://www.opendemocracy.net/od-russia/richard-sakwa/ukraine-and-postcolonial-condition.

30 Mykola Riabchuk, 'Culture and cultural politics in Ukraine: a postcolonial perspective', in Taras Kuzio and Paul D'Anieri (eds), *Dilemmas of State-led Nation Building in Ukraine* (Westport, CT: Praeger, 2002), p. 48.

31 Mikhail Pogrebinskiy, 'Russians in Ukraine: before and after Euromaidan', in Agnieszka Pikulicka-Wilczewska and Richard Sakwa (eds), *Ukraine and Russia: People, Politics, Propaganda and Perspectives* (Bristol: E-International Relations, March 2015), p. 91. Available at http://www.e-ir.info/2015/03/06/edited-collection-ukraine-and-russia-people-politics-propaganda-perspectives/.

32 Anton Shekhovtsov, 'The spectre of Ukrainian "fascism": information wars, political manipulation, and reality', in Andrew Wilson (ed.), *What Does Ukraine Think?* (London: European Council on Foreign Relations, 2015), p. 84.

33 Nicolai Petro, 'Bringing Ukraine back into focus: how to end the new Cold War and provide effective political assistance to Ukraine', *Carnegie Council for Ethics in International Affairs* [website] (19 August 2015). Available at http://www.carnegiecouncil.org/publications/articles_papers_reports/742.

34 Ibid.

35 Sergei Baryshnikov, 'Donbas is returning to its Russian roots', *Counterpunch* [website] (1 July 2015). Available at http://www.counterpunch.org/2015/07/01/donbas-is-returning-to-its-russian-roots/.

36 Anna Matveeva, 'Polarisation of identity and guerrilla movement in Donbass' [article submitted but unpublished as of November 2015].

37 Gordon Hahn, 'Working paper – violence, coercion and escalation in the Ukrainian crisis and civil war: escalation point 8 – ATO: civil war or Putin's war?', *Russian and Eurasian Politics* [website] (12 August 2015). Available at http://gordonhahn.com/2015/08/12/

working-paper-violence-coercion-and-escalation-in-the-ukrainian-crisis-and-civil-war-escalation-point-8-civil-war-or-putins-war/.

38   'Ukrainian education ministry strips academic ranks from 12 people for separatism – deputy minister', Interfax-Ukraine [news agency] (25 August 2015). Available at http://en.interfax.com.ua/news/general/285849.html.

39   For a recent study, see Grzegorz Rossoliński-Liebe, *Stepan Bandera: The Life and Afterlife of a Ukrainian Nationalist* (Stuttgart: Ibidem, 2015).

40   Jared McBride, 'How Ukraine's new memory commissar is controlling the nation's past', *The Nation* (13 August 2015). Available at http://www.thenation.com/article/how-ukraines-new-memory-commissar-is-controlling-the-nations-past/.

41   Denys Kiryukhin, 'Roots and features of modern Ukrainian national identity and nationalism', in Agnieszka Pikulicka-Wilczewska and Richard Sakwa (eds), *Ukraine and Russia: People, Politics, Propaganda and Perspectives* (Bristol: E-International Relations, March 2015), p. 65. Available at http://www.e-ir.info/2015/03/06/edited-collection-ukraine-and-russia-people-politics-propaganda-perspectives/.

42   'Open letter from scholars and experts on Ukraine', *Krytyka* [website] (April 2015). Available at http://krytyka.com/en/articles/open-letter-scholars-and-experts-ukraine-re-so-called-anti-communist-law.

43   A. V. Guschin, S. M. Markedonov and A. N. Tsibulina, *The Ukrainian Challenge for Russia* [Russian International Affairs Council Working Paper 24/2015], p. 16. Available at http://www.slideshare.net/RussianCouncil/wp-ukrainerussia24eng.

44   Matthew Rojansky and Mykhailo Minakov, 'The new Ukrainian exceptionalism', *YaleGlobal Online* [website], 23 June 2015. Available at http://yaleglobal.yale.edu/content/new-ukrainian-exceptionalism.

45   Rajan Menon and Eugene B. Rumer, *Conflict in Ukraine: the Unwinding of the Post-Cold War Order* (Boston: MA, MIT Press, 2015).

46   Gordon Hahn, 'One day in the life of "Ukrainian democracy"', *Russian and Eurasian Politics* [website] (21 June 2015). Available at http://gordonhahn.com/2015/06/21/one-day-in-the-life-of-ukrainian-democracy/.

47   Ivan Katchanovski, 'Interview with Jyllands-Posten (Denmark) concerning the "Snipers' Massacre" on the Maidan and its investigation in Ukraine' (19 June 2015). Available at https://www.academia.edu/13844648/Interview_with_Jyllands-Posten_Denmark_Concerning_the_Snipers_Massacre_on_the_Maidan_and_its_Investigation_in_Ukraine_Full-Text_English_Version.

48   Ivan Katchanovski, 'The "Snipers' Massacre" on the Maidan' [paper presented at the conference of the American Political Science Association, San Francisco, 3–6 September 2015]. Available at https://www.academia.edu/8776021/The_Snipers_Massacre_on_the_Maidan_in_Ukraine. Katchanovski has placed much important material on the sniper shootings and trials on his social-media sites. For example, he posted an updated version of his earlier study, 'The "Snipers' Massacre" on the Maidan in Ukraine', which was referred to in Chapter 4, to Academia.edu, on 20 February 2015, and on Facebook he posted 'New striking revelations in the massacre trial are again ignored' on 12 August 2015. Available at https://www.facebook.com/ivan.katchanovski/posts/1075861679110384.

49   As well as Katchanovski, see also detailed studies by Gordon Hahn, notably 'Violence, coercion and escalation in Ukraine's Maidan revolution: escalation point 6 – the snipers of February', *Russian and Eurasian Politics* [website] (8 May 2015). Available at http://gordonhahn.com/2015/05/08/violence-coercion-and-escalation-in-ukraines-maidan-revolution-escalation-point-6-the-snipers-of-february/.

50 'UN: 6,800 killed, 17,100 wounded since beginning of conflict in Donbas', Interfax-Ukraine [news agency] (17 August 2015). Available at http://en.interfax.com.ua/news/general/284354.html.

51 '2015 UNHCR subregional operations profile – Eastern Europe', UNHCR [website]. Available at http://www.unhcr.org/pages/49e48d456.html.

52 Lev Golinkin, 'Eastern Ukraine needs help, not isolation', *Washington Post* (14 August 2015). Available at https://www.washingtonpost.com/opinions/eastern-ukraine-needs-help-not-isolation/2015/08/14/c9b61d90-4073-11e5-b2c4-af4c6183b8b4_story.html.

53 Henry E. Hale, Nadiya Kravets and Olga Onuch, *Can Federalism Unite Ukraine in a Peace Deal?* [PONARS Eurasia Policy Memo 379, August 2015], p. 5.

54 See for example Vladimir Frolov, 'Will Moscow push for settlement in Ukraine?', *Moscow Times* (6 July 2015). Available at http://www.themoscowtimes.com/opinion/article/will-moscow-push-for-settlement-in-ukraine/525059.html.

55 Personal comment to the author, Sochi, 22 October 2015.

56 Alexander Dugin, 'Shestaya kolonna', *Vzglyad* (29 April 2014). Available at http://vz.ru/opinions/2014/4/29/684247.html. See also his 'Rozhdenie Novorossii', *Evraziya* (19 May 2014). Available at http://med.org.ru/article/4805.

57 Thomas de Waal, 'The new siege of Crimea', *National Interest* (9 July 2015). Available at http://nationalinterest.org/feature/the-new-siege-crimea-13291.

58 Vladimir Putin, 'Vstrecha s predstavitelyami natsional'nykh obshchestvennykh ob"edinenii Kryma', *President of Russia* [website] (17 August 2015). Available at http://kremlin.ru/events/president/transcripts/50140.

59 This is my impression in discussions with Crimean Tatars during a research visit in February 2015, as well as in talks with Crimean people in other locations.

60 Thomas D. Grant, *Aggression against Ukraine: Territory, Responsibility, and International Law* (New York: Palgrave Macmillan, 2015), p. 1.

61 For a recent exploration, see Milena Sterio, 'Self-determination and secession under international law: the new framework', *ILSA Journal of International and Comparative Law* xxi/2 (spring 2015), pp. 293–306.

62 Poll conducted by the Sofia Centre for Social Research, reported by Alexander J. Motyl, 'Anti-Donbas sentiment growing in Ukraine', *World Affairs Journal* (21 August 2015). Available at http://www.worldaffairsjournal.org/blog/alexander-j-motyl/anti-donbas-sentiment-growing-ukraine.

63 Samuel Charap, 'Forcing Kiev's hand: why Russia won't accept a frozen conflict in Ukraine', *Foreign Affairs* [website] (9 September 2015). Available at https://www.foreignaffairs.com/articles/ukraine/2015-09-09/forcing-kiev-s-hand.

64 For a good review of the issues, see Shaun Walker, '"There's shooting all the time" – Ukrainian ceasefire in which guns never fall silent', *Guardian* (1 July 2015).

65 Andrew Wilson, 'Introduction', in Andrew Wilson (ed.), *What Does Ukraine Think?* (London: European Council on Foreign Relations, 2015), p. 12.

66 Dmitri Trenin, 'The disturbing legacy of the Ukraine crisis', *National Interest* (12 February 2015). Available at http://nationalinterest.org/feature/the-disturbing-legacy-the-ukraine-crisis-12237.

67 *Disrupted Trade Relations between the EU and Russia: The Potential Economic Consequences for the EU and Switzerland* (Vienna: WIFO, July 2015). Available at http://www.wifo.ac.at/jart/prj3/wifo/resources/person_dokument/person_dokument.jart?publikationsid=58220&mime_type=application/pdf.

68   'US may keep sanctions for years, Russia to run economy, trade accordingly – PM',
      Interfax [Russian news agency] (24 July 2015). Available at http://russialist.org/u-s-
      may-keep-sanctions-for-years-russia-to-run-economy-trade-accordingly-pm/.

69   Niklas I. M. Nováky, 'Why so soft? The European Union in Ukraine', *Contemporary
      Security Policy* xxxvi/2 (August 2015), p. 244.

70   Andrew Monaghan, 'US should resist calls to provide Ukraine with more weapons',
      Chatham House [website] (23 July 2015). Available at http://www.chathamhouse.org/
      expert/comment/us-should-resist-calls-provide-ukraine-more-weapons.

71   'Most Ukrainians would vote for joining NATO in referendum – poll', Interfax-Ukraine
      [news agency] (17 August 2015). Available at http://www.kyivpost.com/content/ukraine/
      most-ukrainians-would-vote-for-joining-nato-in-referendum-poll-395809.html.

72   'New military doctrine calls Russia Ukraine's military adversary, stipulates NATO
      membership', Interfax-Ukraine [news agency] (3 September 2015). http://en.interfax.
      com.ua/news/general/287787.html.

73   Zbigniew Brzezinski, 'We are already in a cold war', *Der Spiegel* [website] (2 July 2015).
      Available at http://www.spiegel.de/international/world/interview-with-zbigniew-
      brzezinski-on-russia-and-ukraine-a-1041795.html.

74   'The interview: Henry Kissinger', *National Interest* (19 August 2015) [conducted by
      editor Jacob Heilbrunn in early July 2015]. Available at http://www.nationalinterest.
      org/feature/the-interview-henry-kissinger-13615.

75   Ibid.

76   Anna Nemtsova, 'Chechen jihadis leave Syria, join the fight in Ukraine', *Daily Beast*
      [website] (9 April 2015). Available at http://www.thedailybeast.com/articles/2015/09/04/
      chechen-jihadists-leave-syria-join-the-fight-in-urkaine.html.

77   Organized Crime Observatory, *Ukraine and the EU*, p. 125.

78   Nikolas K. Gvosdev, 'Why waiting for Russia to collapse is a terrible Ukraine policy',
      National Interest (1 September 2015). Available at http://www.nationalinterest.org/
      feature/why-waiting-russia-collapse-terrible-ukraine-policy-13750.

79   See Miquel Puertas's Facebook post of 19 July 2015. Available at https://www.facebook.
      com/mykolasalutis/posts/10153493797443659.

80   These options are outlined by the political commentator Viktor Shapinov. See Dmitry
      Rodionov, 'Victor Shapinov: the Novorossiya ideal isn't dead', *Red Star over Donbass*
      [blog] (18 August 2015). Available at http://redstaroverdonbass.blogspot.co.uk/2015/08/
      the-novorossiyan-ideal-isnt-dead.html.

SELECT BIBLIOGRAPHY

Anderson, Perry, 'Imperium' and 'Consilium', *New Left Review* 83 (September–October 2013), pp. 5–111, pp. 113–67.

Åslund, Anders, 'Oligarchs, corruption, and European integration', *Journal of Democracy* xxv/3 (July 2014), pp. 64–73.

——, *Ukraine: What Went Wrong and How to Fix It* (Washington, DC: Institute for International Economics, 2015).

Åslund, Anders, and Michael McFaul (eds), *Revolution in Orange: The Origins of Ukraine's Democratic Breakthrough* (Washington, DC: Carnegie Endowment for International Peace, 2006).

Baburin, Sergei, *Krym naveki s rossiei: Istoriko-pravovoe obosnovanie vossoedineniya Respubliki Krym i goroda Sevastopol' s Rossiiskoi Federatsiei* (Moscow: Knizhnyi mir, 2014).

Balmaceda, Margarita M., *Energy Dependency, Politics and Corruption in the Former Soviet Union* (London and New York: Routledge, 2008).

—— *The Politics of Energy Dependency* (Toronto: University of Toronto Press, 2013).

Bechev, Dimitar, *Turkey's Illiberal Turn* [ECFR Policy Brief 108, July 2014].

Belaya kniga narushenii prav cheloveka i printsipa verkhovenstva prava na Ukraine (aprel' – seredina iyunya 2014) (Moscow: Ministry of Foreign Affairs, June 2014).

Belyakov, Anatoly, and Oleg Matveichev, *Krymskaya vesna: 30 dnei, kotorye potryasli mir* (Moscow: Knizhnyi mir, 2014).

Blockmans, Steven, 'Ukraine, Russia and the need for more flexibility in EU foreign policy-making' [CEPS Policy Brief 320, 25 July 2014]. Available at http://www.ceps.be/book/ukraine-russia-and-need-more-flexibility-eu-foreign-policy-making.

Bromwich, David, 'The world's most important spectator', *London Review of Books* xxxvi/13 (3 July 2014), pp. 3–6.

Brzezinski, Zbigniew, *The Grand Chessboard: American Primacy and its Geostrategic Imperatives* (New York: Basic Books, 1997).

—— *Strategic Vision* (New York: Basic Books, 2013).

Byshok, S. O., and A. V. Kochetkov, *Evromaidan imeni stepana bandery: ot demokratii k diktature* (2nd edn, Moscow: Knizhnyi mir, Narodnaya diplomatiya, 2014).

Carr, E. H., *The Twenty Years' Crisis, 1919–1939: An Introduction to the Study of International Relations*, reissued with a new introduction and additional material by Michael Cox (London: Palgrave, 2001 [1939]).

Clark, Christopher, *The Sleepwalkers: How Europe Went to War in 1914* (London: Penguin, 2013).

Clinton, Hillary, *Hard Choices* (New York: Simon & Schuster, 2014).

Copsey, Nathaniel, and Karolina Pomorska, 'The influence of newer member states in the European Union: the case of Poland and the Eastern Partnership', *Europe–Asia Studies* lxvi/3 (May 2014), pp. 421–43.

Croan, Melvin, 'Lands in-between: the politics of cultural identity in contemporary Eastern Europe', *East European Politics and Societies* iii (March 1989), pp. 176–97.

D'Anieri, Paul, *Understanding Ukrainian Politics: Power, Politics, and Institutional Design* (Armonk, NY: M. E. Sharpe, 2007).

——'Legitimacy, force, and the Ukrainian state: the legacy of the Orange Revolution in 2014' [paper delivered at the ASN conference, New York, 26 April 2014].

Diuk, Nadia, 'Ukraine: a land in-between', *Journal of Democracy* ix/3 (July 1998), pp. 97–111.

Dower, John W., *Embracing Defeat: Japan in the Wake of World War II* (New York: Norton, 2000).

Dragneva, Rilka, and Kataryna Wolczuk (eds), *Eurasian Economic Integration: Law, Policy and Politics* (Cheltenham: Edward Elgar, 2013).

Dutkiewicz, Piotr, and Richard Sakwa (eds), *Eurasian Integration: The View from Within* (London and New York: Routledge, 2015).

Fesenko, Vladimir, 'Ukraine: between Europe and Eurasia', in Piotr Dutkiewicz and Richard Sakwa (eds), *Eurasian Integration: The View from Within* (London and New York: Routledge, 2015), pp. 126–49.

Furman, Ekaterina, and Alexander Libman, 'Europeanisation and the Eurasian economic union', in Piotr Dutkiewicz and Richard Sakwa (eds), *Eurasian Integration: The View from Within* (London and New York: Routledge, 2015), pp. 173–92.

Gaddy, Clifford G., and Barry W. Ickes, 'Ukraine: a prize neither Russia nor the West can afford to win' (22 May 2014). Available at http://www.brookings.edu/research/articles/2014/05/21-ukraine-prize-russia-West-ukraine-gaddy-ickes.

Gaddy, Clifford G., and Barry W. Ickes, 'Ukraine, NATO enlargement and the Geithner doctrine' (10 June 2014). Available at http://www.brookings.edu/research/articles/2014/06/10-ukraine-nato-geithner-doctrine-gaddy-ickes.

Gessen, Keith, 'Why not kill them all?', *London Review of Books* xxxvi/17 (11 September 2014), pp. 18–22.

Glazyev, Sergei, 'Nastoyashchee i budushchee evraziiskoi integratsii', *Izborskii klub: Russkie strategii* iv (2013), pp. 11–39.

Goodby, James E., *Europe Undivided: The New Logic of Peace in US–Russian Relations* (Washington, DC: US Institute of Peace Press, 1998).

Grant, Thomas D., *Aggression against Ukraine: Territory, Responsibility, and International Law* (New York: Palgrave Macmillan, 2015).

Griffin, Roger, and Matthew Feldman (eds), *Fascism: Critical Concepts* (London: Routledge, 2004).

Grigor'ev, M. S., *Evromaidan* (Moscow: Kuchkovo pole, 2014).

Grytsaienko, Oleg, 'The crisis in Ukraine: an insider's view', *Russie.Nei.Visions* lxxviii (June 2014). Available at http://www.ifri.org/?page=contribution-detail&id=8135.

Guschin, A. V., S. M. Markedonov and A. N. Tsibulina, *The Ukrainian Challenge for Russia*, Moscow, Russian International Affairs Council (RIAC) Working Paper 24/2015. Available at http://www.slideshare.net/RussianCouncil/wp-ukrainerussia24eng.

Hale, Henry E., Nadiya Kravets and Olga Onuch, 'Can federalism unite Ukraine in a peace deal?', PONARS Eurasia Policy Memo No. 379, August 2015, p. 5.

Hill, William H., *Russia, the Near Abroad and the West: Lessons from the Moldova–Transdniestria Conflict* (Washington, DC: Woodrow Wilson Center Press; Baltimore, MD: Johns Hopkins University Press, 2012).

SELECT BIBLIOGRAPHY

Horvath, Robert, *Putin's 'Preventive Counter-revolution': Post-Soviet Authoritarianism and the Spectre of Velvet Revolution* (London and New York: Routledge, 2013).

Howard, Colby, and Ruslan Pukhov (eds), *Brothers Armed: Military Aspects of the Crisis in Ukraine* (Minneapolis, MN: East View Press, 2014).

Huntington, Samuel P., 'The clash of civilizations?', *Foreign Affairs* lxxii/3 (summer 1993), pp. 23–49.

—— *The Clash of Civilizations and the Remaking of World Order* (New York: Simon & Schuster, 1996).

Ignatieff, Michael, *Blood and Belonging: Journeys into the New Nationalism* (New York: Farrar, Straus and Giroux, 1995).

Ikenberry, G. John, 'The illusion of geopolitics: the enduring power of the liberal order', *Foreign Affairs* xciii/3 (May–June 2014), pp. 80–90.

Ishchenko, Volodymyr, 'Maidan Mythologies', *New Left Review*, No. 93, May–June 2015, pp.151–9.

Jervis, Robert, *Perception and Misperception in International Politics* (Princeton, NJ: Princeton University Press, 1976).

Jones, Bruce, *Still Ours to Lead: America, Rising Powers, and the Tension between Rivalry and Restraint* (Washington, DC: Brookings Institution, 2014).

Kagan, Robert, *Of Paradise and Power: America and Europe in the New World Order* (New York: Knopf Doubleday, 2007).

Katchanovski, Ivan, 'The separatist conflict in Donbas: a violent break-up of Ukraine'. Available at https://www.academia.edu/9092818/The_Separatist_Conflict_in_Donbas_A_Violent_Break-Up_of_Ukraine.

Korosteleva, Elena, 'The EU, Russia and the eastern region: the analytics of government for a sustainable cohabitation', *Journal of Common Market Studies* [forthcoming].

Kozub, Taras, 'Compromising material about Putin's circle: Tymoshenko's revenge or a redistribution of property?', *Reporter: Vesti* x (21–27 March 2014). Available at http://reporter.vesti.ua/43287-firtash-po-kom-zvonit-avstrijskij-kolokol#.U3HVJ3aoXRw.

Kozyrev, Andrei, 'Partnership or cold peace?', *Foreign Policy* xcix (summer 1995), pp. 3–14.

Kramer, Mark, 'The myth of a no-NATO-enlargement pledge to Russia', *Washington Quarterly* xxxii/2 (2009), pp. 39–61.

Kuchma, Leonid, *Ukraina – ne Rossiya* (Moscow: Vremya, 2003).

Kudelia, Sergei, 'The house that Yanukovych built', *Journal of Democracy* xxv/3 (July 2014), pp. 19–34.

—— 'Domestic Sources of the Donbas Insurgency', PONARS Eurasia Policy Memo No. 351, September 2014.

Kupfer, Matthew, and Thomas de Waal, 'Crying genocide: use and abuse of political rhetoric in Russia and Ukraine' (28 July 2014). Available at http://carnegieendowment.org/2014/07/28/crying-genocide-use-and-abuse-of-political-rhetoric-in-russia-and-ukraine/his9.

Kuzio, Taras, *Ukraine: State and Nation Building* (London: Routledge, 1998).

—— 'History, memory and nation building in the post-Soviet colonial space', *Nationalities Papers* xxx/2 (2002), pp. 241–64.

—— *The Crimea: Europe's Next Flashpoint?* (Washington, DC: Jamestown Foundation, 2011).

—— (ed.), *Democratic Revolution in Ukraine: From Kuchmagate to Orange Revolution*, special issue of the *Journal of Communist Studies and Transition Politics* xxiii/1 (March 2007); also book by the same title (London: Routledge, 2008).

Kuzio, Taras, and Paul D'Anieri (eds), *Dilemmas of State-led Nation Building in Ukraine* (Westport, CT: Praeger, 2002).

Kuzio, Taras, Paul D'Anieri and Robert Kravchuk (eds), *State and Institution Building in Contemporary Ukraine* (Basingstoke: Macmillan, 1999).

La Neuville, Thomas Flichy de (ed.), *Ukraine: Regards sur la crise* (Lausanne: L'Âge d'Homme, 2014).

Lambroschini, Sophie, 'Genèse, apogée et métamorphose du présidentialisme clientéliste en Ukraine', *Revue d'études comparatives Est-Ouest* xxxix/2 (2008), pp. 117–48.

Lane, David, 'The Orange Revolution: "people's revolution" or revolutionary coup?', *British Journal of Politics and International Relations* x/4 (November 2008), pp. 525–49.

Lehne, Stefan, *Time to Reset the European Neighbourhood Policy* (Brussels: Carnegie Europe, February 2014).

Lendman, Stephen (ed.), *Flashpoint in Ukraine: How the US Drive for Hegemony Risks World War III* (Atlanta, GA: Clarity Press, 2014).

Lieven, Anatol, *Ukraine and Russia: A Fraternal Rivalry* (Washington, DC: US Institute of Peace Press, 1999).

Likhachev, Viacheslav, 'Right-wing extremism on the rise in Ukraine', *Russian Politics and Law* li/5 (September–October 2013), pp. 59–74.

——'Social-nationalists in the Ukrainian parliament', *Russian Politics and Law* li/5 (September–October 2013), pp. 75–85.

Lo, Bobo, *Axis of Convenience: Moscow, Beijing and the New Geopolitics* (London: Blackwell for RIIA; Washington, DC: Brookings Institution, 2008).

Loizides, Neo, *Politics of Majority Nationalism: The Framing of Peace, Stalemates and Crises* (Stanford, CA: Stanford University Press, 2015).

McMeekin, Sean, *July 1914: Countdown to War* (London: Icon, 2014).

MacMillan, Margaret, *The War That Ended Peace: How Europe Abandoned Peace for the First World War* (2013; paperback edn, London: Profile, 2014).

Mal'gin, Andrei, *Ukraina: Sobornost' i regionalism* (Simferopol: Sonat, 2005).

Mankoff, Jeffrey, 'Russia's latest land grab: how Putin won Crimea and lost Ukraine', *Foreign Affairs* xciii/3 (May–June 2004), pp. 60–8.

Marples, David, *Belarus: A Denationalized Nation* (London: Routledge, 1999).

—— *Heroes and Villains: Creating National History in Contemporary Ukraine* (Budapest: Central European University Press, 2007).

Matuszak, Sławomir, *The Oligarchic Democracy: The Influence of Business Groups on Ukrainian Politics*, OSW Studies 42 (Warsaw: Centre for Eastern Studies, September 2012).

Mead, Walter Russell, 'The return of geopolitics', *Foreign Affairs* xciii/3 (May–June 2014), pp. 69–79.

Mearsheimer, John J., 'Why the Ukraine crisis is the West's fault: the liberal delusions that provoked Putin', *Foreign Affairs* xciii/5 (September–October 2014), pp. 77–89.

Meister, Stefan, *A New Start for Russian–EU Security Policy: The Weimar Triangle, Russia and the EU's Eastern Neighbourhood*, Genshagener Papiere 7 (Brandenburg: Stiftung Genshagen, July 2011).

Menon, Rajan and Eugene B. Rumer, *Conflict in Ukraine: the Unwinding of the Post-Cold War Order* (Boston: MA, MIT Press, 2015).

Motyl, Alexander, *The Turn to the Right: The Ideological Origins and Development of Ukrainian Nationalism, 1919–1929* (New York: Columbia University Press, 1980).

Nováky, Niklas I. M., 'Why So Soft? The European Union in Ukraine', *Contemporary Security Policy* xxxvi/2 (2015), pp. 244–66.

Obydenkova, Anastassia, and Alexander Libman, 'Understanding the foreign policy of autocratic actors: ideology or pragmatism? Russia and the Tymoshenko trial as a case study',

Contemporary Politics xx/3 (May 2014), pp. 347–64. Available at http://www.tandfonline. com/doi/full/10.1080/13569775.2014.911500#.VDf-ZufY2Dk.

Onuch, Olga, 'Who were the protesters?', *Journal of Democracy* xxv/3 (July 2014), pp. 14–51.

Otte, Thomas, *July Crisis: The World's Descent into War, Summer 1914* (Cambridge: Cambridge University Press, 2014).

Pastukhov, Vladimir, *Ukrainskaya revolyutsiya i Russkaya kontrrevolyutsiya* (Moscow: OGI, 2014).

Petro, Nicolai N., 'Ukraine's ongoing struggle with its Russian identity', *World Politics Review* (6 May 2014), pp. 4–10.

Pikulicka-Wilczewska, Agnieszka and Richard Sakwa (eds), *Ukraine and Russia: People, Politics, Propaganda and Perspectives* (E-International Relations, March 2015). Available at http://www.e-ir.info/2015/03/06/edited-collection-ukraine-and-russia-people-politics-propaganda-perspectives/.

Pirani, Simon, Jonathan Stern and Katja Yafimava, *The Russo-Ukrainian Gas Dispute of January 2009: A Comprehensive Assessment* (Oxford: Oxford Institute for Energy Studies, 2009).

Plekhanov, S. N. (ed.), *Novorossiya: Vosstavshaya iz pepla* (Moscow: Knizhnyi mir, 2014).

Plokhy, Serhii, *The Last Empire: The Final Days of the Soviet Union* (New York: Oneworld, 2014).

Polikarpov, Mikhail, *Igor' Strelkov: uzhas banderovskoi khunty – oborona Donbassa* (Moscow: Knizhnyi mir, 2014).

Prusin, Alexander V., *The Lands Between: Conflict in the East European Borderlands, 1870–1992* (Oxford: Oxford University Press, 2010).

Puglisi, Rosaria, 'Heroes or Villains? Volunteer Battalions in Post-Maidan Ukraine' (Rome, Isttituto Affari Internazionali Working Papers No. 8, March 2015.

Remnick, David, 'Watching the eclipse: Ambassador Michael McFaul was there when the promise of democracy came to Russia – and when it began to fade', *New Yorker* (11 August 2014).

Riabchuk, Mykola, 'Culture and Cultural Politics in Ukraine: A Postcolonial Perspective', in Taras Kuzio and Paul D'Anieri (eds), *Dilemmas of State-Led Nation Building in Ukraine* (Westport, CT: Greenwood Publishing, 2002), pp. 47–69.

Rieber, Alfred J., *The Struggle for the Eurasian Borderlands: From the Rise of the Early Modern Empires to the End of the First World War* (Cambridge: Cambridge University Press, 2014).

Rogov, Kirill (ed.), *Osnovnye tendentsii politichesgo razvitiya v 2011–2013gg.: Krizis i transformatsiya rossiiskogo avtoritarizma* (Moscow: Fond 'Liberal'naya Missya', 2014).

Rossoliński-Liebe, Grzegorz, *Stepan Bandera: The Life and Afterlife of a Ukrainian Nationalist* (Stuttgart: Ibidem-Verlag, 2015).

Rudling, Per Anders, '"The honor they so clearly deserve": legitimizing the Waffen-SS Galizien', *Journal of Slavic Military Studies* xxvi/1 (Spring 2013), pp. 114–37 [review article of Bohdan Matsiv (ed.), *Ukrains'ka dyviziia 'Halychyna': Istoriia u svitlynakh vid zasnuvannia u 1943 r. do zvil'nennia z polonu 1949 r.* (Lviv: ZUKTs, 2009)].

Sakwa, Richard, '"New Cold War" or twenty years' crisis?: Russia and international politics', *International Affairs* lxxxiv/ 2 (March 2008), pp. 241–67.

——— 'Conspiracy narratives as a mode of engagement in international politics: the case of the 2008 Russo-Georgian war', *Russian Review* lxxi (October 2012), pp. 2–30.

——— 'The cold peace: Russo-Western relations as a mimetic cold war', *Cambridge Review of International Affairs* xxvi/1 (2013), pp. 203–24.

———*Putin and the Oligarch: The Khodorkovsky–Yukos Affair* (London and New York: I.B.Tauris, 2014).

———*Putin Redux: Power and Contradiction in Contemporary Russia* (London and New York: Routledge, 2014).

Sasse, Gwendolyn, *The Crimea Question: Identity, Transition, and Conflict* (Cambridge, MA: Harvard University Press, 2007).

Semenov, E. V. (ed.), *Evromaidan i Russkaya vesna: sbornik statei* (Moscow: Traditsiya, 2014).

Sergunin, Alexander, 'Russian views on the Ukrainian crisis', in Thomas Flichy de La Neuville (ed.), *Ukraine: Regards sur la crise* (Lausanne: L'Âge d'Homme, 2014), pp. 55–82.

Shekhovtsov, Anton, and Andreas Umland, 'Ukraine's radical right', *Journal of Democracy* xxv/3 (July 2014), pp. 58–63.

Sherr, James, 'The mortgaging of Ukraine's independence' [briefing paper for Chatham House, the Royal Institute of International Affairs, August 2010]. Available at http://www.chathamhouse.org/sites/files/chathamhouse/public/Research/Russia%20and%20Eurasia/bp0810_sherr.pdf.

Snyder, Timothy, *Bloodlands: Europe Between Hitler and Stalin* (New York: Basic Books, 2010).

Solzhenitsyn, Alexander, *Rebuilding Russia: Reflections and Tentative Proposals* (London: Harvill, 1991).

Starikov, Nikolai, *Ukraina: Khaos i revolyutsiya – oruzhie dollar* (Moscow: Piter, 2014).

Stepan, Alfred, Juan J. Linz and Yogendra Yadav, *Crafting State–Nations: India and Other Multinational Democracies* (Baltimore, MD: Johns Hopkins University Press, 2011).

Sterio, Milena, 'Self-Determination and Secession under International Law: the New Framework', *ILSA Journal of International & Comparative Law* xxi/2 (spring 2015), pp. 293–306.

Titarenko, Larissa, 'Belarus between the Eurasian Union and the European Union: material and symbolic options' [paper delivered at the ASN conference, New York, 25 April 2014].

Tolksdorf, Dominik, 'The EU, Russia and the Eastern Partnership: what dynamics under the New German government?', *Russie.Nei.Visions* lxxiv (February 2014). Available at http://www.ifri.org/?page=contribution-detail&id=8000.

Trenin, Dmitri, *The Ukraine Crisis and the Resumption of Great-power Rivalry* (Moscow: Carnegie Moscow Center, 9 July 2014). Available at http://carnegie.ru/2014/07/09/ukraine-crisis-and-resumption-of-great-power-rivalry/hfgs.

Tymoshenko, Yuliya, 'Containing Russia', *Foreign Affairs* lxxxvi/3 (May–June 2007), pp. 69–82.

Umland, Andreas, 'Starting post-Soviet Ukrainian right-wing extremism studies from scratch', *Russian Politics and Law* li/5 (September–October 2013), pp. 3–10.

Umland, Andreas, and Anton Shekhovtsov, 'Ultraright parties in post-Soviet Ukraine and the puzzle of the electoral marginalism of Ukrainian ultranationalists in 1994–2009', *Russian Politics and Law* li/5 (September–October 2013), pp. 33–58.

Wawro, Geoffrey, *A Mad Catastrophe: The Outbreak of World War I and the Collapse of the Habsburg Empire* (New York: Basic Books, 2014).

White Book on Violations of Human Rights and the Rule of Law in Ukraine (November 2013– March 2014) (Moscow: Ministry of Foreign Affairs, April 2014).

Wilson, Andrew, *Ukrainian Nationalism in the 1990s: A Minority Faith* (Cambridge and New York: Cambridge University Press, 1996).

——*The Ukrainians: Unexpected Nation* (New Haven, CT: Yale University Press, 2000).

——*Ukraine's Orange Revolution* (New Haven, CT: Yale University Press, 2006).

——*Ukraine Crisis: What It Means for the West* (New Haven, CT: Yale University Press, 2014).

——'Ukraine under Poroshenko', in Andrew Wilson (ed.), *Protecting the European Choice* (London: European Council on Foreign Relations, July 2014), pp. 10–25.

——(ed.), *What Does Ukraine Think?* (London: European Council on Foreign Relations, 2015).

Wilson, James Graham, *The Triumph of Improvisation: Gorbachev's Adaptability, Reagan's Engagement, and the End of the Cold War* (Ithaca, NY: Cornell University Press, 2014).

Wood, Tony, 'Back from the edge?', *London Review of Books* xxxvi/11 (5 June 2014), pp. 37–8.

Zaitsev, Oleksandr, 'Ukrainian integral nationalism in quest of a "Special Path" (1920s–1930s)', *Russian Politics and Law* li/5 (September–October 2013), pp. 11–32.

—— *Ukraïns'ky integral'nyi natsionalizm* (Kiev: Krytyka, 2013).

Žižek, Slavoj, 'Barbarism with a human face', *London Review of Books* xxxvi/9 (8 May 2014), pp. 36–7.

Zotkin, A. A., 'Gosudarstvennaya vlast' i politicheskie elity Ukrainy v kontekste otnoshenii mezhdu tsentrom i regionami', in A. V. Duka (ed.), *Vlastnye struktury i gruppy dominirovaniya* (St Petersburg: Intersotsis, 2012), pp. 286–306.

INDEX